SHAKESPEARE
STUDIES

SHAKESPEARE STUDIES
Volume XXXVII

EDITED BY

SUSAN ZIMMERMAN

Queens College

The City University of New York

and

GARRETT SULLIVAN

Pennsylvania State University

ASSISTANT TO THE EDITORS
LINDA NEIBERG
The Graduate Center, CUNY

Madison • Teaneck
Fairleigh Dickinson University Press

Associated University Presses
2010 Eastpark Boulevard
Cranbury, NJ 08512

The paper used in this publication meets the requirements of the American National Standard for Permanence of Paper for Printed Library Materials Z39.48-1984.

International Standard Book Number 978-0-8386-4253-5
International Standard Serial Number: 0-0582-9399

All editorial correspondence concerning *Shakespeare Studies* should be addressed to the Editorial Office, *Shakespeare Studies,* English Dept., Queens College, CUNY, Flushing, NY 11367. Orders and subscriptions should be directed to Associated University Presses, 2010 Eastpark Boulevard, Cranbury, New Jersey 08512.

Shakespeare Studies disclaims responsibility for statements, either of fact or opinion, made by contributors.

Contents

Review Articles

Reviews

Foreword

FOR OVER TEN YEARS, beginning with Volume XXII in 1996 under the editorial direction of Leeds Barroll, *Shakespeare Studies* has featured Forums, or scholarly discussions, on issues important to the field of early modern culture. These issues have been wide-ranging, from psychoanalytical theory, to English cosmopolitanism, to racial identities, to Renaissance manuscript studies, to the return of the author; and over time such Forums have helped to focus come of our best scholarly minds on pressing concerns. The Forum in Volume XXXVII, organized and moderated by John H. Astington, takes up yet another such topic, exploring important connections between "The Universities and the Theater," and featuring contributions by Sarah Knight, Andrew Gurr, Christopher Marlow, and Alan H. Nelson.

As a complement to the Forum, this issue also features an article by S. P. Cerasano, entitled "The Fortune Contract in Reverse" which provides a newly detailed interpretation of the contract's importance to the theatrical scene. Other articles include David B. Goldstein's analysis of cannibalism in *Titus Andronicus,* Martin Orkin on "Speaking Process," and Clare McManus on "Women and the Early Modern Stage," which considers several recent publications on this subject.

The seventeen reviews in Volume XXXVII are deliberately wide-ranging in topic, chronological range, and theoretical approach. For example, Kristen Poole reviews Peter Marshall and Alexandra Walsham's edition of *Angels in the Early Modern World;* in accordance with a recent emphasis on medieval antecedents of the Renaissance, Susan Phillips examines *Reading the Medieval in Early Modern England,* edited by Gordon McMullan and David Matthews; and Christopher Pye comments on Richard Wilson's *Shakespeare in French Theory: King of Shadows.* Other books included in this issue focus on such topics as Foxe's *Book of Martyrs,* male friendship, Shakespeare and the nature of love, literature and anatomy, the "unfinished business" of cultural materialism, race and performance, and the representation of Elizabeth I in seventeenth-century England. It gives us special pleasure to include also a review by John Drakakis of a collection of essays in honor of Leeds Barroll, the founder of *Shakespeare Studies.* This collection, edited by Lena Cowen Orlin, is entitled *Center or Margin: Revisions of the English Renaissance in Honor of Leeds Barroll.*

SUSAN ZIMMERMAN and GARRETT SULLIVAN, Co-Editors

Contributors

JOHN H. ASTINGTON is Professor of English and Drama at the University of Toronto. He is currently completing a book on actors and acting in the Shakespearean period.

S. P. CERASANO is the Edgar W. S. Fairchild Professor of Literature at Colgate University and the editor of *Medieval and Renaissance Drama in England.* She is currently editing Edward Alleyn's diary for Oxford University Press.

JOHN DRAKAKIS is Professor of English Studies at the University of Stirling. He is the editor of *Alternative Shakespeares* (1985), the general editor of the Routledge New Critical Idiom series, and the joint editor of *Gothic Shakespeares* (2008). His Arden3 *The Merchant of Venice* will be published in 2009–10, and he has been appointed general editor of the revision of Bullough's *Narrative and Dramatic Sources of Shakespeare.*

MARY FLOYD-WILSON is Associate Professor of English and Comparative Literature at the University of North Carolina at Chapel Hill. She is currently writing a book on preternatural phenomena in early modern drama.

DAVID B. GOLDSTEIN is assistant professor of English at York University. He is currently at work on a book about food and ethics in early modern England.

ANDREW GURR, Professor Emeritus at the University of Reading, has been publishing work on Shakespearean theater for more than forty years. His books include *The Shakespeare Stage* (now in its fourth edition), *Playgoing in Shakespeare's London* (now in its third), and editions of *Richard II, Henry V, The Knight of the Burning Pestle,* and *The Spanish Tragedy.*

GRAHAM HAMMILL is Associate Professor of English at SUNY-Buffalo. He is currently completing a book on political theology and emergent liberalism in political and literary writings from Machiavelli to Spinoza.

ELIZABETH D. HARVEY is Professor of English at the University of Toronto. She is currently completing a book on early modern medicine and literature.

MARGARET JANE KIDNIE is Professor of English at the University of Western Ontario. She is author of *Shakespeare and the Problem of Adaptation* (2009), and is currently editing *A Woman Killed with Kindness* for the Arden Early Modern Drama series.

SARAH KNIGHT is lecturer in Shakespeare and Renaissance Literature at the University of Leicester. Her research centers on satire and drama in English and Latin, and on the intellectual and literary culture of the early modern universities.

THERESA KRIER is Professor of English at Macalester College. She is the author of works about Renaissance literature.

CAROLE LEVIN is Willa Cather Professor of History and the Director of the Medieval and Renaissance Studies Program at the University of Nebraska. Her most recent book is *Dreaming the English Renaissance: Politics and Desire in Court and Culture* (2008).

ARTHUR L. LITTLE, JR. is Associate Professor of English at the University of California, Los Angeles. He is currently working on a multidisciplinary cultural study of *Hamlet.*

CHRISTOPHER MARLOW is Senior Lecturer in English at the University of Lincoln in the UK. He is currently completing a book on friendship and masculinity in early modern university drama.

CLARK McMANUS is Reader in English Literature at Roehampton University, London. She is currently editing John Fletcher's *Island Princess* for Arden Early Modern Drama.

MICHAEL NEILL is emeritus Professor of English at the University of Auckland. He is the author of *Issues of Death* and is editing Massinger's *The Renegade* for Arden Early Modern Drama.

ALAN H. NELSON is Professor of English Emeritus at the University of California, Berkeley. His next Records of Early English Drama project is the county of Essex.

MARTIN ORKIN is Professor in the Department of English and of Theatre at the University of Haifa, Israel. Author of *Shakespeare Against Apartheid, Drama and the South African State,* and *Local Shakespeares: Proximations and Power,* and editor of the collection *At the Junction: Four Plays by the Junction Avenue Theatre Company,* and with Ania Loomba, editor of *Post-Colonial Shakespeares,* he is currently working on theatrical reinscriptions of hatred.

SUSAN E. PHILLIPS is Associate Professor of English at Northwestern University. She is currently writing a cultural history of premodern polyglot dictionaries, phrase books, and guides to conversation.

KRISTEN POOLE is Associate Professor of English at the University of Delaware. She is currently completing a book on supernatural environments in early modern England.

CHRISTOPHER PYE is Professor of English at Williams College. He is currently completing a book on Renaissance political aesthetics.

NICHOLAS F. RADEL is Professor of English at Furman University. Author of numerous articles on sexuality theory and early modern drama, he is currently working on a book-length study of sodomy and homophobia in Shakespeare and his contemporaries.

DAVID SCHALKWYK is currently Professor of English at the University of Cape Town and a long-term Mellon Fellow at the Folger Shakespeare Library. He becomes Director of Research at the Folger Library in July 2009. His latest book is *Shakespeare, Love and Service* (2008) and he is working on humanism and love in the Renaissance.

ALISON SHELL is Professor of English at the University of Durham. She is currently completing a book on Shakespeare and religion.

ALAN STEWART is Professor of English and Comparative Literature at Columbia University. His latest book is *Shakespeare's Letters*.

ANDREA WALKDEN is Assistant Professor of English at Queens College, the City University of New York. She is currently completing a book on biography, historiography, and early narrative fiction during the later Stuart period.

SHAKESPEARE STUDIES

FORUM
THE UNIVERSITIES
AND THE THEATER

Introduction

John H. Astington

*H*AMLET TWICE REMINDED its original audiences of another tragedy recently performed at the Globe, that of *Julius Caesar,* a central subject of the classical history studied in Elizabethan schools and universities. Horatio thinks that the ghost, like the apparitions which appeared before Caesar's fall, "bodes some strange eruption to our state," and, proleptically, Polonius is prompted to recall that he once acted at "th'university," taking the role of the doomed Caesar, "kill'd i' th' Capitol." While the action of Polonius's play might be imagined to have corresponded to Shakespeare's own play of Caesar, first audiences of *Hamlet* are likely to have inferred that the youthful student Polonius of thirty or forty years previously had learned and spoken his part in Latin, the academic language of school and university instruction and study, as well as of the less formal "exercises," such as college plays: both Stephen Gosson and Thomas Heywood use that term to refer to university drama. When *Hamlet* was played at Oxford, as the title page of the 1603 quarto assures us it had been, older university hands may have been reminded of the Latin play *Caesar Interfectus* (The Assassination of Caesar), written by Richard Edes and acted at Christ Church at some time in 1582, roughly twenty years earlier. In the Shakespearean period university plays were written for and seen by a select audience, and performance in them was, at least in part, regarded as contributing to the training of orators destined for the law courts and the pulpit, or in the case of the fictional Polonius, the council chamber. Many university actors at Oxford and Cambridge subsequently rose to high positions in the church. William Laud, archbishop of Canterbury and chancellor of Oxford University in the sixteen thirties and early forties, was proud of the dramatic prowess of his own Oxford college, St. John's, and he may in his undergraduate days, in the fifteen eighties, have taken roles in plays and entertainments there.

The third in the famous series of *Parnassus* plays, written in English and performed at St. John's College, Cambridge, at the very
end of the sixteenth century, gives clear evidence that the university community had its eyes and ears open to the thriving contemporary theatrical culture based in London. Among the careers a pair
of unemployed graduates consider is that of going on the professional stage, and they are auditioned by Kemp and Burbage, the
chief comic and tragic specialists of the Chamberlain's Men,
played, naturally, by the amateurs of the college. Such facetious
fun, in the everyday vernacular, formed one aspect of university
entertainments. More solemn occasions called for other genres, and
the high-mindedness of the classical languages. Both Oxford and
Cambridge were, in Elizabethan times, fairly remote provincial
towns (although their relative isolation is distinguished by Alan
Nelson, below); modern travelers from London can reach either
university in roughly an hour by train, rather than journeying for
two days or more. None the less, university students and dons read,
and occasionally saw, the plays of Shakespeare and his contemporaries. One other important contact with the metropolis was constituted by the patronage of the court. Queen Elizabeth visited each
university in turn early in her reign: Cambridge in 1564 and Oxford
in 1566; both occasions were marked by elaborate theatrical shows,
and set a pattern for royal visits which persisted until the civil
wars. University drama was one index of the achievements of English culture; when the visiting Polish prince Albert Laski came to
England in 1583 he was entertained independently at Oxford, his
hospitality overseen jointly by the officials of the university and
leading figures of the queen's court. Theatrical entertainment for
important occasions at the universities was supported by contributions of equipment and experienced staff from the royal Offices of
the Revels and Works, and staging could be ambitious and avant-
garde, from the elaborate scenic effects at the theater at Christ
Church, Oxford, in 1566 to the stylish *Royal Slave* in the same
venue seventy years later.

For this Forum, contributors were invited to write about theatrical activity at the universities (and at the "third university," the
Inns of Court in London, which were in many ways similar to university colleges) in the aftermath of the important publications in
the series of the Records of Early English Drama, *Cambridge*
(1989), and *Oxford* (2004), which give an up-to-date scholarly
census of university entertainments from the medieval period up

to 1642. Alan Nelson's edition of the Cambridge records also led him to an independent book on the college theater structures at Cambridge, *Early Cambridge Theatres* (1994), which provides an important comparative guide to those contemplating the physical management of early modern plays on the stage. Following on John Orrell's identification of the plan of the theater built within Christ Church Hall in 1605 (1982), Nelson's survey of the Cambridge playing places further emphasized that the layout of the Globe was not the universal model for academic players. The forthcoming REED volume on the Inns of Court will round out our picture of "collegiate" drama and theatrical patronage in the "Shakespearean" period, from the mid-sixteenth to the mid-seventeenth centuries; as senior scholar involved in the entire series Alan Nelson here offers his own view of some chief features of that large picture.

The papers which follow examine the particular cultural conditions of university entertainments, and the extrinsic influences on them: the very special circumstances of university performance and its reception meant that it was not, apart from some rare occasions, itself an influence on the wider theatrical culture which surrounded it. Sarah Knight begins with Sir Philip Sidney's invocation of the demonstrative power of Greek tragedy in performance, an exploration of which the early modern universities might have taken up, but largely did not: only in Victorian times did "the Greek play" become a Cambridge tradition. Performances in Greek, Knight shows, became less frequent as the Elizabethan reign continued, so that the play Sidney admired, Sophocles' *Ajax,* was represented only in two Latin adaptations, and the first, at Cambridge in 1564, not performed, at least before its projected audience of the monarch and her entourage, although it had undoubtedly been cast and rehearsed for the occasion. The second, *Ajax Flagellifer,* certainly was performed before King James at Oxford in 1605, in a Serlian theater built within Christ Church Hall, and equipped with changing scenery painted on revolving *periaktoi,* a classicized theater which didn't bear much resemblance to the Athenian theater of Dionysus but was otherwise *au courant,* and in relation to the contemporary London stage distinctly spectacular. The performance lasted for four hours, which makes one wonder about the elements which contributed to such a length, apart from the recital of a memorized text: were there, for example, musical passages, in the spirit of contemporary European experiments in the revival of ancient tragedy? The lack of surviving texts of either play limits such speculations, but Sarah Knight demonstrates the surrounding expectations about reception that would have governed plays for learned monarchs, and the likely effects on their composition.

Andrew Gurr examines, first, some of the consequences of the culture of enclosed male celibate communities on the sexual politics of the plays they produced. Although the kind of regulation of their members' lives was nominally similar, however, it must have in fact been far harder to enforce strict rules of conduct in the London Inns than in Oxford and Cambridge colleges, surrounded as the first were by the fleshpots of the city; their authorities otherwise seem to have been more laissez-faire in their attitudes to their nominal residents, who were free, for example, to dress as they liked and to study, or not, as they chose. The matter of sexual seclusion raises the larger question of the ways in which college drama, and specifically that at Cambridge, was open to the world beyond its enclosing walls. While the practice of performing plays in English might suggest accessibility and inclusion, in fact many of the attitudes revealed in play texts are those of an elite in-group, skeptical if not downright scornful of those outside it. The nucleus of the Cambridge audiences was formed from the college fellowship, in its communal sense, and its outlook was that of its peculiar community of celibate gentleman scholars.

Christopher Marlow considers how experience of such an ethos may have colored the composition and reception of two plays written and performed at Cambridge and Oxford in the 1630s, Hausted's *The Rival Friends* and Mead's *The Combat of Love and Friendship.* On the evidence of the surviving texts, Mead's is the better play, but we know next to nothing about the precise date of its performance or its reception, whereas *The Rival Friends,* performed by Queen's College actors in Trinity College Hall on March 19, 1632, before the visiting king and queen, was something of a Cambridge scandal, involving an authors' row, collegiate rivalry, reported royal displeasure, and the consequent suicide of a vice-chancellor. Very little of ideal friendship seems to have attended such events, as it equally did not the occasional violent riots which marked the sparring between the neighboring Trinity and St. John's colleges at the time of plays, a reminder that both Cambridge and Oxford were filled with excitable and perhaps rather bored adolescents, as ready to cut loose as were London apprentices. Looking beyond such accidents of production to the thematic concerns of

Hausted's text, Marlow identifies its satirical view of excessively idealized human relationships, both in love and friendship, which may have contributed to royal distaste for the play. Mead's later play, probably acted at Christ Church, Oxford, in 1634 or the years immediately following, has neoplatonic idealism more firmly in its sights, and is further evidence of critical university response to cultural fashions in the wider world.

Alan Nelson, finally, draws on his thorough familiarity with the various forms of academic drama and entertainment to characterize some of the differences between the two universities in respect of their theatrical activities, and the distinction of the Inns of Court from either. Part of the difference was the consequence of geography: the Inns were close to Whitehall and the royal court, as they were to the professional theaters of London, which indeed began to operate in their immediate vicinity after 1608. Oxford was on the road to other places, making it a strategic center, and the seat of royal administration, after 1642; Cambridge, equally vital to the country's intellectual life, was off the main road to the north and surrounded by the fens, at a topographical dead end. Both universities produced drama of one kind and another, acted by their members, right up to the time of the wars: the Inns, however, were patrons rather than performers of drama from at least the 1580s onward, their resident gentlemen choosing rather to display their skills in the unvocalized art of formal dancing, framed in the elaborately costumed and scenically decorated masques, many of which were taken to the royal court. The immediate connection of the community of the Inns with that of the royal household is signaled, Nelson points out, as early as the 1540s in a document noting the function of the Christmas "prince" ceremonies periodically observed in the Inns, ceremonies which also copied the royal court in commissioning professional players, as at Gray's Inn in Christmastime 1594. The mock courts were a kind of training ground for the real thing, among younger men with social and political expectations; they were also, undoubtedly, an enjoyable holiday spoof of ceremonial solemnity.

The signs that Oxford, rather than Cambridge, emulated such activities Nelson considers an indication of the closer ties of the former place to the royal court, so that Christ Church, the regular site of entertainment and hospitality for royal visitors throughout the Stuart period, became an easy choice for the accommodation of the

exiled court after late 1642. Together these papers demonstrate the centrality of drama and other performative activity to the cultural life of English academic communities before that date, and widen our sense of the many functions of play and playing in Shakespeare's time.

"Goodlie anticke apparrell"?: Sophocles' *Ajax* at Early Modern Oxford and Cambridge

SARAH KNIGHT

I︎N HIS DISCUSSION OF TRAGEDY in the *Defence of Poesy* (*ca.* 1580), Philip Sidney mentions Sophocles' fifth-century play Αἴας (Latinized as *Ajax*) to illustrate the impact that tragedy should make on its audience.[1] Αἴας depicts the frenzy of the famous Greek warrior who became so frustrated after the dead Achilles' armor was given to Odysseus that he went mad:

> let but Sophocles bring you Ajax on a stage, killing or whipping sheep and oxen thinking them the army of Greeks with their chieftains Agamemnon and Menelaus, and tell me if you have not a more familiar insight into anger than finding in the schoolmen his *genus* and difference.[2]

Sidney compares theatrical performance with study, evoking two responses to tragic action: psychological involvement with the protagonist's fall, and academic dissection of his type; he prefers the experience of watching "Ajax on a stage," and the personal "insight into anger" thereby gained to reading the commentaries of "the schoolmen" which dryly anatomize rather than vividly represent Ajax's rage. Sidney's discussion of these different responses to Αἴας is part of the *Defence*'s wider satire of pedantically misguided reactions to literature, but can also be read as a critique of his contemporaries' attitudes towards Greek tragedy. Sophocles was embedded within the curriculum at early modern Oxford and Cambridge, and as a Christ Church undergraduate during the late 1560s Sidney would have probably heard the Greek lectures, in which Sophocles was one of the authors taught.[3] Sidney interro-

gates an engagement with Sophocles only for his didactic useful-
ness, and suggests that the Greek dramatist should be more than
just a worthy pillar of the curriculum, but should instead be
watched "on a stage" to make an audience think and empathize.

Αἴας may well have occurred to Sidney as a good example both
because of Sophocles' place within the academic curriculum and
because the play had recently been prepared for the university
stage. Just before Sidney went up to Oxford in 1568, a Latin production of Sophocles' play under the expanded title *Ajax Flagellifer*
(Ajax the Scourger) had been included in a high-profile royal progress visit to Cambridge.[4] On August 9, 1564, after various sermons,
debates, and perambulations, the Queen pleaded fatigue, and so, in
the stark words of one eyewitness, "This nyght sholde haue byn
pleyed Aiax flagellifer in Latin and was not."[5] In 1605, nearly
twenty years after Sidney's death, *Ajax* was again staged, this time
at his alma mater, Christ Church, on an expensive, innovative Inigo
Jones-designed stage, yet despite being overseen by powerful courtiers and the Office of the Works, accounts of its reception were
mostly negative. The performance lasted from 9 p.m. until 1 a.m.,[6]
and an observer again noted bad-tempered royal fatigue: apparently
James "was verye weary before he came thither, but much more
wearied by that, and spake manye wordes of dislike."[7] Although
another eyewitness enthused that "the King shewed himselfe verie
well pleased, and content with it," we might be skeptical, since this
comes from the official panegyric *Oxfords Triumph* (1605), authored by Anthony Nixon, "freelance Jacobean hack."[8] So both versions of *Ajax* were either canceled or apparently unsuccessful:
could this failure have been predicted?

On the contrary—there were sound reasons for the play's selection. Like all progress visits, the university entertainments were
primarily intended to impress the monarch, and with court advi-
sors such as William Cecil (in 1564) and Thomas Howard, earl of
Suffolk (in 1605), breathing down their necks, Cambridge and Oxford pitched their entertainments squarely at two monarchs who
prided themselves on scholarship, both to pay a compliment to a
learned prince and to imply that university and monarchy shared
priorities. Siobhan Keenan and Linda Shenk have both recently
demonstrated the extent to which Elizabeth's Privy Council sought
to micromanage the 1564 visit, to ensure proof of institutional conformism.[9] This controlling zeal was seen in 1605, too, and best epitomized in Cecil's July 1564 letter to Edward Hawford, Master of

Christ's, in which Cecil articulated his "desyer . . . that twoe thynges may specyally appeare in that vniuersitie / Order/ and lernyng: and for order I meane bothe for religionn and Civyll behavour."[10] The "hands-on" approach that the courtiers often took is further encapsulated in an account of Howard's involvement, along with the earls of Worcester and Northampton, and Lord Cary, in the 1605 Christ Church staging, and the resulting conflict:

> They (but especiallie Suff*olk* vtterlie disliked the stage att Christchurch . . . this dislike of the Earle of Suff*olk* much troubled the Vicechancelor, and all the workmen, yet they stood in defence of the thinge done."[11]

The two productions of Sophocles' play tell us much about the adaptation of Greek drama for the progress visits: the monarch's presence, institutional practice, and contemporary notions of how such plays might be *used* combined to create a unique kind of dramatic performance.

Greek tragedies on the university stage were not as common during Elizabeth's reign, nor half a century later under James, as they had been during the reigns of Edward and Mary, when in the wake of a new humanist interest in Greek rhetoric, college statutes at both universities had advocated the playing of Greek drama.[12] The painstaking efforts made earlier in the sixteenth century by scholars such as John Cheke, Thomas Smith,[13] and Roger Ascham—who, as her tutor, was to be so pedagogically influential on Elizabeth—to reconstruct "authentic" Greek in pronunciation and performance had given way by the 1560s to the translation of Greek texts into institutionally omnipresent Latin.[14] Dramaturgical priorities as well as linguistic register had changed by 1564, as we see from the account of Nicholas Robinson, Queens' Fellow and future bishop of Bangor: Robinson, who seems to have known of the preperformance arrangements of *Ajax,* suggests that this production was impressive not for its historical authenticity, but rather for its use of "Arma namq*ue* bellica vestes splendore illustres apparatumq*ue* omnem reliquu*m* Londino alijs remotissimis locis" (arms of war, clothes shining in splendor, and all the rest of the gear from London and other very remote places). Continuing on the subject of lively visuals, Robinson also writes of "Aiax ille flagellifer, que*m* furentem cernere desiderabamus" (that scourging Ajax, whom we were longing to see raging in his madness).[15] Robinson's emphasis on glittering properties and costumes and on the burly "furentem" protagonist suggests a very different set of theatrical priorities in 1564 to those prized in the Greek plays orchestrated by Cheke and Smith earlier in the century. Authentic pronunciation and even the original linguistic medium were sidelined for spectacle, and so although Robinson refers to the play as a *lucubratio* (nocturnal study), appropriately for its academic context, his description, as Bruce R. Smith has recently discussed, suggests a "visually splendid and aurally exciting" production of *Ajax* rather than a bookish exercise in Greek to Latin translation.[16] Robinson also makes clear the extent to which Elizabeth was the cynosure of performance, which reminds us sharply of how different the original performance context of Αἴας, before an audience of about fifteen thousand at the City Dionysia, would have been to this production of a Latin version within the closed, hierarchical world of the university theater.

The accounts of the 1605 visit echo this impression of academic exclusivity and court control. The Orders for the Delegates of Convocation enjoined that scholars excluded from the plays were not "to make any outcryes or vndecent noyse about ye hall stayres or within ye Quadrange of christchurch as vsually they weare wont to doe": then as now, this is a very large area in which to demand silence.[17] So important was the royal presence that the original seating had to be dismantled because "the Kinge [had been] soe placed that the Auditory could see but his Cheeke onlie."[18] The scenography was of the utmost importance: under the critical gaze of a king fond of the elaborate world of the court masque, Inigo Jones reconstructed classical stagecraft as filtered through Vitruvius and Serlio in Christ Church hall. John Orrell has argued that Jones was eager to "rise to the learning of the academy with a suitable classicism of his own," a kind of architectural humanism, and suggests that Jones chose *Ajax* because of Vitruvius's mention of the play's staging in the fifth book of the *De Architectura*.[19] Jones's classicism may have been even more impressive than Orrell records: in the *Poetics,* Aristotle notes that Sophocles was the first to introduce "scene-painting" (σκηνογρᾰφία), and Jones may have picked up on this association when constructing the "artificiosus apparatus" of *Ajax*.[20] In any case, both painted scenery and the Vitruvian revolving backdrops (*periaktoi*) were adopted:

> a false wall fayre painted and adorned with statelie pillers which pillers
> would turne about, by reason whereof with the helpe of other painted

clothes, their stage did varrie three tymes in the Actinge of one Tragedye.[21]

Orrell's discussion of Jones's classicizing experimentation is borne
out by Isaac Wake's *Rex Platonicus,* a Latin panegyric account of
the visit:

> Quae omnia, quàm mirificâ, & aures, & oculos varietate pascerent, facilè
> non est dicere; eoque magis, quòd pro materiæ varietate, tota Scenae
> fabrica, & artificiosus peripetasmatum apparatus, iterum atque iterum,
> mirantibus omnibus, innouaretur.

> [It is not easy to say with how marvelous a variety all these things fed
> both the eyes and the ears, all the more so because, on account of the
> variety of the matter, the whole fabric of the stage and the artful appara-
> tus of the embroidered hangings were renewed again and again to the
> amazement of all.][22]

These accounts suggest that 1605's emphasis fell on inducing visual "amazement"—"mirantibus omnibus"—and certainly spectators seem to have marveled at the sight, even if they didn't like the
production. Bruce R. Smith has persuasively argued that the 1564
production—judging by Nicholas Robinson's account, particularly—seems to have aimed at stimulating a sense of wonder: judging by the audience reactions, even the negative ones of those who
"vtterlie disliked" it, such an assessment can be applied to the
1605 production too.[23]

Because *Ajax* was not actually performed in 1564, we have to
base our reconstruction of its staging chiefly on Robinson's account. We have more evidence for 1605, particularly in Wake's account, which goes into detail about the plot and characterization.
Wake suggests that Sophocles' play was significantly altered for the
1605 performance, that "titulo ex Sophocle mutuato, sed re, tam
diversa, quàm idiomate" (although the title was borrowed from
Sophocles, still [the play] was as different in matter as in expression).[24] Two of these alterations are particularly important. The
chorus of Αἴας consists of sailors from Salamis, where Ajax was
king, but the 1605 adapters transformed this collective choric voice
into the recognizably Senecan device of a ghost who comments on
the play's action. We see this character in Seneca's *Agamemnon,*
for example, where—in the Cambridge student John Studley's 1566
translation—the ghost of Thyestes speaks of being "sent out again /

from Tartar dungeon depe" to watch his dysfunctional household and comment on the action.[25] Similarly, in 1605 "Vmbra Hectoris . . . Chori praebebat vice*m*" (the shade of Hector . . . provided the function of the Chorus), "Aiaci insenssissima" (completely undetectable to Ajax), and Hector's ghost "exultat" (rejoices) at his death. This choric substitution sets the 1605 adaptation more squarely within Senecan tragic tradition, recalibrating the more dialectical function that the chorus performs in Αἴας.[26] Another fashionable supernatural element was also added as a second radical change to the *dramatis personae;* Wake tells us that one of Inigo Jones's three *periaktoi* depicted the "furiarum domicilia" (dwellings of the Furies), a physical setting that we never see in Sophocles' play. In Sophocles' play, Ajax invokes the Furies as he is about to commit suicide, but this is a prayer flung into the ether: he does not physically visit their dwellings.[27] A scene was probably added in 1605 enacted in front of these "domicilia': Wake cites the moment when Ajax "Furias euocat" (calls upon the Furies), and this was probably the moment at which the *periaktoi* revolved and the actors stood before the "horrenda antra" (fearful caves) of the Furies.[28] In Sophocles, the Furies are bodiless symbols of revenge, invoked rather than seen, while in 1605 the dread goddesses seem to have been embodied, and presented, perhaps, as an onstage manifestation of Ajax's madness.[29] These two changes described by Wake strongly imply that this play "so different" from Sophocles' original was turned into a more visual, literalized dramatic performance, redolent of the more fashionable Senecan form. The presence of Hector's ghost watching and laughing at Ajax's dementia, particularly, reminds us of the ghost of Don Andrea in Kyd's *Spanish Tragedie,* who declares—as the 1605 audience unfortunately did not– that "these were spectacles to please my soule."[30] So we get a sense of Sophocles' *Ajax* transformed into two productions that echo contemporary dramatic trends. Nixon describes the "goodlie anticke apparrell" of the 1605 production,[31] but far from prioritizing a historically accurate reconstruction of Attic drama, these Elizabethan and Jacobean adapters of *Ajax* for the progress visits seem to have updated the play to satisfy the tastes of its contemporary audience, particularly the monarch.

Regina Literata, Rex Platonicus

Illic laeta parat pubes spectacula, Scenae
Materiam veteris, multiplicesque iocos,

Et Tragicam ferri rabiem, querelosque Cothurnos,
Moesta quibus tristi funera clade sonant.
Quis Maiestati nugas praebere canoras
Ausus, quis mimos apposuisse leues?

[In that place, the young men prepare happy spectacles,
The subject of the ancient stage and many jests;
Also the tragic rage of iron, the complaining tragic actors,
Mournful funerals in which they sound in sad misfortune.
Who (would) dare to offer (her) Majesty melodious trifles,
To have placed before her petty pantomimists?]

Abraham Hartwell, *Regina Literata* (1565)[32]

Ajax's antiquarian cachet, and the contemporary perception of tragedy as an elevated genre—"high and excellent," in Sidney's terms[33]—also rendered it suitable for staging before the monarch. Oxford and Cambridge were uniquely placed to showcase humanistic learning through their progress entertainments, alongside the standard progresses provision of hospitality and compliment, and so during these visits the universities sought to appeal directly to the monarch's sense of erudition, an institutional agenda exemplified by the titles of progress narratives such as Abraham Hartwell's *Regina Literata* (London, 1565) and Isaac Wake's *Rex Platonicus* (Oxford, 1607). The University Orders for Elizabeth's 1564 visit specify that Cambridge was "to provide Hercules furens, Troas, or some *Princely Tragedy*" (my emphasis): Alan H. Nelson has pointed out that we don't know whether the Order refers to Euripides' plays or Seneca's, but what is clear is that the organizers wanted to offer a story that involved ancient Greek heroes.[34] A clue to their motivation might be the word "Princely," which does double duty here, referring *both* to the typical *dramatis personae* of Greek tragedy (heroes, gods, royalty—Aristotle's "those who are in high station or good fortune"[35]) *and* to the queen in the audience.[36] By asking whether "trifles" (nugas) and "petty pantomimists" (mimos . . . leues) could entertain someone as intellectually serious-minded as the Queen, Hartwell's poem echoes the more explicit compliment paid in the University Order which described the queen as "adorned with all kinde of good literature, which is rare & mervelous in a woman."[37] Hartwell's rhetorical question represents a marked effort on the part of the university to *perform* its own learning, and the plays were squarely a part of that humanistic performance.[38]

During the progress visits, Elizabeth and James played up to a picture of themselves as the ideal consumers of such "Princely Tragedye." Elizabeth delivered speeches in Latin, "rendred thankes in greeke" for a Greek oration at Christ's, and, despite her "foeminilis pudor" (womanly modesty), delivered an oration in Latin at St Mary's Church.[39] Despite multiple references in the Orders and accounts to the king's short attention span—the stipulation of "very briefe and short oration" recurs[40]—James gamely responded to the university's fashioning of him as a *Rex Platonicus,* reportedly declaring during a visit to the new Bodleian Library that "if I were not a King, I would be an University man."[41] While the universities complimented royal learning, the monarch reciprocally performed erudition, to reassure the institutions that their values and teaching were prized, and thereby to invite loyalty. One reason why the organizers included a classical play like *Ajax* in the entertainment program was to offer the *Regina Literata* or *Rex Platonicus* the gift of the university's erudition, and thereby to pay the monarch the compliment of acknowledging his or hers.

Both Elizabeth and James had been taught by influential humanist tutors who were ardent advocates of Greek tragedy, and awareness of the monarch's own intellectual formation, particularly at Cambridge in 1564, may also have prompted the universities to stage *Ajax.* Elizabeth's tutor Roger Ascham had been involved in the Greek reforms initiated by Cheke and Smith in the 1540s; more specifically, he had translated Sophocles' *Philoctetes* in 1543,[42] and he articulated throughout his writing a particular fondness for Sophocles. In *Toxophilus* (1545) too, Ascham's bow-lover quotes one of Teucer's speeches from *Ajax,* which Ascham translated into English.[43] In *The Scholemaster* (published 1570), Ascham recommends Sophocles among a select few other Greek and Latin authors as a model of "what is fitte and *decorum* in euerie one, to the trew vse of perfite Imitation" (sig. 57[r]). At the start of her reign, Elizabeth and Ascham still read Greek and Latin together after dinner, and he was indirectly involved in the 1564 visit, writing to the Earl of Leicester that he should learn from the plays he saw at Cambridge: "I truste you beinge at Cambrige and hearinge Comedies, Tragedies and Disputacions there will moue you . . . to thincke as I doe."[44] All in all, her former tutor's predilection for Sophocles may well have prompted the staging of *Ajax* before Elizabeth in 1564.

The association between monarch, tutor, Greek tragedy, and university context is less strong in James's case, but his tutor George Buchanan's involvement in the king's education, and influence on the king's classicism,[45] was as well-known in 1605 as Elizabeth's relationship with Roger Ascham had been fifty years beforehand. Buchanan had worked extensively on Greek tragedy, translating Euripides' *Medea* and *Alcestis* at the Collège de Guyenne in Bordeaux during the 1540s, and Ascham had singled out Buchanan's Latin biblical play *Iephthe* as one of the few contemporary tragedies "able to abyde the trew touch of *Aristotles* preceptes, and *Euripides* examples" (*Scholemaster,* sig. 57ʳ). Buchanan died in 1582, but his association with James only strengthened the new monarch's claims to erudition as "University man" and *Rex Platonicus.* Echoing Buchanan's influence, one of James's earliest published works, 1584's *The essayes of a prentise, in the diuine art of poesie,* is full of classical mythological allusions and meditations on the workings of literary genre, and the poem "The Vranie, or heavenly Mvse" makes clear the fascination of Homeric and Greek tragic stories: here, the speaker talks of the pleasure of using Greek to give "a lusty glaise / For to descryue the *Troian* Kings of olde, / And them that *Thebes* and *Mycens* crowns did holde."[46] The stories of ancient Troy, Thebes and Mycenae, particularly their depiction of kingship, all held considerable fascination for the poem's speaker: knowledge at the universities of the king's well-attested classical scholarship, often remarked upon in orations and debates during the 1605 visit, as well as Jones's impulse to reconstruct Vitruvian stagecraft and the "high and excellent" status of tragedy, must all have suggested themselves to the Oxford organizers as compelling reasons for staging a Greek tragedy before the king.

"Goodliest Argument and vse"

We have already seen how the progress visits were meant to reassure the monarch of the universities' good faith, how the entertainments were to reflect "Order and lernyng," and how the elevation of tragedy as a genre rendered it appropriate—in theory, if not in practice—for staging before the monarch, so that *Ajax* at the universities, as "Princely Tragedye," became an institutionally acceptable form of intellectual compliment. In a discussion of receptions of Euripides' *Iphigenia,* Pantelis Michelakis has discussed how theater, particularly Greek tragedy, can be used both "as a conservative force, a force of closure thought to pose a threat to the disruptive potential of radical art," and "as a metaphor for division and difference."[47] This dichotomy is helpful for thinking about two of the main ways in which Greek tragedy was viewed by theorists and adapters of the form. At the early modern universities during the progress visits, no "disruptive potential" featured within the plays chosen, but instead, rather than aiming to make the spectator feel personally "struck so to the soul," in Hamlet's words, and experience individualized "insight into anger," in Sidney's, the two performances of *Ajax* at the universities aimed at collective conformism—that "conservative force"—rather than individual emotional response, guaranteed to disrupt and provoke. The interventions of university authorities, Privy Council, and leading courtiers ensured that the play would have to be received in an orderly manner, and this reception rested on how theater during the royal progresses was meant to function: first, the monarch had to be visibly impressed, and then the whole of the courtly and academic hierarchy fanning out below the monarch should be entertained. Within the performances of *Ajax,* at least, there was no room for disruption.

To craft a "Princely Tragedye" appropriate for the progresses, adapters of *Ajax* had to subdue in their new versions the more disquieting elements that contemporary theorists like Sidney and many later commentators have seen as central to the play.[48] If we look at Sidney's definition of a politicized tragedy, its intended impact on royalty and its unsettling aftermath from the spectator's perspective, we see how far *Ajax* on the progresses deviated from this view:

> [Tragedy] that openeth the greatest woundes, and . . . maketh kings fear to be tyrants, and tyrants manifest their tyrannical humours, that with stirring the affects of admiration and commiseration, teacheth the uncertainty of this world, and upon how weak foundations gilden roofs are builded.[49]

Rather than teaching uncertainty and "stirring the affects," the university progresses sought to *perform* unity, order, loyalty. While university dramatists during a progress visit would never have emphasized these more troubling elements of tragedy, of course, Sidney's words make us reflect on what he and other literary contemporaries thought tragedy could, even *should* be, and how toothless a subgenre the academic tragedies performed during the progresses must have seemed to them. Bruce R. Smith has argued that early modern academic drama flattens out Greek tragedy and its "awkward" ethics, and substitutes a simplified "Christianized" morality,[50] and to modern readers and spectators perhaps more familiar with politicized adaptations of Sophocles, as recently discussed by Edith Hall and Lorna Hardwick,[51] the fact that Greek tragedy was *not* perceived as radical, *not* as politicized at the early modern English universities might seem odd, particularly when contemporaries like Sidney were starting to argue for a more ethically engaged form of theater. Yet we have to acknowledge that all readings of classical texts are "mediated, situated, contingent,"[52] and it was the *situation* of these two performances of *Ajax* that rendered "disruptive potential" impossible. The very arguments that Sidney posits for a more explosive kind of tragic performance— ambivalent ethics; emotive characterization; empathy with anger— disqualify such tragedy from ever being staged during the progresses. Avoidance of these more complicated elements might suggest *why* the adapters foregrounded other elements such as staging, properties, and larger-than-life Senecanism over Sophocles' drama of a once admired warrior deteriorating into a suicidal madman, a narrative which certainly "teacheth the uncertainty of this world." If we acknowledge the sharply "situated" nature of the progress tragic adaptations, rather than dwell on what these two versions of *Ajax* were *not,* it makes more sense to consider the ideological reasons behind their staging, besides their status as "Princely Tragedy," or their function as an opportunity for Inigo Jones to show off his reading of Vitruvius.

For humanists such as Roger Ascham, Greek tragedy was to be taken to heart, to enrich the learner's intellect and improve his (or her, in Elizabeth's case) rhetorical skill. For Ascham, Greek tragedy offered a language of wonderful richness and polish, certainly, but it also offered lessons for *use,* more than epic and lyric poetry, as much as philosophy and history:

> In Tragedies, (the goodliest Argument of all, and for the vse, either of a learned preacher, or a Ciuill Ientleman, more profitable than *Homer, Pindar, Virgill,* and *Horace:* yea comparable in myne opinion, with the doctrine of *Aristotle, Plato,* and *Xenophon,*) the *Grecians, Sophocles* and *Euripides* far ouer match our *Seneca* in *Latin.*[53]

Compare Ascham with Sidney: rather than a genre that "teacheth the uncertainty of this world," tragedy becomes "profitable" for the "learned preacher, or a Ciuill Ientleman." Modern scholars have rightly viewed as more complicated the relationship between Attic tragedy and Athenian *polis*,[54] but for Ascham, Athens was unequivocally an ideal:

> The remembrance of soch a common welthe, vsing soch discipline and order for yougthe, and thereby bringing forth to their praise, and leaning to vs for our example, such Capitaines for warre, soch Councelors for peace, and matcheles masters, for all kinde of learninge, is pleasant for me to recite. (sig. 17ᵛ)

Ascham offers an ideal of Greek culture, manifest in the "goodliest Argument . . . and vse" of its tragedies, and this became a strong reason for staging such plays before the monarch. His idea of weaving the rhetorical fabric of tragedy into religious and secular (vernacular) discourse hearkens back to an earlier humanistic idealism, found in the revival of Greek tragedy at St. John's College, Cambridge, in the 1530s, and in his hope for what tragedy should do, as Jonathan Walker has recently argued.[55] Ascham's terms ("discipline and order"; "all kinde of learninge") echo Cecil's program for the 1564 visit, and Ascham clearly views Greek tragedy as the ideal product of an ideal state, the Athenian "common welthe." His case for the genre's "profitable . . . vse" seems to ignore much of the actual content of Greek tragedy—all of the incest, cannibalism, awful, often innocent deaths, horrendous families, vendettas, and ruthless gods—to construct an idealized version of the rhetorical and literary elements such plays offer, that are, to Ascham, handily ripe for extraction by the shrewd Elizabethan humanist, whether "learned preacher" or "Ciuill Ientleman."

Isaac Wake, like Ascham, glosses over the more unsavory aspects of Greek tragic plot. Wake, as the only chronicler to offer an interpretation of why *Ajax* was chosen, argues that its plot renders it particularly suitable for an academic, courtly audience:

> The choice of its argument was made not only because it provided, with a splendid and stately variety of representations, abundant delight for such great spectators, but because the matter also seemed to be very appropriate for both courtly and academic ears and minds.[56]

Wake states that the play was thoroughly suitable—"perquàm accomodata"—in its 1605 context because Odysseus gets Achilles' armor for his *eloquence:*

Ajax claimed those arms as a reward for military prowess, but Ulysses obtained [them] as the deserts of [his] wisdom and learned eloquence.

Like Ascham's championing of Greek tragedy through presenting it as an exemplary ideal for both rhetoric and the state, Wake's interpretation seems curiously one-sided when compared with how Odysseus' eloquence is actually represented in Αἴας. However different the 1605 adaptation was "in matter as in expression," the adapters must have worked hard to excise the other characters' ambivalence toward Odysseus's smooth tongue. The chorus in the Greek original speaks of his "whispered words," for instance, against Ajax, implying, if not making explicit, that he engages in insidious, destructive gossip;[57] to Ajax, Odysseus is a κίναδος, a "cunning fox," for his scheming and his silver tongue. Ajax, of course, is Odysseus' enemy in the play, and due to his anger his judgments are extreme, but Sophocles posits the idea that eloquence—Wake's "literata facundia"—can be manipulative and pernicious, not unequivocally praiseworthy. Wake's interpretation of *Ajax* is so doggedly straightforward that it at first seems like a willful misreading, but then we have to remember that he's commenting on the altered Latin adaptation rather than Αἴας, and that his reading of the play was based on what was performed in front of him in Christ Church hall.

Nonetheless, we are left with a sense that the progress adaptations offered only simplified versions of the original. G. Zanker has argued that Αἴας takes its questioning of heroic values from Homer's *Iliad,* and that "the problems inherent in heroism that lie at the very heart of the *Iliad* were ones which were perceived by Greek society in Sophocles' day not as any mere poetic construct, but as live issues."[58] As evidence of the "mediated, situated, contingent" nature of the progress performances of *Ajax* and their distance from the original play, those "live issues" that Zanker identifies in Homer and Sophocles do not seem to have been particularly compelling to the play's Elizabethan and Jacobean adapters, nor does Sidney's case for the play's potential behavioral lessons, the "insight into anger" Ajax's plight could provide, seem to have been a factor. For Wake, rather than the "live issues" of what constitutes heroism and proper heroic behavior, it is Odysseus's "prudentia" and "literata facundia" which fit the play for an academic audience, his wisdom and his learned eloquence which unquestionably qualify him for the prize of Achilles' armor above the *flagellifer* Ajax's "militaris virtus" (soldierly strength, courage). Just as the 1564 performance seems to have relied on its properties and "furentem" protagonist to impress, so the 1605 production rested on its stagecraft and the reassuring, orderly message that spectators like Wake appear to have derived from it: eloquence always triumphs, and force must always be subordinated to superior intelligence. In Ascham's terms, and implicitly in Wake's, Greek tragedy teaches skills as necessary to statecraft as to university life: rhetorical facility, persuasive words. The play's interests in verbal register and eloquence's power would clearly appeal to audiences at the institutions bent on teaching rhetorical polish and linguistic self-awareness, but to convey this message, Sophocles' representation of words' potentially destructive power had to be flattened out, as did the play's potential for "teaching of the uncertainty of this world." Stripped of its *ambivalence* toward rhetorical facility, and its potential for "stirring the affects of admiration and commiseration," then, *Ajax* seems to have been rendered "profitable"—in Ascham's terms—both as visual extravaganza and as unequivocal praise of the arts of rhetoric. Nixon, as we have seen, described the play as clothed in "goodlie anticke apparrell": this apparel, though visually impressive and "goodlie," profoundly altered Αἴας through the act of context-specific adaptation.

Notes

1. For ease of reference, I will refer to Sophocles' play as Αἴας and the two university adaptations as *Ajax.*

2. Philip Sidney, *The Defence of Poesy,* ed. Gavin Alexander (London: Penguin, 2004), 17.

3. James McConica, "The Rise of the Undergraduate College," in *The History of the University of Oxford* (Oxford: Clarendon Press, 1986), 3:1–68 (22); see also G. D. Duncan, "Public Lectures and Professorial Chairs,'" ibid., 335–61 (340–41).

4. See Frederick S. Boas, *University Drama in the Tudor Age* (Oxford, 1914; repr. New York: Benjamin Blom, 1971), 97.

5. See Alan H. Nelson, ed., *Records of Early English Drama: Cambridge* (Toronto: University of Toronto Press, 1989) (hereafter *REED: Cambridge*), 1:231.

6. Anthony Nixon, *Oxfords Triumph,* quoted in *REED: Oxford* (Toronto and London: University of Toronto Press/British Library, 2004) ed. John R. Elliott, Jr., and Alan H. Nelson (University); Alexandra F. Johnston and Diana Wyatt (City), 1:303.

7. See the anonymously written manuscript "The preparacion at Oxford in August 1605" (*REED: Oxford,* 1:299).

8. See Anthony Nixon's published account *Oxfords Triumph* (London, 1605) (*REED: Oxford,* 1:303); see also Anthony Parr, "Nixon, Anthony (fl. 1592–1616)," *Oxford Dictionary of National Biography,* http://www.oxforddnb.com/view/arti cle/20206 (accessed September 1, 2008).

9. Siobhan Keenan, "Spectator and Spectacle: Royal Entertainments at the Universities in the 1560s," in *The Progresses, Pageants, and Entertainments of Queen Elizabeth I,* ed. Jayne Elisabeth Archer, Elizabeth Goldring, and Sarah Knight (Oxford: Oxford University Press, 2007), 86–103 (87–90); Linda Shenk, "Gown before Crown: Scholarly Abjection and Academic Entertainment under Queen Elizabeth I," in *Early Modern Academic Drama,* ed. Jonathan Walker and Paul Streufert (Aldershot: Ashgate, 2008), 19–44 (22–26); see also Penry Williams, "State, Church and University 1558–1603," in *The History of The University of Oxford,* 3:397–440 (397–401); Patrick Collinson, *The Elizabethan Puritan Movement* (1967; repr., London: Jonathan Cape, 1971), 67–83; C. M. Dent, *Protestant Reformers in Elizabethan Oxford* (Oxford: Oxford University Press, 1983), 47–73; H. C. Porter, *Reformation and Reaction in Tudor Cambridge* (New York: Cambridge University Press, 1958).

10. See the section entitled "Queen Elizabeth I at the University of Cambridge, 5–10 August 1564," in *John Nichols's The Progresses and Public Processions of Queen Elizabeth I: A New Edition of the Early Modern Sources,* ed. Jayne Elisabeth Archer, Elizabeth Clarke, and Elizabeth Goldring. (Oxford: Oxford University Press, forthcoming). I would like to thank the editors of the Cambridge material, Elisabeth Leedham-Green, Jayne Elisabeth Archer, and Faith Eales, for their permission to cite from this material prior to publication.

11. *REED: Oxford,* 1:295.

12. See, for example, the 1554–55 decree by the "Dean and Chapiter" at Christ Church that discusses four plays at Christmas, which had to include "a comedy in greke" and "a tragedy in greke" (*REED: Oxford,* 1:96); at Cambridge, see, for instance, the stipulation in the Queens' College statutes for 1544–55 for the playing of Greek (*REED:* Cambridge, 1:205).

13. For evidence of Greek plays performed at Cambridge, particularly during the 1530s, see *REED: Cambridge,* vol. 2, app. 8; for details of Cheke and Smith's involvement in Greek language performances, especially at Queens and St. John's, see *REED: Cambridge,* 2:766 and 769. See also Streufert, "Christopherson at Cambridge: Greco-Catholic Ethics in the Protestant University," in *Early Modern Academic Drama,* 45–64.

14. The 1564 Latin version of *Ajax* may well have been based on the Dutchman Georg Rotaller's 1550 translation: Rotaller, following the 1502 Aldine edition of *Sophoclis tragaediae septem cum commentariis,* translates the play's Greek title into *Aiax Flagellifer,* and this combination of title plus epithet was used in both progress performances. For a facsimile edition of Rotaller's translation, see the digitized version on the Bibliothèque Nationale de France Web site: http://gallic a2.bnf.fr/ark:/12148/bpt6k74932g.image.f2.langEN.odeAffichageimage.

15. *REED: Cambridge,* 1:238 (trans. Abigail Ann Young 2:1138).

16. *REED: Cambridge,* 1:238; Bruce R. Smith, *Ancient Scripts and Modern Experience on the English Stage* (Princeton: Princeton University Press, 1988), 216.

17. *REED: Oxford,* 1:286.

18. Ibid., 1:295.

19. John Orrell, *The Theatres of Inigo Jones and John Webb* (Cambridge: Cambridge University Press, 1985), 30.

20. Aristotle, *Poetics*, 1449a 16, trans. W. Hamilton Frye (Cambridge: Harvard University Press, 1946).

21. *REED: Oxford,* 1:296.

22. *REED: Oxford,* 1:308, and 2:1022 (trans. Patrick Gregory).

23. Smith, *Ancient Scripts and Modern Experience,* 216.

24. *REED: Oxford,* 1:307, trans. Patrick Gregory 2:1023.

25. John Studley, *The eyght tragedie of Seneca. Entituled Agamemnon. Translated out of Latin in to English, by Iohn Studley, student in Trinitie Colledge in Cambridge* (London: Thomas Colwell, 1566), sig. Bir.

26. *REED: Oxford,* 1:308; 2:1023.

27. See Sophocles, Αἴας (*Ajax*), ed. and trans. Hugh Lloyd-Jones (Cambridge: Harvard University Press, 1994) 108–9.

28. *REED: Oxford,* 1:308 and 2:1023.

29. Later in the seventeenth century, the Furies are among the cast in plays such as James Shirley's *The Traytor* (1635) and Thomas Nabbes's *Microcosmus* (1637).

30. Thomas Kyd, *The Spanish Tragedie* (published 1592), ed. Emma Smith (London: Penguin Books, 1998), Act 4. Scene 5 (91).

31. *REED: Oxford,* 1:299.

32. *REED: Cambridge,* 1:238 and 2:1138 (trans. Abigail Ann Young).

33. Sidney, *Defence of Poesy,* 27.

34. *REED: Cambridge,* 1:229; 2:1216.

35. Aristotle, *Poetics,* 1453a 5.

36. The adjective "princely" is often used in progress narratives, as we might expect: in Christ Church in 1566, one eyewitness, the Corpus Christi student Miles Windsor refers to the Hall's "Princelie lightes of wax" (see Corpus Christi College MS 257 fols. 104–23 (107r). Windsor adds in the margin that "Lights provyded for 5 nightes woulde serve but one nighte," implying that the lights' princeliness clearly came at a cost beyond the projected lighting budget. For my edition of Windsor's account, see the section "Queen Elizabeth's Visit to the University of Oxford, 31 August–6 September 1566" in the new edition of John Nichols' *Progresses* (see n.10).

37. *REED: Cambridge,* 1:227.

38. *Ajax* was staged alongside one Roman comedy (Plautus' *Aulularia*) and two tragedies, Edward Halliwell's *Dido,* based on book 4 of Virgil's *Aeneid,* and Nicholas Udall's *Ezechias,* derived from 2 Kings 18–19. The emphasis shifted during James's visit from tragedy to comedy and pastoral. In 1605, *Ajax* sat alongside Robert Burton's Latin "pastorall . . . Comedie" *Alba,* Matthew Gwynne's Latin "Comoedia faceta" (witty Comedy) *Vertumnus,* and Samuel Daniel's "english playe . . . drawn out of fydus pastor"; this was first entitled *Arcadia Reform'd,* tellingly renamed *The Queen's Arcadia,* which was "presented to her Maiestie and her ladies." See *REED: Oxford,* 1:298–99 (anonymous commentator on *Alba*); 1:307 (Isaac Wake on *Vertumnus*); 1:299 (anon. on *The Queen's Arcadia*).

39. See the Cambridge 1564 section of the new edition of John Nichols's *Progresses* (n.10).

40. See, for instance, *REED: Oxford,* 2:283 (Orders of the Delegates of Convocation): "att ye topp of Quatervois ye greeke professor shall make a very breife and short oration in greeke not exceedinge twentie lynes to his maiestie."

41. See Robert Burton, *The Anatomy of Melancholy,* ed. Thomas C. Faulkner, Nicolas K. Kiessling, and Rhonda L. Blair, commentary J. B. Bamborough and Martin Dodsworth, 6 vols. (Oxford: Oxford University Press, 1989–2000), 2:88, and 6:434.

42. See Paul Streufert, "Christopherson at Cambridge: Greco-Catholic Ethics in the Protestant University," *Early Modern Academic Drama,* 46–47.

43. Roger Ascham, *Toxophilus* (London: Edward Whytchurch, 1545): "And therfore it is true that Teucer sayeth in Sophocles. Seldome at all good thinges be knowen how good to be / Before a man suche thinges do misse out of his handes" (sig. 11r).

44. See *REED: Cambridge,* 1:229 (letter from Ascham to Robert Dudley, August 5, 1564).

45. See Rebecca W. Bushnell, "George Buchanan, James VI, and Neo-Classicism," in *Scots and Britons: Scottish Political Thought and the Union of 1603,* ed. Roger A. Mason (Cambridge: Cambridge University Press, 1994), 91–111; see also Roger Mason, "George Buchanan, James VI and the Presbyterians," in *Kingship and the Commonwealth: Political Thought in Renaissance and Reformation Scotland* (East Lothian: Tuckwell Press, 1998), 187–214.

46. James VI and I, *The essayes of a prentise, in the diuine art of poesie* (Edinburgh: Thomas Vautrollier), sig. Dir.

47. Pantelis Michelakis, "Reception, Performance, and the Sacrifice of Iphigenia," in *Classics and the Uses of Reception,* ed. Charles Martindale and Richard Thomas (Oxford: Blackwell, 2006), 216–26 (217).

48. For studies of *Ajax* that discuss these elements, see, for instance, P. E. Easterling, "Character in Sophocles," *Greece & Rome,* 2nd ser., 24, no. 2 (Oct. 1977): 121–29; Bernard M.W. Knox, "The *Ajax* of Sophocles," *Harvard Studies in Classical Philology* 65 (1961): 1–37; Jean-Pierre Vernant and Page duBois, "Ambiguity and Reversal: On the Enigmatic Structure of *Oedipus Rex,*" in *New Literary History,* 9, no. 3 (Spring 1978): 475–501.

49. Sidney, *Defence of Poesy,* 27–28.

50. Smith, *Ancient Scripts and Modern Experience,* 201.

51. See Edith Hall, "Sophocles' *Electra* in Britain," in *Sophocles Revisited: Essays Presented to Sir Hugh Lloyd-Jones,* ed. Jasper Griffin (Oxford: Oxford University Press, 1999), 261–306; Lorna Hardwick, "Remodelling Receptions: Greek Drama as Diaspora in Performance," in *Classics and the Uses of Reception,* 204–15.

52. Charles Martindale, "Thinking through reception," in *Classics and the Uses of Reception,* 3.

53. Roger Ascham, *The Scholemaster* (London: Iohn Daye, [1570]), sig. 52v.

54. For a critical overview of such recent ideological interpretations of Attic tragedy, see Jasper Griffin, "The Social Function of Attic Tragedy," *Classical Quarterly,* n.s., 48, no. 1 (1998): 39–61.

55. Jonathan Walker, "Learning to Play," in *Early Modern Academic Drama,* 2.

56. See *REED: Oxford,* 2:1022, translated from Wake's Latin by Patrick Gregory. Wake's original description is as follows, as in *REED: Oxford,* 1:307–8: "Cujus argumenti factus est delectus, non tantùm quòd splendidâ pomposáque representationum varietate, tantis spectatoribus delectationem affluentem ministraret; sed quòd materia etiam videretur Aulicis, Academicisque auribus, animisque perquàm accomodata. Celebris enim representatur illa de Achillis defuncti armis con-

tentio, quae sibi pro militaris virtutis praemio vendicauit Aiax sed obtinuit Vlysses, prudentiæ meritò, & literatae facundi*ae*."

  57. Sophocles, Αἴας, 46–47.

  58. G. Zanker, "Sophocles' *Ajax* and the Heroic Values of the *Iliad*," *Classical Quarterly*, n.s., 42, no. 1 (1992): 20–25. (20, 21).

Professional Playing in London and Superior Cambridge Responses

Andrew Gurr

My real subject is sex. To be a little more precise it is about the effect of living in the monastic conditions of the chambers at either of the two universities or the Inns of Court in late Tudor and early Stuart times. Both of these points have a lot to do with playwriting and playgoing through this period. There are many associations between being an Inns man and playgoing beyond what Henry Fitzgeoffrey mockingly versified in 1616 and Francis Lenton's claim that by the late 1620s law students preferred Ben Jonson's plays to their law books. Some of the stories are very intimate, like the one by Bernard Capp about an Inns man losing his place at the Inner Temple for trying to smuggle his girlfriend in dressed as a page, an obvious adaptation of theatrical disguise to life at the Inns. The Oxbridge students were more remote, but kept a keen eye on what went on at the playhouses in London. The key question, perhaps too deep for a brief survey of this kind, is what the all-male seclusion that went with a bachelor's residence at a university or an Inn did to the thoughts (and feelings) about the other sex in the minds of the men who wrote plays while living there.

First the sociology. For all the recent transformation of collegiate life from monosexual to bisexual, there are some peculiar blanks in the minds of Oxbridge historians. Their familiarity with the seven-century-old tradition of collegiate life which they inherited seems to have prevented them from commenting on how peculiar the practice was in the sixteenth century, as it is now. Surviving from before the English Reformation, the concept of the monastic single-sex college lasted until the 1980s. First-degree graduates are still called bachelors because university students had to be unmarried if they were to live in their ostensibly monastic colleges. Single-sex colleges only recently gave up the requirement that their residents must remain unmarried for the duration of their stay at university.

The chief reason why Oxbridge retained the monastic principle in this form for so long after the Reformation was of course that to male Catholics and Protestants alike women were thought unfit for study. That prejudice has somehow concealed the anomaly where for so long after the demolition of the monasteries the Oxbridge colleges maintained the same principle of a necessarily celibate existence. Another was the equally prejudicial view that wedded life provided too many distractions for a youth whose duty was to read and think. One of the many reasons why Shakespeare never went to Oxford or Cambridge was because he married at the unnaturally early age for his time of eighteen. As Ann Hathaway's husband he was debarred from ever becoming a student. Ben Jonson, who also married early, did receive an honorary degree in 1619 at the age of forty-seven, but that was a master's, not a bachelor's degree. Shakespeare himself made fun of the idea of a monastic male enclave given over exclusively to academic study in *Love's Labours Lost,* a title possibly containing a hint of a personal comment on his own choice of marriage in place of learning. The play starts by mocking the Catholic idea that a man should and could successfully spend his youth entirely secluded from normal life and the society of women. That, of course, was the principle on which the Oxbridge colleges were based.

It is predictable that historians of the Inns of Court should equally have ignored the existence of the identical rules for celibate monastic life in the four major societies of the Inns of Court in London. The Inns had the same concerns as the colleges about their students being kept undistracted by the presence of women, or at least of nubile ones, and their records are more explicit than those of the colleges about the consequent problems. All the Inns banned women and boys, even from attending sermons in chapel. In 1581 Gray's Inn issued an order that no laundresses and victuallers— kitchen women—who were under the age of forty were to be employed. Two years before that the Inner Temple had been more restrictive still, recording in its parliament that "first, it is ordered that the cooks or any other officer in the kitchen shall not have any woman or woman-kind to come or resort into the kitchen or kitchen door for any cause, upon pain that the officer to whom such person shall resort to lose his office or place, or otherwise be punished by amercement."[1] Seven years later this idea was made still

clearer, "It is ordered that there shall be in the kitchen but one un-
dercook and three turn broaches [turnspits], and all women to be
avoided." A recent edition of the *Oxford English Dictionary News*
(September 2005) quoted what seems to have been a stock masculinist joke, as prevalent now as it was in 1762 when the statement
was made. It said " 'Tis a point of great prudence in the governors
of colleges, that the bed-makers should be bothe aged and uninviting." The laws varied, but always denied the possibility of sex. According to Wilfred Prest, Lincoln's Inn in 1478 fined a member who
was found with a woman in his chamber "at the forbidden time."[2]
In the 1480s fornication brought a fine of £5 for the act in a room,
and £1 in the garden or in Chancery Lane.

This kind of masculinism calls in question an assertion made by
Edward Sharpham, a member of the Middle Temple from 1594,
who wrote *The Fleire* in 1605 for the Blackfriars Boys and *Cupid's
Whirligig* in 1606. In the opening scene of the former play a young
gallant says he is a gentleman "for I was both born and begotten in
an Inns a Court." To which the comment is "he that's but admitted
to the house is a gentleman, much more he that's begotten in the
house." Another "puny" or beginner student in the same play is
said to claim that he sleeps with citizen's daughters but actually
does so with his laundress. We do not know whether she was expected to be aged and uninviting, but the social sneer is self-evident. In *Ruff, Band, and Cuff*, a manuscript and a printed quarto of
about 1615,[3] a passage (134–35) has Ruff replying to a question if
he served in the low countries with "Where I served its noe matter,
I'me sure I have bin pressed often." To which Cuff replies "Truly
his laundresse will beare him wittnesse of that." The erotic innu-
endo gives a strong underlay to the dialogue's elaborate joke about
ironing cuffs. There was an inherently theatrical aspect to such
jokes and the activities they reported on, not least in the use of male
disguise for the women who were smuggled into the male preserve
of London's chambers. Bernard Capp reports a story about Katherine Cuffe, a servant girl who had an illegitimate child by Ambrose
Jasper in 1599.[4] The London Bridewell minute-books record that
Jasper was a cook living in the serving quarters at the Inner Temple.
After Katherine's child was born, Jasper went back to Katherine at
her employer's house and told her she must come to see him in his
lodgings at the Inner Temple dressed in "boyes apparrell . . . lest
that she should be espyed." She was observed entering the Inn
dressed flamboyantly like a gentleman with a cloak and hat cover-

ing her doublet and hose, that is, posing as a young resident Templar. That was not far removed from the sensation that Arbella Stuart caused in 1610 when she fled from Whitehall Palace disguised as a male page, and was thought by one observer to be Moll Frith, the notorious transvestite soon to be made the heroine of the Fortune's *Roaring Girl* in her male attire.[5] The incident does signify Mistress Cuffe's need if she was to get into the Temple to disguise herself as a gentleman, not just a junior servant of the kitchens. It was normal for the porters at the Temple doors to block the entry of any woman. Females were not even allowed to hear sermons in the chapel.

It is worth considering why such segregative rules prevailed, and more to the point what were its effects on the young men who became residents with bachelor status at the university colleges and London's Inns of Court. The writings of such Londoners as Edward Sharpham, a Middle Templar who seems never to have actually lived in his Inn's chambers, John Webster, and his peers such as John Ford and William Davenant tell us something about the effects of living in the ostensibly monastic seclusion of the London Inns. But on a different tack we can also learn something about student sexual attitudes from the plays written to be staged in English at the university colleges.

Staging plays in English was an exercise with some peculiar functions in Cambridge at the turn of the century and after. In the Prologue to his *Albumazar,* staged before King James at Trinity College in 1615, Thomas Tomkis said his play was to be recited in "this forraigne language," English, for the sake of the ladies in the audience, "for whose sake / Wee now speake English (*For Latine is our mother tongue)."* An earlier play, *Club Law,* staged at Clare College in 1599–1600, was allegedly written in English so that the uneducated citizens of the town would understand it. Such social prejudice was an integral part of the outlook of Cambridge students, whatever their own social origin. They knew that by gaining an academic degree they automatically became gentlemen, making them socially superior to every citizen.[6]

Club Law, which was well edited a century ago by G. C. Moore Smith, is a college play based on the public row that had been raging for some years between the mayor of Cambridge and the university authorities, and is a good example of the student outlook of the time.[7] From its foundation Cambridge used its royal charters to claim the right to control all supply and pricing of provisions, food, wine, fuel, and candles to the colleges. The town had no reciprocal rights. A statute issued in 1561 under Elizabeth added that the university's officers "as well by day as by night, at their pleasure, might make scrutiny, search and inquisition, in the town and suburbs, and in Barnwell and Sturbridge [location of the biggest annual fair in England], for all common women, bawds, vagabonds, and other suspected persons . . . and punish all whom on such scrutiny, search, and inquisition, they should find guilty or suspected of evil, by imprisonment of their bodies, banishment, or otherwise as the Chancellor or his Vice-Gerent should deem fit."[8] It is hardly surprising that self-respecting mayors of the town should object to such comprehensive control, as many of them did. In 1596 that year's mayor drew up a list of complaints against the university, and his successor, Robert Wallis, elected at Michaelmas, refused to take the oath for conserving the university's privileges. Lord Burghley, who was chancellor, ordered him to take the oath, but he again refused at a meeting in December.

The conflict rolled on without any letup. In June 1597 the vice-chancellor, Dr. Jegon, complained to Burghley that the town had been "more factious and stirringe now of late then in former tymes, making choise of suche to be governours amongst them, as are most boulde and forward in attempts against this University."[9] Burghley died soon after, which did not help the university's cause. Lawsuits were taken out by both sides, without much effect. The mayor elected in 1599, John Yaxley, was quite as ardent as his predecessors in holding out against the university's rights. It was around this time that *Club Law* was composed at Clare Hall.

In act 2, scene 5 (page 37 of Moore Smith's edition), the student hero Philenius says to his fellow-student Musonius, after two citizen wives have made sexual passes at them, "as for them let us feede them with vaine delayes, least the Muses be not propitious unto us in our studies, being such profest enemies to Venus." Musonius replies "I hope my thoughts are of a higher pitch then to enter into such kennell thoughts." What they actually get from the two wives is only information, but news vital to the plot, which is about the threat of a citizen attack on the student body. From the citizen wives they learn specifically that some citizens have concealed a set of clubs to assault the students with. So informed, the students go on to find and hide them before beating the would-be attackers with their own clubs. Moore Smith gives ample information about the play's context of opposition between city and university in Cambridge at the time. We can easily accept his conclusion that *Club Law* was written from a student perspective about the current acts of some citizen gangs taking sides in the running affray between city and university.

Sex is not kept out of consideration, but it is put firmly, though with obvious prurience, to one side. In the previous scene, act 2, scene 4, Mistress Colby had told her fellow-wife "why, but theise gentle Athenians [Cambridge students] are such maiden fac't fellowes, ne're credit me, if I did not carrie Mr Musonius up into my bedchamber and shewed him my bed and arras hanging, and shutt the doore, and asked him if it were not a faire and soft bed and yet the foole understood mee not. And thereupon I fell of talking of fyne lynnen, and therupon I had him see if my smocke was not fyne Holland, and yet the foole understood me not. What could have a woman done more? Unless—" This affirmation of the sexist divide of men from women and the citizen women's alienated attitudes to their own males was an obvious feature used to decorate the current dispute between Cambridge's mayor and the university authorities. The women's interest in sex with the students is something the men ignore, with what credibility is left to our own imaginations.

According to Moore Smith, Fuller's history of Cambridge said that citizens went to see the play, obviously accessible to them because of its use of English rather than the Latin which was used for most student plays at the time. Smith is skeptical of that claim, and we must concede that the plot of the play in its overt hostility to the citizens and their wives clearly did not anticipate a major citizen presence. The wives are shown in ways hardly complimentary to the major citizens of Cambridge. That point goes with several other oddities in *Club Law* as it relates to the local politics of the time. The final speech was certainly written and addressed solely to the university members: "for your sakes kind Gentlemen some of our company have shed their bloud and have thought it well shed for your sakes." That amounts to an apology for using clubs in the street fights with the citizen gangs. The speaker invokes Plato as a philosopher favoring club law.

Club Law's explicit favoring of the university population against the citizenry raises a further question, how and why so many performances for and by students were composed in English, not Latin. In 1615 Thomas Tomkis in *Albumazar* excused its presentation to the courtiers of its royal audience at Cambridge not in Latin but English, which he called "this forraigne language." But why was it originally written in English when Tomkis composed it four or five years before? Was the snobbery of university versus town and against London professional playing quite as two-faced as that makes it seem? Did the colleges routinely expect to admit citizens to their performances? Such questions bring us to the most famous, or notorious, of the Cambridge plays written in English at the height of the success in London of the duopoly companies at the Rose and the Globe.

Of all the Oxbridge plays that take note of London theater by far the most celebrated are the Parnassus plays, written for the students of St. John's at Cambridge. Their sneers at London players such as Burbage and Kemp and their use of Shakespeare against Ben Jonson are commonly cited as the stock hearsay of the time. What they really provide us with is the downside of student thinking about life after they graduate from Cambridge. The three plays use some of the modes current in London at the time, chiefly Juvenalian satire and what Jonson called the comedy of "railing," made popular by graduates such as John Marston (who the second play perhaps parodies for his neologisms), Everard Guilpin, and the others whose books of railing satires were burned by the bishop of London in May 1599.

The first play, *The Pilgrimage to Parnassus,* takes the allegorical route to describe the ambitions of two young men aiming at the seductive graduate career of rhetorician and poet. Despite the likelihood and the promises made by failed students that all they will find is poverty, they persevere, and after four years of travels with a variety of adventures find themselves at the foot of Mount Parnassus. In the second play, *The First Part of the Returne from Parnassus,* they seek employment, and consider either writing for the press, joining the church, or taking to alcohol. None of these attracts the two venturers, so at the end they resolve to go to "Rome or Rhems," that is, to make the escape from Protestant poverty by joining the Catholic church abroad. The third and last play begins by summing up the story of the previous pair. Momus, an actor, declares that "these same *Philomusus* and *Studioso* have beene followed with a whip and a verse like a Couple of Vagabonds though *England* and *Italy.* The Pilgrimage to *Pernassus,* and the returne from *Pernassus,* have stood the honest *Stagekeepers* in many a Crownes expence for linckes and vizardes: purchas'd many a Sophister a knock with a clubbe, hindred the buttlers boxe, and emptied the Colledge barrells." Now they are back from Parnassus, and firmly in England, so the scene "lookes not good invention in the face."

It shows some inside knowledge of how graduates might try scratching a living from London printers. The two students, returned from overseas, reject the struggle with hostile printers, and take up cony-catching by pretending to be a French physician and his servant, looking for rich gulls who they can deceive by their ostensible learning. In the process they meet other ex-students who have failed to make their fortunes in various ways. They all fail to make much by their pretenses. The two end up offering their services to the players Burbage and Kemp in what they call "the basest trade." Failing in that, they turn to working as traveling fiddlers, and the play concludes with them both becoming shepherds on the Kentish downs. Their series of misadventures does not offer much hope of a good livelihood to would-be graduates. Perhaps that was one of the reasons for writing it in English, the language of the poor and uneducated.

Why these three plays appeared in English perhaps does reflect the feeling that Latin was an unprofitable course for study. But they were written for student audiences, who might have expected Latin to be the mode. The plays lack *Club Law*'s ostensible reason for making itself accessible to an audience including citizens, and I suspect that they show evidence that the popularity of the plays appearing at the two licensed London playhouses, the Rose and the Theatre, was impacting on at least some Cambridge students. The derision the third play shows for Burbage and Kemp must have more than a touch of jealousy in it.

Perhaps the most intriguing case of a play written in English and displaying anti-London theater prejudices is Tomkis's *Albumazar*.[10] Tomkis was the youngest son of a vicar at Bilston in Staffordshire, and educated at Shrewsbury School and then Trinity College, Cambridge. Both places were famous for its students staging plays. Tomkis stayed at Cambridge till at least 1610, when he wrote the play, before he inherited substantial wealth, and left the university, buying property near Wolverhampton, and working there as a lawyer, dying in 1634. His university plays, both in English, started with *Lingua* (1607), which went through six editions before the Restoration. It is a sprightly dialogue, burlesquing styles and academic arguments. Tomkis has been not very plausibly claimed also as the author of the similar *Band Cuff and Ruff* and *Work for Cut-*

lers. His second acknowledged play, *Albumazar,* was very largely a translation of Giambattista della Porta's *Lo Astrologo,* published in Venice in 1606. For his version Tomkis chose to cut out what its editor Hugh Dick calls *Lo Astrologo*'s "boisterous pornography." He also cut away a character whose "humor" is to speak in old proverbs, a clown type found in *Two Angry Women of Abingdon,* which may have been the reason Tomkis chose to omit him. The satire is partly based on the idiocies of astrology, also used by Middleton in 1612 as the chief humor of Weatherwise and his almanacs in *No Wit? No Help Like a Woman*'s at the Fortune. Albumazar mocks the pretentious speech of astrologers like Subtle, who are "Now then declining from *Theourgia, / Artenosoria, Pharmacia,* rejecting / *Necro-puro-geo-hydro-cheiro-coscinomancy,* / With other vaine and superstitious sciences, / Wee'l ancor at the Art Prestigiatorie, / That represents one figure for another, / With smooth deceit abusing th'eyes of mortals." When Ronca starts spouting astrological terms Pandolfo asks him "Pray you speake English." Charlatanry and gulling are the main targets of Tomkis's play, though he adjusts his main aim from the abuse of parental authority to social climbing. King James was known to be interested in astrology, so there was some adventurousness in presenting such a play before him. Tomkis revised his translation in 1614 before it was staged, probably when he knew the king would see it.

John Chamberlain accompanied the king to Cambridge, and afterward wrote about the visit to Dudley Carleton on March 16, 1615. After St. John's *Aemilia,* on the first night, and Clare Hall's *Ignoramus* (also based on a Porta play) on the second, both in Latin, Trinity staged *Albumazar.* Chamberlain reported, "On the third night was exhibited an English comedie called Albumazer, of Trinitie Colleges action and invention, but there was no great matter in yt more then one goode clowns part."[11] Tomkis's adaptation of Porta's play gives the focus to Trincalo as a yeoman-clown, who climbs socially thanks to a successful use of disguise. Milton seems to have seen the play when he was at Cambridge, since he refers in *An Apology for Smectymnuus* as regretting having seen clowns such as "Trinculo's, Buffons, and Bawds; prostituting the shame of that minestery, which either they had, or were nigh having, to the eyes of Courtiers and Court-Ladies." He would hardly have seen *The Tempest*'s Trinculo there. It is Trincalo who announces that he will deliver compliments to his mistress that he has learned from going to the Fortune and the Red Bull (TLN 586–89, act 2, scene 1). "O 'tis *Armellina:* now if she have the wit to beginne, as I meane shee should, then will I confound her with complements drawne from the Plaies I see at the Fortune, and Red Bull, where I learne all the words I speake and understand not." He also misquotes from *The Spanish Tragedy,* "O lippes, no lippes, but leaves besmear'd with mel-dew! O dew, no dew, but drops of Hony combs! O combs no combs, but fountains full of teares! O teares no teares, but—" (TLN 624). It is Trincalo who speaks the epilogue, hailing the new income he has gained from his disguising tricks.

The plays written in English were certainly less academic in subject as well as in style from those written to be spoken in Latin. They give ample evidence of student prejudice over social status, some of which is evident in *Club Law*'s mockery of its citizen wives, and the prurient assertions accompanying the rejection of them by Musonius and Philenius that they have no sexual interest in the women. Perhaps more pertinently, we should renew the question why the Parnassus plays were written in English, "this forraigne language," not *"our mother tongue,"* Latin, and why they have an exclusively male set of characters. None of the three plays has any women's parts in it. Can this be ascribed just to the male prejudice that excluded women from college and from learning? *Albumazar*'s omission of Porta's bawdy jokes, a related issue, might simply reflect a version of English conservatism, of course, particularly if Tomkis knew that the prurient King James might be in attendance. Much of the standoffish attitude of student writers to women, like their contempt for male citizens, must have come from the ostensible superiority that their learning gave them, typified as it was by Latin being their "mother" tongue, and the distance that took them from their actual mothers. The retreat by Philomusus and Studioso in *Returne from Parnassus* to looking after sheep shows a desire for peace after the struggle to use their learning in books. Such an impulse to the pastoral might, of course, imply an interest in shepherdesses too.

Notes

1. Frederick Andrew Inderwick, *A Calendar of the Inner Temple Records,* vol. 1 (1505–1603) London, 1896, 299 (Parliament, July 5, 1579), 341 (Parliament, November 3, 1586).

2. W. R. Prest, *The Inns of Court under Queen Elizabeth I and the Early Stuarts, 1590–1640* (Towtowa, NJ, Rowman and Littlefield, 1972), 91.

3. *Malone Society Collections* 14 (Oxford, The Malone Society, 1988), 133–47.

4. Bernard Capp, "Playgoers, Playing and Cross-Dressing in Early Modern London: The Bridewell Evidence," *The Seventeenth Century* 18 (2003): 159–71 (166).

5. Sarah Gristwood, *Arbella Stuart, England's Lost Queen* (New York: Bantam Press, 2003), quotes a description of Arbella wearing "a man's doublet, a man-like peruque, with long locks over her hair, black cloak, russet boots, and a rapier" (3). The shipmaster who observed her said she looked like Moll Cutpurse (5).

6. Barnaby Rich grumbled about such forms of social climbing in *Roome for a Gentleman:* "there are comprised under the title of Gentry, all Ecclesiastical persons professing religion, all Martial men that have borne office, and have command in the field; all Students of Artes and Sciences, and by our English custome, all Innes of Court men, professors of the Law; it skills not what their Fathers were, whether Farmers, Shoomakers, Taylers or Tinkers, if their names be inrolled in any Inne of Court, they are all Gentlemen" (E1).

7. G. C. Moore Smith, ed., *Club Law. A Comedy Acted in Clare Hall, Cambridge about 1599–1600* (Cambridge, 1907).

8. Ibid., xiv.

9. Ibid., xx.

10. A good edition is *Albumazar: A Comedy [1615] By Thomas Tomkis.* Hugh G. Dick, ed., (University of California Publications in English, Berkeley, CA, 1944).

11. N. E. McClure, ed., *Letters,* 2 vols. (Philadelphia, 1939) 1:586–87.

A Crisis of Friendship?:
Representation and Experience
in Two Late University Plays

CHRISTOPHER MARLOW

IN THE SIXTEENTH and seventeenth centuries the universities of Oxford and Cambridge were almost unique in accommodating semi-autonomous communities of young men, and I will argue that this rare social circumstance leaves its mark upon the dramatic work in which those communities were engaged. In this paper I will show how two university plays of the 1630s stage a moment of crisis for the predominant discourse of perfect friendship, and I go on to suggest some ways in which this can be accounted for. In the plays, the classical view of perfect friendship—as an absolute similitude between two friends who commonly understand their relationship to be that of "one soul in two bodies"—is put into question by the emergence of a more pragmatic view of friendship that recognizes the importance of strategic alliances and the significance of the group. This moment of crisis has an irreverent, satirical impulse, and I am particularly interested in thinking about why that impulse emerges in university drama, and what it might say about early modern masculinity.

In terms of plot, both Peter Hausted's *The Rivall Friends* (1631–32) and Robert Mead's *The Combat of Love and Friendship* (1634–38?) fit comfortably into the popular subgenre of friendship literature that deals with the conflict between friendship and heterosexual desire. The classical world was replete with pairs of friends who each wish to sacrifice their own lives in order to save their friend, with Damon and Pithias, and Orestes and Pylades perhaps the best-known examples. An early modern twist upon this desire for mutual self-sacrifice was introduced into the English vernacular tradition in 1531 by Thomas Elyot, whose conduct book,

The Book Named the Governor, included a brief fictional illustration of perfect friendship in what it calls "the wonderful history of Titus and Gisippus." Although self-sacrifice in the face of execution remains present in the narrative, the text also provides an opportunity for Titus and Gisippus to sacrifice for each other their own equal romantic interests in Sophronia, a beautiful Athenian gentlewoman.[1] The central action of a friend resigning his interest in his mistress reappears in a number of early modern texts that postdate Elyot's, including Lyly's *Euphues: The Anatomy of Wit* (1578), Shakespeare's *The Two Gentlemen of Verona* (ca. 1594), and Hausted's *The Rivall Friends.*

The play, performed by members of Hausted's own Queens' College, Cambridge, in front of Charles I, Queen Henrietta Maria, and numerous Cambridge students, concerns two friends who are love rivals, and the twist here is that they both actively attempt to favor the suit of the other in increasingly outlandish ways. Since it was performed in 1632, the play arrives a century into the tradition of English writing on self-sacrificing friends and it is careful to indicate its awareness of the convention. In fact, at the same time that the play acknowledges the friendship tradition, it emphasizes that tradition's incompatibility with the world encountered by the early modern university student. The plot of *The Rivall Friends* is composed of four overlapping narrative strands, and is too complicated to be explained here in full. I return to the titular plot below, but one of the subplots involves a mock battle of wits between four young men, arranged by two of the play's gentleman malcontents, Lovell and Anteros. These four young men can be seen to represent a variety of subject positions commonly available to young Englishmen in the seventeenth century. One identifies himself as an elder brother; one is an Inns of Court man; one an attorney's clerk; and one a Bachelor of Arts. As we might expect, given that this play was performed in front of an audience full of Cambridge university students, the Inns of Court character is given a rather hard time of it: his name is Nodle Emptie. But the relationship between Hammershin, the scholar, and Mungrell, the elder brother, has the most to tell us about the play's view of friendship. In act 3, scene 8, Mungrell comes to the defense of his friend Hammershin, who has insulted Nodle Emptie:

Loveall.	No more Scholler, you haue met with him sufficiently, . . . and here's a brave *Pylades* too, that

	would not see his *Orestes* opprest by multitude. (*Hee claps him on the backe*)
Mungrell.	Arrest mee Sir? Soft, and easily Sir, more words to a bargaine; s'duds! . . . As I'm a Gentleman, and an elder brother, I owe no man a farthing that I mean to pay him. Nay come Sir, I am flesh'd now i'faith.
Loveall.	You will not quarrel with your friends Sir, will you?
Mungrell.	Friends Sir? I know not whether you be my friend, or no; I am sure you use no friendly language.
Loveall.	Pri'thee Scholler, tayle off Mr. Mungrell a little, hee'l never leave now hee has drawne blood once.
Hammershin.	Come, you'r a foole: the Gentleman's of worth, and our friend.[2]

This is perhaps the best joke in the play. Smugly assured of his privileged position in the system of primogeniture, Mungrell does not have a university education and has thus never heard of Orestes. He thinks that Loveall has instead threatened to arrest him. Ironically, Mungrell cannot understand the friendly language that has indeed been used, and it is left to Hammershin the scholar to point out his foolishness.[3] In the context of a university performance, this is potentially a very effective moment because it represents the triumph of education over birth. With this exchange, Hausted's audience experiences the satisfying thrill of having the superiority of the scholar emphasized at the expense of the elder brother. However, the scholar's success is fleeting, because it is possible to detect a sense of anxiety in his insistence upon Loveall's "worth." Hammershin's conciliatory attitude to Loveall testifies to the insecure position of the impoverished scholar, for it is he, not the elder brother, who needs as many alliances with gentlemen of worth as he can get. Thus Loveall's idealistic reference to Orestes and Pylades soon gives place to Hammershin's far more pragmatic interest in preserving a potentially useful connection with a witty gentleman.

This is not the only part of the play that draws attention to the harsh realities of life for university graduates. In another of the play's subplots, one that satirizes the practice of simony, the local parsonage is being used by Sacriledge Hooke as a dowry to attract a husband for his disfigured daughter Ursely.[4] The offer entices six suitors, three of whom are university men desperately seeking a church living. Their three competitors are a box-maker, a cloth-worker, and a scrivener. In these scenes, the humiliation of the scholars is not ameliorated at all, as they are ridiculed just as effectively as the other suitors. Of course, *The Rivall Friends* is not the only academic play to point out the precarious nature of life after university, as the most familiar university plays of all, the *Parnassus* trilogy, also concentrate upon the difficulty of translating learning into a living.[5]

But if, in its subplots, the play reveals anxieties about the financial efficacy of a university education, its main plot is squarely concerned with pointing out the stalemate that occurs when the similitude of perfect friendship is pushed to its logical conclusion. The two rival friends are Lucius and Neander, who have each abandoned their previous mistresses in order to pursue the affections of Hooke's other daughter, Pandora. The play makes it clear that these men are to be understood as friends in the classical mold by giving Lucius a speech, early in the first act, which clarifies the type of friendship that they share:

> *Lucius.*   When I do violate
> That loue, that more then mortall bond, wherewith
> My soule is ty'd vnto Neander, may
> I fall vnpittied, may no gentle sigh
> Be spent at my last obsequies, may I want
> A man to wish me againe, would that preuaile.[6]

Hausted satirizes perfect friendship tales like "Titus and Gisippus" by having neither friend accept the other's offer of Pandora. In *The Rivall Friends*'s many precursor texts, perfect friends must take turns in offering and accepting sacrifices, and the tales usually end with the debt incurred by the first friend being recompensed in one way or another by the second friend. Hausted removes the turn-taking element and thus makes the principle of self-sacrificial friendship entirely farcical. He also recognizes that the object of exchange in such tales, the woman, might well have something to say about being passed from one friend to another. Unlike Elyot's Sophronia, who meekly accepts her status as chattel, Hausted's Pandora soon tires of the passivity of the perfect friends, and attempts to spur them into action by offering her affections to Lucius's page. In an echo of Shakespeare's *Twelfth Night,* Pandora ultimately falls in love with the page, and when he unexpectedly inherits three thousand pounds, their marriage is confirmed. Lucius and Neander finally return to their previous mistresses, and a precarious happy ending is suggested.

There are a number of ways in which the events of the main plot can be interpreted. In keeping with the worldly pessimism present in the subplots, we might see the failure of Lucius and Neander as an early modern version of the familiar maxim "faint heart never won fair lady." However, things become a little more interesting if we recognize the presence of a competing literary tradition in Hausted's construction of these scenes. That tradition is Platonism, especially as it appears in the Platonic drama favored by the wife of Charles I, Queen Henrietta Maria. The popularity of Platonic drama at the court of Charles I, especially during the 1630s, is inextricably linked with the patronage wielded by Henrietta Maria, and often associated with the pastoral mode, as in one of the most famous examples of the genre, Thomas Montagu's *The Shepherd's Paradise* (1629). Platonic drama was concerned, in the words of Graham Parry, with "honour and duty entangled with love, usually expressed in an elegant, slightly affected language that reflected the Queen's fondness for a preciosity of manner that she had acquired in her youth."[7] Parry also describes the tradition, rather more forcefully, as involving "starry-eyed debate about the refining effects of non-sensual love," and it is in these terms that the intersection with perfect friendship can be more plainly perceived.[8] The friendship of Lucius and Neander is nothing if not idealistic, and their mutual loss of Pandora is repeatedly represented in terms that emphasize both the feminizing potential of perfect friendship and the frustratingly ethereal nature of Platonic love. In the last of such references, Pandora tells Lucius:

> *Pandora.*   I care not this for all your loue, nor yet
>   For your friend *Ianus* there with the two faces;
>   Nor do I think ye men.
> *Lucius.*   So quickly?
> *Pandora.*   Yes
>   I doe confesse I am a woman; see,
>   Here is the man has wonne what ye haue lost;
>   Stout souldiers sure, that when the Citie gates
>   Were open to yee, durst not enter in.[9]

The play certainly contains a powerful strain of misogyny that needs to be taken into account when reading lines such as these, but it is also difficult to deny that Pandora is a far more interesting and sympathetic character than either of the rival lovers simply by virtue of the fact that she plays an active role in the plot. In effect, the play satirizes perfect friendship, the triumphant expression of homosocial bonding, by pointing out its similarity to Platonic drama, often seen because of its association with Henrietta Maria as a "feminine" genre more at home in Parisian salons than at the English court. *The Rivall Friends* reveals, then, that a crisis has always already existed at the conceptual heart of perfect friendship, but that this crisis is easier to perceive when the discourse is read alongside that of Platonic love and within the context of a tradition of cynical university plays that emphasize the lack of fit between the ideal world of philosophy and the actual world of the scholar's lived experience.

The influence of Platonic drama can be detected even more strongly in Robert Mead's *The Combat of Love and Friendship.* The play is full of the conventional terminology of Platonic drama, in which love is described as the transfusion of souls, and mistresses are mortal reflections of immortal perfection. According to the title page of the 1654 edition, the play was performed at Christ Church, Oxford, where its author studied from 1634 until at least 1639, and it was probably written during the early years of his academic career.[10] The play is far shorter than *The Rivall Friends* and the competing merits of love and friendship are subjected to a more sustained level of analysis. The "combat" of the title arises because Lysander, who is in love with Artemone, is persuaded by his friend Theocles to woo Panareta, the sister of Theocles's cruel mistress Ethusa. Panareta is in love with Lysander, and Theocles hopes that Lysander can persuade her to encourage Ethusa to love him. So if he is to be true to his friend, Lysander must at least appear to be false to his mistress. In the soliloquy that opens the play, Lysander laments his position and contrasts the spirituality of friendship with the materiality of love:

> *Lysander.* Instruct me some kinde Power
> To which I may most Lawfully prove false:
> My friend, or Mistress.
>
> . . . .
>
> Friendship, thou art a name, and nothing real,
> A meer and empty word. And
> Here I quit thee,
> Ile be not fetter'd in fantastick chains,
> To court *Ideas,* nothings, and adore
> A strange *Platonic Cupid.* Give me Love,
> That has some life and vigor in it: Love
> That shall delight our bloods as well as Fancies.[11]

Although he takes these words back almost as soon as he has spoken them, and thus reestablishes the primacy of a classical model of spiritual friendship here attributed to Plato, Lysander nevertheless articulates once more the same crisis of friendship that was at the center of *The Rivall Friends*. Again, perfect friendship is, albeit momentarily, revealed to be a "starry-eyed," self-defeating ideology. It is worth noting in passing what this moment has to say about the increasingly privileged place given in the culture to heterosexual relationships, especially marriage, as opposed to homosocial ones like friendship. This episode is interesting because the terms of Lysander's argument are unexpected. Rather than borrowing the spiritual discourse of perfect friendship in order to describe heterosexual relations, according to the standard strategy of Caroline Platonic drama, Lysander here preserves the ancient dichotomy between spiritual friendship and material love while simply reversing the privileged term in the relationship.[12] The play thus demonstrates a willingness to critique the assumptions made about love and friendship in Platonic drama, and this critique emerges most powerfully in act 3 of the play.

Although in his opening speech Lysander struggles to understand the relative importance of friendship and love, Theocles does not hesitate to sacrifice friendship for love. In order to make Ethusa more likely to accept his suit, Theocles encourages Artemone to believe that Lysander's feigned love for Panareta is in fact genuine. Theocles begins his attempt to make Artemone jealous by invoking Lysander's status as perfect friend:

> *Theocles.*   Men talk of *Pylades,* and I know not what
> Strange Enterprizes of rash *Theseus;*
> But this *Lysander,* how he out-goes all story?
> Give me a man made up of all the Extractions
> And quintessence of all who ever yet
> Fame with her lowdest Trumpet hath proclaim'd
> For Men of Loyal Breasts, and this same Man,
> This Man thus fill'd with Friendship, shall yet learn
> A way to love from our *Lysander.*[13]

Just as *The Rivall Friends* included an allusion to Orestes and Pylades in order to emphasize the exhaustion of the concept of perfect friendship in the contemporary world of the scholar, *The Combat of Love and Friendship* also recalls the discourse in order to demonstrate the ease with which it can be subverted. Theocles praises the perfect friendship of Lysander so that his supposed betrayal of Artemone will appear more plausible. Playing on the traditional primacy afforded to friendship at the expense of love, Theocles posits that an exchange of lovers can be seen as a reasonable aspect of the continuum of friendship. Since Lysander is a perfect friend, and perfect friends are identical in all things including virtue and honesty, Artemone cannot doubt Theocles's story for a moment. If Lysander is so honest in his friendship to Theocles that he is willing to sacrifice his mistress for him, the tradition tells us that Theocles must be just as honest in his relationship to Lysander, and that his story must therefore be true. This unquestioned assumption of the truthfulness of perfect friends is at the center of the play's convoluted plot, and the trick is played on the audience as well as Artemone, because the fact that Theocles is lying only becomes clear later in the play. However, it is not long before we learn that, ironically, Lysander has indeed fallen in love with Panareta, and their union is confirmed at the play's conclusion. Nevertheless, when Theocles's behavior is revealed in act 4 it leads to a duel between the two friends, during which Lysander makes it clear that it is Theocles's betrayal of the spirit of friendship, not the loss of Artemone, that is the greater crime.

It is impossible not to detect a satirical tone in all this, especially since the play ends with the revelation that all the friends and lovers have proven themselves false in one way or another. Although we know that Robert Mead was a staunch royalist—he would go on to serve both Charles I and Charles II—*The Combat of Love and Friendship* must be seen as a play that ridicules the conventions of Platonic drama, popular of course at the royal court. However, these two impulses need not be seen as contradictory because, as Karen Britland argues, it is entirely possible that Henrietta Maria was herself aware of the pretensions of Platonic drama and their ripeness for ridicule.[14] But beyond its skeptical engagement with Platonic drama, Mead's play is also a critique of friendship. Indeed, it is an even more serious critique than Hausted's, because the behavior of Theocles is active rather than passive; whereas Lucius and Neander suffer because they take the conventions of friendship too seriously, in *The Combat* those conventions are not taken seriously enough. Or, to be more precise, the seriousness with which they are traditionally taken is exploited to such an extent that it is not just the friendship of Theocles and Lysander that reaches crisis point but the discourse of friendship itself. Mead explodes the absolute association of friendship with truth, present throughout the classical tradition, so that in the play friendship simply becomes nothing more than a convenient cover for falsehood. It is revealing that the physical similitude that was such an integral part of classical friendship tales like "Damon and Pithias" and "Titus and Gisippus" has disappeared entirely from the play; indeed, the fact that Theocles and Lysander do not love the same woman also testifies to a lack of emphasis placed upon the similitude trope. We might see this as evidence for a movement away from what Michel Foucault calls the "classical episteme," a period during which, he argues, knowledge was thought to be structured according to the principle of similarity.[15] Indeed, the play can even be read as a nostalgic lament for a vanished world in which exterior appearances were a credible guide for interior principles. Alternatively, we might read the play's critique of friendship as contributing to the ideological ground-clearing exercise in which discourses of friendship were replaced by those of companionate marriage, although since all the main characters are consistent only in their inconsistency, the future of marriage in the world of the play seems just as gloomy as that of friendship.

How can we account for the fact that these two university plays, ostensibly about perfect friendship, both emphasize the problematic nature of that concept? For Hausted perfect friendship is in crisis when it invests too much energy in similitude; for Mead, it is in crisis when similitude is neglected. The satirical treatment of the theme, and especially Mead's failure to punish his false friends, seems to move the plays beyond the realm of conventional complaint literature: they do not simply assert that "no real friendships exist nowadays," but instead call perfect friendship itself into question.[16] As I have said, we can see this impulse as nothing more than a reaction to the excesses of Platonic drama. It is also tempting to read the cynicism of the plays as an expression of a general sense of dissatisfaction with the absolute rule favored by Charles I, although this risks falling into what Martin Butler calls the ex post facto perspective in which every literary artefact of the 1630s foreshadows the events of 1642.[17] But perhaps it is not coincidental that the discourse of perfect friendship should be called into question by university men. If anyone was living in circumstances matching those espoused by the tradition of perfect friendship, it was they. Studying, eating, and sleeping in the company of young men very like themselves, students at the colleges of Oxford and

Cambridge were placed within an institutional framework that should have been an incubator for perfect friendship. No doubt close, perhaps even perfect, friendships did arise between pairs of university students, as Alan Bray for one has shown.[18] But the universities were also places that encouraged their students to approach friendship in terms broader than those offered to them by the humanist reinvigoration of the perfect friendship trope. The organization of students into colleges, for instance, may well have encouraged them to conceive of themselves as part of a discrete and exclusive community of many, rather than a partner in a perfect friendship of two. The violence that often accompanied performances of student drama underlines the seriousness with which many university men took their college affiliations.[19]

Within colleges, further group attachments were encouraged. Differences of social status were no less important, and no less visible, inside the college walls than they were outside them, and students were allocated to various categories depending upon their social or intellectual status. Three major groups of undergraduate students may be identified. Firstly, fellow-commoners (or gentleman-commoners) were students of aristocratic origin who paid for their education but were set above the majority of the undergraduate body because of their social rank. The colleges visibly marked this difference of status every mealtime, as fellow-commoners were given special dispensation to dine with the fellows—graduate members of a college whose tuition and expenses were covered by an endowment, and who would usually be expected to tutor undergraduates—at the fellows' table, which was usually situated on a raised dais.[20] The second group, who formed the majority of fee-paying undergraduates at the universities, were known as commoners at Oxford and pensioners at Cambridge. The existence of a third set of undergraduates called servitors at Oxford and sizars at Cambridge was again visually displayed when members of the college gathered together to eat: sizars and servitors waited at the tables of the fellows, fellow-commoners, and commoners or pensioners. These young men were paid for their services, and were also entitled to any leftover food that could be found. Stephen Porter notes that at the end of the sixteenth century servitors were employed by commoners or fellow-commoners to perform "tasks which were regarded as degrading for students of their standing, such as bedmaking, lighting fires, fetching wood and water, sweeping chambers, and buying provisions," and that some students brought their own servitors or sizars with them upon arriving at university.[21] Others, like Simonds D'Ewes, had them allocated upon arrival. In common with most young men of humble origins, D'Ewes's sizar Thomas Manning was at the university in order to gain the qualifications that would allow him to pursue a career in the church. Unlike D'Ewes, who stayed at Cambridge for two and a half years and did not take a degree, those like Manning destined for the clergy needed to attain the degree of MA if they were to be successful in their chosen vocation. The clear demarcations of student rank, as well as students' very different career destinations, may also have suggested that the cultivation of practical networks of influence and interdependence were more important than the idealistic notion of a perfect friendship with one single individual.[22]

If performances of drama encouraged an almost tribal sense of communal feeling among members of a college, taking a role in such a play must have similarly emphasized the importance and efficacy of small-group interdependence. Interestingly, all the available evidence suggests that the men who performed in plays represented a microcosm of the larger college community to which they belonged. Each of the twenty-eight extant and complete university drama cast lists shows pensioners or commoners and sizars or servitors performing together, and the majority of casts also seem to have included at least one fellow- or gentleman-commoner.[23] Such patterns of association bear out the findings of Alexandra Shepard, who in her work on male bonding and antisocial behavior in early modern Cambridge concludes that students of every rank were involved in episodes of misrule.[24] Emphasizing the distinction between perfect amity and the comradeship formed in the college or tavern, Shepard notes: "These were not the bonds of friendship, however. The status and personalities of the participants in the camaraderie of excess were ultimately irrelevant beyond a desire to perform and applaud this alternative theatre of manhood."[25] If the disruptive camaraderie of students outside the college can be understood in some sense as a "performance" of homosocial bonding in an "alternative theatre," may not actual performances of drama in a real—albeit somewhat makeshift—college theater be understood in an analogous way? If *The Rivall Friends* and *The Combat of Love and Friendship* suggest a degree of skepticism about the tenets of perfect friendship, perhaps this arises from an enthusiasm for the sort of friendship that "was issue of the Taverne, or the Spit," in Ben Jonson's phrase, and which was surely experienced by most young men during their time at university.[26] Perhaps, too, we can thus begin to see university drama as a site of conflict not just between love and friendship but also between conventional and innovative modes of early modern masculinity.

Notes

1. Thomas Elyot, *The Book Named The Governor,* ed. S. E. Lehmberg (London: Dent, 1962), 135–48.

2. Peter Hausted, *The Rivall Friends: A Facsimile of the 1632 Edition* (Amsterdam: Da Capo Press, 1973), 3.8.19–34.

3. For an alternative reading of this scene and the play, see my "Friendship, Misogyny and Antitheatrical Prejudice: A Reading of *The Rivall Friends,*" *Peer English* 1 (2006): 25–33.

4. For a detailed discussion of this aspect of the play, see Laurens J. Mills, *Peter Hausted: Playwright, Poet, and Preacher* (Bloomington: Indiana University Press, 1944), 18–20.

5. See my "Scholarly Interiority in the *Parnassus Trilogy,*" *The Dalhousie Review* 85 (2005): 275–84.

6. Hausted, *Rivall Friends,* 1.3.49–54.

7. Graham Parry, *The Golden Age Restor'd: The Culture of the Stuart Court, 1603–42* (Manchester: Manchester University Press, 1981), 203.

8. Graham Parry, *The Seventeenth Century: The Intellectual and Cultural Context of English Literature, 1603–1700* (London: Longman, 1989), 29.

9. Hausted, *Rivall Friends,* 5.11.98–104.

10. Charles Brayne, "Mead, Robert (1615/16–1653)," in *Oxford Dictionary of National Biography,* http://www.oxforddnb.com/view/article/18468 (accessed August 27, 2008).

11. Robert Mead, *The Combat of Love and Friendship* (London, 1654), 1.1.1–3, 15–22 (lineation mine).

12. For an overview of the relationship between friendship and marriage in the literature of the period, see Thomas Luxon, *Single Imperfection: Milton, Marriage and Friendship* (Pittsburgh, PA: Duquesne University Press, 2005). The trope is also discussed in Catherine Belsey, "Disrupting Sexual Difference: Meaning and Gender in the Comedies," in *Alternative Shakespeares,* ed. John Drakakis (London: Methuen, 1985), 166–90; Lisa Jardine, *Reading Shakespeare Historically* (London: Routledge, 1996); and Gregory Chaplin, "Friendship and Miltonic Marriage," *Modern Philology* 99 (2001): 266–92.

13. Mead, *Combat of Love,* 3.2.47–55.

14. Karen Britland argues "I find it impossible to accept that she could have sponsored two major theatrical productions by two separate authors in relatively quick succession without being aware of their irreverent stance towards neo-Platonism," *Drama at the Courts of Queen Henrietta Maria* (Cambridge: Cambridge University Press, 2006), 130.

15. Michel Foucault, *The Order of Things: An Archaeology of the Human Sciences* (London: Tavistock, 1970), especially 17–25.

16. Laurens J. Mills, *"One Soul in Bodies Twain": Friendship in Tudor Literature and Stuart Drama* (Bloomington, IN: Principia Press, 1937), 112.

17. Martin Butler, *Theatre and Crisis, 1632–1642* (Cambridge: Cambridge University Press, 1984), 7–11.

18. See Bray's discussion of the memorial to the friendship of Sir John Finch and Sir Thomas Baines at Christ's College, Cambridge, in *The Friend* (Chicago: University of Chicago Press, 2003), 144–45.

19. Violent clashes at performances of university drama were common, but most famously occurred at Cambridge in 1611 when fighting between St. John's and Trinity College men escalated into a full-scale riot. See *Records of Early English Drama: Cambridge,* ed. Alan H. Nelson, 2 vols. (Toronto: University of Toronto Press, 1989), 2:424–86 and J. W. Clark, *The Riot at the Great Gate of Trinity College, February 1610–11,* Cambridge Antiquarian Society, Octavo Publications 43 (London: George Bell, 1906).

20. Christopher Brooke, ed., *A History of the University of Cambridge,* vol. 2, Victor Morgan, ed., *1546–1750* (Cambridge, MA: Cambridge University Press, 2004), 325.

21. Stephen Porter, "University and Society," in *History of the University of Oxford,* ed. T. H. Aston, vol. 4, *Seventeenth-Century Oxford,* ed. Nicholas Tyacke (Oxford: Clarendon, 1997), 37. See also Morgan, 318.

22. On social interaction at the universities see Rosemary O'Day, "Room at the Top: Oxford and Cambridge in the Tudor and Stuart Age," *History Today* 34 (1984): 31–38 and Elizabeth Hanson, "The Interiority of Ability," *Dalhousie Review* 85 (2005): 257–73.

23. Academic rank or class status is not recorded for all students, and not all students included on cast lists can be definitively identified. However, out of the twenty-eight plays for which cast lists survive, fourteen definitely included students of all three academic ranks and ten definitely did not. The four remaining cast lists include some performers with popular names who cannot be identified with certainty. For a full breakdown of these results see my *Friendship and Masculinity in English University Drama* (forthcoming). Cast lists are published as appendices in *Records of Early English Drama: Oxford,* ed. John R. Elliot and others, 2 vols. (Toronto: University of Toronto Press, 2004), 2:841–45 and *Records of Early English Drama: Cambridge,* 2:942–62.

24. Alexandra Shepard, *Meanings of Manhood in Early Modern England* (Oxford: Oxford University Press, 2003), 110.

25. Ibid., 113.

26. Ben Jonson, "An Epistle to Master Arthur Squib," in *Ben Jonson,* ed. C. H. Herford and Percy and Evelyn Simpson, 11 vols., *The Poems, The Prose Works* (Oxford: Clarendon, 1947), 216.

Emulating Royalty: Cambridge, Oxford, and the Inns of Court

Alan H. Nelson

As EDITOR OR COEDITOR of three collections for Records of Early English Drama (REED), I have surveyed entertainment records to 1642 from Cambridge, Oxford, and the Inns of Court.[1] Both Oxford (University and Colleges) and Inns of Court I inherited from my very good friend John R. Elliott, Jr., following his incapacitating stroke in 2002 and subsequent death. From conversations over many years I know that both Professor Elliott and I initially assumed that entertainment at all three institutions would have been much of a muchness. Sir George Buc's oft-quoted characterization of London and its Inns of Court as "The Third Universitie of England"[2] doubtless contributed to our assumptions.

Having worked over all three institutions, I now realize (and I think Professor Elliott realized, though I cannot in fairness speak for him) that in respect to entertainment, the Inns of Court were more the odd man out than a third university. While Cambridge and Oxford reflected a tradition of academic drama shared with England's grammar schools, the Inns of Court tended to emulate entertainment at the royal court.

From 1587–88, and perhaps earlier, the Inns of Court tended to concentrate on revels and masques rather than on plays. Plays continued to be performed at the Inns, but by professional companies rather than gentlemen members. Lincoln's Inn, for example, played host to the Children of the Chapel, led by Richard Edwards in 1564–65 and 1565–66, and by Richard Farrant in 1579–80. Shakespeare's *Comedy of Errors* was famously acted at Gray's Inn in 1594–95, his *Twelfth Night* at Middle Temple in 1601–2, both presumably by Shakespeare's company.[3] For most of the seventeenth century, indeed, the Inner Temple and the Middle Temple paid for two professionally performed plays each per year, on All Souls Day (November 1) and Candlemas (February 2).[4]

Of the two universities, Oxford more than Cambridge shared the Inns of Court emulation of royalty. Geography clearly played its part. The Inns of Court owed their very existence to their proximity to the royal courts of justice in Westminster. Oxford, which lies near Woodstock, a royal palace, naturally enjoyed both formal and casual connections with the royal court. As an example, royal trumpeters passed through Oxford so frequently that the city fathers declared as a matter of record that they would not be awarding a gratuity on the trumpeters' every transit through the town.[5] While Cambridge lay not far from two locales dear to the heart of James I—Royston, site of a royal hunting lodge, and Newmarket, a horse-racing venue—it was not on the direct route from London to either place.

Neither Cambridge nor Oxford was of course totally independent from royalty. The chancellorship of each university lay in the gift of the English monarch, who sometimes interfered in the annual appointment of the vice-chancellor. Several colleges in each university were royal foundations, whose heads were directly appointed by the monarch: at Cambridge, King's, Queens', and Trinity colleges; at Oxford, Oriel College, Queen's College, and Christ Church.

Both Cambridge and Oxford were the sites of important royal visits. Though monarchs visited more or less informally throughout the history of the universities, theater historians trace the tradition of formal visits to 1564 at Cambridge and 1566 at Oxford. Subsequent visits were both rare and fairly distributed between the universities. Elizabeth came to Saffron Walden in 1578, where she was entertained by members of Cambridge University; she paid a formal visit to Oxford in 1592. James I visited Oxford in 1605, Cambridge in 1614/15. Charles I visited Cambridge in 1627–28 and 1631–32, Oxford in 1635–36. In other years the two universities were invaded by visiting ambassadors and noblemen in approximately equal numbers.

The relatively equal distribution of formal royal favors between the two universities belies the advantage enjoyed by Oxford, where Christ Church was treated, especially by James and Charles, as a virtual extension of the royal court. This advantage may be appreciated by comparing Oxford to the Inns of Court.

Though no English monarch paid a formal visit to any Inn of

Court, plays and masques from the Inns of Court were frequently repeated at the royal court, starting with the Inner Temple play *Gorboduc,* performed over the 1561–62 Christmas season, first in the Inner Temple hall on an unknown date in January, and then at court on January 18. The most productive period of visits to the royal court began with two masques performed in the "Old" Banqueting House following the marriage of Princess Elizabeth to Frederick of Bohemia, which occurred on February 14 (Valentine's Day), 1612/13. The next day, February 15, witnessed the performance of a joint masque by Middle Temple and Lincoln's Inn; five days later, on February 20, occurred a joint masque by Inner Temple and Gray's Inn. Similar masques were performed in subsequent years, above all *The Triumph of Peace* by all four Inns on February 3, 1633/34 in the "New" Banqueting House in Whitehall (designed by Inigo Jones).

Many Inns of Court masques, though not all, were performed at court and drew on court resources. Thus both the joint masque of Middle Temple and Lincoln's Inn performed in February 1612/13 and the joint masque performed by all four Inns in February 1633/34 were designed by Inigo Jones; music was composed by Robert Johnson for the first of these masques, by William Lawes and Simon Ive for the joint masque performed by all four Inns in February 1633/34, and by Henry Lawes and William Lawes for the Middle Temple masque of February 1635/36, called *The Triumphs of le Prince d'Amour,* performed in Middle Temple hall. Though the latter was not the occasion of a formal royal visit, Queen Henrietta Maria and her ladies attended, wearing hats to support the fiction that they were citizens' wives.

No comparable connection to the royal court can be documented for any Cambridge entertainment, but several Oxford entertainments during the reigns of James I and Charles I were essentially "royal." This point was made, though without a nod to the Inns of Court, in the Introduction to REED: *Oxford* (605–7):

King James, Queen Anne, and the young prince Henry all participated in a royal visit to Oxford in August 1605. The Records show that four plays were presented in Christ Church, three in Latin for the king, all written or adapted by Oxford men, and one in English especially written for the queen and prince by the queen's favourite court poet, Samuel Daniel. Costumes were imported from the master of the revels in London. [The theatre erected in Christ Church hall was designed by Inigo Jones.] . . .

Of all plays performed by students of Oxford through 1642, the most notorious by a wide margin was Barton Holyday's *Technogamia,* which earned its dubious fame not for its original performance at Christ Church on 13 February 1617/18 but for a repeat performance before James I and his court at Woodstock on 26 August 1621. . . .

The opulence of the 1605 plays at Christ Church was perhaps more than matched by the entertainment of Charles I at the same hall in 1636, the last occasion on which plays were presented to a monarch in Oxford. The plays were William Strode's *The Floating Island* and William Cartwright's *The Royal Slave.* . . . The 1636 royal plays, although written and acted by Oxford men, were in all other respects the product not of Oxford but of the king's purveyors of court entertainment. The scenery and costumes were provided by the office of the works and the office of the revels; the music was written by William and Henry Lawes and performed by the king's musick and other professional musicians; student actors were specially coached by Joseph Taylor, leader of the king's men at the Globe; candelabra were brought from Whitehall Palace and reassembled in Oxford to provide lighting. In contrast to the choice of learned, academic plays for King James, all of the 1636 plays were comedies, and all, by royal command, were written in English, thus confirming William Cartwright's remark in the epilogue to *The Royal Slave:*

> There's difference twixt a Colledge and a Court;
> The one expecteth Science, the other sport.

. . . *The Royal Slave* . . . got a warm reception from the entire court, especially the queen, who asked to see it again performed at Hampton Court. What she saw both there and in Oxford, however, was not representative of Oxford culture but an imitation of the usual type of Stuart court entertainment.

Queen Henrietta Maria's interest in Oxford's *The Royal Slave* paralleled her interest in Middle Temple's *The Triumphs of le Prince d'Amour* the same year.

Indirect evidence of a connection to royalty may be discerned in the curious production of *The Christmas Prince* by students of St. John's College, Oxford, in 1607–8, whose text bears an important and apparently unique relation to the Inns of Court in London, and thence to the royal court.

The Christmas Prince survives in a manuscript still at St. John's College, Oxford (MS 52.1). This is a handsome, folio-sized volume, beautifully bound in brown calf, carefully written in several hands, interspersed with historiated roundels and other illustrations. The photographic facsimile published in the Renaissance Latin Drama in England series (ser. 1, vol. 11, 1982)[6] is vastly better than nothing, but is reduced in size and starkly black-on-white, unlike the original which is written in black-brown ink on creamy rag paper. The Malone Society print-facsimile edition of 1623 gives a better overall impression.[7] Neither source attempts to reproduce the red ink used in the original for decorations, including roundels.

Two major Christmas Prince texts survive from the Inns of Court in London: *Gesta Grayorum,* performed at Gray's Inn in 1594–95 but not published until 1688; and *Le Prince d'Amour alias Noctes Templariae,* performed at Middle Temple in 1597–98 but not published until 1660.[8] These two texts must also stand for several others now lost. Following is a list of known Christmas Prince ceremonies prior to 1642:

Gray's Inn:	Prince of Purpoole	William Hatclyff 1587–88
		Henry Helmes 1594–95
		Henry Yelverton 1617–18
Inner Temple:	Prince of Sophy	Robert Dudley 1561–62
Lincoln's Inn:	Prince de la Grange	Edward Smith 1617–18
Middle Temple:	Prince d'Amour	Richard Martin 1597–98
		Richard Vivian 1635–36

Little more than a cast-list survives from the Gray's Inn entertainments of 1587–88 while virtually nothing survives from 1617–18. A secondhand account of the Inner Temple activities from 1561–62 is printed in Gerard Legh's *Accidens of Armory* (1562).[9] Edward Smith at Lincoln's Inn in 1617–18 was not a Prince but rather a Lieutenant. The 1635–36 Middle Temple masque may have stood alone rather than being a subset of a full Christmas Prince ceremony. Other Christmas Prince ceremonies may have been attempted but are now lost from view. They were not forgotten by contemporaries, however: Henry Yelverton in 1617–18 was denominated Henry II, Richard Vivian of 1635–36, Richard II. *Gesta Grayorum* of 1594–95 alludes to an eight-year gap, presumably pointing back to the events of 1587–88, and we may observe a nearly forty-year gap between the Prince d'Amour appointments at Middle Temple from 1597–98 to 1635–36. A thirty-year gap is referenced in the St. John's *Christmas Prince* text, back to the time when Dr.

John Case was Prince, presumably circa 1577–78.[10] Again, the most fulsome festivities in this kind are recognized as both memorable and rare.

At the Inns of Court, the connection between the Christmas entertainment and the royal court was nicely expressed in the report of a commission on the Inns of Court drawn up toward the end of the reign of Henry VIII (d. 1547), in a section entitled "The Manner of Christmas, used amongst them":

> The Readers and Benchers at a Parliament or Pension held before Christmas, if it seeme unto them that there be no dangerous time of sickness, neither dearth of victuals, and that they are furnished of such a Company, as both for their number and appertaines are meet to keep a solemn Christmas, then doe they appoint and chose certain of the house to be Officers, and bear certain rules in the house during the said time, which Officers for the most part are such, as are exercised in the King's Highness house, and other Noble men, **and this done onely to the intent, that they should in time to come know how to use themselves.** In this Christmas time, they have all manner of pastimes, as singing and dancing; and in some of the houses ordinarily they have some interlude or Tragedy played by the Gentlemen of the same house, the ground, and manner whereof, is devised by some of the Gentlemen of the house.[11]

The raison d'être, "that they should in time come to know how to use themselves," serves as a key to Christmas traditions in general, and to the Christmas Prince tradition in particular.

Each Christmas season, which ran from November 1 to February 2 (and sometimes beyond), Inns of Court gentlemen formed themselves into a facsimile of the royal court. At a minimum, a limited number of gentlemen were appointed to the offices of steward, marshall, and master of the revels. At a maximum, dozens of officers were appointed, as at Gray's Inn in 1594–95, as recorded in *Gesta Grayorum,* pp. 6–8 (names of appointees are here omitted):

> The Order of the Prince of Purpoole's Proceedings, with his Officers and Attendants at his honourable Inthronization; which was likewise observed in all his solemn Marches on grand Days, and like Occasions; which Place every Officer did duly attend, during the Reign of his Highness's Government.

| A Marshal. | A Marshall. |
| Trumpets. | Trumpets. |

Pursuevant at Arms,
Towns-men in the Prince's   Yeomen of the Guard,
Livery, with Halberts   three Couples

Captain of the Guard,
Baron of the Grand Port,
Baron of the Base Port,
Gentlemen for Entertainment,
three Couples

Baron of the Petty Port,
Baron of the New Port,
Gentlemen for Entertainment
three Couples

Lieutenant of the Pensioners,
Gentlemen-Pensioners, twelve Couples, . . .
Chief Ranger, and Master of the Game,
Master of the Revels,
Master of the Revellers,
Captain of the Pensioners,
Sewer,
Carver,
Another Sewer,
Cup-bearer,
Groom-porter,
Sheriff,
Clerk of the Council,
Clerk of the Parliament,
Clerk of the Crown,
Orator,
Recorder,
Sollicitor,
Serjeant,
Speaker of the Parliament,
Commissary,
Attorney,
Serjeant,
Master of the Requests,
Chancellor of the Exchequer,
Master of the Wards and Idiots,
Reader,
Lord Chief Baron of the Exchequer,
Master of the Rolls,
Lord Chief Baron of the Common Pleas,

Lord Chief Justice of the Prince's Bench,
Master of the Ordnance,
Lieutenant of the Tower,
Master of the Jewel-house,
Treasurer of the House-hold,
Knight-Marshal,
Master of the Ward-robe,
Comptroller of the House-hold,
Bishop of St Giles's in the Fields,
Steward of the House-hold,
Lord Warden of the four Ports,
Secretary of State,
Lord Admiral,
Lord Treasurer,
Lord Great Chamberlain,
Lord High Constable,
Lord Marshal,
Lord Privy Seal,
Lord Chamberlain of the House-hold,
Lord High Steward,
Lord Chancellor,
Archbishop of St Andrews in Holborn,
Serjeant at Arms, with the Mace,
Gentleman-Usher,
The Shield of Pegasus, for the Inner-Temple,
Serjeant at Arms, with the Sword,
Gentleman-Usher,
The Shield of the Gryffin, for Grays-Inn,
The King at Arms,
The great Shield of the Prince's Arms,
The Prince of Purpoole,
A Page of Honour,
Gentlemen of the Privy Chamber, six Couples,
A Page of Honour,
Vice-Chamberlain,
Master of the Horse,
Yeomen of the Guard, three Couples.
Towns-men in Liveries.

At a maximum, each gentleman appointee performed duties appropriate to his office; at a minimum, these were empty titles. Probably for most participants the titles made few or no demands; but many took their appointments seriously—or perhaps mock-seriously. The Gray's Inn's Prince of Purpoole in 1594–95 was Henry Helme or Helmes, whose frenetic activities are described at length in *Gesta Grayorum;* in addition, Helmes admitted some dozen individuals, including John Lyly the poet-playwright and John Spenser the current Lord Mayor of London, to membership in Gray's Inn, as recorded in the Admissions Register; his namesake Henry Yelverton authorized similar admissions in 1617–18.[12] A Christmas Prince might also exercise real or mock authority through his Lieutenant of the Tower, who had control of the stocks.

The Christmas Prince and his officers were authorized to raise money for their enterprise. The Oxford manuscript of *The Christmas Prince* (St. John's College) incorporates the texts of "warrants" issued to friends of the college, along with a record of actual monies received.[13] Similar warrants were issued by the Inns of Court. One original warrant survives, issued in 1597–98 over the signature of "Middle Temple" and sent to Gilbert Talbot, Earl of Shrewsbury, who annotated the warrant in his own hand to the effect that he had responded with a payment of £30.[14]

Holders of the office of Christmas Prince also spent their own money on the enterprise. Richard Vivian, for example, Prince d'Amour at Middle Temple in 1635–36, is reported to have spent £3000 of his recent inheritance during his tenure. In return, at least under the Stuarts, Christmas Princes were given knighthoods—not mock knighthoods but literal knighthoods. Henry Yelverton was so knighted in 1618; Thomas Dayrell (or Darrell) of Lincoln's Inn, who served as "Mareschall" for *The Triumph of Peace,* in 1634; and Richard Vivian in 1636. (As late as November 1682, Richard Gipps of Gray's Inn was granted a knighthood in anticipation of a Christmas masque of February 1682/83.)[15]

Though Thomas Tucker was not knighted for his services as Christmas Prince at St. John's College, Oxford, over the 1607–8 Christmas season, parallels between the entertainment over which he presided and similar entertainments at the Inns of Court may be taken as confirmation that Oxford colleges, at least to a greater degree than the college of Cambridge, tended to emulate activities at the court of their sovereign master or mistress.

Notes

1. Records of Early English Drama, a series published by University of Toronto Press: Alan H. Nelson, ed., *Cambridge,* (1989); John R. Elliott, Jr., et al., eds. *Ox-*

ford (2004); Alan H. Nelson and John R. Elliott, Jr., eds., *Inns of Court* (forthcoming). Most items cited in my text are reproduced in these volumes.

2. *The Third Universitie of England,* in John Stow, *Annals of England,* ed. Edmond Howes (1615: STC 23338), 958–88.

3. Evidence for *Comedy of Errors* occurs in *Gesta Grayorum* (1688) pp. 23, 31 ("Play of Errors"); evidence for *Twelfth Night* occurs in *The Diary of John Manningham of the Middle Temple, 1602–1603,* ed. Robert Parker Sorlien (Hanover, NH: University Press of New England, 1976), 48.

4. This pattern of activity was discovered in the course of research forthcoming in REED: *Inns of Court.*

5. REED: *Oxford,* 616.

6. *The Christmas Prince,* prepared with an introduction by Earl Jeffery Richards, in Renaissance Latin Drama in England, ser. 1, vol. 11 (Hildesheim, 1982).

7. Frederick S. Boas and Walter W. Greg, eds., *The Christmas Prince,* Malone Society Reprints (Oxford, 1923).

8. *Gesta Grayorum* (1688); *Le Prince d'Amour, or, The Prince of Love* (1660).

9. Gerard Legh, *Accidens of Armory* (1562), 204–25.

10. St. John's College, Oxford, MS 52.1, pp 5–6, 26.

11. Edward Waterhouse, *Fortescutus Illustratus* (1663), 546.

12. Joseph Foster, ed., *The Register of Admissions to Gray's Inn, 1521–1889, together with the Register of Marriages in Gray's Inn Chapel, 1695–1754* (London, 1889); entries under respective dates.

13. St. John's College, Oxford, MS 52.1, pp 10–13.

14. Lambeth Palace Library MS 3199, fol. 249; printed in Edmund Lodge, *Illustrations of British History, Biography, and Manners* (London, 1791), iii, 91.

15. Knighthoods mentioned in this paragraph are recorded under appropriate dates in William A. Shaw, *Knights of England,* 2 vols. (London, 1906).

ARTICLES

The Fortune Contract in Reverse

S. P. Cerasano

Introduction

In late September 1626, just two months before Edward Alleyn died, he wrote a lengthy "Memorandum" relating to Dulwich College.[1] It is a little-known document, and the state of Alleyn's health at the time of its writing is unclear; but given the contents of the manuscript and the proximity of its writing to Alleyn's demise, it is difficult not to think of the memorandum as a set of instructions outlining the business that was to be carried out upon his death. The first sheet, in Alleyn's handwriting, lists properties that he bequeathed to the college upon his death; the second sheet, also in Alleyn's hand, catalogs the names of persons who owed him money. For most of us, the second list is the most interesting because Alleyn notes that, among others, Richard Gunnell, an actor who had performed at the Fortune with the Lord Palsgrave's Men since 1613, was £50 in debt; and even more impressive, "the kinges Maiestie in the Exchequer" owed Alleyn the staggering sum of £800. Yet an assertion in the preamble to the Memorandum might be more useful for exploring the history of the Fortune playhouse. Here, Alleyn stated that most of his "evidences"—that is, papers verifying entitlement—were kept in "a chest at the bedsfeete in the yellow chamber, the keye where of is in the till of my deske." And although only a portion of the manuscripts relating to Henslowe and Alleyn's theatrical ventures could have been stored within this chest, one of these might have been Alleyn's copy of the contract for Fortune Playhouse which indicated that Henslowe and Alleyn constructed the playhouse in 1600. Moreover, the First Fortune seems to have been important to Alleyn from its inception. As events unfolded, it became the theater that he oversaw following Henslowe's death in 1616; and after its accidental destruction by

79

fire in 1621 Alleyn replaced it with a second playhouse on the same
site (also called the Fortune).

But despite the importance that the Fortune held for Alleyn—as
a site for theatrical artistry, a setting offering opportunities for commercial success, and a home for actors, many of whom became
Alleyn's lifelong friends—we normally study the playhouse from
the standpoint of bricks and mortar, which is only natural in light
of the fascinating specifics that the front of the Fortune contract
provides. I will say a bit about that here, as well, but, I hope primarily to enlarge our sense of the Fortune and its creation by placing
the front of the contract in a different context, one that can only
be produced by a more careful reading of the back of the contract.
Examining historical circumstances from this angle alters our understanding of the physical conditions that produced the playhouse in a unique way; and, also, it has significant ramifications for
our interpretation of the human, economic, and political framework in which the theater was erected. Furthermore, reading the
Fortune in reverse highlights the ways in which the physical fabric
of the playhouse, as we envision it, is bound up in our sense of the
contract. The manuscript of the Fortune, after all, provides the only
setting in which the playhouse finally "exists."

The Manuscript

The Fortune contract is a manuscript measuring under one meter
from side to side, and it is slightly shorter from top to bottom.[2]
Written on parchment, in order to stand the test of time, it would
have been identified by the legal establishment of Henslowe's time
as a document called an "indenture"; that is, the manuscript represents an "agreement between two or more parties with mutual cov-
enants" (that is, in legal terms, "accords").[3] The part of the
manuscript that has survived would have been only half of the original document because the term "indenture" takes its name from
both the legal purpose and the *shape* of the manuscript. Originally,
identical copies of the agreement were written on a single piece of
parchment or vellum, and then these were cut apart in a serrated or
sinuous line. Hence, after it was cut, the border of the manuscript
was notched or "indented." The purpose for this procedure was
simple: if, for any reason, there was a dispute over the agreement
that had been made by the parties involved, the manuscripts could

be brought together, and the edges tallied, indicating that they were parts of *one* and the *same* document. Additionally, both parts were authenticated by a custom that called for the signatures to be witnessed by two persons, with the addition of formal seals attached to the manuscript with cord or a thin piece of parchment. But contrary to the way in which the Elizabethans often used the word "letters" (from the Latin *litterae*) to refer either to a single, or several missives, the word "indenture" referred only to an individual piece of the original manuscript. Therefore, the phrase "a pair of indentures" referred to a reassembled, multipart document, although, occasionally, an agreement came to involve more than two parts. This is the process described by Edmund Mortimer, Earl of March, in act 3, scene 1, of *Henry IV, Part 1,* when Mortimer and the other conspirators envision their upcoming campaign against the royal forces and the tripartite division of the country that will follow the victory they anticipate. Mortimer explains the plan this way:

> The Archdeacon hath divided it [the country]
> Into three limits very equally:
> England, from Trent and Severn hitherto,
> By south and east is to my part assigned;
> All westward, Wales beyond the Severn shore,
> And all the fertile land within that bound,
> To Owen Glendower;—and, dear coz, to you
> The remnant northward lying off from Trent.
> And our indentures tripartite are drawne,
> Which being sealèd interchangeably—
> A business that this night may execute—
> Tomorrow, cousin Percy, you and I
> And my good Lord of Worcester will set forth
> To meet your father and the Scottish power,
> As is appointed us, at Shrewsbury.
>
> (3.1.70–84)[4]

Among the hundreds of theatrical manuscripts in the collection amassed by Philip Henslowe and Edward Alleyn are three building contracts, and all of them are indentures. These include the contract for the Fortune Playhouse, written in 1600; the contract for the renovation of some portion of tenements at the Bear Garden, written in 1606; and the contract to pull down the Bear Garden and to erect, in its place, a combination theater and gaming arena, known to history as the Hope, in 1613. The contract to build a playhouse in the Blackfriars district, undertaken by Alleyn in 1615 after Philip

Rosseter had failed in a similar venture, is no longer extant; but if it had existed, we have every reason to expect that it too would have been an indenture.[5] Of the three existing contracts, that for the Fortune offers the most detailed picture both of the construction that was agreed on, and the terms of the project. The indenture for the renovation of the tenements at the Bear Garden offers some intriguing structural details and an elaborate schedule for the way in which payments were made at various stages during the actual building process; but neither it, nor the later contract for the Hope playhouse, assist us in answering many of the abiding questions regarding the reconstruction of the Bear Garden. In fact, the indenture for the construction of the Hope is the most unclear of the three because, in it, the parties agreed that many key elements of the playhouse—for example, the compass, form, width, height, boxes, and staircases—should be "as the Plaie house Called the Swan in the libertie of Parris Garden."[6] (And, of course, there is no extant contract for the Swan.) Consequently, the Fortune contract is a valuable manuscript offering, as it does, dimensions for so many significant architectural details.

The front page (or recto) of the manuscript was prepared, and probably written, by a professional scribe named William Harris. The level of his training is indicated not only by the fact that he wrote his title—"Pub Scr," the English version of the Latin *scriba publica,* "Public Scrivener"—after his name; but Harris's training is also illustrated by the clear hand in which the contract was written, in the manuscript's even lineation, and in the ornamental letter "T" on the first word in the opening line, the word "this" in the phrase that customarily introduces indentures: "This Indenture made . . ." Furthermore, Harris's expertise is demonstrated in the correct use of customary phrases—such as "in witness whereof," "now theiruppon," or "in consideracon." And in typical fashion these are written in a bolder hand than the rest of the text in order to identify the beginnings of important sections within the document. Finally, Harris's training is confirmed in the form of the indenture, which employs a common pattern for the ordering of information within the deed.

Despite the existence of such traditional elements, the indenture was anything but conventional in other ways. As was the case with all scriveners of his time, Harris framed the agreement in a hodgepodge of architectural shorthand, what was thought of as standardized legal terminology, and quasi-legal rhetoric of his own invention. Any legal practitioner of the period would have recognized the opening statement ("This indenture made," etc.), as well as the closing statement ("In witness whereof the parties abovesaid to these present indentures interchangeably have set their hands and seals/ given the day and year first abovewritten"). Architectural shorthand emerges in well-known descriptors—"according to the manner and fashion of the said house called the Globe"—as well as in phrasing such as "for the erecting, building, & setting up" or "suchlike stairs, conveyances, & divisions, without and within." The many references to "[X] number of feet of lawful assize" is also builder's shorthand, calling, as it did, for Peter Street to use measurements that corresponded to those set by the local assize of weights and measurements. Lastly, phrases such as "bargained, compounded & agreed," "at his proper costs and charges," and "reputed, accepted, taken & accompted" are all rhetorical turns that Harris employed in an attempt to describe the complexity of the agreement that Henslowe and Alleyn entered into with their builder.

Additionally, Harris participated in defining the agreement in other ways. At the end of the manuscript he served as witness to the indenture, and Francis Smyth served as the second witness to the contract, signing his own name behind Harris's and identifying himself as "app[rentice] to the said Scr[ivener]." Interestingly, Harris's relationship with Henslowe and Alleyn was more complex than the Fortune contract alone would indicate. For over a decade he had been employed by the two men, on various occasions, to draw up the legal paperwork relating to land transactions; and, like many scriveners of the time, Harris was probably involved in the legal negotiations that led up to the agreements in the contracts. Harris's first appearance in the Dulwich papers occurs in 1595 when he witnessed the bargain and sale of a share in a jointly held messuage, from John Alleyn (Edward's brother) to Edward.[7] During the following year Harris witnessed the transfer of more Alleyn family property from John's widow to Edward.[8] After 1600, Harris was involved in miscellaneous legal work—both for the Admiral's Men and for their financiers.[9] And in 1605, Harris served as the central agent for Edward Alleyn in the negotiations leading up to his purchase of Dulwich Manor. So over time, it appears that Harris played an increasingly important role in Henslowe and Alleyn's legal affairs, serving as counselor, head negotiator, and writer of documents, particularly to Edward Alleyn.[10]

Given this context, together with an understanding of the ways in which public scriveners generally operated, it would be reasonable to speculate that Harris assisted in working out the details of the negotiations that went into the Fortune contract in advance. He certainly met with each of the parties, separately or together, and took careful notes or "minutes," as they were called. Following this, he would have prepared one or several drafts of the final concord. Following all of the negotiations, the final indenture was copied onto the parchment so that it could be signed. Whether or not all of the signators were present at the time of the signing was immaterial because Harris and his apprentice witnessed both copies of the indenture, and they could easily have run the paperwork around to Peter Street and the playhouse owners at separate times. However, in order for the contract to go forward, all parties had, theoretically speaking, to agree on every detail contained therein. Therefore, it was only when all was signed and settled, and when the signed copies were cut apart, that the contract became a binding agreement.

The copy of the Fortune contact that has come down to us represents the final agreement between Street, of the one party, and Henslowe and Alleyn, of the other. As we might expect, Peter Street, the builder, signed the document with his tradesman's mark: a capital "P" for "Peter," with a backward "S" written over it, for "Street." An examination of other documents indicates that this was Street's customary way of signing documents, and it comes, of course, from the practice adopted by carpenters, in which they identified their work on a building project by "signing" the posts and beams with a unique mark. However, legally speaking, it is the holograph signatures of William Harris and Francis Smyth which verified that Street's signature was valid and that his copy of the document was signed and sealed in their presence. The other portion of the indenture—which seems to have been lost over time—would have been signed by Henslowe and Alleyn, and also witnessed by Harris and Smyth. From the sinuous cuts across the top of the Fortune manuscript, we can tell that the copy of the document located on the upper part of the parchment (the copy signed by Henslowe and Alleyn) was kept by Street. He also retained the famous "plot" of the theater, which apparently indicated the positions of various design elements. The lower copy of the contract, signed by Street, was kept by Henslowe and Alleyn; and this provides the explanation as to why it has survived. Whereas the manuscripts that Street received were viewed as working copies—the plot probably taken out onto the site where the actual building work was done—Henslowe and Alleyn removed their copy of the indenture to the safekeeping of one of their houses where the "evidences" for the rest of their businesses were stored.

Reading the Contract in Reverse

The front of the Fortune indenture is the most familiar side to those of us who study theater architecture. Here, as the terms of the contract are laid out, we find the basic elements of an actual playhouse characterized in detail. The external dimensions, internal dimensions, the heights of the galleries, the number of divisions for gentlemen's rooms and two-penny rooms, the size and shape of the stage (along with how it is to be paled in), specifications for the kinds of boards and gutters to be used in various parts of the building, even a few elements of the internal decoration (including a tiled roof over the stage)—all give a vivid impression of what one Elizabethan playhouse might well have looked like, in size, appearance, and texture. The front of the contract also offers us a sense of what level of expense the owners intended to undertake; and it even lays out the schedule for the distribution of the money that was allocated for the construction. The final cost was estimated at £440—which seems high by comparison with the £360 set aside to build the Hope thirteen years later, and perhaps a bit modest by comparison with the estimates for other playhouses of the period.[11] However, what I am interested in, before discussing what we think we know best, are the notes on the back side, or verso, of the contract, and what we can glean from them that will help us to place the more familiar side in a different context.

The back of the Fortune contract consists of sixty-eight separate annotations in the hands of Edward Alleyn and Philip Henslowe, who framed them using the kinds of standard abbreviations that were used for accounting purposes, such as "pd" for "paid," and "dd" for the Latin "dedit" or "given" (that is, money laid out [for any reason, whether related to materials, or labor, or other things]). These are the same abbreviations that we see written throughout Henslowe's well-known theatrical *Diary*, and in the personal memorandum book that Alleyn kept between 1617 and 1622;[12] and we find the same abbreviations in other account books and memorandum books of the period as well. Also in evidence on the back of the Fortune contract are customary terms such as "lent," which refers to money that was borrowed for purposes other than funding construction. The majority of entries simply begin with "paid" or the word "more," as in "more money paid out." The most common phrase employed is "in parte of payment" by which Henslowe and Alleyn meant to signal that they were advancing only a fraction of what would eventually add up to a much larger total (i.e., the £440 set aside to cover construction costs). Last of all, it is worth noting that the annotations—dated between January 17, 1600, just over a week after the contract was signed, and June 11, roughly a month before the July 25 deadline for the building phase of the project— are relatively complete. They offer a clear sense of the pace of the work, and also suggest that all of the parties involved apparently underestimated the final expense of the theater.

Most of the entries are, in the legal language of the time, "acquittances" (from Old French *acquittance*) or receipts offered as evidence for the discharge of debt." In the procedure employed by Henslowe and Alleyn, money was advanced to Peter Street who, as head carpenter, purchased many of the materials and paid his assistants' wages. Acquittances also refer to sums laid out to those tradesmen who constructed parts of the building in Middlesex while Street worked out in the country. These included the bricklayer who built the foundation and the men who carted and hauled building materials to the site where the playhouse would eventually stand. In and of themselves, the annotations seem a rather mundane list of bricks, timber, and mortar; however, the information that can be gleaned from them increases our understanding of the Fortune, as a building and as a project, more than we might at first imagine; and, in some ways the list of annotations is more revealing about some details of the construction, than is the well-known front side of the contract. In addition to providing us with a partial account of the kinds and amounts of building materials, the annotations calendar the progress of the production throughout the many months that Street and his crew were building what was identified in the contract as a "house" and "stage." Moreover, the acquittances also project a sense of the ways in which Henslowe and Alleyn might have interfaced, on a financial and personal level, with the project.

In terms of the building materials, we learn that the bricks seem to have been made locally (perhaps at the nearby brick works in

Islington). We also learn that the timber for the theater was cut somewhere out in the country, probably from forests near Windsor, fitted together temporarily, and then disassembled, transported to Middlesex, and erected on a foundation as a permanent structure. (Like the stipulation in the Hope contract—that builder Gilbert Katherens should "new build" the playhouse—the Fortune is also referred to as a "new house." This made for expensive construction costs.) And although the winter conditions would have delayed the construction of a foundation for the theater, cold weather provided an ideal time to fell trees. Consequently, it seems that Peter Street began the preparation of the wood frame almost immediately after he signed the contract, riding out into the country, from whence he would return from time to time; and during the periods when he was away from London his assistants couriered sums of money to him; or, on occasion, Alleyn delivered money to Street, which gave Alleyn the opportunity to see how the work was progressing. As John Orrell determined, in his essay entitled "Building the Fortune Playhouse," published in 1993, the accounts on the contract, supplemented by three leaves of accounts that were written into Henslowe's *Diary,*[14] suggest a working schedule for the construction. While I will not attempt to repeat the weighty details of this chronology here, it seems that the Fortune contract was signed on January 8. By January 24 Street was out in the country beginning his work there. By March 20, barge loads of timbers (representing the prefabricated playhouse) began to arrive in Middlesex. If the annotations are accurate the foundations were completed around May 8th, and it seems likely that the prefabricated building rose fairly quickly thereafter although, five weeks later, in the middle of June, when the annotations break off, the playhouse had not yet been completed.

Complementing these nuts-and-bolts impressions, the annotations on the back of the Fortune indenture create a human picture, suggesting, first and foremost, the utter centrality of Peter Street to all phases of the operation. With timber, bricks, sand, and such arriving on the scene in batches throughout the project, the master carpenter was vital since, in acting as the general contractor, it was his job to make certain that materials and workmen were coordinated in a well-defined order so that the project didn't lag behind due to material or human delays. Moreover, several of the acquittances indicate that the tradesmen who worked on the project were hired by Street who served as overseer for all phases of the project;

for instance, William Shepherd, bricklayer, and Richard Deller, bargeman, were both paid "at the appointment of Peter Street." And if the schedule of payments in the annotations is at all accurate, despite a few delays, the work on the Fortune ticked along fairly regularly. However, it also appears that Street began to show signs of strain as the project went beyond its deadline and its budget. Perhaps in response to Street's volatile temperament (a characteristic for which he was well-known), or simply owing to everyone's heightened anxiety level, Henslowe and Alleyn noted that they began to purchase drink for the workmen, starting around the middle of May; and throughout much of the summer, Henslowe frequently noted that he laid out money to purchase both food and drink for Street.[15] At times, Henslowe and his bailiff—Gilbert East—even breakfasted and/or dined with Street. Finally, on June 10, barely over a month before the project was to be completed Henslowe and Alleyn gave Street 4s., as they said, "to pasify him."

In human terms, the list of acquittances on the back of the Fortune contract also offers a directory of Street's crew and the craftsmen with whom he worked. John Benion, referred to as "M[aste]r Street's man," and William Blackbourne were fellow members of the Carpenters Company, who appear alongside Street in manuscripts detailing the history of the company during the same period.[16] (Street was serving as a warden in the Carpenters Company in 1599 when he helped to move the theater from Hollywell to Southwark where it was rebuilt as the First Globe.)[17] Also mentioned is Street's apprentice Robert Wharton who was probably supervised, in part, by Benion, and who appears a fair number of times as the boy who collected money for Street.[18] Another man, William Wharton, is named only once; but he appears to have been related to Robert. Then there are the names of nine men and women who supplied and/or transported timber, as well as the names of five sawyers who cut timber. One of these, Robert Deller, also appears as a supplier of boards in records of the Carpenters Company for 1610.[19] Additionally, Henslowe's records identify two bargemen who moved the timber to a point where it was carted to the building site. And lastly, in and among the many entries for payments that Henslowe made directly to Street are the anonymous "workmen" who performed unspecified tasks, but whose labor was doubtless fundamental to the construction of the Fortune.

Complementing what we can tell about economic arrangements from the front of the contract, the annotations on the reverse of the indenture reveal some concrete information regarding Street's physical whereabouts during the Fortune project. On the front of the contract we read that Street was to be given the first half of the money owed, or £220 "Att suche tyme And when as the Tymberwoork of the saide fframe shalbe rayzed & sett upp . . . Or w^{th}in Seaven daies then next followeinge." But it is on the back of the contract that we learn that Street received the first advance for 40s. at the sealing of the contract nine days later (January 17). Moreover, the annotations reveal that, over the course of the next two months, most of the payments were transferred to Street by intermediaries; and then, from March 20 on, because Street was apparently spending more time in London, payments were made directly to him, and he, in turn, paid his workmen—frequently, though not always, on a Saturday.[20] The back side of the contract reveals, as well, that the price of timber, as calculated per load, could vary and that the fee for the carriage of a "faer" (or bargeload of timber) could differ as well, along with the periods of time that it took to transport timber or the prefabricated sections of the playhouse into Middlesex. All which variations made it difficult for Street to keep costs within the limits set out on the front of the contract, even if, as is stated there the second half of the payment would be delivered "att suche time and when as the saide fframe & woork*es* shalbe fullie effected & ffynished . . . Or w^{th}in Seaven daies then next followeinge." According to John Orrell's final estimates, over the course of the six months that Henslowe and Alleyn financed the project they laid out a minimum of £509 (£69 over the anticipated expense of the theater), without accounting for the costs of labor involved in tiling the roof, plastering the walls, or hiring glazers, plasterers, plumbers, and smiths to complete the finish work on the building.[21] In Alleyn's own list of expenses he claimed that he laid out £520 on the playhouse alone, a further £240 to secure the lease on the property, and £120 for other private buildings of his own, bringing the initial costs to a hefty £880, which only covered the construction of the theater and the development of the surrounding property in a preliminary fashion.[22] Nevertheless, it was probably worth the price for men like Henslowe and Alleyn, who would become court servants and aspired to even greater things. And also, they had years of experience as entrepreneurs. For them, the high costs were justified by the commercial and artistic success that they anticipated in return on their wager. Surely it was no accident that the new playhouse was named "The Fortune," which alluded not only

to the fact that the owners had pinned their hopes on the good favors of Dame Fortuna, but to the "fortuna" that the investors hoped
to reap as benefits, both in the arena of London commerce and at
court.

The Fortune in the Context of Its Owners

The coming and going of people preserved in the annotations on
the back of the Fortune contract remind us that Henslowe and
Alleyn were also coming and going from the building site, as well
as from the location where Street framed and created the playhouse. In fact, the placement of some annotations on the back side
of the indenture, and the preservation of others within Henslowe's
Diary suggest that while both men seem to have been committed
equally to the success of the project, each investor took responsibility for managing the finances for the construction at different times,
dependent upon whatever other responsibilities they were handling. And here is another point at which the back of the contract
offers evidence that is absolutely unique to our understanding of
the Fortune's history. In looking over the list of acquittances it appears that both Henslowe and Alleyn kept accounts, but Henslowe's hand predominates. John Benion, who located suppliers of
timber, wrote one entry, and various payees and witnesses to payments wrote their signature below the entries inscribed by Henslowe and Alleyn. At the opening of 1600 it is Edward Alleyn's
clear, open hand that we see down much of the left side of the
manuscript. Then from the twentieth of March to the eleventh of
June, Henslowe's hand is prominent as he copies a list of payments
onto the right side of the page. At this point Henslowe ran out of
space on the manuscript, but he had already started keeping another listing of expenses in his *Diary,* starting at some point previous to June 2 and ending on the eighth of August. However, the
latter is not a simple continuation of building costs. Following one
entry—a payment of 10s. for removing dung with a cart—and another—for going to Greenwich with Robert Shaw, an actor, which
might be utterly unrelated to the Fortune project—Henslowe produced a list of some thirty-seven entries in which he recording
nothing more than the expenses for food and drink for Street and
his crew. From this we are led to conclude either that Henslowe
and Alleyn either stopped keeping building accounts in the middle

of June or—what is more likely—that they continued on separate sheets of paper, or in another book. But these have been lost. Either way, what have been lost to us are the acquittances relating to the final phases of the project, about which we know very little. In this aspect we can only acknowledge that for certain periods, the Fortune contract, even when supplemented with the odd pages from Henslowe's *Diary,* renders a very incomplete picture.

But if the manuscript evidence supplied by Henslowe's portion of the back of the contract hints at anything, it is that Henslowe had commitments elsewhere that made it inconvenient for him to attend to the construction at every phase. Furthermore, as it turns out, these were substantial, primarily because, since 1593, Henslowe had spent a fair amount of time as a servant of the Chamber in the royal household, a responsibility that required that he divide his time between his business interests in London and wherever the Court might take him. Early in his career Henslowe began his service as one of fourteen Grooms of the Chamber, twelve of which were usually in service. The men who held these positions were men like Henslowe who were members of the gentry; and some of them, like Henslowe, also had family ties to the Court that went back in time to former generations. Edmond Henslowe, Philip's father, had been appointed Master of Ashdown Forest by the Crown, and he received a pension under Queen Mary for unspecified service to the Crown. Henslowe's uncle, Raphe Hogg, was licensed by the Queen to operate an iron foundry in Sussex, a business that was not only lucrative but which allowed him to gather further privileges, including a patent to make gunshot and to sell surplus cannons on the Continental market. In addition, Hogg supplied advice on the design of heavy weaponry, and is credited particularly with the invention of the best iron cannon of his day, many of which were used for guarding the Sussex coast against foreign invasion. As a result of these factors, Henslowe was socially and economically privileged, which led to his own appointment at Court; and he was apparently useful enough in that setting that by 1599 he had been promoted to the position of Gentleman Sewer (i.e., Steward).[23]

All this bears importantly on our characterization of Henslowe as an actor in the Fortune drama, especially as this drama was played out over the first months of 1600; and also it shapes our image of him as we seek to understand how his London investments came together with his ambitions in the more exalted setting of the Court. But, initially, it is useful for us to piece together what we can know of Henslowe's life within this chronological framework. During the Christmas season that stretched from December 1599, through the early part of 1600, the Court was sitting at Richmond. Four plays were performed, two each by the Chamberlain's Men and the Lord Admiral's Men companies. The latter performed *The Pleasant Comedie of Old Fortunatus* on December 27, and they performed *The Shoemaker's Holiday* on New Year's Day. The titles of the plays by the Lord Chamberlain's Men are unknown.[24] On January 8 the Fortune contract was signed; and sometime, soon thereafter, the Justices of the Peace in Middlesex attempted to stop the construction of the playhouse. The situation escalated so quickly that on January 12, Charles Howard, the Lord Admiral and patron of the acting company that hoped to move into the Fortune upon its completion, sent a warrant to the Justices of the Peace of Middlesex, authorizing Edward Alleyn to continue with his project. In justifying the need for a new playhouse, Howard made three claims: that the Rose was in a state of decay, that Alleyn had already "provided Tymber and other necessaries for theffectinge therof to his great chardge," and that "her Ma[tie] (in respect of the acceptable Service, w[ch] my saide Servant and Companie have doen and presented before her Highenes to hergreate likeinge and Contentmen[t] aswell this last Christmas as att sondrie other tymes) ys gratiouslie moved toward*es* them wth a speciall regarde of favor in their proceedings."[25] Five days later, from January 19 to 21, the Queen spent three days at the Chelsea home of Charles Howard, the Lord Admiral, patron of the company that would move to the Fortune upon its completion.[26] Nevertheless, for whatever effectiveness Howard's warrant might have had initially, the Middlesex justices continued to bring pressure to bear on the construction project, because on April 8, three months after work on the project had been done, a second warrant defending Alleyn was addressed "To y[e] Justices of Peace of y[e] Countye of Midd[le]s[ex,] especially of S[t] Gyles w[th] out Creplegate, and to all others whome it shall Concerne."[27] Like the previous warrant, this one made much of the Queen's favorable disposition toward Edward Alleyn. It recapitulated that Alleyn had spent quite a lot of money on the project too, and noted that the location was very "convenient" for theatergoers. The warrant—written "frome the Courte at Richmonde"—was signed by Howard, Robert Cecil, and George Carey Lord Hunsdon, who was the patron of Shakespeare's company; and while the manuscript was written by one of the Court secretaries, all of the signatures are autograph signatures. Interestingly, when we mesh this calendar with the construction calendar on the back of the Fortune contract it appears that, ultimately, the censure of the Middlesex justices produced little more than inconvenience for the playhouse owners. The payments to Street, and other tradesmen, occurred regularly, more or less without interruption, from mid-January to mid-June, including payments indicating that the workmen continued through Lent, and probably through all of the week leading up to, and including Holy Saturday, the day when they were given their wages. Because the following day was Easter, the workmen broke for two days, Easter Sunday and Easter Monday. They were paid again the next day, on Tuesday, the feast of the Annunciation.

But to return to politics: why didn't the justices seem to have more authority in the situation? And why is it that despite periodic attempts to close down the Fortune, throughout its history, the justices failed on every occasion? Looking more carefully at the particular moment which is the spring of 1600, we would be missing an important clue if we didn't recognize that not only was Alleyn popular with the Queen, but that Philip Henslowe—who had been promoted from a Groom of the Chamber to a Steward of the Chamber—probably had a role to play in the internal politics surrounding the construction phase of the project. In fact, one tax certificate, written from Court at Richmond on the tenth of October, 1600, notes that "Phillip Henslowe esqr, one of the Shewers of her ma*es* chamber," was "most resyaunt and abiding here at the court in the time of Taxeacon and for the most part of the yeare before."[28] As a result, many of the payments on the back of the Fortune contract were copied in batches, from another source, probably from accounts kept by Alleyn who, on at least two occasions during the project (March 13, May 15), rode to Windsor to make payments to Street.

Moreover, there are other links between the Fortune contract and those who either served at Court or held Court-appointed positions. Early in the life of the Fortune project (January 21) the owners made their largest payment in the list—£20—to purchase timber from two men: "m*r* winche of the scaldinge howsse & m*r* Baylle kep*ere* of the stare chamb*er* dore." Another substantial payment—for £10 10s.—was made to Winche and Baylle in early March. And it is also instructive to realize that, by 1600, Peter Street was not only well connected within the Carpenters Company, but that, as early as

1597–98, he was employed by the Royal Works; and a year earlier, in a lawsuit adjudicated in the Court of Requests, Street identified himself as an ordinary servant in the Queen's household.[29] Given these circumstances, it is entirely possible that Henslowe and Street, probably with Alleyn, had come together in other circumstances. Nor was the building of the Fortune the first construction-related encounter that Henslowe had with Street. Henslowe became the manager of the Royal Barge House, built by Street, which was constructed from 1597 to 1598, not far from the Rose Playhouse.[30] Furthermore, in the middle of December 1599, Henslowe lists sums laid out for construction on a house, possibly his own residence. He heads his list: "for bylldinge of my howsse vpon the bancksyd w[ch] was goodman deres . . . wth mr strette carpenter."[31] Although we associate Street with the large-scale building and jobbing work that he did on the Globe and the Fortune, and later on, on the tenements at the Bear Garden, we need only remind ourselves that Henslowe and Alleyn generally became well acquainted with their builders; and there is some likelihood that Street caught their attention through Court connections, before the Globe was built. John Griggs, who was employed as the master builder on the Rose Playhouse, in 1587, later renovated part of Edward Alleyn's house, becoming part of the friendship circle that grew up around Henslowe and Alleyn.[32] When Alleyn was on tour during the summer of 1593, Henslowe regularly included news of Griggs and his wife in his letter to Alleyn; and on August 1, Alleyn—who was still in the country—sent a letter to his wife and father-in-law, conveying his "harty commend[ations] to m[r] grigs and his wife and all his houshould."[33]

Both Sides of the Contract Taken Together

If we return to the front of the Fortune contract, the side that we know well, we can determine a few things about the appearance of the playhouse that are unique. Assuming that the owners' intentions were followed precisely, the playhouse measured eighty feet square, on the outside, and fifty feet square on the inside, all which were to be calculated in "feet of lawful assize." The front of the indenture also stipulates that there will be three galleries, of twelve feet in height, then of eleven feet, and finally, of nine feet, growing shorter as the workmen built from the ground upward. And all of the stories were to be twelve and a half feet wide, from the back wall to the front side, nearest to the pit, the top two with a jetty forward of ten inches. The builders were also to create divisions within the galleries for gentlemen's rooms and two-penny rooms; and, of course, stairs, conveyances, and divisions "like the Globe's." Not least of all there was to be a stage that measured forty-three feet in breadth, and which extended halfway out into the yard, or twenty-two and a half feet; and it was to be paled in below. Behind this would be a tiring house, and the house would also incorporate the usual windows, lights that were at the Globe; and there would be tiling on the stage and staircases with sufficient gutters to carry the water away from the covering of the stage. Lastly, after the structure was finished with the customary "lathe, lyme, & haire," the main posts on the stage, shaped as squares, would be decorated with carved satyrs, of the kind that one typically found on pilasters of the period. And the kind that Henslowe and Alleyn called for again to be included by Street on the reconstructed tenements at the Bear Garden six years later.

Of course, this description doesn't tell the whole story; and, in the final scene, although no manuscript ever seems "complete," the primary purpose of the Fortune indenture is to describe the intentions of the parties involved at the time of its signing, not necessarily to create a full picture of the Fortune Playhouse and the surrounding property, in all of its manifest complexity. Nor do the copious annotations on the back of the Fortune clarify some of the questions that the front of the contract raises. To a great extent, both sides of the contract are separate snapshots, illuminating only the playhouse and telling us nothing about Alleyn's subsequent investments, developments, and renovations on the Golding Lane property. For instance, we know that there was a taphouse near the theater, run by Mark Brigham,[34] although there is no provision for a taphouse in the contract; and over time, Alleyn created housing near the playhouse, possibly for the several players from the Admiral's Men who moved from Bankside to St. Giles when the playhouse was completed, presumably to help manage the Fortune. Nor does either side of the contract really elaborate on the reasons as to why Henslowe and Alleyn decided to design the First Fortune as a square building, abandoning the traditional polygonal structure typified by the Globe or the Swan. And why did they alter—also, perhaps—the shape of the stage? Granted, the Fortune stage might have offered more space for the actors. Yet the "quinque angle" to which Tamburlaine refers when he explains the necessity of changing the order of battle relative to different terrains is modeled so vividly by the shape of the Rose's trapezoidal stage where the play was being performed in the 1590s.[35] Were other nuanced allusions to the Rose theater lost in the move to a different architectural model?

Conclusion

Obviously, there are questions that no side of the Fortune contract can illuminate; and the back of the indenture that was signed in 1600 by the playhouse owners and its builder, prompts questions that bear ultimately upon both Fortune Playhouses, the first and the second. For, in many ways, it is important to look ahead; after all, the Second Fortune Playhouse was so important to Edward Alleyn that he made a special trip to visit the Earl of Arundel in order to show him the plot for the construction of the new playhouse.[36] But while we are busy looking forward we must concurrently look backward and sideways as well. For, as is commonly the case, the history of a playhouse often stands somewhere between portions of a manuscript that seem directly relevant to it, and other bits of the manuscript, which might at first seem less directly relevant. In the contract that we have been examining here, the manuscript points us not only to the physical playhouse, with which we are already familiar, but to new and original contexts which, prism-like, allow us to see fresh possibilities for the interpretation of the entire Fortune project. In this, we are reminded of Edward Alleyn's manuscript chest, with its many treasured "evidences," in the yellow chamber, the key to which was hidden in the till of his desk. As is the case with Alleyn's chest, we have yet to unpack fully the Fortune contract which is, in itself, a treasure chest, one full of mesmerizing detail, enticing suggestion, and alluring implications.

Notes

1. Folger Library, MS X.d.255. This essay was first read as a lecture at Shakespeare's Globe on November 4, 2006.

2. The manuscript citation for the Fortune contract is Muniment 22 in G. F. Warner, *Catalogue of the Manuscripts and Muniments of Alleyn's College of God's*

Gift at Dulwich (London: Spottiswoode, 1881), 234–35. A "muniment" is a title deed or charter where rights are defended.

3. *OED. Oxford English Dictionary Online,* s.v. "indenture," #2, http://dictionary.oed.com/cgi/entry/50115154?query_type = word&queryword = indenture &first = 1&max_to_show = 10&sort_type = alpha&result_place = 1&search_id = hkkY-KsJtf1-11748&hilite = 50115154.

4. William Shakespeare, *King Henry IV Part 1,* ed. David Scott Kastan (London: Thomson, 2002).

5. S. P. Cerasano, "Competition for the King's Men?: Alleyn's Blackfriars Venture," *MaRDiE* 4 (1989): 173–86.

6. W. W. Greg, *Henslowe Papers* (London: A. H. Bullen, 1907), 19–22, quotation from p. 20. (Hereafter cited as *HP.*)

7. Warner, *Catalogue,* 254.

8. Ibid., 255–56.

9. R. A. Foakes, *Henslowe's Diary,* 2nd ed. (Cambridge: Cambridge University Press, 2002), 43, 166, 174, 244–45. (Hereafter cited as *HD.*)

10. Edward Griffin (Griffen) is scribe who worked frequently with Philip Henslowe. Ibid., 65, 230 and Warner, *Catalogue,* 42, 46, 48, 77, 102.

11. E. K. Chambers, *The Elizabethan Stage* (Oxford: Clarendon Press, 1923), 2:406, 468. (Hereafter cited as *ES.*)

12. Warner, *Catalogue,* MS. IX, transcribed as pp. 165–95.

13. *OED Oxford English Dictionary Online,* s.v. "acquittance," #3, http://dictionary.oed.com/cgi/entry/50002004?query_type = word&queryword = acquittance&first = 1&max_to_show = 10&sort_type = alpha&result_place = 1&search_id = hkkL-MYo20g-11881&hilite = 50002004.

14. Ff. 98v–99r, which are Foakes, *HD,* 191–93. All of my references to the Fortune contract, throughout this essay, are to Foakes's transcription, *HD,* 306–15.

15. Foakes, *HD,* 191–93.

16. See, for example, the references to William Blackbourne in vol. 7 of *Records of the Worshipful Company of Carpenters,* ed. A. M. Millard, (Isle of Wight: Pinhorns, 1968), 42, 47. "Benion" is presumably the "John Benison" who became a freeman in 1577 (see vol. 5 of *Records of the Worshipful Company of Carpenters,* ed. Bower Marsh and John Ainsworth [London: Phillimore, 1937], which is Wardens' Account Book, 1571–91, p. 90).

17. B. W. E. Alford and T. C. Barker, *A History of the Carpenters Company* (London: George Allen and Unwin, 1968), 180.

18. Wharton's apprenticeship to Street is recorded in the Wardens' Account Book (1592–1614), transcribed and edited by A. M. Millard as vol. 7 of *Records of the Worshipful Company of Carpenters,* 7:151.

19. Richard Deller is referred to twice in 1610 entries of the Wardens' Account Book (1592–1614), transcribed and edited by A. M. Millard as vol. 7 of *Records of the Worshipful Company of Carpenters,* 7:341, 361.

20. The Saturday wage payments occurred on Feb. 22, March 8, March 22, May 24 (2), May 31, and June 7. Other Saturday payments were given out on January 19, April 26, and May 10. Other payments made late in the week, on Friday, occurred on Feb. 15, Feb. 29, April 25, May 30, and June 6 (3).

21. John Orrell, "Building the Fortune," *Shakespeare Quarterly* 44 (1993): 144.

22. Foakes, *HD,* 302.

23. S. P. Cerasano, "The Geography of Henslowe's Diary," *SQ* 56, no. 3 (2005): 328–53.

24. Chambers, *ES,* 4:112.

25. Greg, *HP,* 49–50.

26. Chambers, *ES,* 4:112.

27. Greg, *HP,* 51–52; citation from p. 52.

28. NA, E115/219/79.

29. NA, REQ 2/91/57.

30. NA, E351/3233.

31. Foakes, *HD,* 66–67.

32. Ibid., 233–34.

33. Greg, *HP,* 35, 36, 41.

34. The reference to the taphouse is recorded in a later lease (Warner, *Catalogue,* 242–43).

35. Christopher Marlowe, *Tamburlaine the Great, Parts One and Two,* ed. Anthony B. Dawson (New York: W. W. Norton, 1997), 126–27 (*2 Tamburline the Great,* 3.2.62–67.)

36. Warner, *Catalogue,* 192 (June 12, 1622).

The Cook and the Cannibal:
Titus Andronicus and the New World

David B. Goldstein

IN ANY DISCUSSION OF SHAKESPEARE and the New World, it seems *The Tempest* "must follow, as the night the day." I propose instead to analyze the use of American exploration narratives in Shakespeare's earliest tragedy. In its preoccupations with Rome, Ovid, Virgil, and Seneca, *Titus Andronicus* is usually read in dialogue with Renaissance humanism. Without discounting its classical context, we may profit by examining the play alongside representations of New World cannibalism in sixteenth-century writings about American conquest. These representations involve a distinctly different set of conventions from those of classical stories. Crucially, accounts of Old World anthropophagy emphasize the physical act of eating, while in visual and verbal depictions of New World cannibalism the act of eating occurs as an afterthought or a leftover of the ritual killing that precedes it.[1] The sources available to Shakespeare frame questions of anthropophagic behavior and ethics in ways that are highly relevant to the play's dynamics. An examination of these conventions sheds new light upon one of the play's cruces, the apparent anticlimax of the cannibal banquet scene that closes the play's action. An analysis of *Titus* in an American context shows us a play organized around misuses of cooking and eating with roots not only in classical literature but in the behaviors of Iberian, Brazilian, and Aztec warriors. Cannibalism, the play's central metaphor, provides a mechanism by which victims and victors debase each other, producing an ethical landscape controlled by variegated forms of devourment and dismemberment. In any act of eating, one organism is destroyed to serve another, and the resulting collapse of self and other provides sustenance and regeneration for both. In *Titus,* eating destroys, but produces neither sustenance nor regeneration for eater or eaten. In such a world, the collapse of the self/other boundary that eating necessitates does not liberate, but rather degrades all parties. In *Titus,* the heuristic of consumption is the uncovering of one's own inhumanity.

Revenge and Anticlimax

In the final scene of *Titus,* the title character presents the Gothic queen Tamora with a pie in which he has baked her sons, which she proceeds unwittingly to eat. When asked to account for the sons' whereabouts, Titus reveals his plot in the gloating tones of the Renaissance revenger:

> Why, there they are, both baked in this pie;
> Whereof their mother daintily hath fed,
> Eating the flesh that she herself hath bred.
> 'Tis true, 'tis true, witness my knive's sharp point.
> *He stabs the Empress* (5.3.59–62)[2]

In the space of twenty lines occur Titus's killing of his daughter Lavinia, the twin revelations quoted above, Titus's murder of Tamora, the emperor Saturninus's killing of Titus, and the retaliatory stabbing of Saturninus by Titus's son Lucius. Tamora has only a few seconds of horror, and no time for anguished speech, before Titus kills her.

For most writers of revenge tragedy through the Renaissance, Shakespeare included, the dilated moment at which the revenger reveals the victim's crime and subsequent punishment constitutes a hallmark of the genre, inherited directly from Seneca and ultimately from Aeschylus.[3] Seneca's *Thyestes,* which Shakespeare used as a major source for *Titus,* draws out the revelation in an extended dialogue between Thyestes and his revenger, Atreus. Jasper Heywood's 1560 translation of the play dilates the revenge still further by giving Thyestes an extra scene in which he meditates on having eaten his children. In *The Spanish Tragedy,* Hieronymo volunteers a lengthy catalog of the events that have brought him to his revenge before killing the Duke of Castile and himself. *The Revenger's Tragedy,* which appeared over a decade after *Titus,* maintains and heightens the Senecan convention. Vindice spells out his careful revenge and its origins while poison slowly eats away at the mouth of his victim, the lecherous duke; Vindice then holds the duke down to witness the duchess's adultery before he dies. Marston's *Antonio's Revenge,* whose quasi-cannibalist climax closely parallels Shakespeare's in other ways, strays from its source in prolonging the act of recognition: Antonio uncovers a dish containing the limbs of his victim's child, after which the stage direction indicates that "Piero seems to condole his son."[4] Several lines of dialogue allow Piero to digest the horror of his situation before Antonio and his compatriots stab the duke to death. Even Shakespeare follows the Senecan model in his other foray into the genre: the tempo of the fencing match in *Hamlet* allows most characters time to register their own and each other's misdeeds even as they hurtle toward death.

The abruptness of the revenge scene in *Titus,* by contrast, has created challenges for critics and especially directors. Alan Dessen identifies the issue of "how to deal with the staccato murders so as to avoid an unwanted audience reaction" as one of the play's most severe staging problems. Peter Brook's 1955 production magnified the killings' rapidity to the point of farce, cutting many of the scene's lines and enacting the killings, as Richard David described it, "like a row of ninepins." Deborah Warner's otherwise realistic 1987 version set the killings against a stylized chorus reaction; meanwhile, Estelle Kohler's Tamora struggled to eat as much of the pie as possible but found that the speed of the events made it hard to consume much of the meal.[5] Julie Taymor's cinematic version freezes the drama at the moment of Saturninus's death and digitally rotates the resulting tableau, thus cinematically dilating the act of revenge. The final stage picture, a mixture of tragedy and farce, offers a stage scattered with bodies, "the poor remainder of Andronici" (5.3.130) struggling off to mourn, and the poor remainder of Tamora's pie sitting forlornly amid a half-eaten banquet.

My answer to the question of why *Titus*'s final scene seems anticlimactic lies in the recipe for its half-eaten pie. By recipe, I mean the sources the playwright has drawn upon in order to invent his pasty, or "coffin," as Titus calls it—sources comprised of stories in which humans consume other humans in order to consummate revenge. Critics have traditionally focused upon two antecedents of the play's cannibalism: Seneca's play of Atreus and Thyestes, and Ovid's narrative of Tereus, Procne, and Philomela. Let us turn our attention instead to another popular strand of anthropophagy in Shakespeare's time, the New World cannibal narrative.[6] As European ethnography absorbed American cannibalism, its modes increased in number and variety. Old World notions influenced New World narratives and vice versa. Shakespeare inherits several ways of depicting and understanding cannibalism. *Titus Andronicus* mingles aspects of the anthropophagic imaginary without integrating them. Divergent narratives and structures coexist and exert force upon each other.

Old World and New

The two species of cannibalism, or anthropophagy, that Shakespeare inherited are as distinct but interrelated as the terms "cannibalism" and "anthropophagy" themselves.[7] One strand involves stories about person-eating derived from the founding myths of the Greco-Roman tradition, as well as from early ethnographic descriptions by Herodotus and Pliny of tribes who ate human flesh.[8] The Greek term for these tribes, Anthropophagi or Androphagoi ('Ανδροφάγοι, "person-eaters"), had been known through editions of Herodotus and Pliny for centuries, though the *OED* cites the first English language use of the term only in 1552. The mythical background of cannibalism stems largely from the stories of Kronos and Tantalus. In his *Theogony,* Hesiod describes how the king of the Titans and father of Zeus swallows his children one after another in order to prevent any of them from conquering him. His wife Rhea and his mother Gaia trick him into vomiting up his children, thereby engendering a second "birth." Zeus conquers Kronos and his reign over humankind begins.[9] Like father like (grand)son: we find a similarly transgressive act in the legend of Tantalus, Zeus's son. An original *chef de cuisine humaine,* Tantalus prepares and serves his son Pelops to the gods in order to test whether they can distinguish the taste of human from beast. His punishment, echoed by Aaron's at the end of *Titus,* is one of proverbial tantalizing desire: the apples are always just out of reach; the water beneath him recedes when he stretches down to it. Tantalus, like Kronos, is an overreacher, violating boundaries between self and other, between one generation and the next, between civilized and savage. In both cases, cannibalism is an ambivalent act, mixing destruction and regeneration: the golden age gives way to the silver, innocence to discernment.

The word "cannibal" first appears in Christopher Columbus's journal to describe the fearsome man-eating inhabitants of an island near Hispaniola. The term would seem to describe an ethnographic, rather than a mythical phenomenon, and thus a set of associations separate from those of Greco-Roman anthropophagy. But as David Beers Quinn reminds us, "In relation to the New World, new geographical ideas were largely old ideas shifted westwards; genuine novelty emerged only very slowly."[10] Columbus's "discovery" of cannibals was shaped by his knowledge of ancient travel narratives and by his belief that he had found Cathay; he first mentions the tribe in relation to the "canine" dog-headed Scythians of Herodotus and Pliny, and then becomes convinced that they are people of the great "Khan."[11] Within the term "cannibal," therefore, lies buried a trove of conflicting and symbolically rich etymologies that connect the Old World with the New through a rapt fascination with the taboo of person-eating.

What do we know of Shakespeare's familiarity with these cannibals and the sensationalist narratives about them that arrived in Europe along with corn, tomatoes, and potatoes? *The Tempest* famously provides proof of Shakespeare's knowledge of New World cannibalism; Caliban anagrammatizes cannibal, and Gonzalo paraphrases Michel de Montaigne's essay "Des Cannibales" in 2.1 of the play.[12] Montaigne's *Essais* appeared in John Florio's English translation in 1603 and seem to inform both *Hamlet* and *Troilus and Cressida,* both likely composed between 1600 and 1602, but scholars have been hesitant to credit Shakespeare with knowledge of Montaigne before 1600.[13] I think it plausible that Shakespeare knew and responded to Montaigne's book (first published in French in 1580) in *Titus,* and will return to Montaigne later in these pages. But one does not have to prove an early link between the two authors to show that knowledge of cannibalism in both the Old and New Worlds had circulated widely in Shakespeare's England prior to the publication of the *Essais.* Many of the sources used by Montaigne were also available to Shakespeare, and by the time *Titus* was first printed, in 1594, ethnography of the Americas had taken on new urgency in the wake of key explorations and publications.

In Europe, news of American cannibals closely followed news of America itself. The first visual image of the New World in Europe, found on the Portuguese Kunstmann II map of 1502, reprinted in Sebastian Münster's popular *Cosmographia Universale,* shows a man being spit-roasted by a naked native. It is based on Amerigo Vespucci's account of his 1501–2 voyage to South America.[14] The Munich woodcut of 1505 or 1506, which introduced Europe to a somewhat more ethnographically accurate picture of Brazilian cannibalism, was republished several times, first appearing in English between about 1511 and 1523, in the undated printed work *Of the Newe Landes.*[15] Columbus's fantasy of Caribbean cannibalism entered English with Richard Eden's translations of Münster's *A treatyse of the new India* (1553) and *The decades of the newe worlde* (1555) by Pietro Martire Anghiera (known in England as Peter Martyr), if not before. Martyr's *Decades,* republished by Hakluyt in 1587, also contains numerous and meticulous, if often fanciful, depictions of Brazilian and Venezuelan cannibals stemming from the reports of Balboa and other conquistadores. André Thevet's *The New found vvorlde,* which was published in France in 1557 and served Montaigne as a source, was translated in 1568. His longer *Cosmographie Universelle,* published in France in 1575, may have been part of the Elizabethan MA program of study (as Münster's *Cosmographia* was), and Marlowe relied on it for the second part of *Tamburlaine.*[16] Descriptions of Aztec human sacrifice appear in Eden's translation of Peter Martyr and in Thevet's *Cosmographie,* and are luxuriously described in Francisco López de Gómara's detailed account of Cortés's conquest of Mexico (an explicit source for Montaigne's "Of Coaches"), Englished in 1578 and reprinted in 1596.[17] Thus we may establish that texts relating to Caribbean, Brazilian, Venezuelan, and Mexican cannibal practices were all circulating in England by the time Shakespeare sat down to write *Titus.*[18]

Eating Scenes

At least two aspects of the sixteenth-century discourse of New World cannibalism bear upon *Titus.* The first involves the subtle ways in which, from the very first reports, the ritual and spectacle of anthropophagy function differently in representations of the New World from those of the Old. This is a paradoxical claim since, in general, and also from the first, notions of cannibals were so deeply enmeshed in prior representations. Yet the difference remains: ethnographic and mythical representations of European anthropophagy focus upon the physical act of eating, while in representations of American cannibalism physical eating is rarely the point, with the focus instead centering upon the spectacle of dismemberment and cooking, or upon the remains of the meal. Although exceptions arise, the distinction tends to hold true both in visual and verbal depictions of cannibalism, starting with Hesiod, Ovid, and Thyestes, and continuing through and beyond the sixteenth century. Visual renderings of Kronos eating his children, for instance, usually emphasize the moment at which a child becomes an ingested food. Thus Peter Paul Rubens's *Saturn Devouring his Children* (1623) shows the savage god tearing into his son with his teeth (fig. 1). Other pre-conquest visual representations of anthropophagy bear out this distinction. The famous thirteenth-century Hereford map of the world depicts the Essedones, a legendary people who ritually consumed their parents, with an illustration in which two figures, seated at a pile of bloody limbs, hack with one hand and eat with the other.[19] In literature too, anthropophagic narratives focus on eating as the primary spectacle. Thyestes' banquet takes up 140 lines in Seneca's play, and lasts even longer in Heywood's translation; the table itself shakes and "leap[s] from trembling ground."[20] Ovid's Philomela story reaches its climax only after Tereus has finished half his meal. An extraordinary example of this focus on literal consumption occurs in *The Bloody Banquet,* a play published in 1639, attributed cautiously to Thomas Dekker, and based on William Warner's 1584 classically inspired romance *Pan his Syrinx.* A "bloody banquet" does indeed end the play, with the queen of Cilicia forced to gnaw upon her illicit lover's raw skull and limbs. The play presents no surprise revelation, as in Seneca and Ovid; instead, the queen eats with full knowledge of her act, and she keeps at it doggedly throughout the scene until her husband stabs her to death.[21]

Accounts of colonial cannibalism, like stories of classical anthropophagy, focus on ritual and spectacular elements, such as violent dismemberment and the transformation of a living body into food. But if classical anthropophagy depends upon the spectacle of eating, accounts and images of cannibalism in both Africa and the New World make a point of substituting for literal cannibalism either its remains or the ritual performances that precede it. The first visual depiction of cannibalism, the Kunstmann II map, inaugurates the tradition by showing a native turning a spit to which a European man has been bound: the cooking signifies and replaces the eating. Likewise, in the first printed excursus on New World cannibalism, chronicled (in slightly different versions) both in Münster's *Treatyse* and in Martyr's *Decades,* it is the cooked leftovers and kitchen utensils that stand in for the cannibalism itself. Here is Martyr:

Fig. 1. Peter Paul Rubens, *Saturn Devouring His Children* (1623). Used by permission of Art Resource, Inc.

Our men found in theyr houses [the cannibals', the cannibals themselves having fled], all kyndes of erthen uessels, not muche unlike unto
oures. They founde also in theyr kichens, mannes flesshe, dukes flesshe, and goose flesshe, al in one pot: and other on the spittes redye to
be layde to the fire. Entrynge into theyr inner lodgynges, they founde
faggottes of the bones of mennes armes and legges, which they reserue
to make heades for theyr arrowes, bycause they lacke iron. The other
bones they caste awaye when they haue eaten the flesshe. They founde
likewise the heade of a yonge man fastened to a poste and yet
bledinge.[22]

At the primordial scene we find only the displacing logic of the
sign: cooking pots, flesh on spits, bones, and—to establish the referent for all these signifiers—the "yet bledinge" "heade of a yonge
man." What draws the reader's rapt attention is the material evidence of the crime, from which the reader must (and inevitably
does) reconstruct the violent act. At the same time, Martyr shocks
us with a frisson of domesticity: the earthen vessels are "not muche
unlike unto oures," and the detail that the human, duck, and goose
flesh lie "al in one pot" suggests a hodgepodge, olla podrida, or
other one-pot stew of assorted and often leftover meats, a common
household dish in Tudor-Stuart England.[23] The publisher of the
Decades emphasizes the connection to English housewifery further
by drolly glossing the passage "fine cookery."

Martyr's and Münster's descriptions of Caribbean cannibalism
differ in many ways from accounts of Brazilian cannibalism by
Thevet, Jean de Léry, and other travel writers, but they agree in sub-
ordinating the consumption of bodies to the prep work for or aftereffects of that consumption. The final woodcut from Thevet's series
on Brazil in the *Cosmographie* (fig. 2) typifies the phenomenon: a
group of cannibals chop and cook body parts, but there is little sign
(yet) of the eating that the scene implies. Colonial cannibalism
turns out to be about its leftovers, its "poor remainder": the tools
and residues of the act (the body parts, the kettle) stand in for the
act itself.[24]

The displacement of consumption by spectacular ritual reaches
an apotheosis in narratives of Aztec and Central American cannibalism. The first printed account in English, again by Martyr,
chronicles idolatrous practices in the "Islandes of Sacrifice," situated west of the Yucatan. Martyr describes a ritual of child sacrifice
in excruciating detail, warning his readers before he begins: "But
oh abhominable crueltie: Let euery godly man close the mouth of
his stomake lest he be desturbed."[25] He then devotes several sen-

Fig. 2. André Thevet, from *La Cosmographie Universelle* (1575). Used by permission of the Fogler Library, University of Maine.

tences to the method by which the child's heart is ripped from its breast. Its still-warm blood having been used to "anoynte the lyppes of their Idoles," the priests "suffer the residue to faule into the synke." Eventually "they eate the fleshe of the armes, thighes, and legges, especially when they sacrifice an enemy taken in the warres," but the narrative rests only for a sentence on the meal, moving quickly to the contemplation of "a streame of congeled blud" presumably located on the temple grounds. Body and blood become "residue," with the description of the sacrifice itself taking the place of the banquet of flesh: "Let euery godly man close the mouth of his stomake" lest he partake of such an unholy visual spectacle. To "eat" the description becomes a kind of anthropophagy— Martyr's audience metaphorically consumes the people whose consumption they peruse.

Francisco López de Gómara's *The pleasant historie of the conquest of the West India, now called new Spaine,* whose 1596 English title page calls the work "most delectable to reade," gives the most lurid accounts of Aztec and Mexican cannibalism available in 1590s England. Throughout the work, Gómara sprinkles his accounts of spectacular ritual and spectacle with descriptions of food, cannibalistic and otherwise, with the meal always grammatically or narratively subordinated to the show. After describing temples with walls "an inch thicke with blood," Gómara segues directly into a description of the temple kitchen, with its "gardens of hearbes and sweete trees."[26] Following this, he describes a festival during which the natives prepare "a certaine past, tempered with childrens bloud," whose recipe Titus might have found useful.[27] The charnel house at the base of one temple is "made lyke unto a Theater, more larger than broade," and is surrounded by 133,000 sacrificed men's heads stuck on poles.[28] When, almost at the end of the book, Gómara finally describes an Aztec sacrificial ritual in detail, eating takes up only a sentence of a page-long account mostly focused upon the flaying of prisoners. In fact the passage's syntax collapses the act of eating with those of sacrificing and worshipping. Gómara (or Thomas Nichols, his translator) tells us that "the last day of the first moneth is called Tlacaxipeualizeli, on the whiche day were slaine a hundred slaues, which were taken in the warres, and after the sacrifice, their flesh was eaten in this order." But the text goes on to describe the sacrifice rather than the meal: each slave is laid out on a stone and his heart, which is removed with a flint knife, is then offered to one of the idols. Then priests strip each sacrifice of his skin and "the king himself" joins the priests in dancing clothed in the skins, "and an infinite number followed him to behold his terrible iesture." Finally,

> the owner of the slaues did carry their bodies home to their houses, to make of their fleshe a solemne feaste to all their friendes, leauing their heades and hartes to the Priests, as their dutie and offering. And the skinnes were filled with cotten wooll, or strawe, to be hung in the temple, and kings pallaice, for a memorie.[29]

The account repeats, with varying actors and slight changes in spectacular content, but with an unvarying adherence to the subordinated importance of literal cannibalism, throughout the chronicles of sixteenth-century European observers of Mexican ceremonial life. A 1521 eyewitness account of Cortés's Aztec conquest, which circulated throughout Europe in manuscript before its 1632 publication, describes a similar ritual that ends with the victims' flesh eaten in a stew—the ultimate repository of leftovers, as every thrifty cook knows—and with their remains thrown to packs of carnivores, as is Tamora's body at the end of *Titus*.[30] An account by the early ethnographer Bernardino Sahagún ends with the victim's body being rolled down the temple steps, where "some old men, whom they called Quaquacuiltin, laid hold of it and carried it to their tribal temple, where they dismembered it and divided it up in order to eat it."[31] The true climax of the Aztec performance as reported by European observers thus centers not upon the act of human-eating, but upon the removal of the victim's heart atop the sacrificial altar. Held aloft before the populace and offered to the god, the human heart becomes a synecdoche for the edible human, the ultimate proof of a communion of body and blood. According to Sahagún, the Aztec priests called the displayed heart a "precious eagle-cactus fruit," further emphasizing the nature of this transubstantiation; Gómara describes the virgin hearts offered to Quecalcouatl as "first fruites unto the Idoll."[32]

Whether or not Shakespeare read all of these accounts, it should be clear that when travel writers reported cannibalism, and especially Aztec cannibalism, to a European audience, they did so in terms of a framework that gave pride of place to the spectacular killing of the victim, with eating relegated to a potent but delayed aftereffect, the bodies acting as "poor remainders" of a feast for the eyes. One possible reason for this pattern lies in such a narrative's tantalizing effect upon the audience: cannibalism, the supposed marker of absolute otherness, is both referenced and withheld, offered as a symbolically potent act of violence and then coyly removed. In an ironic sense, this dramatic structure both parallels and reverses the conventions of Greco-Roman tragedy. In the latter, the violence occurs offstage so that the audience witnesses its remainders—the verbal violence of the messenger's report, the physical evidence of the violated body. In textual and visual depictions of New World cannibalism, the violence surrounding cannibalism is described or viewed in vivid detail, but the anthropophagy itself must be gleaned from brief reference or by implication, as if from a messenger's lips. But both tragedy and New World narrative are fundamentally concerned with displaying the remainder of violence, the human body with marks of violence upon it—Oedipus blinded, Thyestes wracked by supernatural digestive pain, the cauldron of bones, the skin hung up "for a memorie." In both modes of spectacle, the greatest violence is withheld not to protect the audience's delicate sensibilities, but to excite those sensibilities, to make the violence all the more potent because it is not seen but imagined.

The "memorie" of that skin suggests another reason for this pattern. Whether or not the Aztecs themselves imagined sacrifice in this way, in the minds of its European observers the ritual displaces the literal eating of bodies onto an act of visual cannibalism.[33] In other words, at the same time that ritual performance pushes literal eating to its margins, it places the audience in the position of anthropophagite. The scene's readers or viewers consume the bodies presented to them. The main course of the New World cannibal banquet consists of the moment at which the audience feasts upon the actors. The flesh is eaten later in private, but the heart is devoured by all.

Romans, Goths, Spaniards, Aztecs

From the beginning, narratives of New World conquest circulate in the background of the structure and plot of *Titus*. Most striking of these concerns the echoes of Hernándo Cortés's attack on Mexico City in the play's opening scene, as narrated by Gómara. In Gómara's account, the ultimately victorious siege starts with an apparent defeat. Cortés's major assault on the city ends in chaos: his lieutenant dies while saving him (by chopping the arms off Cortés's captor) and many Spaniards are killed or taken prisoner. That night, thinking they have won the battle, the Aztecs thank the gods by entering the main temple and sacrificing fifty Spanish soldiers in sight of Cortés's troops:

> and with their fine razors [the priests] opened them in the breastes, and pluckt out their hartes for an offering to the Idols, and sprinckled their bloud in the ayre. Our men seeing before their eies the dolefull sight, would fain haue gone to reuenge the cruel custome.[34]

After the sacrifice, the Aztec king holds a debauched feast, and the following day sends "two Christians heads, and two horse heads" (each a species recently introduced to the New World from the Old) to the neighboring provinces, "to signifie their victorie."[35] Shakespeare's play opens in an eerily similar way: after a hard-fought battle seemingly resolved, the conquerors enter the city and sacrifice an important prisoner. We find the Goths in the role of Spaniards, and the Romans playing the Aztecs. From Tamora's perspective, the play begins with the Goths' apparent defeat—which turns out to be a deferred victory—and with the sacrifice of one of their own. Although the place of sacrifice is not noted, the scene soon switches to the tomb of the Andronici, a symbolic locus both of death and political power that, like Aztec temples in the face of Spanish conquest, become steadily marginalized throughout the narrative. Of the impending sacrifice, Lucius announces:

> Give us the proudest prisoner of the Goths,
> That we may hew his limbs and on a pile
> *Ad manes fratrum* sacrifice his flesh
> Before this earthly prison of their bones,
> That so the shadows be not unappeased,
> Nor we disturbed with prodigies on earth.
>
> (1.1.99–104)

While the description and motive of the event, with its Latin tag and emphasis on the shades of Hades, conforms to Elizabethan views of Roman religion, the act of human sacrifice itself was generally unknown in the Roman Empire, and may have been suggested as much by the genre of the New World conquest narrative as by ideas about Roman ritual or by the occasional sacrifices of Roman myth.[36] As in Gómara's account, the brethren of those slain witness the event, or at least its directive (to stage such a sacrifice might have taxed the resources of Tudor theater). And like Gómara's narrator, the witnesses must defer their "opportunity of sharp revenge" (1.1.140). Although no messenger returns with the head of Alarbus, this symbolic action is deferred until later in the play, when a messenger fresh from Saturninus's raucous court arrives carrying the heads of Titus's sons.

Lest we jump too quickly to the conclusion that Shakespeare's play cleanly aligns Goths with Spaniards and Romans with Central Americans, we should examine Tamora's most sympathetic moment in the play—her importuning of her captors for a stay of execution. "Stay, Roman brethren," she declaims, implying a notion of universal brotherhood, "gracious conqueror / Victorious Titus, rue the tears I shed / A mother's tears in passion for her son" (1.1.107–9). We will not read anything like this speech in Gómara, who never sees the need for Spaniards to plead for mercy. Rather we find it in the mouths of the Indians in Bartolomé de Las Casas's *The Spanish Colonie or Briefe Chronicle,* published in Spain in 1552 and in En-

gland in 1583, a work viciously critical of the conquistadores' behavior in the Americas. Las Casas's narrative of Cortés's conquest
almost exactly reverses Gómara's. Las Casas offers not a single account of human sacrifice by Aztecs or any other Indian nation. For
Las Casas, Native Americans are the proverbial noble savages,
"peacefull, without brawles and struglings, without quarrelles,
without strife, without rancour or hatred, by no meanes desirous of
reuengement."[37] Rather than vicious revengers, Las Casas's Indians
feature frequently as suppliants, begging the Spaniards not to do
the unimaginably cruel things to them that the Spaniards then invariably do. When the Queen of the Goths pleads with Titus that
"sweet mercy is nobility's true badge" (1.1.123), she echoes the Pe-
ruvian emperor Attabalipa, who is captured by the Spaniards, ran-
somed, and then condemned to be burned alive even after he has
provided the ransom. King Attabalipa responds incredulously,
"What trespasse haue I done yee?" and asks to see the king of
Spain.[38] Queen Tamora and King Attabalipa both speak from the
position of a victimized other, conquered in war and now made to
suffer the cruel and unusual punishment of human sacrifice for
their loss.

To allow the possibility that both Gómara and Las Casas, with
their radically opposed views of Spanish conquest, inflect and in-
fect *Titus Andronicus* (as they have both been shown to influence
Montaigne's *Essais*),[39] is to add another layer of nuance to the division and intertwining of the Goths and Romans. In accounts of New
World conquest, two apparently irreconcilable narratives domi-
nate: on one side, the vengeful and irredeemably savage Indians
rightfully subdued and converted by noble and civilized Europeans, and on the other, the noble and gentle Indians wrongfully subdued and converted by vengeful and irredeemably savage Spanish
or Portuguese Catholics. Given this division, Montaigne addressed
each in turn, but concerned himself more with the latter. In "Of
Moderation," he draws upon Gómara to paint a horrific picture of
the Aztec treatment of their prisoners: "Some are burnt alive, and
halfe roasted drawne from the fire, that so they may pull out their
hearts and entrails."[40] But the final sentences of the essay suggest a
New World nobility that segues into his next chapter, "Of the Cannibales," in which the literal cannibalism of Brazilians is prefera-
ble to the metaphorical cannibalism of the conquistadores—in
which, in effect, so-called barbarians are more civilized than West-
erners who act barbarously.[41] He may receive this idea in part from
Las Casas, who makes the point with characteristic intensity:

> The Spaniardes doe sucke from the Indians the whole substaunce of their bodies, because they haue nothing else in their houses. . . . To put the Indians into the Spaniardes handes . . . it were as good to throwe them among the hornes of wilde Bulles, eyther to deliuer them vnto hunger starued Wolues, Lions, and Tygres, and as much good shoulde they gette by any lawes, precepts, or threates made to the saide hungrye beastes, for the forbidding of them to deuoure them, as much do we say any lawes, threates, or precepts, stay the Spaniardes, when they haue authoritie ouer the Indians from murdering them for their golde.[42]

If the Indians are elsewhere accused of cannibalism, here it is the Spaniards who devour, and who, more generally, engage obsessively and compulsively in the violation of Indian bodies through rape, the use of hungry dogs, burning alive, and, above all, dismemberment. A characteristic example of the latter, from the invasion of Hispaniola, engages in the kind of heavy irony that runs through the dismemberment jokes in *Titus*:[43] "cutting off their two handes as neere as might bee, and so letting them hang, they sayd: Get you with these letters, to carry tydinges to those which are fled by the mountaines."[44] The hanging hands, unable to carry letters, become the letters themselves—a message that, written upon the body, is both unmistakable in its inscription of power relations and mystifying in the savagery of its motives. Likewise Marcus, upon seeing Lavinia with her limbs "lopp'd," is both bewildered and quite clear about what has happened: "what stern ungentle hands / Have lopped and hewed and made thy body bare / Of her two branches" gives way to "But sure some Tereus hath deflowered thee / And, lest thou shouldst detect him, cut thy tongue" (2.3.16–27). Titus expands upon the idea that messages can be read in a body marked by violence when he calls Lavinia a "map of woe" (3.2.12). And when Titus cuts off his own hand for Aaron, it is because Aaron has offered the prospect that the hand will become a message that, sent to the king, will act as "ransom" for Titus's sons—a visual sign better read than a verbal one because it is written both on and by the body.

For Montaigne, the message of Las Casas and other anticonquest narrators such as the Catholic André Thevet and the Huguenot Jean de Léry is one of cultural reversal. Using the same catalog of cruelties found in Las Casas, Montaigne writes, in an oft-quoted passage that has as much to do with the French wars of religion as with Brazil:

I thinke there is more barbarisme in eating men alive, then to feed upon them, being dead; to mangle by tortures and torments a body full of lively sense, to roast him in peeces, to make dogges and swine to gnaw and teare him in mammockes (as wee have not only read, but seene very lately, yea and our owne memorie, not amongst ancient enemies, but our neighbours and fellow-citizens; and which is worse, under pretence of pietie and religion) than to roast and eat him after he is dead.[45]

Montaigne demonstrates extreme skepticism toward colonial and theological justifications for conquest, but is less distrustful regarding depictions of Indians as noble savages, since he allows them to have their cake and eat it too—they retain their cannibalism, along with the idea that such culinary habits are undertaken not for nourishment but to satisfy "an extreme, and inexpiable revenge," while manifesting at least a marginally higher ethical standard than their Iberian conquerors.[46] For Montaigne's purposes, as Tzvetan Todorov has famously argued, "the Indians here are hardly more than an allegory."[47]

Shakespeare's interest (in *Titus* and, for that matter, in *The Tempest*), like Montaigne's, lies not in American cultures per se, but rather in how the emerging paradigms of American travel narratives help his compatriots see themselves. And Shakespeare may take a cue from Montaigne's juxtaposition of the Aztecs in "Of Moderation" with the Brazilians in "Of Cannibals" when he distributes the best and worst qualities of both the Indians and the Catholic Europeans across the play. But the result is more radical. Watching *Titus* is like reading Gómara and Las Casas simultaneously, with the point of view oscillating violently, sometimes within a single scene. The Goths might be pitied in the first act like the Spaniards in Gómara, or like the Indians of Las Casas, made to suffer the sacrifice of a brother. But they eagerly take on the roles of Las Casas's rapacious, dismembering Spanish—or Gómara's savage Indians—in the second act, and by the fourth act have been performatively transformed into rape, murder, and revenge, recalling what by the end of Las Casas's *Spanish Colonie* has become the proverbial cruelty of the conquistadores. Meanwhile the Romans move in the first act from Gómara's Aztecs, trafficking in human sacrifice and fixating abnormally upon death and dead bodies, to (in the person of Lavinia especially) inhabiting the victimized, dismembered body of Indian nobility in the second. Meanwhile characters like Saturninus and Lucius, Romans who ally themselves

with Goths, and Tamora, who allies herself with Romans, complicate further the dynamic of conquest, tightening like a noose the
cords that bind these two apparently opposed subnarratives.[48]

Cooks and Cannibals

The fifth act of *Titus* intertwines so completely the cultural perspectives articulated by Gómara and Las Casas that they become
nearly indistinguishable—Romans and Goths are inextricably identified with both ends of the colonial spectrum. The central stage
vehicle and metaphor for this paradoxical fusion is cannibalism,
the unnatural breakdown of the boundary between others and
selves. In the fifth act we witness Shakespeare's full working out of
the notion of mutual degradation that underlies the play's ontology
of eating, its replacement of a heuristic model with one of dynamic
debasement. The Goths' revenge upon Lavinia renders her un-
reachable, a kind of sealed book from which an alphabet must be
"wrested," as Titus says of her. The Andronici respond in kind, re-
venging themselves upon the Goths by rendering Tamora a cannibal, a vertiginous other whose humanity is tautologically called
into question by her unwitting act. To read Gómara and Las Casas
alongside each other produces the same sort of vertigo, with Indians turning Spaniards into cannibals and vice versa. In both narratives, body parts speak louder than words: messages are encoded
in hanging hands, in severed heads, in cooking pots and streams of
blood. The New World travel narratives deconstruct the human
body, not to reintegrate it into a new whole, but to leave it lying
around, a body in pieces signifying nothing, or nothing more than
an inexpiable revenge.

First there is Tamora, the play's definitive if unwitting cannibal.
I have already discussed her parallels with Las Casas's Indians in
the first act; in the second, her role is explicitly reversed through
her cruelty in the face of Lavinia's plea, which paves the way for
the elaboration of an identity between the Goths and the stereotypically pathological Spaniards, and for Tamora to become the person-
ification of revenge. Tamora's movement from margin to center,
from outsider Goth/Indian to incorporated Roman, occurs in tandem with this transformation. "Titus, I am incorporate in Rome,"
she declares late in the play's first scene, "A Roman now adopted
happily" (1.1.467). The triple entendre of "incorporate in Rome"

indicates not only a negative process of assimilation that breaks down individuality (Rome as digester), and a positive relocation from margin to center, but also a Eucharistic blending—Tamora is in Rome, and Rome is in Tamora. In all three senses, the phrase implies a sudden turnabout for a character who arrived at the beginning of the scene as a powerless outsider witnessing the sacrifice of her son.

We may contrast this absorption with the total rejection of Tamora at the play's end, her transformation into something more beast than human, tossed to the edges of Roman and Goth society:

> As for that ravenous tiger, Tamora,
> No funeral rite, nor man in mourning weed,
> No mournful bell shall ring her burial,
> But throw her forth to beasts and birds to prey:
> Her life was beastly and devoid of pity,
> And being dead, let birds on her take pity.
>
> (5.3.194–99)

Tamora's punishment reinscribes her body, like that of Lavinia in Titus's eyes (5.3.36–46), as one so defiled that it must be ejected from life and society. By engaging in anthropophagy, Tamora has crossed a threshold that, although both definitively human and narratively familiar (through New World, classical, and folk literature, not to mention as a recurring accusation against the Irish, Scots, and Jews), simultaneously lies a priori beyond the bounds of human behavior. The punishment enacts a parody of Eucharistic incorporation—having become a beast of prey, she will be quasi-cannibalistically eaten by those beasts at the play's end. The discomfiting repetition of "pity" is mimetic of the play's doubled, cannibalistic mindset, in which like devours like. The birds recall the metamorphosis of all the characters into birds at the end of Ovid's tale, suggesting an endless continuation of the play's fruitless digestions. As Maggie Kilgour puts it, "In the struggle between desire and aggression, between identification and the division that creates power over another, a struggle which is finally that between communion and cannibalism, cannibalism has usually won."[49]

Tamora's trajectory—from outsider, to incorporation into the cannibal maw of Rome, to being vomited out of it—suggests another of Shakespeare's problematically incorporated Romans, Coriolanus, who is mentioned in *Titus* (4.4.67) and who, upon receiving his own play late in Shakespeare's career, finds himself

in a position not dissimilar to Tamora's. Having fallen from fully
incorporated Roman hero to "a disease that must be cut away," Coriolanus is defended by Menenius, who accuses the Plebeians of
turning Rome into a cannibal mother, who "like an unnatural dam /
Should now eat up her own!"[50] In rejecting this characterization of
Rome, Menenius hits upon its truth: in both plays, Rome functions
as a mother who eats her children, whether that child is Titus,
whose sons, daughter, sanity, hand, and finally life are swallowed
up; or Lavinia, whose wounds function as a Lucrece-like allegory
for the dismemberment of the body politic; or the adopted and
ejected Tamora. Subscribing to an idea of Romanness in these plays
means agreeing to a cannibalizing notion of empire in which the
imperium absorbs and destroys what it can, and ejects and destroys
what it cannot. Like Las Casas's Spanish conquistadores who hun-
grily feed upon both enemies and allies in the quest for a New
World empire, Rome demands a fealty of its citizens and captives
that frequently ends in the body's dismemberment and destruction.

Tamora, the cannibal mother of Titus's Rome, both crystallizes
this phenomenon and turns it inside out. Her Eucharistic absorption begins in a parody of the Augustinian notion that "you shall
not change Me into yourself as bodily food, but into Me you shall
be changed."[51] Like a Christian suppliant, Tamora sups on Rome
through the sexual and political body of Saturninus, and in so
doing becomes part of the Roman body politic. But when Tamora
mimics Rome's cannibal behavior by incorporating her own sons
back into herself, she reifies the costs of this model of political control. Her literal consumption is "unnatural" in that it reverses the
normative vector of female generation, turning birth into devourment. But what seems repugnant on the bodily level is business as
usual on the political one: Tamora's consumption of her sons is an
abomination, but Rome's consumption of her subjects is a necessary act of statecraft. Like Lavinia's, Tamora's body becomes a
"map of woe" on and *in* which the anxieties of empire are literally
inscribed.[52]

In order to understand Lavinia's role in the final act of the drama,
and to explore her surprising kinship with Tamora, let us return to
the fundamental iconographical difference between Old and New
World depictions of anthropophagy: that the former can't do without the eating scene, while the latter shuns it in favor of more symbolic and spectacular forms of consumption, relegating the eating
itself to a remainder or leftover of the narrative. The brevity with

which Tamora samples the pies in the final scene mirrors this New World model—her behavior unwittingly parallels, for example, that of the Aztecs in Gómara's account of Tlacaxipeualizeli, in which the "solemne feast" that concludes the festival is accorded relatively little narrative importance.

If this model helps determine the dramatic structure of the final act, then we should be able to identify a scene immediately prior in which the spectacular bodily violence that precedes cannibalism is fully staged, providing the alternative climax familiar to colonial cannibalism. And indeed such a scene does precede the banquet—the ritual killing of Chiron and Demetrius by Titus and Lavinia. Like the upraised heart atop Gómara's Aztec pyramids, the river of blood polluting Peter Martyr's Islands of Sacrifice, or Thevet's cannibals dismembering a body for the feast, Titus and his daughter's killing of Tamora's sons uses the languages of ritual and spectacle to condense the play's discrete performances of revenge into a single moment of distilled violence. Like the heart or the river, it fashions a symbol from a set of complex relationships between the characters and the symbolic world they inhabit and shape. But here, rather than attempting to stage a still-beating heart or a stream dyed red, Shakespeare focuses attention on the bowl that Lavinia clutches between her stumps. The bowl helps fashion an iconography that transforms Lavinia from object to participant, or more precisely, from food to cannibal.

The ritual begins with an overdetermined set of stage directions and verbal cues that mirror and reverse not only Alarbus's sacrifice in act 1, but also Lavinia's rape and dismemberment in act 2, an event that itself closely parallels Las Casas's charges of Spanish treatment of American Indians. In *The Briefe Chronicle,* Las Casas often accuses Spaniards of coupling rape with dismemberment as tools of colonial domination, and the charges combine in more than one instance. One mother attempts to stop an "euill Christian" from raping her daughter; both are gruesomely punished: "the Spaniarde drawing his dagger or rapier, cutte off her hande, and slue the young girle with slashes of his weapon: because shee woulde not consent to his appetite."[53] Although the act of rape is unconsummated, the violence is transferred to the mother's dismemberment and the slashing of the girl's body, the creation of another "map of woe." In *Titus,* the rape draws most directly from its Ovidian source, but resonates too in the New World context: in both cases, the iconography and the politics of the relationships indicate that empire and its uses of power are at stake.

The scene of the brothers' killing recapitulates both the "map of woe" and, symbolically, the bloodletting of rape. Titus begins by having the brothers bound and gagged (5.1.154ff), thus rendering both their hands and mouths useless, as they had rendered Lavinia's. Titus and Lavinia exit, then immediately reenter, Titus with a knife and Lavinia with a basin. After delivering a catalog of the play's physical horrors, especially those visited upon Lavinia, Titus describes what he will do to the brothers, as Gómara's Montezuma explains what he will do to Cortés's men:

> Hark, wretches, how I mean to martyr you:
> This one hand yet is left to cut your throats,
> Whiles that Lavinia 'tween her stumps doth hold
> The basin that receives your guilty blood.
>
> (5.2.180–83)

Having described the stage picture, Titus repeats and extends it:

> Hark, villains, I will grind your bones to dust,
> And with your blood and it I'll make a paste,
> And of the paste a coffin I will rear,
> And make two pasties of your shameful heads,
> And bid that strumpet, your unhallowed dam,
> Like to the earth swallow her own increase.
>
> (5.2.186–91)

And for good measure, he repeats his plans a few lines later:

> Lavinia, come,
> Receive the blood, and when that they are dead
> Let me go grind their bones to powder small,
> And with this hateful liquor temper it,
> And in that paste let their vile heads be baked.
>
> (196–200)

If Tamora's eating happens in brief, Shakespeare compensates in these passages through parodic exaggeration. The scene's dilated Senecan rhetoric forms a better companion to the drawn out scenes of revenge I detailed in this essay's opening paragraphs than does the banquet that follows. Chiron and Demetrius are constructed in this scene as the play's primary criminals, and therefore the ones upon whom revenge must be taken in the most extreme and heightened fashion. The fact that this dramatic function is not borne out across the play—that the brothers tend to operate more as Tamora's and Aaron's henchmen than as the masterminds behind the Andronicus family's destruction—underscores the ghostly New World antecedents of this scene. For Gómara and Thevet, it is always the secondary figures—soldiers, slaves, children, lieutenants—who are ritually slaughtered and eaten, not the rulers or leaders. Shakespeare uses this parallel to create a palimpsest of revenge, in which Old and New World models are superimposed over each other to create the multiplying effect of the play's last two scenes.

Titus cuts the brothers' throats with his remaining hand, while Lavinia catches their blood in the bowl held between her arms. Titus closes the scene by announcing, "So, now bring them in, for I'll play the cook, / And see them ready against their mother comes" (5.2.204–5). Titus's curious construction "I'll play the cook" further emphasizes the New World elements of the scene: in the last few minutes, Titus has played the parts of madman, priest, and butcher in quick succession. In the following scene, he will play the host. In fact, the one role that Titus does *not* play onstage is that of cook, though he arrives at the banquet dressed as one. His announcement that he will "play the cook" presages his departure. As in many of the cannibal narratives we have examined, most notably those of Gómara, the cooking of the brothers will happen offstage.

If Titus appropriates the role of cook, Lavinia takes on the role of cannibal. Up until this point in the play, she appears as an Indian out of Las Casas, whose missing hands are "letters" or "tydinges," whose mute silence marks and conveys the loud voices of her conquerors. This scene exposes the opposite aspect of Lavinia's character, the voracious and destabilizing energy of the New World eater. The stage props of the knife and bowl suggest this correlation. Knife and bowl are objects indispensable both to ritual murder and to dinner, and as such herald the banquet of the next scene.[54] But the fact that Titus holds the knife and Lavinia the bowl is significant. Balanced in Lavinia's arms, the bowl becomes metonymic for Lavinia's own work as a vessel, as both a mouth and a womb. In collecting the blood of the brothers, Lavinia positions herself simultaneously as mother and consumer, incorporating the blood of her tormentors back into her body. This image arises not from Ovid's version, which emphasizes the tearing apart of the child Itys's body, but from the gendered logic of colonial cannibalism.

In her analysis of Jan van der Straet's ca.1575 engraving *America,*
Anne McClintock writes that "the inaugural scene of discovery is
redolent not only of male megalomania and imperial aggression but
also of male anxiety and paranoia. . . . [It] becomes a scene of ambivalence, suspended between an imperial megalomania, with its
fantasy of unstoppable rapine—and a contradictory fear of engulfment, with its fantasy of dismemberment and emasculation." Indeed, depictions of cannibalism often included women cannibals,
sometimes as voracious blood-drinkers.[55] Thevet relates a scene in
which "the blood from the victim and what flowed from the head
were scarcely on the ground before an old woman scooped it up
into an old gourd, and as soon as she had collected it, she drank it
raw."[56] A copperplate from Theodore De Bry's influential series on
Brazilian cannibalism draws a similar connection between women,
domesticity, and cannibalism (fig. 3). While two men hack apart a
dismembered body, women swarm the scene, waving a foot here,

Fig. 3. Theodor De Bry, from *Americae tertia pars* (1592). Used by permission of
the Royal Ontario Museum; photograph by Mindy Stricke.

an arm there, loading a bowl and a cauldron with entrails and a head. As in the scene in *Titus,* here a man holds a knife and butchers, while a woman piles guts into a bowl. The story that McClintock tells of rape fantasies giving way to a fear of female "engulfment" in cannibal narratives and drawings describes Lavinia's role at this point in *Titus.* McClintock's description of "the gendering of America as simultaneously naked and passive *and* riotously violent and cannibalistic" parallels the iconographic translation of Lavinia's silent and passive body after act 2 into the vengeful mother figure of the play's penultimate scene. Lavinia takes on the absorptive characteristics of the American cannibal in the play's economy of retribution. Her act of symbolic consumption does not nourish but rather, according to cannibalism's logic of "extreme and inexpiable revenge," furthers that retribution. Lavinia becomes the mother who consumes the strength of her victims, taking possession of their blood in a ritualized transfer of power. In co-opting the role of cannibal, Lavinia both plays upon and complicates the connection in the Renaissance mind between cannibal savagery, motherhood, and female sexuality.[57]

Lavinia's identification with the female cannibals of De Bry, Thevet, and other writers is ironically underscored by her apparent powerlessness—lacking voice or hands, she yet can personify the *vagina dentata* that critics have located both in the pit of the second act and in Lavinia's body. As Heather James comments, "Shakespeare's play and especially the pit and Lavinia's body seem compulsively to contaminate and digest literary sources and, indeed, all possible referents."[58] This association forms one indication that Shakespeare has rehearsed Lavinia for this role throughout the drama, and that she fulfills her dramatic function only once she has played it. Shakespeare weaves Lavinia's cannibalism into the play's symbolic structure, implicating her as a devourer of rhetorical and literary modes and sources as well as of characters. The gruesome yet plaintive act to which Titus encourages her in the first scene of act 3, the carrying of his recently severed hand between her teeth as they exit the stage, adumbrates this connection, as well as associating her further with the cannibal iconography of dismemberment. That the human body part in Lavinia's mouth belongs to Titus presages the incorporative role she will play in the symbolic ingestion of the brothers' blood, as well as hinting at Tamora's indigestive incorporation of her sons in the form of pie. The "fly-killing" scene that follows neatly develops the

theme. Titus "wrests" from her daughter's "alphabet" the sentiment that "she drinks no other drink but tears" (3.2.36–37), with
the implication that she starves herself because she requires no
other food but that of a cannibalistic revenge.[59] When she kisses the
severed heads of her brothers, Marcus comments, "that kiss is
comfortless / As frozen water to a starved snake" (3.1.251–52), an
image that combines pathetic, devouring, and sexually dangerous
elements, assuming that Lavinia is the snake. The following scene,
the last in which Lavinia appears before the sacrifice of the brothers, opens with young Lucius fleeing his aunt as she tries to obtain
his volume of Ovid's *Metamorphoses.* The boy's fright may be understood simply as the unnerving experience of being chased by
the admittedly spooky Lavinia. His protestation, "Alas, sweet aunt,
I know not what you mean," however, reminds a Renaissance audience of another scene. Lucius in this moment takes on the character
of Itys, the Ovidian son destined for dinner, while Lavinia steps
into the doubled role of Procne and Philomela, both of whom stab
Itys when only one stroke would have sufficed (6.642–43). The obe-
dient schoolboy knows the story full well, and flees, perhaps, for
his life.

Logics of Eating

Is it more degraded to eat one's own child (as do Kronos, Thyestes, and Tamora), or to engineer such an act (as do Procne, Atreus,
and the duo of Titus and Lavinia)? Is it worse to eat your offspring
or to feed someone else's offspring to her? Is there "more barbarisme in eating men alive, then to feed upon them, being dead?" The
grotesque question that the fifth act of the play posits is, at its core,
a question about the ethics of eating. "The eating of one species by
another," writes Georges Bataille, "is the simplest form of luxury."
For "the fragility, the complexity, of the animal body" to be destroyed in the service of another being marks an explosive, "glori-
ous" expenditure of energy.[60] The eating of one's own species, of
one's own son, marks an even more spectacular expenditure, an expression of redundancy that forecloses all possibility of familial or
generational growth. Shakespeare underscores the extremity of
such eating by changing the gender of the eater from that of Seneca
and Ovid. Performed by anyone, cannibalism is both inhuman and
fully human, since only humans can eat their own and call it a

crime. Performed by a mother, the act resides symbolically at nature's edge, at the point where human and inhuman meet, where carnivores gather at the fringes of the polis.

Yet to *create* a cannibal, to feed a son to his mother, one needs already to have labeled the other "inhuman" (5.2.177). To commit revenge, one must challenge the other's human subjectivity—to other the other, as it were. This is the ethical impoverishment into which Titus and, to the extent that she is an active participant, Lavinia, enter when they embark upon the plan of killing Chiron and Demetrius, just as it is the ethical error that Montaigne condemns in both Portuguese conquerors and French religious zealots. Shakespeare marks this transition through his borrowings from New World iconography. The Romans begin the play as Gómara's Aztecs sacrificing a Goth/Spanish prisoner. They spend the middle acts as Las Casas's Indians pleading for justice in a world whose only code is one of scheming cruelty. When Titus regains power in the fifth act, it is not by asserting a new ethics of justice, but by returning to the position of Aztecs engaging in human sacrifice. The difference now is that the Goths are assimilated into both roles through Titus's machinations; by the end of the play they are both rapacious Spaniards and literal New World cannibals, inhabiting all points on the continuum of American revenge. The final actions of Titus, Lavinia, and Tamora solve nothing, establish no new communion; instead they enact a complex parody of communion, in which transubstantiation becomes grotesquely literal—the incorporated Son—but presages no Augustinian assimilation of the human into divinity.

Las Casas, for all his ethnographic simplifications, makes one central point continually in *The Spanish Colonie:* by treating the Indians like savages, the Spanish become savages themselves, defined by a narrative that leaves no room for moderation or community, in which all players are either eating or eaten. The final scene of *Titus* makes a similar point. The law of revenge constitutes a *reductio ad absurdum* of selfhood in which the only possible mutuality is the mutuality of otherness—the mutuality of objects bound to be consumed or destroyed. In showing Tamora to be a cannibal, Titus and Lavinia turn themselves into metaphorical anthrophagites. The result of these acts is a series of nonliberating consumptions, in which the grotesque body provides grounds not for regeneration but for fragmentation.[61]

The play's final fragment functions in precisely this way, providing the play with both a leftover of violence and a hint of further revenges. As the "poor remainder of the Andronici" gather themselves to depart, Titus's brother Marcus calls to mind the infant child of Aaron and Tamora: "Behold the child: / Of this was Tamora delivered, / The issue of an irreligious Moor" (5.3.120–21). Aaron is found with the child in "a ruinous monastery," a "wasted building," thus identifying the child not only with remains in general but those in particular of Catholicism, with its fine line between communion and cannibalism.[62] Lucius calls the child "the base fruit of her burning lust" (5.1.43), eliciting an image both of edibility and revulsion. Aaron refers to him in terms of force-feeding and coarse, unrestrained consumption: "I'll make you feed on berries and on roots, / And feed on curds and whey, and suck the goat" (4.2.179–80). Editors generally amend the second "feed" to "fat" or "feast" out of unease with the repetition, but on the other hand, such repetition forces us to think of even the child as one of the play's obsessive consumers, carrying its cannibalism into the next generation—a Cortés or a Montezuma. It is difficult to see the baby, as have some recent directors and critics, as a possible symbol of healing, though we rebel against the idea that the sins of the parents should be visited upon the child. The play does not specify exactly what happens to the infant. The dangling plot thread simply ratifies the nature of the play throughout: the child becomes another leftover of the play's machinations, unaccounted for and uncounted. It is what survives.

Notes

The list of people who have nourished this essay along its slow path to maturation is much longer than I can express here; I am grateful for the generous conversations and emendations that helped shape it. I would like especially to thank Stephen Orgel, Lars Engle, David Riggs, Heather James, Bill Worthen, Adam Zucker, Joel Burges, and my Renaissance graduate cohort at Stanford University for their patient attention to drafts of the essay. Earlier versions were presented at, and revised in light of, the USC-Huntington Early Modern Studies Institute in 2004 and the Performances/ Modernities/ Shakespeares conference at Berkeley in 2001. I am thankful for the support of Stanford, a faculty summer development grant at the University of Tulsa, and York University. Finally I am indebted to Deanne Williams, Elizabeth Pentland, Douglas Saunders, Mindy Stricke, and an anonymous reader at *Shakespeare Studies* for helping guide the essay to its final form.

    1. Barker et al. suggest that depictions of American cannibalism are usually post-prandial, but do not draw a contrast with classical representations. See Fran-

cis Barker, Peter Hulme, and Margaret Iversen, *Cannibalism and the Colonial World* (Cambridge: Cambridge University Press, 1998), 2.

2. All line references to the play are to William Shakespeare, *Titus Andronicus*, in *The Arden Shakespeare*, ed. Jonathan Bate (London: Routledge, 1995).

3. My use of the term "dilation" is indebted to Patricia A. Parker, *Shakespeare from the Margins: Language, Culture, Context* (Chicago: University of Chicago Press, 1996).

4. John Marston, *Antonio's Revenge: The Second Part of Antonio and Mellida*, ed. G. K. Hunter (Lincoln: University of Nebraska Press, 1965), 5.3.81.

5. Alan C. Dessen, *Titus Andronicus* (Manchester: Manchester University Press, 1989), 68, 91–92.

6. The only critic I have come across who places *Titus* in a New World context is Hillary Nunn, who generously shared with me a conference paper in which she argues for a reciprocal exchange between Shakespeare and depictions of the Tupinambá. Louise Noble's work draws parallels between English "medical cannibalism" (but not American cannibalism) and that of the play. See Louise Noble, "'And Make Two Pasties of Your Shameful Heads': Medicinal Cannibalism and Healing the Body Politic in *Titus Andronicus*," *ELH* 70, no. 3 (2003); Hillary Nunn, "*Titus Andronicus* and the Tupinamba: Staging Cannibalism in a New World," conference paper, The Ohio Shakespeare Conference (Akron, OH: 2002).

7. A third strand, that of survival cannibalism, dates back in literature to Josephus's account of the siege of Jerusalem, but I think that Shakespeare's concern in *Titus* relates more to the desperation of revenge than that of starvation.

8. Herodotus (*The Histories,* 4.18 and 4.106) describes the Anthropophagi as a people living near but unrelated to Scythia, well north of Greece. Pliny, following Herodotus, refers to them in *The Natural History,* 7.2.11–12.

9. Hesiod, *Theogony,* ed. and trans. Apostolos N. Athanassakis (Baltimore: Johns Hopkins University Press, 1983), 2:459–506.

10. David Beers Quinn, "New Geographical Horizons: Literature," in *First Images of America: The Impact of the New World on the Old,* ed. Fredi Chiappelli, Michael J. B. Allen, and Robert Louis Benson (Berkeley: University of California Press, 1976), 635. See also Edmundo O'Gorman, *The Invention of America: An Inquiry into the Historical Nature of the New World and the Meaning of Its History* (Bloomington: Indiana University Press, 1961).

11. Frank Lestringant, *Cannibals,* trans. Rosemary Morris (Berkeley: University of California Press, 1997), 16.

12. See especially Charles Frey, "*The Tempest* and the New World," *Shakespeare Quarterly* 30, no. 1 (1979); Stephen Orgel, "Shakespeare and the Cannibals," in *Cannibals, Witches, and Divorce: Estranging the Renaissance,* ed. Marjorie B. Garber (Baltimore: Johns Hopkins University Press, 1987).

13. Cf. Hugh Grady, who finds strong similarities between the *Essais* and Shakespeare's early history plays but leaves open the question of the work's direct influence. Hugh Grady, *Shakespeare, Machiavelli, and Montaigne: Power and Subjectivity from Richard II to Hamlet* (Oxford: Oxford University Press, 2002), 114.

14. Quinn, "New Geographical Horizons: Literature," 644. For an account of the dissemination of cannibal narratives in Europe, see Lestringant, *Cannibals,* chap. 2.

15. Quinn, "New Geographical Horizons: Literature," 643.

16. David Riggs, *The World of Christopher Marlowe* (New York: Henry Holt, 2004), 160–61.

17. For a thorough and invaluable chronology of these texts' publication history in England and Europe, see John Eliot Alden and Dennis C. Landis, *European Americana: A Chronological Guide to Works Printed in Europe Relating to the Americas, 1493–1776* (New York: Readex Books, 1980); Edward Godfrey Cox, *A Reference Guide to the Literature of Travel: Including Voyages, Geographical Descriptions, Adventures, Shipwrecks and Expeditions,* 3 vols. (New York: Greenwood Press, 1969).

18. The first quarto is dated 1594; see *Titus Andronicus,* ed. Bate, 69–79 for a summary of the controversy over the play's date of composition and for Bate's own argument that *Titus* was begun in late 1593. While I incline toward the later date, even the earliest dates suggested for *Titus*'s origins would not hamper my argument for Shakespeare's access to most of these texts.

19. See P. D. A. Harvey, *Mappa Mundi: The Hereford World Map* (Toronto: University of Toronto Press, 1996), 5; Scott D. Westrem, *The Hereford Map: A Transcription and Translation of the Legends with Commentary* (Turnhout, Belgium: Brepols, 2001), 70.

20. Jasper Heywood, "Seneca's Thyestes," in *Five Elizabethan Tragedies,* ed. A. K. McIlwraith (London: Oxford University Press, 1963), 5.3.20.

21. T. D., *The Bloody Banquet, 1639* (Oxford: Printed for the Malone Society by V. Ridler at the University Press, 1961).

22. Pietro Martire di Anghiera, *The Decades of the Newe Worlde or West India Conteynyng the Nauigations and Conquestes of the Spanyardes, with the Particular Description of the Moste Ryche and Large Landes and Ilandes Lately Founde in the West Ocean Perteynyng to the Inheritaunce of the Kinges of Spayne,* trans. Richard Eden (London: 1555), B1v.

23. Thomas Hariot depicts the native Virginians as cooking a similar dish, sans human, that they "lett all boyle together like a galliemaufrye, which the Spaniarde call, olla podrida." See Thomas Hariot, *A Briefe and True Report of the New Found Land of Virginia of the Commodities and of the Nature and Manners of the Naturall Inhabitants* (Francoforti ad Moenum, 1590), B8v.

24. Thevet's *Cosmographie* contains some of the rare written descriptions of the physical act of eating, but no images of it. When, in those few exceptions to the pattern I have sketched out, eating is pictured, it still tends to be relegated to the margins of the picture, as in the dog-headed cannibals of an early Strasbourg woodcut (see Lestringant, *Cannibals,* 18). A more complex exception is found in Theodor De Bry's *Americae tertia pars,* whose frontispiece shows highly classicized New World Indians gnawing on body parts. I hope to address the cannibal iconography of that influential work in a later essay.

25. Anghiera, *Decades of the Newe Worlde,* Qq1r.

26. Francisco López de Gómara, *The Pleasant Historie of the Conquest of the West India, Now Called New Spaine. Atchieued by the Most Woorthie Prince Hernando Cortes, Marques of the Valley of Huaxacac, Most Delectable to Reade,* trans. T. N. [Thomas Nichols] (London, 1596), 203–4.

27. Ibid., 205.

28. Ibid., 206.

29. Ibid., 393–94.

30. Bernal Díaz del Castillo, *The Discovery and Conquest of Mexico, 1517–*

1521, trans. and ed. A. P. Maudslay, intro. Irving A. Leonard (New York: Farrar, Straus and Cudahy, 1956), 436.

31. Bernardino de Sahagún, *Florentine Codex: General History of the Things of New Spain, Book 2: The Ceremonies,* trans. A. J. O. Anderson and C. E. Dibble (Santa Fe, NM: School of American Research and University of Utah, 1981), 3; see also 184–85.

32. Ibid., 47; López de Gómara, *Pleasant Historie,* 205.

33. My notion of displacement here is indebted to Joseph Roach's idea of the "effigy." See Joseph R. Roach, *Cities of the Dead: Circum-Atlantic Performance* (New York: Columbia University Press, 1996). For an attempt "to discover how ordinary [Aztecs] understood 'human sacrifice'" see Inga Clendinnen, *Aztecs: An Interpretation* (Cambridge: Cambridge University Press, 1991).

34. López de Gómara, *Pleasant Historie,* 334.

35. Ibid., 335.

36. On Roman sacrifice see Ronald Broude, "Roman and Goth in *Titus Andronicus,*" *Shakespeare Studies* 6 (1970), 30. Nunn draws a comparison between this scene and Tupinambá sacrifice rituals.

37. Bartolomé de Las Casas, *The Spanish Colonie, or Briefe Chronicle of the Acts and Gestes of the Spaniardes in the West Indies, Called the Newe World, for the Space of xl. Yeeres,* trans. M. M. S. (London, 1583), A1r. For a discussion of Las Casas's anticolonial vehemence and the pro-Protestant strategies to which it was put, see José Rabasa, *Writing Violence on the Northern Frontier: the Historiography of Sixteenth Century New Mexico and Florida and the Legacy of Conquest* (Durham, NC: Duke University Press, 2000), 254ff.

38. Las Casas, *Spanish Colonie,* K3v.

39. Gómara's influence is undisputed; see for example Deborah N. Losse, "Rewriting Culture: Montaigne Recounts New World Ethnography," *Neophilologus* 83, no. 4 (October 1999). On Las Casas see Juan Durán Luzio, "Las Casas y Montaigne: Escritura y Lectura del Nuevo Mundo," *Montaigne Studies* 1, no. 1 (1989); Géralde Nakam, *Montaigne et Son Temps, les Événements et les Essais* (Paris: A. G. Nizet, 1982), 40–41.

40. Michel de Montaigne and J. I. M. Stewart, *The Essayes of Montaigne,* trans. John Florio (New York: Modern Library, 1933), 159.

41. This idea has been explored by various critics, but see also David Quint's argument that the Brazilians' culture of revenge exposes the flaws of stoic philosophy, especially in the context of the French wars of religion. David Quint, *Montaigne and the Quality of Mercy: Ethical and Political Themes in the Essais* (Princeton: Princeton University Press, 1998), 75–101.

42. Las Casas, *Spanish Colonie,* O4v.

43. Gillian Murray Kendall, "'Lend me thy hand': Metaphor and Mayhem in *Titus Andronicus,*" *Shakespeare Quarterly* 40 (1989); Katherine Rowe, *Dead Hands: Fictions of Agency, Renaissance to Modern* (Stanford: Stanford University Press, 1999).

44. Las Casas, *Spanish Colonie,* A3v.

45. Montaigne and Stewart, *Essayes of Montaigne,* 166–67.

46. Ibid., 166.

47. Tzvetan Todorov, "The Morality of Conquest," *Diogenes* 125 (1984), 93.

48. It should be noted that while this mixing may radicalize Montaigne, it is in keeping with Quint's analysis of the *Essais,* which points out that the Brazilians

"have readily adopted the more sadistic methods of executing prisoners taught them by the Portuguese conquistadores as an even better form of vengeance than their own" (81), just as Tamora and her sons swiftly apply the cruelties visited upon them to their captors.

49. Maggie Kilgour, *From Communion to Cannibalism: An Anatomy of Metaphors of Incorporation* (Princeton: Princeton University Press, 1990), 7.

50. 3.1.291–93. All line references to *Coriolanus* are to William Shakespeare, *The Riverside Shakespeare,* ed. G. Blakemore Evans, 2nd ed. (Boston: Houghton Mifflin, 1997).

51. Augustine, *The Confessions of St. Augustine, Books I–X,* trans. F. J. Sheed (New York: Sheed & Ward, 1942), 118.

52. Cf. Heather James, who argues that "the raped and mutilated Lavinia is transformed into a visual palimpsest of the textual struggles that reflect the loss of cultural integrity in an empire mythically founded on rape." Heather James, *Shakespeare's Troy* (Cambridge: Cambridge University Press, 1997), 106.

53. Las Casas, *Spanish Colonie,* F2v.

54. The fork arrived from France during Elizabeth's reign, but was considered more of a court fad than a serious utensil. See Betty Wason, *Cooks, Gluttons & Gourmets: A History of Cookery* (Garden City, NY: Doubleday, 1962), 176–77.

55. See Bernadette Bucher, *Icon and Conquest: a Structural Analysis of the Illustrations of De Bry's Great Boyages* (Chicago: University of Chicago Press, 1981), 46–51.

56. André Thevet and Suzanne Lussagnet, *Les Français en Amérique pendant la deuxième moitié du XVIe Siècle,* vol. 1 (Paris: Presses Universitaires de France, 1953), 281, qtd. in Bucher, *Icon and Conquest,* 49.

57. See also Raymond J. Rice's argument that "the relationship of women to the symbolic order . . . is analogous to cannibalism's function as a threatening specter behind/beyond the last act of revenge." Raymond J. Rice, "Cannibalism and the Act of Revenge in Tudor-Stuart Drama," *SEL* 44, no. 2 (Spring 2004): 302–3, 306.

58. James, *Shakespeare's Troy,* 292. See also John Kerrigan, *Revenge Tragedy: Aeschylus to Armageddon* (Oxford: Clarendon Press, 1996), 196–98.

59. The fly-killing scene appears first in the folio edition of the play. Its careful development of the trope of Lavinia's cannibalism suggests that whoever was responsible for the addition of the scene into the printed text, whether Shakespeare or other actors or revisers, may have been aware of and wished further to elaborate upon this aspect of Lavinia's character.

60. Georges Bataille, *The Accursed Share: An Essay on General Economy,* trans. Robert Hurley, 1st paperback edition, vol. 1 (New York: Zone Books, 1991), 33–34.

61. My phrase recalls, of course, Bakhtin. But in Bakhtin's reading of Rabelais the grotesque body is always unfinished and reciprocal, both destroying and regenerating, both tomb and womb. Shakespeare's parody of Rabelaisian logic results in a terrifyingly closural body, a womb that becomes a tomb, but not the other way around. See Mikhail Bakhtin, *Rabelais and His World,* trans. Hélène Iswolsky (Bloomington: Indiana University Press, 1984), 26 and passim.

62. For readings of this passage with reference to the play's attitude toward Catholicism, see Lukas Erne, " 'Popish Tricks' and 'a Ruinous Monastery': *Titus Andronicus* and the Question of Shakespeare's Catholicism," in *The Limits of Textuality,* ed. Lukas Erne and Guillemette Bolens (Tübingen: Gunter Narr Verlag, 2000); Nicholas R. Moschovakis, " 'Irreligious Piety' and Christian History: Perse-

cution as Pagan Anachronism in *Titus Andronicus,*" *Shakespeare Quarterly* 53, no. 4 (2002), 481–82.

Works Cited

Alden, John Eliot, and Dennis C. Landis. *European Americana: A Chronological Guide to Works Printed in Europe Relating to the Americas, 1493–1776.* New York: Readex Books, 1980.

Anghiera, Pietro Martire di. *The Decades of the Newe Worlde or West India Conteynyng the Nauigations and Conquestes of the Spanyardes, with the Particular Description of the Moste Ryche and Large Landes and Ilandes Lately Founde in the West Ocean Perteynyng to the Inheritaunce of the Kinges of Spayne.* Translated by Richard Eden. London, 1555.

Augustine. *The Confessions of St. Augustine, Books I–X.* Translated by F. J. Sheed. New York: Sheed & Ward, 1942.

Bakhtin, Mikhail. *Rabelais and His World.* Translated by Hélène Iswolsky. Bloomington: Indiana University Press, 1984.

Barker, Francis, Peter Hulme, and Margaret Iversen. *Cannibalism and the Colonial World.* Cambridge: Cambridge University Press, 1998.

Bataille, Georges. *The Accursed Share: An Essay on General Economy.* Translated by Robert Hurley. 1st paperback edition. Vol. 1. New York: Zone Books, 1991.

Broude, Ronald. "Roman and Goth in *Titus Andronicus.*" *Shakespeare Studies* 6 (1970): 27–34.

Bucher, Bernadette. *Icon and Conquest: A Structural Analysis of the Illustrations of De Bry's Great Voyages.* Chicago: University of Chicago Press, 1981.

Clendinnen, Inga. *Aztecs: An Interpretation.* Cambridge: Cambridge University Press, 1991.

Cox, Edward Godfrey. *A Reference Guide to the Literature of Travel: Including Voyages, Geographical Descriptions, Adventures, Shipwrecks and Expeditions.* 3 vols. New York: Greenwood Press, 1969.

D., T. *The Bloody Banquet, 1639.* Oxford: Printed for the Malone Society by V. Ridler at the University Press, 1961.

De Bry, Theodor. *Americae Tertia Pars.* Frankfurt, 1592.

Dessen, Alan C. *Titus Andronicus.* Manchester: Manchester University Press, 1989.

Erne, Lukas. "'Popish Tricks' and 'a Ruinous Monastery': *Titus Andronicus* and the Question of Shakespeare's Catholicism." In *The Limits of Textuality,* edited by Lukas Erne and Guillemette Bolens, 135–55. Tübingen: Gunter Narr Verlag, 2000.

Frey, Charles. "*The Tempest* and the New World." *Shakespeare Quarterly* 30, no. 1 (1979): 29–41.

Grady, Hugh. *Shakespeare, Machiavelli, and Montaigne: Power and Subjectivity from Richard II to Hamlet.* Oxford: Oxford University Press, 2002.

Hariot, Thomas. *A Briefe and True Report of the New Found Land of Virginia of* the Commodities and of the Nature and Manners of the Naturall Inhabitants. Francoforti ad Moenum, 1590.

Harvey, P. D. A. *Mappa Mundi: The Hereford World Map.* Toronto: University of Toronto Press, 1996.

Hesiod. *Theogony.* Translated and edited by Apostolos N. Athanassakis. Baltimore: Johns Hopkins University Press, 1983.

Heywood, Jasper. "Seneca's Thyestes." In *Five Elizabethan Tragedies,* edited by A. K. McIlwraith. London: Oxford University Press, 1963.

James, Heather. *Shakespeare's Troy.* Cambridge: Cambridge University Press, 1997.

Kendall, Gillian Murray. " 'Lend Me Thy Hand': Metaphor and Mayhem in *Titus Andronicus." Shakespeare Quarterly* 40 (1989): 299–316.

Kerrigan, John. *Revenge Tragedy: Aeschylus to Armageddon.* Oxford: Clarendon Press, 1996.

Kilgour, Maggie. *From Communion to Cannibalism: An Anatomy of Metaphors of Incorporation.* Princeton: Princeton University Press, 1990.

Las Casas, Bartolomé de. *The Spanish Colonie, or Briefe Chronicle of the Acts and Gestes of the Spaniardes in the West Indies, Called the Newe World, for the Space of Xl. Yeeres.* Translated by M. M. S. London, 1583.

Lestringant, Frank. *Cannibals.* Translated by Rosemary Morris. Berkeley: University of California Press, 1997.

López de Gómara, Francisco. *The Pleasant Historie of the Conquest of the West India, Now Called New Spaine. Atchieued by the Most Woorthie Prince Hernando Cortes, Marques of the Valley of Huaxacac, Most Delectable to Reade.* Translated by T. N. [Thomas Nichols]. London, 1596.

Losse, Deborah N. "Rewriting Culture: Montaigne Recounts New World Ethnography." *Neophilologus* 83, no. 4 (October 1999): 517–28.

Luzio, Juan Durán. "Las Casas y Montaigne: Escritura y Lectura del Nuevo Mundo." *Montaigne Studies* 1, no. 1 (1989): 88–106.

Marston, John. *Antonio's Revenge: The Second Part of Antonio and Mellida.* Edited by G. K. Hunter. Lincoln: University of Nebraska Press, 1965.

Montaigne, Michel de, and J. I. M. Stewart. *The Essayes of Montaigne.* Translated by John Florio. New York: Modern Library, 1933.

Moschovakis, Nicholas R. " 'Irreligious Piety' and Christian History: Persecution as Pagan Anachronism in *Titus Andronicus." Shakespeare Quarterly* 53, no. 4 (2002): 460–86.

Nakam, Géralde. *Montaigne et Son Temps, les Événements et les Essais.* Paris: A.-G. Nizet, 1982.

Noble, Louise. " 'And Make Two Pasties of Your Shameful Heads': Medicinal Cannibalism and Healing the Body Politic in *Titus Andronicus." ELH* 70, no. 3 (2003): 677–708.

Nunn, Hillary. "*Titus Andronicus* and the Tupinamba: Staging Cannibalism in a New World." Conference Paper, The Ohio Shakespeare Conference. Akron, OH, 2002.

O'Gorman, Edmundo. *The Invention of America: An Inquiry into the Historical*

Nature of the New World and the Meaning of Its History. Bloomington: Indiana University Press, 1961.

Orgel, Stephen. "Shakespeare and the Cannibals." In *Cannibals, Witches, and Divorce: Estranging the Renaissance,* edited by Marjorie B. Garber, 40–66. Baltimore: Johns Hopkins University Press, 1987.

Parker, Patricia A. *Shakespeare from the Margins: Language, Culture, Context.* Chicago: University of Chicago Press, 1996.

Quinn, David Beers. "New Geographical Horizons: Literature." In *First Images of America: The Impact of the New World on the Old,* edited by Fredi Chiappelli, Michael J. B. Allen, and Robert Louis Benson, 636–58. Berkeley: University of California Press, 1976.

Quint, David. *Montaigne and the Quality of Mercy: Ethical and Political Themes in the Essais.* Princeton: Princeton University Press, 1998.

Rabasa, José. *Writing Violence on the Northern Frontier: The Historiography of Sixteenth Century New Mexico and Florida and the Legacy of Conquest.* Durham, NC: Duke University Press, 2000.

Rice, Raymond J. "Cannibalism and the Act of Revenge in Tudor-Stuart Drama." *SEL* 44, no. 2 (Spring 2004): 297–316.

Riggs, David. *The World of Christopher Marlowe.* New York: Henry Holt, 2004.

Roach, Joseph R. *Cities of the Dead: Circum-Atlantic Performance.* New York: Columbia University Press, 1996.

Rowe, Katherine. *Dead Hands: Fictions of Agency, Renaissance to Modern.* Stanford, CA: Stanford University Press, 1999.

Rubens, Peter Paul. *Saturn Devouring His Children.* 1623.

Shakespeare, William. *The Riverside Shakespeare.* Edited by G. Blakemore Evans. 2nd ed. Boston: Houghton Mifflin, 1997.

———. *Titus Andronicus. The Arden Shakespeare,* edited by Jonathan Bate. London: Routledge, 1995.

Thevet, André. *La Cosmographie Universelle.* Paris, 1575.

Todorov, Tzvetan. "The Morality of Conquest." *Diogenes* 125 (1984): 89–102.

Wason, Betty. *Cooks, Gluttons & Gourmets: A History of Cookery.* Garden City, NY: Doubleday, 1962.

Westrem, Scott D. *The Hereford Map: A Transcription and Translation of the Legends with Commentary.* Turnhout, Belgium: Brepols, 2001.

Speaking Process

MARTIN ORKIN

IDENTIFICATION OF ETHICAL ACTION may be an inescapable "human" compulsion, evident at least in part, as we all know, in Hamlet's "to be, or not to be," (3.1.56).[1] But the act of speaking the ethical into being, as early modern humanists understood only too well, is in itself no guarantee of the ethical. Human speaking just as easily may be duplicitous, manipulative, in its effects also deadly. Moreover, it remains frail. The tradition that, as Erica Fudge points out, maintained that "speaking is the site of the human" (65) and that placed the "animal" as "the thing which the human is constantly setting itself *against*,"[2] acknowledges simultaneously and by implication that "human-ness" is "a quality which must be learned and can be lost" (65). Humans, according to early modern humanists, have to learn to speak, and so, become "human". Even so, the "human," as Thomas Adams sermonized in the first half of the seventeenth century, remains dangerously proximate to the "animal," in the case of wrongful action, particularly, to "mysticall *wolues;* rauenous beasts in the formes of men. . . . The wicked haue many resemblances to *wolues.*"[3]

Indeed skepticism about the possibility of establishing any distinction between the "human"—and the human power of speech—and the "non-human," reaches a point of particular intensity in the late twentieth century in, for example Howard Brenton's *The Romans in Britain,* performed at the National Theater in London, 1980, when, just after he has been raped by Roman soldiers the Druid priest speaks of survival in a manner that infers rejection of speech as means to the ethical, the "human," and the humane:

> We must have nothing to do with them. Nothing. Abandon the life we know. Change ourselves into animals. The cat. No, an animal not yet heard of. Deadly, watching, ready in the forest. Something *not human.* (Part 1, Scene 6, p.60, my emphasis)[4]

Such a blurring of the distinction between the "human" and the "animal" sounds one of many notes of finitude for that term "humanism" that, invented, as Tony Davies argues, in the nineteenth century,[5] had certain of its origins in the early modern period, one that vested particular importance in the concept of human (meaning "male") intellection or reason, and human (meaning "male") speaking as marks of the "human."

In putting his now famous question, Hamlet attempts of course to speak (ethical) action into being by way of a binary: he juxtaposes the possibility of "being"—suffering "the slings and arrows of outrageous fortune" (3.1.58)—against "not-being" but taking "arms against a sea of troubles" (3.1.59). Significantly and famously for Hamlet, though, that search for singularity in agency, which initial enunciation of a simple binary infers to be also (easily) decidable, proves, as the soliloquy unfolds, impossible to achieve.

I want in this essay to consider other examples of the use of this binaric mode habitual to human speaking, but ones which, in contrast to Hamlet's usage, propose simple oppositional singularities that go unquestioned. Such a habit of speaking, which seeks to conceptualize the world in terms of a putative, easily identifiable, and resolvable binary singularity suggests, I would argue, one possible reason for the fears expressed in different ways by both Thomas Adams and Howard Brenton. In attempting in this essay a reading of a number of diverse examples of such a binaric mode of speaking reality into being, I will also draw briefly on one aspect of a habit of speaking evident in the Southern African Tswana conceptualization of human and "humane" action—though patently in no way "early-modern," and itself arguably a version of what we understand to be deconstruction. What I want to foreground is the particular stress, within this Tswana analytic procedure, upon ongoing multiplicity of relevance. I call such a stress "processual," and want to suggest that such an emphasis may be useful to us for our own (deconstructive) readings. It may help to provide for, or more consistently facilitate, the putative possibility of understanding or effecting the "ethical" and especially the "humane"—just those outcomes which the early modern humanists or perhaps certain present-day human rights activists might have wanted, or still want the terms "human" speaking or "human" action, in differing ways, to resonate. Having noted this, I will seek evidence of processual utterance amid those dominantly patriarchal and misogynist gender binaries apparent in Ben Jonson's writing in *Timber or Discoveries* as well as in one instance of the scholarship that deals with Hamlet's famous declaration, "Frailty, thy name is woman" (1.2.146). I will then explore evidence of processual utterance amid certain occasional, proto-racist binaries involving the colors "black" and "white" operative in the language of *Hamlet*. Turning, finally, to a very different set of examples, I will juxtapose, against what I notice in these instances of early modern writing, representative instances of the mode of political and religious enunciation to be found in the early twenty-first century writing of the Anglo-Kuwaiti Sulayman Al-Bassam, in his *Al-Hamlet Summit*. My aim throughout will be to explore whether attention to the processual potential sometimes apparent in human utterance might counterbalance or help to diminish those deadlier implications or consequences evident from the more dominantly used or recognized mode of (unquestioning) binary singularity.

I

It may be worth prefacing discussion of this predilection for unquestioning binary singularity in human speaking by way of brief recall of certain early-modern shibboleths concerning speaking in general. In *Timber or Discoveries,* Ben Jonson articulates early modern faith in speech as, potentially, ideally accurate referential tool. Words are therefore carefully "to be chose[n] according to the persons wee make speake, or the things wee speake of."[6] This is because "*speech* is the only benefit man hath to expresse his excellency of mind *above other creatures*. It is the *Instrument of Society*" (620–21, my emphases). Used properly, then, speech will show exactly what is there. As an "instrument of society," it reveals also the social and commonly held ethical truths or norms that inform what it describes. Such usage confirms the importance of human speaking, revealing a (masculine) "excellency of mind above other creatures." If rational and ethical "human" action is attainable only by the eloquent speaking human being then also "*language* most shewes a man: speake, that I may see thee" (625). What, for the early modern humanist, would be *inhuman* would be a way of speaking that obscures not only what happens but the conventional truth content or expected norms held to inform what happens.

I want, for a moment or two, to juxtapose such desire for a transparent route to a singular and homogenous kind of normative "truth," against aspects of the speaking of human action into being, to be found amongst the Tswana people of southern Africa.[7] This is to step—very briefly—beyond current, scholarly, metropolitan insistence on the primacy of early modern texts together with recovery of their "materiality." I do this not to conflate in any way obvious differences. But if human beings are similar to as well as different from one another, local knowledges from one culture or moment may provocatively intersect with the knowledges of another, on occasion even extend or enrich particular (in this case deconstructive) enterprises. The Tswana do postulate a set of putative ethical norms underlying their common culture, but they pay as well empirical, or what I would call "processual," respect to what they conceptualize as the enigmatic nature of a "reality" that can never fully be held in place, solely by articulated "norms." This means that in the attempt to discern the ethics that might define a moment of particular conflict, they take into account complicating incidents that in the event actually, in process, occur. They do not simply impose upon what happens, or read into what happens, commonly held preconceived notions of truth content. They recognize that particular incidents in the event itself may indeed glimpse or posit different (ethical) possibilities, that might deviate from, complicate or even contradict the ethical articulation in conventional norms—without, either, it must be emphasized, simply dismissing or erasing those norms. Such a conceptualization, registers that there is always a "reality" beyond commonly held "truth content" in or "knowledge" about human experience—something which words such as the "unknown," the "mysterious," the "unpredictable" seek to indicate. That which lies beyond what human speaking until then has been able to propose as true, is in the processual mode of conceptualizing human action given tendentious or profound *potential relevance.*

From this I extrapolate a way of reading that attends, similarly, not only, "teleologically," as it were, to indications in a text of normative cultural moorings germane to it and its location—especially those simple opposites informing a particular value system—but also *processually,* to what actually happens in the particular language of that text. Nor is this in order to register a putative "difference" or endless deferral of meaning, against which certain norms might be (temporarily) fortified or exposed. Nor, again, to register contradictions or reveal or confirm some underlying fixed dialectic.

The Tswana never deny the norms that exist within their culture, and that help to determine the speaking or the reading of ethical human action into being. But they set these norms against a simultaneous resolve processually to take seriously into account everything that, *in the actual event,* exceeds, or stretches, or may alter in particular ways conventional norms, or current, commonly held notions of "truth content," A Tswana, or processual mode of reading respects particular cultural frameworks but simultaneously tolerates, meditates, and especially attempts to *process and absorb* complicating evidence. It meditatively registers that language which, inadvertently or otherwise, points elsewhere, resonates implications prompted by the enigmatic, the inexplicable, or the unpredictable in experience, which no cultural framework or ideological system can ever fully anticipate.

For instance, to read Jonson's recycling of a classical commonplace about "fortune" in *Timber or Discoveries* processually, is, on the one hand, to register an early modern ("teleological") impulse to assert certain—what we imagine to be—early modern English norms of patriarchy, but, on the other hand, to attend as well to that in his prose which, perhaps inadvertently, admits a more complicated and mixed set of conditions. Let us consider the following passage:

> Ill *Fortune* never crush't that man, whom good *Fortune* deceived not. I therefore have counselled my friends, never to trust to her fairer side, though she seem'd to make peace with them: But to place all things she gave them so, as she might aske them againe without their trouble; she might take them from them, not pull them: to keepe alwayes a distance betweene her, and themselves. He knows not his own strength, that hath not met Adversity. Heaven prepares *good men* with *crosses;* but no ill can happen to a *good* man. Contraries are not mixed. Yet, that which happens to any man, may to every man. But it is in his reason what hee accounts it, and will make it.[8]

Jonson avers on the one hand that "Ill *Fortune* never crush't that man, whom good *Fortune* deceived not," recommending (masculinist) consistency and neo-stoicism in the face of a falsely based trust in what might happen.[9] He argues that "Heaven prepares *good men* with *crosses*"; and that "no ill can happen to a *good* man." Especially noteworthy, he asseverates explicitly that *"Contraries are not mixed"* (my emphasis). Such language clearly strives for a patriarchal assertion of binary singularity. This is implicitly also binarically poised against inferred complication, changeability, or difference—all also posited as negatively oppositional and, usually, feminine. On the other hand, Jonson's next sentence, qualifies this urge to binary singularity. To observe this is to read processually, to register how Jonson's own prose admits complexities that complicate the binaries upon which he appears to rely. Even as Jonson offers a normative assertion of the inviolability of boundaries between good men and bad men, good and ill fortune, his language admits a more complex reality than what the normative postulate of binarically insulated singularity allows: *"yet, that which happens to any man, may to every man"* (my emphasis). This concession opens the door to recognition of a potential for heterogeneity that lies within and without the human subject, within and without "any" man, "every" man (or, of course, woman). The teleological urge returns though, in his very next sentence: "But it is in his *reason* what hee accounts it, and will make it" (my emphasis). This at once draws on the early modern humanist telos of the "rational," to contain and shut out that enigma of inner mixedness or complexity, the potential for multiplicity: both within the human subject as well as in the world she inhabits. Although there are good men, there is reason and contraries are *not* mixed, nonetheless, "that which happens to *any* man may *to every* man" (my emphasis). Language that insists on singularity and homogeneity, simultaneously and processually registers the *contrariness* of contingency.

Jonson's language may be read processually as well as teleologically everywhere in *Discoveries*. He targets vanity and arrogance in:

> No man is so foolish, but may give an other good counsell sometimes; and no man is so wise, but may easily erre, if hee will take no others counsell, but his owne. But very few men are wise by their owne counsell; or learned by their owne teaching. For hee that was onely taught by himselfe, had a foole to his Master. (563)

The admittedly traditional conflation of wisdom and folly he draws on here is nonetheless one that may be seen simultaneously to disrupt the urge to binary singularity. He writes

> A man should so deliver himselfe to the nature of the subject, whereof hee speakes, that his hearer may take knowledge of his discipline with some delight: and so apparell faire, and good matter, that the studious of elegancy be not defrauded; redeeme Arts from their rough, and braky seates, where they lay hid, and overgrowne with thornes, to a pure open

and flowry light: where they may take the eye, and be taken by the hand. I cannot thinke Nature is so spent and decay'd, that she can bring forth nothing worth her former yeares. She is alwayes the same, like her selfe: And when she collects her strength, is abler still. Men are decay'd, and *studies:* Shee is not. (566–7)

Even as Jonson poses the ideal of artistic integrity in the midst of what is self-evidently writing in patriarchal vein, he resorts to philogyny—nature "is always the same, like her selfe . . . Men are decay'd and *studies:* Shee is not"—a somewhat startling, what Alan Sinfield would call, "faultline."[10] Again, Jonson asserts that

a *wise tongue* should not be licentious and wandring; but moved, and (as it were) govern'd with certaine raines from the heart, and bottome of the brest: and it was excellently said of that Philosopher; that there was a Wall, or Parapet of teeth set in our mouth, to restraine the petulancy of our words: that the rashnesse of talking should not only bee retarded by the guard and watch of our heart; but be fenced in, and defended by certaine strengths, placed in the mouth it selfe, and within the lips. (573).

When Jonson asseverates that wise speaking needs restraint, his language simultaneously concedes predilection to "wander" beyond the known and legitimate, informing even the "wise" tongue; it registers a potential for innovatory or transgressive speaking, admits that lying within—not, typically for the early modern period, the female, but—the male body, is a heterogeneity that necessitates "a Wall or Parapet of teeth," to "restraine" "licentiousness," "petulancy," "rashness."

Indeed, Jonson's concern, everywhere in *Discoveries* with ruly and unruly speaking may be set beside Joseph Bristow's point regarding the struggle of nineteenth century sexologists to establish normative categories of sexuality, which the detail of their language of casebook illustration for the greater part resists.[11] The detail of Jonson's language is processually everywhere punctuated by linguistic eruptions, faultlines that belie the teleological endeavor to idealize (in the context of sexuality, the word would be naturalize) a preferred binary singularity. In such ways the detail of the language of *Timber or Discoveries* returns processually to that in experience that evades, lies beyond, undoes its own speaking into being of "humanist," noticeably patriarchal, binary norms.

Such evidence of processual similitude, proximity, the slippage of "one" into an "other," side by side with dependence on an un-questioning binary singularity invites collocation with, say, Tony Davies's reference to the project of early modern humanism as "an embattled and uncertain construction."[12] Jonson's impulse toward speaking singularity and simple opposition into being in human experience proves never to be entirely comprehensive. Processu-ally, the linguistic tissue of his prose instead entails intimations or uncanny returns of that which renders its assertions of singularity, fabrications of opposites, particular elisions and omissions, always in the end, fictional.

Before I end this section I want to look at one example of how teleological expectations involving the early modern gender binary at least might be unsettled by a more processually inclined kind of scholarly inquiry—this time, though, in the case of *Hamlet,* with which my next section will be mainly concerned. The editors of the most recent Arden Shakespeare edition of the play, Ann Thompson and Neill Taylor,[13] cite for Hamlet's line "Frailty thy name is woman,"(1.2.146)—which occurs in the First Quarto, Second Quarto, and Folio texts—Dent's suggestion that the proverb alluded to here is *Women are Frail* (W700.1, a1400).[14] Neither Dent, Jenkins, nor Thompson and Taylor register the possibility that the proverb *Flesh is Frail* (Tilley, F363, 1575) might just as easily be involved.[15] Why, it might be wondered, do editors register *Women are Frail,* as the likely allusion, rather than the less gender-located one? I would argue that in doing this they conform to the (momentary) conven-tional misogyny evident in Hamlet's painful outburst itself, here. Indeed Dent provides one citation for the proverb he chooses, that points toward a more generically proximate conceptualization of human frailty, "'Damsell leave of dispaire, Nature, humane, *and* women's sex is fraile" (Ariosto, *Orlando Furioso,* 1591, II.71 R4ᵛ, my emphasis). This directs us (I would argue, processually) to the possibility of a more diffuse and nonbinarically gendered referent, one indicated also in Tilley's citation for *Flesh is frail,* "The flesh is weak," (*Matt.,* xxvi, 41). It is worth in this context recalling, too, Falstaff's less misogynist allusion to the more generalized proverb *Flesh is frail:* "I have more flesh than another man, and therefore more frailty" (*I Henry IV,* 3.3.153–54).[16] In this context, it might be possible to argue that Hamlet, in a moment of frustrated anger, plays with the proverbial *Flesh is frail,* by reassigning frailty, sin-fulness, and degradation to the feminine, that is, by projecting a proverbial recognition of human frailty onto the female body (his mother's). That this is momentary anger in Hamlet, not fixed misogyny is made clear elsewhere when he speaks differently in, for instance, the line "Use every man after his desert, and who shall scape whipping?" (2.2.524–55), or in "You should not have believed me; for virtue cannot so inoculate our old stock but we shall relish of it" (3.1.117–78). Such a reading would accord more happily too with the process Janet Adelman discerns in the play's redirection of "ordinary genital sexuality" into the "indiscriminately sexual maternal body."[17]

In any event, the mode of binary categorization evident in the matter of gender construction that I have so far partly been glancing at mainly in Jonson, entails, as is well known, potential consequence of a violent elision of that which exceeds its taxonomies. A processual reading might show what this kind of human speaking cannot everywhere omit, but it cannot free us from the power of its influence, a teleological urge toward binary singularity which Barbara Johnson long since has argued "undergird[s] Western culture's logic about both race and sex."[18] How humane actually, then, is such a habit of speaking binary singularity into being, in Timber or Discoveries (or even in a detail of the scholarship dealing with Hamlet)? For more reasons than his humanist faith in "reasoned" speaking would care to indicate, perhaps, Jonson's own dramatic writing is obsessed by spectres, in the act of human speaking, of violent slippage from the human to the animal.

II

In Hamlet, one of the many ways in which the speaking of unquestioning binary singularity into being may be traced is of course in conventional or traditional uses of the colors "black" and "white," and related terms, as in, to recall a few of innumerable instances in the play, the Pyrrhus whose "sable arms, / Black as his purpose, did the night resemble" (2.2.448–49), Hamlet's sarcastic "[then] let the devil wear black"(3.2.127),[19] or Claudius's sudden, agonized plea, regarding his own "cursed hand," "is there not rain enough in the sweet heavens / To wash it white as snow?" (3.3.45–46).[20] Among others, Kim Hall, Arthur Little, Ania Loomba, and Peter Erickson have traced the semantic shift from patristic and homiletic to more explicitly racist[21] use of these colors,[22] early modern mythic, performative, and dramatic readings of them,[23] and visual representations[24]—all argued to be evidence, too, of an early modern "moment of intensified English interest in colonial travel and African trade," suggestive of incipient empire building.[25] Patricia Parker delineates brilliantly numerous instances of the operation in the play of this binary:[26] in the context of notions of sullying, adulteration, the maculate, and the immaculate, "the postlapsarian decline from 'honesty' figured as the purity of an immaculate or unspotted 'white,' a decline evoked by the post Edenic 'vnweeded' garden of Q2 and F" (133), the contrast "between the 'modesty' and 'whiteness' of Ophelia" (134), the "old Mole . . . in the 'earth' or 'ground'"(135), the dirty and the soiled, "the earthy or abject bodily sense of sullying as muddying . . . sounded [also] in Ophelia's 'muddy' death" (4.7.182)(136). She traces the explicit identification of melancholy, mourning, tragedy, and death with racialized figures of blackness in the period and records presentations of "Melancholy" and "Death" as Moors/Moorish. As interesting, from my present perspective, remarking the "network . . . [of] polarity of 'black' and 'white' that pervades" (145) the quarto and folio versions of the play, she registers, too, albeit perhaps only fleetingly at the end of her essay, its reversibility, positing a "*rhetoric* of distinction, the construction of polarity *where none may exist*" (148, my emphasis). Inadvertently perhaps gesturing toward what I would call the processual elements in the play that complicate and undo the conventional binary, she remarks further, in her concluding section, that "the early texts of *Hamlet* repeatedly construct such oppositions—of white and black, heaven and hell, angel and devil—*and simultaneously undo these polarities*" (149, my emphasis). But regrettably she does not pursue this further.

I want now briefly to sketch, as possible complement to such work, how processual examination of aspects of the text might complicate that racist teleology apparent in it. In a play informed, as the editors of the third Arden edition note, by "contradictions and equivocations"[27] such tendentious possibilities are not difficult to find. If Hamlet desires a way of killing Claudius so that his uncle's soul "may be as damned and black / As hell whereto it goes" (3.3.94–95), the presentation of Hamlet's uncle and much else of what happens in the play, taken as "European" artifact (an early modern English structuration of "Denmark") postulate, rather, a devilish and deceptive murderousness for "*whiteness.*" The balanced inversions of act 3, where the guilty Claudius who attempts to find a moment of forgiveness is juxtaposed against a violent and abrasive, although in aspiration ethical Hamlet, capable of both cruelty and slaughter, interrogate further the reductive nature of the conventional teleology of binary singularity (the "good" Hamlet, the "evil'" Claudius).

Moreover, processual complication in the text is not limited to such instances of inversion, or counter-identification. The black Hamlet who confronts the court at its beginning, or the darkness in which the play opens propose more complex resonances for the color "black" than the traditional binary encourages. If the blackness of Hamlet's clothing is a conventional marker of mourning, it can be argued that it emerges as surely in the play, as also marker of sincerity and honesty. His inky cloak hypothesizes a coherent blackness for that ink that is inscribed upon the meaningless blankness of the empty white page, an ink inscribing the blank and in his view amoral white page of Claudius and Gertrude's o'erhasty wedding with other meanings.

The image of darkness with which the play opens, too, powerfully disrupts conventional signification, setting in motion as this darkness does a movement that seeks to articulate and enact ethical action. Moreover the play moves from the darkness of the first scene, via the "morn in russet mantle clad' '(1.1.171) to where Marcellus has already said he knows Hamlet will "this morning" (1.1.179) be found and where they tell him about events occurring "yesternight" (1.2.189). The kind of "brightness" of Claudius's court, to which the play in this way turns, particularly the literal daylight in which it now in act 1, scene 2, functions, perhaps also the resonance of the (glittering) mystique of power attached to the image of the monarch addressing his entire court as the scene opens,[28] and yet, at the same time, the multiple opacities of language usage simultaneously practiced there, in some senses contrasts with the ethical demand for truth emanating from this darkness. Part of the fascination of this play may well lie in its processual presentation of a partly mysterious and unknowable "reality" into being by way, among other things, of a "darkness" which underlines the limits and inadequacies of the conventional semantics of the word "black" itself, or words related to it. In this regard "darkness" is one metaphor for the human condition, located as it always is in experience that seems partly to lie beyond that "discover'ed bourne" that words attempt to fix. In the face of this, the conventional negative signification attached to the word "black" reads merely as means of speaking away, or containing—erecting a wall or a parapet to keep out—the challenge of epistemological profundity and mystery darkness poses. If, as Catherine Belsey articulates it, "culture is the element we inhabit as speaking beings [and] resides in . . . the meanings we learn,"[29] the darkness in *Hamlet* points to that which exceeds it. Darkness and blackness in this sense bear philosophical or ontological importance and value as denoting that which, potentially positive as well as negative, lies beyond the grasp of known language, or epistemology. If the night can be "made" "hideous"(1.4.54) it must otherwise also be potentially beautiful. Horatio and Marcellus's overtly Christian articulations at the end of act 1, scene 1, cannot fully account for or contain the mystery that threatens their need to proclaim faith in the existence of a time "in joint."[30] The brightness of the dawn (or "whiteness" throughout the play as I have just argued) emerges as equally enigmatic. If we do live in conditions that we do not fully understand, we may be sure the fascination of *Hamlet* comes in part from the extent to which the play makes processual space, as well as in its language and event, through its imagery of darkness for that opaque, sometimes positive, sometimes negative condition of human experience within which human speaking and action has to operate but for which it cannot fully account.[31]

I want to glance here at one other possible direction for a project of reading the colors "black" and "white" processually. Critical discussions of biblical allusions in *Hamlet* often operate with a "teleology" of an uncomplicated black/white color binary in mind to argue the incipiently racist telos for the play's use of the colors "black" and "white." Such discussions draw inevitably on, and so replicate the symbolic figurations found in, one or other version of Christian scriptures, by way, partly at least, of the Septuagint, Vulgate, Geneva Bible, the Authorized King James version of 1611, or versions since then.[32] But examination of the text "recovered" by European Protestants, among them English Hebraists, in the early modern period, known as the Hebrew Bible, which later versions, from the Septuagint and the Vulgate on sought to translate, suggests a more neutral use there of the black-white binary.

For example, critics suggest that Gertrude's, "Thou turn'st my eyes into my very soul / And there I see such black and grained spots" (3.4.89–90) resonates Jeremiah 13:23, "Can the black Moor change his skin? Or the leopard his spots?" Patricia Parker argues that this reference points in turn to "the pollution danger associ-

ated by Douglas, Kristeva, and others with Leviticus."[33] And Parker
specifically indicates here the source of her biblical citation as the
Geneva Bible.[34] Although Michael Neill, in turn, writes that the
prophet Jeremiah "demands" this question and quotes "*Then* may
ye also do good, that are accustomed to do evil" as evidence that,
significantly, "in the biblical text colour has a complex analogical
function: in the first instance it simply stands for that which cannot
be changed," "by implication," he insists, there is also racism to be
read into it.[35] He maintains that "in Jeremiah the black Moor's skin
is shown as a mark of disclosure: making apparent his hereditary
sin and the punitive sentence to which he is subject, it speaks of
death and apocalypse" (147). Again, on Claudius's comment "Is
there not rain enough in the sweet heavens / To wash it white as
snow?" (3.3.45–46) Parker notes "the king . . . invokes for his own
sin the proverbial impossibility of washing the Ethiope white," relating "the language of washing an Ethiope" to the "context of
maimed rites and adulterate mixtures."[36]

But the assumption of a proto-racist binaric singularity operating
here, deriving from the "Bible" itself, is interestingly challenged by
the relevant passages in the Hebrew Bible which, Avraham Melamed argues to be merely rhetorical, positing only "the impossibility of altering natural characteristics," and without racist
inference.[37] Imposing negative resonances onto such imagery may
well reflect a post-Hebrew Bible tradition. Referring to Jeremiah's
"Can the black change his skin?" Melamed contends:

> Consider the well-known Roman proverb "To wash the black (and make
> him) white", and the contrast is clear. The two sayings may appear par-
> allel, but unlike [Jeremiah's formulation], whose words are essentially
> descriptive, the Latin proverb is weighted with negative judgements.
> There are two qualitative differences between Jeremiah and Lucianus.
> One is that Jeremiah, whose complexion is lighter, asks a rhetorical
> question, assuming the empirical fact that skin colour cannot be altered
> and so makes no attempt to do so. In Lucianus, by contrast, the black
> himself stubbornly tries to change his complexion. . . . The second dif-
> ference is in the washing motif, which is very strong in Lucianus and
> totally absent in Jeremiah, who does not allude to a way that the
> "Cushi" is to change his skin colour, since he recognises it as an empiri-
> cal, unalterable fact . . . Only in comparing the black's inability to
> change his skin with the Israelites' inability to mend their ways is there
> a potential for a negative stance regarding the black. In addition, the
> sins of Israel here are linked to drunkenness and promiscuity, two char-

acteristics later attributed to the black in particular as we shall see on many occasions. One might conclude, as did Midrashic authors and medieval commentators, Abarbanel for example, that the analogy between the black and the evil deeds of Israel is no coincidence, and relates to the negative significance of the former's skin colour. But this interpretation comes centuries later and is far from the original literal sense of the words. It is more a testimony to the value system of the commentators than to what the [Hebrew] Bible text originally meant. While the prophet's words are somewhat enigmatic, they do not automatically carry a specifically negative attitude to the black, especially since elsewhere (46:9) Jeremiah refers to them as valiant soldiers, and King Zedekiah's black slave too is described by the prophet as a most positive figure as we note later on. (57)

Racist resonances later scholarship attaches to the color "black," not only do not appear here, but appear almost nowhere in the originary text. In such contexts it is worth glancing, too, at how Parker's argument that Claudius's earlier reference to his offense, that "it hath the primal eldest curse upon't—/A brother's murder" (3.3.36–38) alluding to the biblical story of Cain, is taken up once again in the context of a later tradition, which she and other scholars use retrospectively (so far as the story in the original Hebrew Bible is concerned):

> the "curse" on Cain was conflated by long tradition with the curse of blackness on Canaan or Ham, whose punishment for his own "adulterous" sin figured the origin of "black Moors" as well as the maculation of racial mixing. Chus, son of Ham, identified with southern or "tropic climes," had mingled offspring both white and black . . . The "primall eldest curse" (F/Q2) on fratricide thus recalls the curse that identified Cain with the "curse" on blackness itself.[38]

This "long tradition" may not, however, include the Hebrew Bible, where, Melamed notes,

> the genealogy of the birth of Cush is completely neutral, with no hint regarding his skin colour. There is no reference whatever—positive or negative—to special character traits, his or those of his descendants. Canaan, Cush's brother, is punished by eternal slavery for the sin of his father Ham against his grandfather Noah . . . Cush himself is not mentioned, nor is there any reference to Canaan's skin colour. The passage, however, became the *locus classicus* for perceptions of the black in the literature of the Sages and in the Middle Ages. The identification of Ham and his sons as dark skinned and naturally destined to slavery is

post-[Hebrew Bible], the result of later historical or cultural circumstances, and is by no means to be projected anachronistically onto the [Hebrew] Bible text itself.[39]

Melamed's argument may be collocated, again, with John Gillies's related arguments on the topic[40] and when Gillies cites Best's "this blacknes proceedeth rather of some natural infection of that man, which was so strong, that neither the nature of the Clime, neither the good complexion of the mother concurring, coulde anything alter" to conclude, by implication at the very least, that the biblical story itself signifies, "regardless, then, of where they may be or with whom they may copulate, moors will continue to beget offspring 'polluted with the same blot of infection.'"[41] But Gillies acknowledges that the biblical text he is using is the Cambridge *Revised Holy Bible,* published 1898.[42] His citation of George Best, and use, then, of the (non-Hebrew) Bible suggests a further instance in which later biases in favor of a teleology of binary singularity, inflect claims made about the originary biblical story in the Hebrew Bible itself.

Melamed, it may be added, also points out that the words "Cush" or "Cushi," in the Hebrew Bible[43] have only *geographic* signification, and are "identified with the Nubians who lived in the south of Egypt."[44] Moses takes a "Cushit" wife during his wanderings in the desert, with no hint of the fear of miscegenation that critics subsequently discern.[45] Elsewhere in the Hebrew Bible too, use of the word "black" emerges as "descriptive and not judgemental."[46] The text of the *Song of Songs*[47] "relates ambivalently though not of necessity negatively to dark skin" (43), as is clear from the change later translations were to make of the line which in the Hebrew reads "I am black *and* comely," to "I am black *but* comely."[48] And in terms of a conventional racist binary of black and white it is worth noting briefly that points of contradiction in the use of the word "white" are also to be found in the Hebrew Bible. Although Isaiah describes repentance as becoming white as snow, the punishment Miriam receives for having complained about Moses's black wife, through sibling envy not racism, is that "her own skin [was] turned white but with a disease," that is, "leprous *as white as snow"* (Num. 12:10).[49] Furthermore, when Melamed cites the writing of the Jewish sages he observes that they describe the "Torah as written 'in black fire,' (*Devorim Rabbah,* 3:13; *Song of songs Rabbah,* 5:9)," and quotes R. Berakhiah who said, "Consider the eye-ball; it is not through the white of it that one sees but through the black. Said the Holy One, blessed be He: 'I created light for you out of the darkness'" (*Vayikrah Rabbah,* 31:8; *Bamidbar Rabbah,* 15:5) (19).[50] Moreover, "*shahar* the Hebrew word for dawn, the beginning of light, and 'grew black' (Job 30:30) are exactly the same" (19).

For the sake of achieving a more processual openness toward occurrence of the words "black and white" it may, then, be helpful to be at least aware of Melamed's argument that "a close look at the [Hebrew] biblical attitude [toward] the black shows that it is descriptive and neutral, in special cases enigmatic and ambivalent, sometimes positive, and rarely, if ever, stereotypically, 'racist'"(55). This is in no way of course to suggest that Shakespeare may himself have been an Hebraist. Nonetheless, to register, within the originary text of the Bible itself, a less fixed binaric model, might contribute further to a disabling of the perpetuating effects of, in scholarship too, possible ongoing reiteration, albeit entirely unintentional, of this particular urge toward (discovery of) binary singularity.

III

Sulayman Al-Bassam's *Al-Hamlet Summit,*[51] was first performed at the Edinburgh International Fringe Festival in 2002 and at the International Festival of Experimental Theatre in Cairo.[52] Al-Bassam, born of an English mother and a Kuwaitan father, has lived for the past eighteen years in England and France. He uses Shakespeare's text as an opportunity to dramatize an unnamed present-day Middle Eastern state, presenting, by his own account, "a composite of many Arab problems that affect peoples from the Arabian Gulf to the Atlantic and beyond."[53] His play is concerned, as he indicates, with "the hypocrisy of rulers who act without sympathy for those whom they rule, who care only for the support of Western finance and armaments, who corruptly seek only the perpetuation of their own power." He jettisons Shakespeare's language in his version which is written in modern English. As a result of a Japanese commission, the play has subsequently been translated into Arabic.[54]

How does *The Al-Hamlet Summit* speak ethical action into being? Al-Bassam operates by way of the mode of unquestioning

binary singularity. He indicates that his play is everywhere informed by a sense of how the fate of his own present-day "Arab
world and its people" is inextricably linked to that of the West's.
Al-Bassam reproduces here and everywhere the powerful binary of
Arab and Westerner that already informs, as is well known, much
Western literature. Again, Claudius represents the oppressive ruler
depending on his power by way of Western support. This is suggested in the play, in turn, by the Arms Dealer, an amoral manipulator who deals expediently with anyone, irrespective of their
position or affiliation. After seeking the help of the Arms Dealer,
Claudius declares:

> Oh God: Petro dollars. Teach me the meaning of petro dollars. I have no
> other God than you, I am created in your image . . . I do not try to be
> pure: I have learnt so much filth, I eat filth, I am an artist of filth, I make
> mounds of human bodies sacrifices to your glory, I adore the stench of
> rotting peasants gassed with your technology . . . My nose is not so
> hooked is it, my eyes so diabolical as when you offered me your Wash-
> ington virgins and CIA opium. . . . Your plutonium your loans, your
> democratic filth that drips off your ecstatic crowds, I want them all.
> (21–22)

Al-Bassam's presentation of Fortinbras, who takes over from Claudius, replicates this binary of, on the one hand, exploitative and
vicious ruler (with vicious manipulator behind him) and, on the
other, exploited subjects. At the play's close, Fortinbras broods on
the possibilities of common or popular resistance he in turn, after
Claudius, is likely to face: "it won't be easy, terrorism is not yet
defeated, but the pipeline will be completed within a year" (29).
The word "terrorism" is used here by him to characterize potential
resistance. The play argues that corrupt rulers all use the word or
its variants in order to demonize or interpellate any opponent of
their own corrupt rule. Only after dreaming of the "pipeline" that
will secure his own riches and position does he proceed, hypocriti-
cally to outline a rhetoric of altruism, offered by way of a string of
notably mundane and predictable formulations, "hunger will be
eradicated, the homeless will find refuge, the old will die, and the
young will never forget, the poor will find wealth and this barren
land will be seen to bloom"(29).

In its own concern with the word "terrorism," too, the play thus
also manifests the predilection for unquestioned binary singularity.
In this Al-Bassam relies as well on a binary of "terrorist" and "vic-

tim," although it is true that he does counteridentify or invert this, as Peter Smith has remarked.[55] He does so, firstly, as mask for capitalist Arab or Western economic exploitation and, as I have just noted, as a term to demonize or interpellate any kind of democratic political opposition. Secondly, he relies on the binaric terms as, inversely, indicee of political and ethical purification or liberation. Thus Al-Bassam inverts conventional structurations of "innocent victim" in one of what are several direct allusions to the Palestinian/Israeli conflict in the play, as when Ophelia, dressed in the clothing of fundamentalist Islam declares: "The one who has turned me into a refugee has made a bomb of me . . . I will ex-press with [*sic*] my body what [I cannot] express [in] politics . . . So I go to my God pure in my soul in my dignity I am pure" (25–6).[56] Hamlet, particularly, is given a fiercely retaliatory narrative, again manifesting the urge to binary singularity in the equation, corrupt persecutor/exploiter on the one hand, and purified persecuted/exploited on the other:

i.   I will clean this land, I will make it pure . . . I will cleanse it for you . . . I will clean it, I will purge it, blood will flow, I will make blood flow in torrents. I swear in my father's name, I swear in the name of Allah. (16)

ii. The only way to change the geography of a conflict is to have infantry on the ground firing bullets into flesh. (22)

iii. From Allah we emerge and to Allah we return. Run, blood, across the sewers and the graves, stop up the mouths of vermin and hypocrites, the squall that begins in the East moves with mighty power over the seas. (23)

iv. I bear witness that there is no God but Allah and that Mohammed is his messenger. I Hamlet, son of Hamlet am the rightful heir to this nation's throne. My rule will crush the fingers of thieving bureaucrats, neutralize the hypocrites, tame the fires of debauchery that engulf our cities and return our noble people to the path of God. Our enemies comprehend only the language of blood for this, the time for the pen has passed and we enter the era of the sword . . . Let it be so and may God raise the profile of His martyrs! (28)

IV

What to some extent may be startling here is the proximation of that aspect of a yearning for binary singularity to be found in the early-modern *Timber of Discoveries,* as well as in some uses of the words "black" and "white" in *Hamlet,* to the search here, in the early twenty-first-century anti-Western *Al-Hamlet Summit,* for a singular purity in response to what the play in turn also seeks to register as a singular (again) injustice. This proximity collapses assumptions based on traditional structurations of difference between "East" and "West."

In the face of identification of the teleology of binary singularity to be found in each of the three disparate texts I have glanced at, then, how helpful might the processual mode of reading be? Ewan Fernie seems to touch on this problem when, on the one hand, he registers, in *Hamlet,* language that speaks the messy compromises of human life, but, on the other hand, discerns in it also a language that speaks what he calls a "militant spirituality," one that "seeks emancipation" and an "alternative world" with "real political potential."[57] Fernie himself recognizes that "at this historical juncture, any intellectual engagement with militant spirituality risks being misinterpreted as an endorsement of terrorism" (12). This disclaimer notwithstanding, in his reading of Hamlet in the last act of the play he moves beyond the proscriptions such a form of speaking might enjoin, attempting to discern from what Hamlet says, an "immersion of divinity in the messy human element"[58] which, he argues, enables Hamlet "to act [nonetheless] in favour of the absolute even as a compromised agent in a compromised world" (203):

> Once Hamlet has committed himself to "divinity" rather than the furious spirit of a murdered father, the play dramatizes the enabling power of a complete commitment. After his mystical experience, Hamlet, like Abraham is willing to do whatever is required, and without Abraham's "pang"—which suggests Shakespeare went further than Kierkegaard beyond ordinary good and evil. As if to stress the historical potential of spirituality, Hamlet's mystical commitment to a "special providence" is inseperable from a commitment to intervening in time. His god of "rashness" plunges ethical idealism into the flux and chance of history, abolishing a separate sphere of ethics. Only a pledge to the absolute can combine the violence of a specific commitment with the assurance of doing right. (204)

In this passage, Fernie raises an interesting concept of spiritually valid "rashness" of action. What he writes appears in part as a reading of the final scenes of *Hamlet* through a prism of the "terrorist" as "liberator"—as in Al-Bassam. If this is so, what may be crucially important is the fact that Hamlet's "rashness" does not entail entering the situation with the deliberate intention of killing whoever may be in his path. Laertes's "rashness" takes us much closer to such a stance in that he has with Claudius—"rashly" with regard also to the well-being of his soul, the play's Christianity, in a different sense, seems to have it—agreed to smear his sword with poison, that is, secretly to bear a lethal weapon that will murder Hamlet. Here, his target is, admittedly, not "anyone" but specifically the imagined enemy Hamlet himself, though it is true that such a position might as easily include a contention (or an urge to binaric singularity) that, argues that anyway, all "innocent" targets are in fact "guilty." Furthermore, neither Hamlet nor Laertes construct what they are doing as actively suicidal in nature. I take it that Fernie is aware of all of this when he concedes what he calls a "sinister" potential to his unfolding point. But such distinctions in the matter of "rashness"—as well as the separate equally important meditation upon the issue of "accident" in the play—need in this regard, perhaps, further attention.

What I find deeply troubling in Fernie's language, despite its qualifications, is its persisting connection to the tradition of speaking I have been tracing, to that part of it that seeks to construct out of the rich darkness—(blackness?)—of multiple partly unknown, complex, often surprisingly proximate experiences and predicaments one single light of commitment that will cleanse and in its particular image remake bright (or "white"?) the universe. Writing in my present location of Israel-Palestine invites me—leaving this color code, if that were only possible, aside—to yearn for and recognize an absolute need for commitment to absolute justice. But I have learned simultaneously to doubt the human speaking on all sides that articulates this: an ongoing reiteration of various urges toward binary singularity, noticeable as I have suggested in this essay in the disparate texts I have glanced at. I do not know if focus on a (Tswana) processual understanding of ethical human action can better help us to move beyond the boundaries of one or other kind of binary singularity—help us to conceptualize who we are or what is to be done in a different way entirely—but at the least, it frames and sharpens understanding of the potential human (animal?) deadliness in this persisting, so far apparently inescapable, binaric predilection toward, in "human" speaking, a ferocious singularity.

Notes

1. William Shakespeare, *Hamlet,* ed. Harold Jenkins, Arden Shakespeare edition (London: Methuen, 1982) 277. All quotations from the play are taken from this edition.

2. Erica Fudge, *Perceiving Animals: Humans and Beasts in Early Modern English Culture* (Urbana: University of Illinois Press, 2002) 65, 1 (my emphasis).

3. Cited in Ibid., 75.

4. Howard Brenton, *The Romans in Britain* (London: Methuen, 1981).

5. Tony Davies, *Humanism* (London: Routledge, 1997).

6. Ben Jonson, *Timber or Discoveries Made vpon Men and Matter: As they have flow'd out of his daily Reading, or had their refluxe to his peculiar Notion of the Times,* London, in *Ben Jonson,* ed. C. H. Herford and Percy and Evelyn Simpson, vol. 8 (Oxford: Oxford University Press, 1970), 621. All quotations are from this edition.

7. See John L. Comaroff and Simon Roberts, *Rules and Processes: The Cultural Logic of Dispute in an African Context* (Chicago: University of Chicago, 1981); Martin Orkin, *Local Shakespeares: Proximations and Power* (London: Routledge, 2005).

8. Herford and Simpson, *Ben Jonson,* 563.

9. We are by now well attuned to the discursive privileging of the masculine in the quotations on speech and speaking evident in the quotations I began with, and equally well versed in registering here the misogyny in Jonson's feminization of fortune.

10. See Alan Sinfield, *Faultlines: Cultural Materialism and the Politics of Dissident Reading* (Berkeley: University of California Press, 1992).

11. See Joseph Bristow, *Sexuality* (London: Routledge, 1997).

12. Davies, *Humanism,* 100.

13. William Shakespeare, *Hamlet,* ed. Ann Thompson and Neil Taylor, (London: Arden Shakespeare edition, Thomson Learning, 2006).

14. Ibid., 177 fn146. Citation of proverbs is followed by proverb number in the dictionary mentioned, and then date of first cited usage. See R. W. Dent, *Shakespeare's Proverbial Language: an Index,* Berkeley: University of California Press, 1981.

15. See M. P. Tilley, *A Dictionary of the Proverbs in England in the Sixteenth and Seventeenth Centuries* (Ann Arbor: University of Michigan Press, 1966).

16. Stephen Greenblatt et al. eds., *Henry IV Part 1,* Norton Shakespeare edition. (New York: Norton, 1997).

17. Janet Adelman, *Suffocating Mothers: Fantasies of Maternal Origin in Shakespeare's Plays Hamlet to The Tempest* (London: Routledge, 1992), 19, 14.

18. Barbara Johnson, *A World of Difference* (Baltimore: Johns Hopkins University Press, 1987), cited in Kim F. Hall, *Things of Darkness: Economics of Race and Gender in Early Modern England,* Ithaca: Cornell University Press, 1995, 2.

19. See also Hamlet's reprimand to the actor playing the murderer Lucianus to "leave thy damnable faces and begin . . . the croaking raven doth bellow for revenge" (3.2.247–48); Lucianus's "Thoughts black, hands apt, drugs fit, and time agreeing" (3.2.249); Claudius's reference to his own "bosom black as death" (3.2.67).

20. I refer briefly to these lines again below.

21. This is not to claim that patristic and homiletic traditions are innocent of racist effects.

22. Hall, *Things of Darkness,* 3.

23. See Arthur Little, *Shakespeare Jungle Fever: National-Imperial Re-Visions of Race, Rape, and Sacrifice,* (Stanford, CA: Stanford University Press, 2000); "'An Essence That's Not Seen': The Primal Scene of Racism in *Othello,*" *Shakespeare Quarterly* 44 (1993).

24. Peter Erickson, and Clark Hulse, *Early Modern Visual Culture: Representation, Race and Empire in Renaissance England* (Philadelphia: University of Pennsylvania Press, 2000).

25. See Hall, *Things of Darkness,* 3; Patricia Parker, "Black *Hamlet:* Battening on the Moor," *Shakespeare Studies,* 31, 2007; and Ania Loomba, *Shakespeare, Race, and Colonialism* (Oxford: Oxford University Press, 2002).

26. Parker, "Black *Hamlet,*" 127–64.

27. Shakespeare, *Hamlet,* ed. Thompson and Taylor, 33.

28. Thompson and Taylor, eds. *Hamlet,* note (164n) that the SD *Flourish,* which most editors including them include for the SD introducing act 1, scene 2, and emphasizing this power, is not in F/Q.

29. Catherine Belsey, *Culture and the Real* (London: Routledge, 2005), 9

30. "Poetry and spirituality are kin," Ewan Fernie argues, "in that both traffic beyond the known world." Ewan Fernie, introduction to *Spiritual Shakespeares* (London: Routledge, 2005), 4.

31. Catherine Belsey notes the psychoanalytic sense that if "we are speaking beings," we nonetheless inhabit a "silent or silenced exteriority, which is also inside us, and which we cannot symbolize, delimit, specify or know, even when we can name it the real'" (14). And John D. Caputo recently asseverates, in the context of current Shakespeare criticism, "There are more things in heaven and earth, Horatio, than are dreamt of in secular materialism, theology, or contemporary theory." John D. Caputo, foreword to *Spiritual Shakespeares,* ed. Ewan Fernie (London: Routledge, 2005), xix.

32. Jaroslav Pelikan, *Whose Bible Is It? A Short History of the Scriptures* (London: Penguin, 2005), writes, "the Authorized Version was by far the most successful of all English translations of the Bible" (174).

33. See Parker, "Black *Hamlet,*" 131.

34. Ibid., 154n15.

35. Michael Neill, *Issues of Death: Mortality and Identity in English Renaissance Tragedy* (Oxford: Oxford University Press, 1997), 146.

36. Parker, "Black *Hamlet,*" 131–32

37. See Avraham Melamed, *The Image of the Black in Jewish Culture: A History of the Other* (London: Routledge, 2003), 56–57, to whom I am grateful for much of the information that follows in this section.

38. Parker, "Black Hamlet," 132.

39. Melamed, *Image of the Black,* 55

40. See John Gillies, *Shakespeare and the Geography of Difference* (Cambridge: Cambridge University Press, 1994), 18–19, 25, 172–73.

41. From "Experiences and reasons of the Sphere, to proove all partes of the world habitable, and thereby to confute the position of the five ones" published in Richard Hakluyt's *The Principle Navigations,* and cited in Gillies, *ibid* 196n74.

42. Gillies, *Shakespeare and the Geography of Difference,* 194n57.
43. Used in Hebrew only later for the word "black."
44. Melamed, *Image of the Black,* 53
45. Ibid. 56, Melamed also writes, "the descriptions of the Queen of Sheba, another descendant of Cush, are positive and full of wonder. From the enigmatic statements about Moses's black wife one cannot be sure what Aaron and Miriam were complaining about. That it was her dark complexion is not at all clear from a literal understanding of the [Hebrew] Bible text, and indeed it puzzled the Sages deeply . . . Whatever the reason that Aaron and Miriam are said to have complained about, the Bible text as it stands shows that God and Moses both took the part of the black woman." Rabbi Joseph Telushkin, *Biblical Literacy* (New York: Harper Collins, 1997), 129–31, describes the story in the relevant passages from the Bible as follows: "Miriam and Aaron are surely not the only sister and brother in history to be periodically annoyed by the great success of a younger sibling. . . . The Bible describes a conversation between Miriam and Aaron in which they criticize Moses because of the Cushite woman he had married. Whether the woman in question is Moses's wife Tziporrah, or a second wife he might have taken we don't know, nor does the Torah seem to care. What matters is that Miriam and Aaron speak negatively about their brother . . . What seems to rankle them is that they are ranked as numbers two and three behind their brother . . . God summons the three to the Tent of Meeting where He appears in a cloud and instructs Aaron and Miriam to step forward . . . the text describes God as incensed (an anger that is reflected in the punishment Miriam soon suffers) . . . Miriam's body is stricken with flaky, snowy scales; it's some sort of horrific skin disease . . . Miriam's punishment suggests a biblical view that exalted and mighty figures are to be punished, just like everyone else, when they act badly."
46. Melamed, *Image of the Black,* observes that blacks are designated as "other and different, but rarely, if ever as inferior and animal-like" (58).
47. Although composed later, in the Second Temple period, and so more susceptible to current emergence of notions of the barbaric and of the "other."
48. See Melamed, *Image of the Black,* 43–44: He argues there for the line, "I am black (*shehorah*) and comely, O ye daughters of Jerusalem, as the tents of Kedar, as the curtains of Solomon: Look not upon me because I am black, because the sun hath looked upon me," that " 'black' and 'comely' are synonymous positive images, reinforcing the speaker's beauty in her own eyes. But she has to contend with the aesthetic norms that saw an advantage in light skin: hence the negative 'Look not upon me. . . '. Indeed, elsewhere (6.10) ideal feminine beauty is identified with white: 'Who is she that looketh forth as the morning, fair as the moon, clear as the sun?' The very existence of such norms indicates the existential dread of anything identified with a darker complexion: hence the efforts to avoid it, and the attempts to have as light a skin as possible, to keep poles apart from those with dark skin and as close as possible to the light-skinned people one wants to resemble. The subject here is suntanned skin, not natural blackness, that cannot become lighter. Shrinking aesthetically from suntanned skin indicates a dread that the individual who has such a complexion could be identified with one who is normally black—with all the negative aesthetic and moral connotations. The female voice in the *Song of Songs* takes a stand against such norms. Her opposition indicates just how rooted, how accepted they were: hence the ambivalence in the text. Possibly she, the village girl, the true daughter of Israel, is speaking out against attempts of her

city counterparts, the daughters of Jerusalem, to look like the gentiles, the fairer 'children of Japheth' and to accept their aesthetic standards, with all the theo-ethnic implications that their stance implies. She it is who represent the ethnic and religious pride of the dark-skinned and comely, an ancient version of 'Black is beautiful,' against the normative dilemmas of those who want to identify with the light-skinned designator, accepting the gentile world view'" (43). Melamed goes on to show how such ambiguities are lost as later biblical commentators, the sages, take on dominant attitudes within the cultures in which they find themselves.

49. Melamed, *Image of the Black,* 56, observes: "The sin was criticizing something concerning the black wife, and the punishment was whitening the skin of the sinner."

50. Melamed, *Image of the Black,* 19. See also scientific accounts of the colors black and white, their (equally positive) effects, and the relationship between them, all subsumed in metaphoric eagerness to convert their "differences" into fixed exclusive binaries.

51. I am very grateful to Peter Smith for kindly sending me a copy of the text of this play, shortly after it was first performed. All quotations from the play are taken from this text.

52. See also Sulayman Al-Bassam, *The Al-Hamlet Summit,* ed. Graham Holderness (Hertfordshire, University of Hertfordshire, 2006), 12–13.

53. See here, and for the quotation that follows, Sulayman Al-Bassam's introduction to the publication of the *Al-Hamlet Summit* in *Theatre Forum* (2003), http://www.zaoum.com/ALH/ALH.html.

54. Al-Bassam, *Al-Hamlet Summit,* ed. Holderness, 12.

55. See Peter J. Smith, "'Under Western Eyes: Sulayman Al-Bassam's *The Al-Hamlet Summit* in an Age of Terrorism,'" *Shakespeare Bulletin* 22, no. 4 (2004): especially for what follows, 72–73.

56. Holderness in his introduction Holderness ed. *Al-Hamlet Summit,* 14, refers on this point to Yvette K. Khoury, "'Glaring Stare': Middle Eastern Presentation of Ophelia," paper presented to the MLA 2005 Annual Convention Seminar on "Gender in Arabic Interpretations of Shakespeare."

57. Arguments anticipated in Ewan Fernie, "Shakespeare, spirituality and contemporary criticism," introduction to *Spiritual Shakespeares,* 8.

58. Ewan Fernie, "The last act, Presentism, spirituality and the politics of *Hamlet,*" in Fernie, *Spiritual Shakespeares,* 202.

REVIEW ARTICLES

Early Modern Women's Performance: Toward a New History of Early Modern Theater?

Clare McManus

Brown, Pamela Allen, and Peter Parolin (eds.), *Women Players in England, 1550–1660: Beyond the All-Male Stage* (Burlington, VT: Ashgate Press, 2005). 352 pp., $49.95. (paper)

Callaghan, Dympna (ed.), *The Impact of Feminism in English Renaissance Studies* (Basingstoke: Palgrave Macmillan, 2007). 346 pp., $84.95. (cloth)

Findlay, Alison, *Playing Spaces in Early Women's Drama* (Cambridge: Cambridge University Press, 2006). 260 pp., $99.00. (cloth)

Tomlinson, Sophie, *Women on Stage in Stuart Drama* (Cambridge: Cambridge University Press, 2005). 294 pp., $101.00. (cloth)

T HE FIRST SCENE OF *King Lear* stages a self-conscious moment of female performance at the heart of the dramatic canon. Asked to speak their love for their father, Lear's daughters are drawn not into a love-test but into an oratorical competition for the kingdom, the winner of which will be the speaker who offers the most skillful and satisfying variation on the theme "Which of you shall we say doth love us most[?]" (*King Lear,* 1.1.42). In Dominic Dromgoole's 2008 production for Shakespeare's Globe Theatre, Sally Bretton as Goneril went to great lengths to frame her oratorical performance. Clearing her throat, smoothing her dress with her hands, she made eye contact with each onstage character, ensuring their attention for the speech she was about to make. So framed, her oration was the spontaneous production of a royal woman educated and trained in the strategies, structures, and techniques of debate, and she herself was a courtier accustomed to performing at royal command. Watching her sisters' performances from behind a pillar, directing her asides at the Globe audience rather than that waiting for her onstage, Jodie McNee's Cordelia pondered how to bring variety to a competition into which she would enter last. Her line, "What shall Cordelia speak? Love and be silent" (1.1.53), here became the thoughts of a performer looking for novelty, seeking for a formal turn to undermine her sisters' productions and win the competition for herself. And here is the catastrophe of Cordelia's performance. It is not that she is silent, for on the contrary, in the public, courtly section of the scene she is by far the most vocal of the three female characters; it is not that she says nothing but that she says "Nothing" (1.1.81) and stakes her claim to the kingdom with a self-conscious performance of unornamented sincerity and plain-speaking which in this courtly context fails her badly. Her fatal mistake is in her choice of register, and her failure to demonstrate the linguistic dexterity required of the female courtier. In this scene, Cordelia is less a truth-teller than a woman who misjudges the requirements of her rank and launches on a risky performance that badly backfires. This gap between rhetorical expectation and execution, and her refusal to produce the variations on the theme that Lear requires—"Nothing will come of nothing: speak again" (1.1.82)—condemns her. Furthermore, this reading suggests that the British court's mistake is not an undervaluing of sincerity, but the failure to properly educate its youngest royal woman to be a successful orator, courtier, and future ruler.

At the opening of this most canonical of plays, Shakespeare brings the figure of the female orator to the all-male stage.[1] In the metatheatrical orations of the elder sisters are the traces of the verbally dexterous English royal and courtly woman, so recently embodied in Elizabeth I herself. The royal woman was required to speak publicly and to speak well.

And yet this eloquent woman is not only English, for the opening scene of *King Lear* stages a fascinating intersection of national performance traditions. In its courtly speakers, the scene conjures the figure of the female orator of Italy or France, women such as Claude-Catherine de Clermont, the Maréschale de Retz, and Madeleine de l'Aubespine, Madame de Villeroy, who, as Julie D. Campbell's chapter in Brown and Parolin's collection demonstrates, were famed for their verbal dexterity, their supple manipulation of figures and register, and their ability to outshine male orators in formal debates and informal conversations in courtly salons and academies.[2] Responses to these women, of course, vacillated between admiration and condemnation, and *King Lear* reflects just this in Cordelia's horror of her sisters' "glib and oily art" (1.1.229) and in the play's own lack of faith in a theatricality it connects to feminine inconstancy through the treachery of Goneril and Regan, its successful performers. Nonetheless, in a play seemingly bound by the limits of island Britain and by the Dover cliffs over which Gloucester will later believe he has fallen, this "British" play is shadowed by the figure of the continental female orator. Cordelia's performance, of course, loses her the crown of England and the right to live within its bounds but it also gains her the crown of France. On her return to England and reunion with her father (4.6), her continental education seems to have trained her in the requirements of queenship, and gives her access to a language that combines a lack of ornament with the expression of true compassion. At their reunion, she can speak to her father as she could not before and it is not only the changes in Lear which make this possible, but those in Cordelia as well.

While it would be stretching a point to suggest that Dromgoole's production was in dialogue with recent work on early modern women's performance, my reading of this opening scene does demonstrate the extent to which *King Lear*'s inherently self-conscious theatricality centers on its female characters and on a broader sense of female engagement with performance. A growing body of work on the early modern theatrical woman is establishing the extent to which English theater audiences and playwrights found contexts for the productions of the all-male stages of the London playhouses in the theatrical women of England and Europe. In addition to interrogating the relationship of feminism to this project, this interdisciplinary scholarship also attends to the inherently transnational nature of women's relationship to the English stage, making very clear the fact that those stages cannot accurately be read in isolation from Continental practice. After all, in *King Lear* we have an instance of the English stage's openness to European influence at the very heart of the English canon.

With all this in mind, it remains the case that an interpretation of Shakespearean tragedy, however briefly sketched, is not the typical starting point for a discussion of studies of early modern female performance. Though Pamela Allen Brown and others are starting to do this work, the emerging body of scholarship which the books reviewed here represent more typically focus on marginal forms of theater and performance (comedy rather than tragedy—or, in Tomlinson's case, Caroline rather than "high Renaissance" tragedy— the masque rather than the stage play) and often on yet still more critically marginalized forms of women's engagement with early modern performance cultures (women as dancers, singers, linen traders, mountebanks, rope dancers, or ballad sellers).[3] Yet these works raise the issue, both explicitly and indirectly, of the relationship of feminist investigations of early modern theater—and indeed of feminism itself—to the canon. Indeed, the decision to open this essay with *King Lear* raises the all-important questions of whether the feminist project is best served attending to the canonical or marginal, whether attending to the marginal cedes the aesthetic centerground, or whether the time is ripe for that centerground to be reshaped and reenvisioned through exposure to the marginal.[4] The recent crop of scholarship on women's performance demonstrates the advantages of both approaches.

Sophie Tomlinson's *Women on Stage in Stuart Drama* is a rich, beautifully written book that teases out what its author calls the "pre-history of the actress." Positing a cultural poetics of the seventeenth-century theatrical woman, the book cuts across arbitrary period boundaries and generic divisions to outline the contours of a particularly prominent kind of English female player. A line of courtly women's performance emerges that transforms the Restoration from a watershed into an integral part of the contours of seventeenth-century theater. Moreover, Tomlinson is very aware of the impact of this newly emerging tradition of female performance, offering clear instances of the differences that accounting for women's cultural activities and for the tropes used to represent the theatrical woman on the stages of the London playhouses can make to our understanding of early modern theatre. In analyzing the cohabitation of Caroline courtly women's performance with the theater of Jonson, Shirley, and Ford, for instance, Tomlinson resists the normative status of the all-male stage, reinterpreting its productions within this alternative context of female theatricality. As her goal of outlining "a new poetics of female performance" suggests, Tomlinson's focus is on the creative role of the theatrical woman in shaping the aesthetics of such complex productions as masques and pastorals as well as those of canonical drama. In dealing head-on with the aesthetic productions of the all-male stage, and in demonstrating them to be part of a culture imbued with female performance, Tomlinson's scrupulous readings offer new visions of seventeenth-century plays and a new sense of the history of seventeenth-century theater.

Pamela Allen Brown and Peter Parolin's edited collection, *Women Players in England, 1550–1660: Beyond the All-Male Stage,* takes a different tack. This collection of essays demonstrates the sheer range of materials and approaches available to scholars of this subject and, in its commitment to deal with central and marginal, elite and nonelite productions, is in an immensely productive dialogue with the work of scholars like Tomlinson. This eclectic collection moves in exciting and sometimes surprising ways. Some essays such as Rachel Poulsen's on *Twelfth Night* and Julie D. Campbell's essay, above, pay close attention to the Shakespearean canon. These chapters sit next to important reassessments of well-known theatrical women such as Natasha Korda's recontextualization of Moll Frith's anomalous appearance on the side of the Fortune stage against her entirely unexceptional status as a female worker in the linen trade, a reading which revises the relationship of the London playhouse stages to the economic world surrounding them. Other chapters reconsider the texts of the all-male playhouse stages in the light of female cultural production: Jean E. Howard reinterprets the theatrical codes of feminine representation in Heywood's *If You Know Not Me, You Know Nobody,* and Bruce R. Smith teases out the implications for a play such as *Othello* of the feminine ballad form and its intersections with the passions. Further essays deal with distinct modes of performance: for instance, Melinda J. Gough writes on Henrietta Maria and amateur female performance, Bella Mirabella on the female mountebank, and M. A. Katritzky on the visual depiction of the commedia actress. With an exemplary insistence on placing the canonical next to the marginal and a commitment to expand the focus of this field of study beyond the activities of the female elite, Brown and Parolin create a dialogue between well-known and more obscure texts which illuminates the mutual effects of each. In so doing, they create an invigorating collection that is far more than the sum of its parts. This structure also tempers the risks inherent in embracing the canonical centerground of being swallowed whole by the model of "Shakespeare and . . . ," while refusing to cede that centerground to nonfeminist investigations.

The impact of this conversation between the central and the marginal is perhaps most clear in James Stokes's stunning synthesis of archival recovery and polemic which opens Brown and Parolin's collection. Outlining the implications of his work for the REED volumes for Somerset and Lincolnshire, Stokes offers a new image of women's relationship to drama which counters a focus on the playhouse institution and disrupts any sense that the English stage's exclusion of women was something easy or seamless. In so doing, he makes a pivotal contribution to a newly emerging history of early English theater which is utterly changed by its inclusion of women. Analyzing what he calls the "copious evidence of dual and co-equal presence by men and women" within the socioreligious guilds prior to their abolition by Edward VI, Stokes compares this "universal suffrage" with the repression of women within later sixteenth-century theatrical cultures (Brown and Parolin, 41). The comparison is instructive and, Stokes insists, should change our perspective of these later cultures: "The suppression, repression, pursuit and exile of women from the stage in sixteenth-century England needs to be seen not as the norm of that culture but as the aberrant historical moment that it was—a genuine religious and political revolution that descended into an unspeakably vicious culture war focusing on the most vulnerable elements of that culture" (Brown and Parolin, 41). This is a remarkable statement in an essay worthy of a broad readership.

The methodological and ideological ramifications of these issues are grist to the mill for Dympna Callaghan's important edited collection, *The Impact of Feminism in English Renaissance Studies.* This book does not focus on female performance throughout, but its tussle with the contours of the past and future of feminist work on the early modern deals head-on with the field of women's performance as a test case for feminism and raises profound questions for the future of the discipline. Callaghan's introduction opens with a witty and telling exposition of the profits and pitfalls of particular approaches to the study of the early modern theatrical woman. Outlining what would seem to be the dream find of a scholar of early modern women's performance, a performative ritual which depended on a woman's presence and a woman's voice for its success, which seems to demonstrate women's agency but which may also express nothing more than female subjugation, Callaghan gives two readings of the ceremony of marriage from the Book of Common Prayer which remind historicist critics that we should be at our most cautious when we find what we are looking for. Callaghan's lesson is twofold: warning against ignoring the pernicious effects of patriarchy, she reserves equal skepticism for those critics who see women only as the victims of a social system rather than its participants. Seeking a mode of feminist criticism which combines the best of each position, she proposes the immensely useful category of the "excluded participant" to describe women's standing within an early modern social hierarchy that certainly required their presence and their participation yet undeniably necessitated their subjection—but not all at once and not all in the same way. In this way, Callaghan calls for "a valuably complex picture of women's simultaneous participation in *and* exclusion from early modern culture" (Callaghan, 7), for "nuanced" thinking rather than the occupation of entrenched positions, and for a clear-sighted reading of the available evidence even while the archives are scoured for more.

One of Callaghan's targets is a utopian mode of revisionist feminist inquiry that, to her mind, ignores the clear evidence of women's oppression. She reserves particular criticism for those scholars of early modern women's performance who seek to recuperate the exclusive zone of the all-male stage for the theatrical woman, using the exceptional woman—almost invariably Moll Frith—as proof that there was no such thing as an all-male stage. There certainly was such a thing as the all-male stage of the London playhouses, and the best work on early modern women's performance does not aim to suggest that women were actors in the London city theaters prior to 1660. Instead, this work exposes "the all-male stage" for the cultural and historiographical formation that it is, and outlines the work that it has done in criticism of early modern theater. This, then, is not a project to insert women into an existing theater history, but to change the terms on which that history is written: to recontextualize "the all-male stage" (now with scare quotes of its own) as only one possible performance venue, and, above all, one that was even more anomalous within its own culture for its exclusion of women than we have previously realized. Of course, one would not want to give the impression that the London playhouses were buildings under constant siege from women clamoring to perform on their stages: the early modern period bore little resemblance to *Shakespeare in Love* and, as she reminds us in her introduction, Callaghan has already made the pertinent point in *Shakespeare Without Women* (2000) that women did not press to be included on the all-male stage precisely because that stage was not a reputable space. To this picture, though, must be added the alternative stages and playing spaces—the masquing stage, the aristocratic house—that were indeed reputable and the stages, like the mountebank platform or the ballad seller's pitch, which were the product of economic necessity. In this way, Stokes's recognition of the sheer, strange anomalousness of the all-male stage and a commitment to recontextualizing it within the theatrical world beyond the playhouse walls is a crucial starting point for future research.

Alison Findlay's *Playing Spaces in Early Women's Drama* perhaps falls into Callaghan's revisionist category. Like Brown and Parolin, Findlay's range is expansive: though she focuses on the cultural elite, she discusses women's participation in theater as writers, producers, and performers from 1376 to 1705 and so admirably works across previously restrictive categories. Indeed, Findlay presents some wonderfully allusive material: her identification of the potential of a performance of Mary Sidney Herbert's *Antonie* (1591) at Wilton "in rooms once frequented by Philip Sidney" (25) is a reading rich in the intersections of the canonical and the marginal, the cultural production of men and women, the mutual interaction of each, and the revelation of something new about each as a result. However, in such generalized claims as "playing spaces (settings and venues) that celebrated sororal communities were invariably subversive forms of early women's drama," Findlay risks simplifying her materials for the sake of a coherent narrative (Findlay, 148). More representative of Findlay's approach, perhaps, is the account of Robert White's 1617 masque *Cupid's Banishment,* which was danced for Anna of Denmark at Greenwich Palace by the schoolgirls of the Ladies' Hall. Focusing on the masque's female performers, Findlay's decision to deal with this masque in her chapter on "Sororities" rather than "Courts" is a fruitful repositioning. However, while she does briefly mention the presence of the characters of Cupid and the King of the Bean, her account otherwise almost completely excises the professional and amateur male performers who populated the antimasque and main masque. This is strange partly because the masque itself survives only in a manuscript copy preserved by Richard Browne, who played the role of Diana, but more importantly this approach obscures this masque's truly radical aspects. *Cupid's Banishment* produces a theatrical discourse of female education in praise of the queen consort and tests the boundary between masquing and playing in the speech of Ann Watkins as Fortune but, crucially, it does all of this via a mixed rather than a single-sex theatrical economy, refusing to separate versions of feminine theatricality off from its masculine counterparts.[5] In neglecting the contribution of male performers in favor of a somewhat overstated idea of female community, Findlay in fact underplays the complexity of White's masque and its importance within both the court of Anna of Denmark and the history of women's performance more generally.

Despite their distinct focuses and investments, the works under review here have several features in common. Above all, these studies make very clear that the archival project is far from complete and that, with the ongoing publication of the monumental REED project, further evidence of the ubiquity of the female performer emerges by the year. Each of the books reviewed here are testament to how crucial it is to remain alive to the possibilities offered by new archival finds. Of course, recovery is only part of the story: it matters enormously what we do with these documents once we have found them. After all, there are instances of female performance in E. K. Chambers's 1923 *Elizabethan Stage* which have gone unstudied over many years, so accessibility is clearly only part of the story.[6] But the exemplary work of scholars like Brown, Korda, Stokes, and Tomlinson points the way for the teasing out of the effects of new materials on better-known theatrical texts, and for this refreshed history of early modern theater. Tomlinson's work is particularly stimulating for its careful avoidance of a progression from the Jacobean to the Restoration theater that would simply reinscribe previous categories of theater history. Implicitly endorsing the point made by Brown and Parolin that the Restoration's self-interested presentation of the actress as a novelty has skewed our sense of the early modern stage (Brown and Parolin, 18), Tomlinson reintegrates the Restoration into seventeenth-century theater, presenting it not as an endpoint but an integral part of the century's theatricals. In doing so, she also avoids a straightforward causality that might read the Restoration actress as a direct result of, say, Caroline courtly theater or Caroline roles for boy actors as a direct response to Henrietta Maria's court productions. Tomlinson's scrupulous attention to her sources and her skepticism of an overarching teleology does not offer easy answers or a clear sense of cause and effect, but her approach better does justice to the complexity of seventeenth-century theater, its reception, reactions, and

interactions than any straightforward, causal trajectory could. Indeed, all the books under review here share a productive skepticism of the conventional (if increasingly outmoded) divisions of
early modern theater history. In particular, Brown and Parolin's
introduction does an especially stylish job of demolishing—
"deconstructing" would be too polite—the milestone, the turning
point, or the female "first" as a means of constructing theater history (Brown and Parolin, 3–4). This demolition sits nicely alongside Natasha Korda's observation that while such markers may
seem to reveal the exceptional theatrical woman, they in fact endorse an exclusionist theater history without shifting its foundation and obscure the utterly unexceptional, ubiquitous theatrical
woman (Brown and Parolin, 71).

Frances E. Dolan's important contribution to Callaghan's collection, "Hermione's Ghost: Catholicism, the Feminine, and the Un-
dead," sees the purpose of the feminist project as being to add to
other forms and organizations of knowledge. She strongly resists
the ghettoization of feminism "through citation practices that suggest that scholarship on gender, women and sexuality yields
knowledge only on these topics and is only of interest to other specialists rather than to everyone working on politics or nationalism
or print culture more generally" (Callaghan, 230). She goes on to
argue that "gender is a question that might be asked even in studies
that are not 'about' it" (Callaghan, 231). Following Dolan's lead, it
should be clear that the ramifications of studies of early modern
women's performance are to be felt in the reshaping of the history
of early modern theater, with significant implications for scholars
of gender and of theater alike. The shared impulse of those working
in gender to look beyond the canonical can be instructive and can
bring to light new materials which should be integrated into studies of early modern theater.

Take, for instance, Terence Hawkes's productive reading of the
mechanicals' embedded play in act 5 of *A Midsummer Night's
Dream*. Taking the First Folio stage direction at the players' en-
trance to their courtly onstage audience, "Tawyer with a Trumpet
before them" (5.1.128), Hawkes reads this blast of the trumpet as
connecting its performer to "an expanded, non-discursive and non-
textual notion of stage performance whose roots reach to a level far
deeper than that plumbed by any modern drama." He then invokes
Robert Weimann in order to argue that there is a "tension between
that older inheritance and a newly emerging text-based notion of

drama, the grounding of the one we inherit."[7] Hawkes rightly interprets the rupture of this trumpet blast as an audible marker of the
transition into an embedded performance. However, nonverbal
performance modes like the blast of Tawyer's trumpet are not, as
Hawkes would have them, only older, primitive avatars of the sophisticated textual creations of the Shakespearean playhouse. As
the work of REED and others has shown, these forms coexisted
with the plays of the Globe stage: Tawyer's trumpet is a version of
the Globe trumpeter announcing the start of the play itself, or of the
town waits, or of musicians in the streets outside the playhouses.[8]
A willingness to account for the vibrant, perhaps more informal
theatrical activities beyond the playhouses can benefit those who
ask "the gender question" and those who do not. Here, it allows us
to begin to replace Hawkes's paradigm in which English theater
takes only from the English past with one in which that theater also
takes from its domestic present, revealing a broad rather than deep
model of early modern theater's relationship to its social context.
In this broad model, English theater is created in the intersections
of contemporary continental and domestic performers and performance modes, as in the simultaneous production by the boy
players of *King Lear* of female characters who are both eloquent English courtiers and the female leaders of French courtly salons.

Yet while attention to the archive is crucial, a healthy skepticism
and a careful attention to the structures and formal techniques of
these records are required at all times. In "Feminist Criticism and
the New Formalism: Early Modern Women and Literary Engagement," which was published after her untimely and tragic death in
late 2006, Sasha Roberts argues that formalist techniques should be
put to the service of feminism, tying a renewed attention to form to
an invigorated awareness of gender (Callaghan, 67–92). Roberts's
approach has much to recommend itself to those of us delving into
the rich findings of recent work in the archives: her focus on form,
rhetorical technique, and tone is crucial for a clear consideration of
the records of performance. The possibilities of such reading strategies are evident in Natasha Korda's chapter on the informal trade of
women working in and around the London playhouses (Callaghan,
259–80). Warning against the temptation to see women everywhere, to "assume that each example [in records of economic and
theatrical activity] is exemplary," Korda makes clear that "we must
also acknowledge that evidence of women working outside sanc-
tioned forms of trade may at times augment their numbers to suit

political purposes," since "informal female traders frequently served as convenient scapegoats" (Callaghan, 266). This formal engagement with the records of performance can lead to findings which, however counterintuitive, extend our knowledge of the practices and intersections of the various early modern stages. In my own work, I have interpreted John Harington's satirical invocation of female performance in his infamous letter on the drunken Theobalds entertainment of 1606 less as a transparent eyewitness account of performance than an invocation of the literary trope of the theatrical woman to criticize the court that supported such a performer—crucially, I argue, in the absence of the real thing.[9] Given that scholarship on the masque often depends on sources such as letters or diplomatic reports, that is, on eyewitness accounts and narrations after the fact, attention to their rhetorical and political strategies is crucial. Korda's work shows very clearly that such caution must also be extended to the rhetorical deployment of seemingly objective numbers. Although it is so obvious as to seem to go without saying, it is nonetheless worth stating that the feminist project requires an approach to the archives that blends close formal attention with a careful theorization of what we find there, for which we require reading strategies which formally engage with records of performance which are themselves the product of a gendered society.

In a subject which depends upon the interdisciplinary investigation of early modern drama, and upon asking what Pamela Allen Brown calls "rude, unsettling, and at times enlightening questions" of several disciplines at once (Callaghan, 171), the complexity of our evidence, whether it be the economic, the textual, the visual, or the bodily requires an equally sophisticated, varied, and theorized methodology to do it justice. Callaghan's interrogation of the potentials and pitfalls of the concept of agency is particularly fruitful here. Though she criticizes a scholarship that seeks female agency everywhere, Callaghan nonetheless does not deny its possibilities as an investigative category, and indeed it is raised implicitly or explicitly in all of these studies. As C. E. McGee has pointed out in his review of Alison Findlay's book, the French ambassador's description of Anna of Denmark in *The Masque of Beauty* (1608) as "the authoress of the whole" (Findlay, 126) is worthy of further investigation since it raises the thorny issue of the relationship of agency and performance.[10]

Certain readings of female playing might approach the female actor, player, dancer, masquer, musician and singer as "merely" the performers, however charismatic and skillful, however improvisatory, of another's script. There are hints of this sense of playing as a secondary activity in Jean Howard's analysis of the female characters of the all-male stage as "prosthetic creations, called into being by white paint, fabric, and pre-penned words" (Callaghan, 278). However, if we think of early modern authorship as a collaborative act embedded in social networks and mediating the influences, traditions, and tropes of previous literary works, and of dramatic texts as being fashioned anew in each performance and as inherently, institutionally collaborative, then the female performer—resituated against this context—is revealed as a cultural authority through the creation of meaning by embodied performance. It is here perhaps that studies of the early modern theatrical woman might engage more actively with the ramifications of the collaborative creation of meaning that takes place in theatrical production and which are teased out by scholars of present-day performance.[11]

Callaghan's own playful reading of the early modern Protestant marriage ceremony, for instance, is open to such an interpretation. Reading the impact of audience interjections and unruliness in the aisles, Callaghan is clear that the meaning of performance lies in its specificity (Callaghan, 8–9). Taking a lead from performance studies, then, one possible way forward is to depend less on the textual record of the marriage ceremony, which we might think of as a script from which the performance was created through the intersection of voice, body, gesture, and playing space. We might, then, work with evidence of how specific performers—male and female—manipulated or were constrained by their basic materials in their embodiment of the position of Callaghan's excluded participant. This would allow us to subject the concept of performance itself to a deep historicizing, and, in so doing, to further explore the idea and the gendered ramifications of agency. Possible questions include the issue of what constituted an early modern performance; whether specific instances of performance necessitated or created agency; of the dynamics of authorship in performances which relied upon the embodied presence of the performer; of the relationship of the performer to script and the ways in which that relationship was gendered?

My opening reading of *King Lear* and its importing of the continental female orator onto the English all-male stage suggests another vital direction for this research: a thoroughgoing consideration of the interactions and mutual transactions between the stages of England and Europe. In many ways, of course, there is nothing new at all about this suggestion, as is demonstrated in De-anne Williams's fascinating chapter on the relationship of the mid-twentieth-century scholar Frances Yates to feminism ("No Man's Elizabeth: Frances A. Yates and the History of History," Callaghan, 238–58). Williams characterizes Yates's impulse to look to Europe as an attempt to offer a reconstructive coherence after the disintegrative impact of the wars that destroyed Yates's family happiness and utterly changed the world around her. And while current scholarship on the early modern theater should avoid any totalizing impulse and remain alive to differences and discontinuities as well as shared practices and ideas, it seems very clear that interdisciplinary work on women's performance has to turn to Europe to broaden its frame of reference and to deal with its materials. As Pamela Allen Brown points out, it is the responsibility of feminism to look through and beyond prevailing organizations of knowledge and, just as this applies to disciplines, so too it applies to the organizing category of nation. Partly this is a requirement of the subject of inquiry: the figures of the foreign actress and foreign queen who shaped so much early work in the field, either as a point of comparison or contact with English practice, had to be traced through their own cultures and into that of England, requiring scholars to work across and between cultures. Karen Britland's work on the court of Henrietta Maria, for instance, is committed to exploring the interaction of French and English courtly cultures, and to revealing the operation of a supranational courtly elite whose communities cut across national boundaries. Her astonishment at scholars for whom a Henrietta Maria outside England is a Henrietta Maria who effectively ceases to exist is an excellent corrective to a somewhat myopic focus in studies of early modern theater which often narrow "England" so far down that it really means only "London."[12]

The writing of this refreshed theater history is moving apace. Even issues such as terminology, the all-important question of how we name the subject of our study, remain open to new developments, and these books are in productive disagreement on this issue. Brown and Parolin's category of the "female player," Tomlinson's focus on "female performance," and Findlay's deliberately inclusive definition of "early women's drama" all retain the potential to change in the light of new findings and discussions. In her reading of Shakespeare's *Twelfth Night* through *La Calandria* and

Gl'Ingannati, Rachel Poulsen invokes the concept, indebted to Judith Butler, of the "actress effect" to express the conjuring of the foreign actress on the English all-male stage. This is an extremely effective means of considering the openness of the English stage to Continental practice, but even here, as the reading of the sisters of *King Lear* with which I opened this essay shows, the term "actress" is too limited to define the practice of theatrical women, even continental ones. The early modern woman constantly oversteps the bounds of "the actress," moving into broader fields of cultural and theatrical activity. "Actress" is a risky term, too, because it implies that scholars of women's performance should seek out a female counterpart to the male actor: in this way it replicates a dangerously revisionist structure which threatens either to exclude the bulk of women's theatrical activities from consideration or to claim that they were everywhere. Indeed, the lack of an English "actress" to parallel the English actor has, in the work of early- and mid-twentieth-century criticism at least, enshrined the all-male stage as the locus classicus of early modern theater and so obscured the vast range of other theatrical labors and practices with which women were indeed engaged.

That said, though, the "actress" remains a potent concept, one which Tomlinson's most recent work has found operating in English theatrical culture as early as 1608. As Tomlinson outlines, Gerardine, the hero of Lording's *Family of Love* (pub. 1608), utters the phrase "To be an Actresse in the Comedy." Tomlinson connects this to Gerardine's "origins in the classical trickster figure, perhaps with a nod at the Italian tradition of the *commedia dell'arte,* in which women were prominent performers."[13] In demonstrating that this term was available to describe what at least some women might have done on a stage, Tomlinson also emphasizes English knowledge of the commedia actresses and the possibility of comparison between theatrical cultures, all of which renders the English experience of the boy actor still less normative, still more anomalous.

The work on early modern women's performance represented here rises admirably to the challenge of Callaghan's call for complexity and nuance in scholarship on early modern gender. The authors reviewed here are clear that their research represents the beginning of the project on early modern women's performance and that we are reading the first fruits of research rather than the final form of the subject. The real impact of this work, one might argue, is in its collective force: its impact lies in the juxtaposition of books on women's elites with essays on the commercial activities of poorer women, with a refreshed appreciation of the vibrant contexts for commercial and informal playing in the towns and cities of early modern England and Europe, with the analysis of the difference this all makes to canonical drama. Rather than lamenting, with the authors of the recent *O.D.N.B.* entry on Anna of Denmark, that "much modern literary scholarship has overemphasized the queen's role in promoting and performing court masques," we should recognize that any work published so far is only the first expression of a much larger project, the full outlines of which we can at the moment only sketch.[14] Given time, this scholarship may offer a much-changed history of early modern theater.

Notes

1. This argument is laid out in more detail in my "Sex, Gender and Performance on the Early Modern Stage," in *The Palgrave Guide to Early Modern Women's Writing,* ed. Suzanne Trill (Basingstoke: Palgrave Macmillan, forthcoming).

2. Julie D. Campbell, "'Merry, nimble, stirring spirit[s]': Academic, Salon and Commedia dell'arte Influence on the *Innamorate* of *Love's Labour's Lost,*" in Brown and Parolin, *Women Players,* 145–70.

3. For work on women as mountebanks, in addition to Bella Mirabella's "'Quacking Delilahs': Female Mountebanks in Early Modern England and Italy," Brown and Parolin, *Women Players,* 89–105, see M. A. Katritzky, *Women, Medicine and Theatre, 1500–1750: Literary Mountebanks and Performing Quacks* (Burlington, VT: Ashgate Press, 2007).

4. I am indebted to Pamela Allen Brown and Melinda Gough for their discussion of these issues at a meeting of the *Theater Without Borders Working Group on Early Modern Transnational Theater* (Kadir Has University, Istanbul, 2005).

5. Clare McManus, *Women on the Renaissance Stage: Anna of Denmark and Female Masquing in the Stuart Court (1590–1619)* (Manchester: Manchester University Press, 2002), 182–99.

6. For one such instance see my "Women and English Renaissance Drama: Making and Unmaking 'The All-Male Stage,'" *Literature Compass* 4, no. 3 (2007): 784–96.

7. Terence Hawkes, *Shakespeare in the Present* (London: Routledge, 2002), 110.

8. See David Lindley, *Shakespeare and Music* (London: Arden Critical Companions, 2006), 90; David Galloway, ed., *Records of Early English Drama: Norwich, 1540–1642* (Toronto: University of Toronto Press, 1984), especially app. 6 (352–54) and intro. (xxxvii–xli).

9. See McManus, "When is a Woman not a Woman? Or, Jacobean Fantasies of Female Performance (1606–1611)," *Modern Philology* 105, no. 3 (2008): 437–74.

10. C. E. McGee, *Shakespeare Quarterly* 59, no. 1 (2008): 103–6.

11. See, for instance, Bridget Escolme's study of metatheatricality in productions of Shakespeare, *Talking to the Audience: Shakespeare, Performance, Self* (London: Routledge, 2005).

12. Karen Britland, *Drama at the Courts of Queen Henrietta Maria* (Cambridge: Cambridge University Press, 2006), 192. This kind of work is also under way in groups like *Theater Without Borders: The Working Group on Early Modern Transnational Drama:* see http://www.nyu.edu/projects/theaterwithoutborders/.

13. Sophie Tomlinson, "A Jacobean Dramatic Usage of 'Actress,'" *Notes and Queries* 55, no. 3 (2008): 1–2.

14. Maureen M. Meikle and Helen Payne, "Anne (1574–1619)," *Oxford Dictionary of National Biography,* http://www.oxforddnb.com/view/article/559.

Center or Margin:
Revisions of the English Renaissance
in Honor of Leeds Barroll

JOHN DRAKAKIS

IN THE INTRODUCTORY CHAPTER to his *Politics, Plague and Shakespeare's Theater: The Stuart Years* (1991), Leeds Barroll lamented the tendency of biographies of Shakespeare to reify "presuppositions about historical causation," thereby resulting in "the freezing of the number of available viewpoints that might otherwise be brought to bear" (7). Barroll's call for the rereading of documents and for the rethinking of patterns of causation comes in the wake of Foucault's account of the "tactical polyvalence of discourses"[1] and of the range of theoretical positions that emphasized discontinuities, instabilities, and the exclusionary forces that underpin the operations of language. In the process, Barroll revisited, and augmented, the stock of those very documents that traditional (and even some revisionary) criticism has reduced to a "uniform" reading. It is precisely this openness, combined with an undiminished appetite for the reinvestigation and the reevaluation of what has hitherto passed for "fact" and critical "truth." that Lena Cowen Orlin's edited collection celebrates. It builds on what Barroll himself inveigled against when he spoke of the sketching of "historical figures making intelligent plans to implement intelligent decisions, experiencing consequences fully anticipated and hoped for" (ibid., 12). Indeed, his initiation and indefatigable editing of major journals such as *Shakespeare Studies,* and *Medieval and Renaissance Drama in England,* his founding of the Shakespeare Association of America, his presence at its annual conferences, combined with the regular appearance of his own further publications, all indicate an exemplary and continually adventurous intellectual energy. Meanwhile, the impressively well-organized Shakespeare Association of

America continues to provide a major international focus for Shakespeare Studies, and has sustained its mission to encourage and provide a nurturing environment for young scholars, while *Shakespeare Studies* continues to adventure beyond the existing boundaries of the discipline. Orlin's collection is an appropriate way to honor the achievement of a major Shakespeare scholar, but it is also a testimony to those various avenues of critical and historical investigation that Barroll has been, in large measure, responsible for stimulating and encouraging.

This collection is organized under four headings, representing consecutively, the title of a paper, a graduate seminar theme, a chapter title of one of Barroll's seminal books, and a book title: "England at the Margins," "Researching the Renaissance," "The Human Figure on the Stage," and "Artificial Persons." In some cases, as in the opening essay by Peter Stallybrass under the heading "England at the Margins" it was one of Barroll's own Shakespeare Association of America seminars (Montreal, 2000) that provided both the occasion and the stimulus. But in others, the essays appear to have been specially commissioned for the volume, and have been grouped under one of these four headings: each group a testimony to the prescience of Barroll's own published work, and to the enduring challenge it continues to provide.

Peter Stallybrass's "Marginal England: The View from Aleppo" aims to perform a strategy familiar to readers of Barroll's writing: an adjustment of perspective, of the kind that some recent examples of postcolonial criticism have taken much further to the point of disturbing the hegemonic foundations of post-Enlightenment historiography. Stallybrass does not quite go that far, since, following a dialectic that he himself has been partly responsible for making familiar, of the relationship between marginality and symbolic centrality, his concern is with some of the ways in which "the Mediterranean figured centrally in the English imaginary" (29). The textual spur for his inquiry is the hero's final speech in *Othello* in which a suicide is figured as the resolution of a conflict "in *Aleppo* once" between "a *Malignant* and a *Turband Turke*" and "*Venetian*." This convergence of "malignancy" and geographical location is, however, not consistent, since, in the later play, *Macbeth,* Aleppo is represented as "a merchant city where one might hope to evade the malignancy whose normal place of residence is Scotland" (27). In the one instance the geographical location of malignancy is the Orient, and in the other it is the Occident. Or to put it more precisely, a "margin" of the kingdom of James I, whose destructively libidinal force is *imagined* as the direction from which a "traduction" of the State might be launched. Stallybrass's quest in this essay is to separate out the "real" Aleppo from its representations, and to investigate the politics that can occasionally make of such locations *either* antitheses, or, more problematically, proximate geographical spaces. Of course, much depends upon the position of the speaker, since this is not simply a question of reassembling documents that tell different stories about, for example, the relationship between Venice and the Ottoman Empire, but also of evaluating English perceptions and imaginings of these geographical locations. Here material cultures clash with the materiality of languages, and the pursuit of the "real" (in a quasi-Marxist sense of the term) is contaminated by an irreducible textuality that is both fundamentally appropriative and dependent on context.

This adventurous gaze through the wrong end of the cultural and geographical telescope, and the attempt to enhance the image via the psychoanalytical device of Freud's "uncanny," traverses lightly over a complex interlocking web of what Foucault would call "statements"[2] that engage drama, historiography, geography, and literary criticism. The "real" Aleppo, or the "real" Venice, are not quite so easily locatable as Stallybrass would have us believe. In *Othello,* for example, both geographical locations (and we might add Cyprus to this list) are already allegorized to the point where they become unstable signifiers, reflecting not a geographical location but a culturally and politically inflected narrative. Indeed, the demonic energy that is allocated to a specific geographical space in the play—or to be more precise, *three* geographical spaces: Venice, Cyprus, *and* Aleppo—points not so much in the direction of the "unheimlich," but toward forces that exist under the surface(s) of early Jacobean English culture that become visible as part of a theologically informed economy. Such a formulation would take care of *Othello* and *Macbeth,* and point us more firmly in the direction of these plays' perplexing recourse to the disturbing congruence of animal and demonic imagery.

Stallybrass's essay began its life as a conference paper and as such is an informed but polemical incitement to further thought. Nevertheless, the argument does invite us to wonder whether phrases such as "global economy," in claims such as the Ottoman Empire "was the westernmost outpost of the intra-Asian trade that dominated the global economy in 1600" (31), are not too extravagant. Also, we need to ponder the formulation of the claim that the Ottomans, Persia, and India "*materialised* [my emphasis] Europeans. That is, they provided much of the *matter* (fibres, textiles, dyes) that shaped European bodies" (33). In the plays to which Stallybrass refers "the view from Aleppo" is obscured by a series of "statements" that materialize the perspectives of English culture: "statements" that occlude the very determinations, discursive and otherwise, that drive them, and from which no amount of over-determined historical curiosity can separate them.

It is a pity that the ghost of Freud is given too free a rein in the cellarage of Stallybrass's argument. His isolation of the term "assassination" in *Macbeth* (1.7.2) correctly locates its first English usage in Richard Knolles's *The History of The Turks* (1603). But his premature conclusion that this naming "was surely to imagine it as, above all, alien and familiar" (32), "heimlich" and "unheimlich," glides over its earlier Latin and Old French usage that linked it etymologically to the alleged use of "hashish" prior to the act of killing in early Moslem culture. The image of the drugged killer is domesticated in *Macbeth* in the drunkenness that becomes a literal and a metaphorical impediment to political success. Here the act of "translation" appropriates what is marginal for a moral economy in which rational surfaces are always liable to disturbance from below. In *Othello* the process is reversed simply *because* the hero is black, indicating a "natural" propensity for a problematic Venetian civilization to correct aberration by presenting a challenge to what surfaces signify. The politics of this process, and the "art" that sustains it, should make modern readers and spectators nervous.

It is a politics of which Philippa Berry is acutely aware in her fine essay, " 'Incising Venice: The Violence of Cultural Incorporation in *The Merchant of Venice*." The editorial juxtaposition of these two essays confirms the proximity of *The Merchant of Venice* and *Othello* to each other in a number of crucial respects. The emphasis in Berry's essay is on "Venice" itself as a space offering "insights into the fragmented and fragmenting character of the Renaissance or early modern culture" (40). She takes up the debate about "surfaces" and suggests that there is a tension in Renaissance culture generally between "the simultaneously alien yet compellingly seductive appeal of diverse forms of ornamentation" (41). It is in *The Merchant of Venice* that what she calls a "persistently troubled awareness" can be traced through the recovery of earlier "texts" from the play, and thence positioned as part of a larger Renaissance culture haunted "by a multiplicity of half-acknowledged fathers: in other words, by a diversity of putative cultural 'origins'" (40). Once again the "uncanny" surfaces briefly, as part of "a powerful surplus of alterity" (44), although here in its Nietzschean guise as "repetition," while the invocation of St. Paul on the "cutting off" and "grafting" of the Jews threatens to draw the argument in a predictable direction. However, and surprisingly, Berry invokes that most anti-Freudian of philosophers, Gilles Deleuze, to draw our attention to what is a lacuna in Stallybrass's argument: the degree to which "incorporeal entities . . . materialise *at the surface of bodies* without being themselves corporeal or substantial materials." Citing Deleuze, she notes that "corporeal bodies are objects, incorporeal entities are effects" that as such, have no origin; the "incorporeal effect has a ghostly or "phantasmatic' property" (45). Her quarry is the trope of writing itself as an incision made upon a surface, "a highly visual form of cultural marking or wounding, performed upon a skin-like surface by an alien hand," and its manifestation in the play through a series of verbs associated with inscription. The "insculpted" coin that Morocco produces is enlisted in this argument, while the death's head that he chooses can be read as both "an emblem of time," and as "a reminder that within this new work of cultural incision, a strangely hybrid double-eyed (a Janus-like) model of cultural temporality is implicit" (46). However, the invocation of Deleuze raises an important question concerning the historicizing bent of the critic, and militates against too straightforward a theory of causality; indeed, as Deleuze says of "the event": "The infinitely divisible event is always *both at once.* It is eternally that which has just happened and that which is about to happen, but never that which is happening (to cut too deeply and not enough)." He continues: "The event, being itself impassive, allows the active and the passive to be interchanged more easily, since it is *neither the one nor the other,* but rather their common result (to cut—to be cut)" (*The Logic of Sense,* 10). The reading of topologies as historical narratives runs a certain risk. Berry negotiates this deftly with her claim that any re-inscription of "textual remains" may never leave "archaic or abjected cultural origins completely behind" (46), or that "once *cut off* from their originating context, and 'inserted' or 'inscrolled' in an alien cultural surface, can acquire new *interest*—an exaggerated significance whose 'incising' effect is 'incorporeal' in that it verges on the uncanny, phantasmic, or spectral—precisely because of the loss of an origi-

nal cultural context or frame." The reversion to a neo-Freudian vocabulary here sits uneasily with Deleuze, but the convergence in
Berry's argument of Morocco, Shylock, and Othello (and she would
also add *Antony and Cleopatra*) suggests a closer topographical
connection between these three figures and the four plays than criticism has hitherto detected.

The Merchant of Venice is full of what appear to be antithetical,
if not paradoxical, formulations, and Berry's dense argument manages to tease out many of them. At a purely phenomenological
level, the final act of the play does, indeed, weave together "several
different figures of the incorporeal effects that are allied to acts of
cultural incision" (51). But what she accomplishes is a model of
the play's concerns that refuses an orderly temporal narrative of its
various "events." The cultural displacements of particular textual
fragments place the play's fabric at the very juncture of what Deleuze identifies as "the boundary between things and propositions"
where "everything happens" (ibid., 11). Consequently, the inci-
sions in the play that Berry makes, amounting, it must be said, to
major surgery, leave pedestrian debates about "materiality" far behind.

Where Berry leaves off, Patricia Parker begins. As if taking her
cue telepathically from Berry's mention of *Antony and Cleopatra,*
Parker explores the "marginal" in a play that contrives to render all
boundaries problematical. The figure that she chooses is "Enobarbus"—*nomen est omen*—whose name resonates throughout the
play and is the focus of comments about "barbering," "beards,"
"cutting," as parts of the more general effect that Egypt has on
Rome. Parker does not depart from the familiar opposition of a
"masculine" Rome versus a "feminine" Egypt, but she is concerned to tease out, and in some textual detail, the play's complex
and persistent association of beards with things Roman. Moreover,
she associates the material beard in the theater, as an index of a
"prosthetic" masculinity[3] that is part of the play's own discourse
of the conditions of its theatrical production of gender identity (80).
Her primary concern, however, is, through a close reading of Enobarbus's "most memorable of Shakespearean speeches" (54), to establish a connection between the "infidel" East and the categories
of "renegade," "witch," and "infidel" (65) that all come together in
the figure and the reported actions of Cleopatra. As in Berry's account of classical analogues in *The Merchant of Venice,* so here;
Parker notes that in *Antony and Cleopatra* such analogues carry

with them "contemporary overtones" (67). Her method is to begin from specific textual references, and then work outward to embrace the provenance of various source texts for the play, and to speculate upon etymologies that become more central to her argument as it progresses. In a play where the view from Egypt is an integral element in the generation of a series of binary oppositions, the customary gloss on Pompey's phrase "salt Cleopatra" (2.1.21) extends the frame of reference beyond familiar editorial associations "of female sexuality or a 'gypsy's lust.'" "Salt" also suggests, Parker argues, "the figure of the *saltator, salter,* or transvestite dancer familiar from Plautus and other Roman writers and from the condemnation of such spectacles in contemporary anti-theatrical literature" (79). But it is Enobarbus, a marginal figure in the dramatic lives of the play's two protagonists, who is symbolically central to the business of drawing the worlds of Rome and Egypt together. He represents Roman virility *and* "the prosthetic stage beard that complicated the very categories of natural and constructed" (80). He violates the Roman masculine principle of military loyalty; he is the "red-bearded renegade" of Knolles's *The History of The Turke* (1603), and the "network of barbering" that he invokes "may have recalled not only Judas or the stage beard of the Jew but the most memorable Red-beard from what *The Jew of Malta* calls the other 'Circumcised nation'—the Barbarossa who reversed not only Actium but the very direction of Enobarbus's defection, and was a renegade who, like Antony, chose never to return" (82). These three adventurous essays set the tone of the volume as a whole, in that they traverse an intellectual terrain whose broad outlines Barroll has done much to define.

The second section, "Researching the Renaissance," was the title of a graduate seminar led by Barroll at the Folger over eight years from 1991 to 1999, and the three essays grouped under this heading focus, among other things, on questions of gender and theatrical representation. In the case of Phyllis Rackin ("Our Canon, Ourselves") and Harry Berger, Jr. ("Artificial Couples: The Apprehensive Household in Dutch Pendants and *Othello*"), the emphasis is very much on Shakespearean texts, though in a comparative setting, whereas in the case of Lena Cowen Orlin ("Spaces of Treason in Tudor England"), the focus is upon the semiotics of space in the wider domestic culture of the period. Both Rackin and Berger begin with an acknowledgment of the Shakespearean text's "unconscious"; Rackin asserts, "For modern scholars, Shakespeare's plays have often constituted a notable site of women's repression" (91), while for Berger, the question of theatricalization is linked to "performance anxiety," both within particular plays, *and* on the part of scholarly commentators (114). Hitherto Rackin has concerned herself with various Shakespearean narratives of masculine "oppression"[4] but the terminological switch to "women's repression" implies a rather different political (and psychological) dynamic that gestures away from "Shakespeare's representations of women" (92), and toward the process of internalizing patriarchal values. Rackin sees the Comedies as the site of "the modern preference for stories in which women are put in their (subordinate) place," and she nominates *The Taming of The Shrew* and *The Merry Wives of Windsor* as two plays that illustrate this tendency "with remarkable clarity" (93). The first of these two plays has long given feminists some difficulty: either the play is, from a modern point of view, a brutal demonstration of women's oppression, or it is a masculine pipe dream that willfully inverts a more complex Elizabethan "reality." Which version of feminism one chooses determines which side of the argument receives most emphasis. Rackin acknowledges that the women's roles are not realistic, but "a wistful fantasy" (98), but she is also skeptical of modern readings that either apologize for Petrucchio's behavior, or credit him with a greater sensitivity than the character possesses (101). It is disappointing that the discussion should settle at the point where the play's status as "the paradigmatic Shakespearean representation of women's place in marriage" is acknowledged (102). Disappointing, because the argument does not fully respond to the fact that in *The Taming of The Shrew* (as in later comedies) the action is double-edged. Kate's shrewish behavior is a response to her situation, just as Petrucchio's strategy is a response to her shrewishness, and it is this complex dynamic that requires further dismantling. What compounds the problem is the unequal distribution of gender roles that is the source of a modern discomfort that no acknowledgment of the erotic frisson of sexual encounter can dispel. Rackin's neat demolition of Quiller-Couch's offensively elegant projection of masculine desire onto the fabric of the play is well-taken, but she deploys it as part of her own strategy to find, in *The Merry Wives of Windsor,* a more fitting paradigmatic example.

What Rackin finds attractive in *The Merry Wives* is its domestic realism (102–3), and the positive empowering roles allotted to its female characters. Masculine "verbal facility" is neither dominant

nor "privileged" (107), and the isolation of Falstaff figures the inadequacy of masculinity in the play. This is a welcome rehabilitation
of a play that Shakespeare scholars have consistently undervalued,
although the extent to which it can counterbalance what Rackin
identifies as "counterfactual fantasies rather than reflections of the
life that the majority of Shakespeare's original audience knew outside the theatre" (110), is questionable, even if we knew much
more about the life that they knew. That the audience was com-
plicit "in the production of theatrical pleasure" (109) is a reasonable assumption to make, but the actual *dynamics* of that process is
another matter altogether. Falstaff's outrageous presumption, allied
with Ford's pathological jealousy in a causal sequence stimulates
the kind of laughter that signals both anxiety and liberation. But
the behavior of Mistresses Ford and Page invites much closer scrutiny, since they act in various ways in support of the institution of
marriage while at the same time interrogating its licit and illicit
practices. As the victim of a ludicrously possessive patriarchy, Mistress Ford negotiates a successful route through a minefield that destroyed one of Shakespeare's later heroines, Desdemona, and her
manner of doing so—in particular the dehumanizing of Falstaff to
a pile of dirty laundry, and then to a cross-dressed "witch"—
deploys the very conceptual materials out of which her own femininity is constructed. In another register, Mistress Page attempts to
engineer the marriage of her daughter to an unsuitable partner, thus
rendering precarious the business of parental choice *tout court.* To
suggest that it is Anne Page who is from the outset "the only figure
who resembles the heroines of the romantic comedies" and that she
is "characterised from the first as a *representation*" (110) is to un-
dervalue the play's own aesthetic dynamic, as it reaches beyond
the quotidian world of marital tension, with its risks, its opportunities for betrayal, and its power games, toward a resolution in which
these tensions are projected onto the figure of Falstaff, at the same
time that the aristocratic impulses of Fenton are transformed as part
of a more egalitarian heterosexual confidence in the new generation. In the end this may be no less of a "wistful fantasy" than that
of *The Taming of The Shrew,* but the extent to which this reflects
the preoccupations of an Elizabethan audience, or those of modern
commentators—after all Rackin's title is: "Our canon, Ourselves"—is never quite resolved.

The question of the efficacy and protocols of the historical study
of texts—and it is one to which Barroll himself has devoted consid-

erable attention—is taken up in Harry Berger, Jr.'s essay, "Artificial Couples: The Apprehensive Household in Dutch Pendants and *Othello*." Unlike Rackin, who deals more directly with the *transmission* of the Shakespeare canon, Berger uses the concept of "performativity" and its capacity to register social change as a cultural barometer of such "techtonic changes of institutional structure as the emergence of new forms of state and family organisation" (114). Read against Rackin's essay, Berger provides a token explanation of what female "repression" might have looked like in medieval Italian society (115), but from which English and Dutch models of the family may well have diverged (115–16). Following in the footsteps of Catherine Belsey's *The Subject of Tragedy* (1985), and *Shakespeare and The Loss of Eden* (1999), he locates desire in the conjugal relation of the nuclear family, which functions to "domesticate a destabilising passion, confining it within the safety of a loving family" (116). But for a variety of reasons, some of which have a demonstrable historical validity, others of which are more speculative, this kind of household in which the male householder is the locus of state authority becomes "a place of danger" (ibid.), and later "a place of theatre" (120). Berger's argument modifies that of Belsey, and it benefits from a comparative dimension, as he moves from medieval Italy to the Dutch Republic, and from domestic manuals such as Jacob Cats's *Houwelyck* (1625), to the roles and psychic lives of women as projections of male fantasy: "men imagine what women desire, and then displace these fantasies onto women as *their* fantasies and desires" (119). At stake here are the very ways in which commentators construct historical images and narrative accounts, and Berger's own methodology amplifies Barroll's "important revisionist account of historical methodology" (120) that challenges the New Historicist model of the relations between theater and the State that underestimates the radical mobility of power. In an essay of considerable intricacy, Berger follows through Louis Montrose's observation that the assertion of "theatricality as a universal condition of social life" (*cited,* 123) made available to all the techniques of the theatricalization of State power. Moreover, the promotion in schools of "the study of grammar, rhetoric and translation" facilitates the mastery of "the ethical skills of mimesis." The consequence is a rethinking of "character" as an *effect* rather than a source, "the product of art rather than nature," thus rendering an act of successful personation or "the production of a convincing 'character'" as "the fictive effect of a performance and closely identified with acts of imitation" (ibid.). Berger tracks Montrose's account of "the complex micro-political negotiations necessary to keep things going behind the ceremonial facades of the Two-Body constitution." But in a disarmingly self-conscious fashion, he goes on to imagine that the tension between "imperial or royalist ideology and statist reality" is actually worked out in "that wonderfully elastic and disorderly and successful system of checks and unbalances, that repressed bad dream of constitutional monarchy, the Dutch Republic" (125). The result is a reading of Dutch marriage portraits (pendants) as offering "an essentially comedic view of spousal competition," particularly "the wife's performance," and a comparison with the representation of Emilia and Iago in *Othello* that foregrounds "the husband's anxiety" (126). The competition for space in one genre that registers "the pull between the two sitters' positional reciprocity and their performative competition" (137) is transformed in Shakespeare's play, and in the relationship between Iago and Emilia especially, into a jostling for power that "presuppose[s] the institutional stabilisation of wifely power" (138). Here Berger's argument revolves around the status of Iago's and Emilia's soliloquies, especially that uttered on the perplexing occasion of the latter's discovery of Desdemona's handkerchief (3.3.294–302). For Berger, it is an example of "the technique of ethical evasion" (145). But more surprising perhaps is the claim that Emilia's refusal "to enlighten Desdemona and Othello is a source of her power over Iago inasmuch as it ratifies and preserves his power over them," and that she belatedly exercises that power at the end of the play (146). This an ingenious attempt to negotiate the apparent inconsistency between an omniscient Emilia, capable of analyzing her own subject-position as the mimetic performer of masculine "ills" (4.3.101–2), and a dramatic character of an inferior social class, who appears to be curiously unconcerned, until it is too late, with the consequences of her own wifely loyalty. Berger provocatively concludes that Iago is both empowered and disempowered by his own internalization of "everyone else's evil desires," and that his final silence in the play represents a gesture associated with the very femininity over which he has failed to exert control. "Mum" may be "the model housewife's word" (149), but the ambassadorial Lodovico has other plans for "this hellish villain" (5.2.366), involving another kind of spectacle, and requiring yet another performance.

This deft and finely illustrated account of Dutch portrait paint-
ing, and of the intensely Jacobean domestic machinations of Iago,
leads directly into Lena Cowen Orlin's essay "Spaces of Treason in
Tudor England," in which she augments what she calls "a familiar
narrative," that of the "so-called 'Ridolphi Plot' ", with another that
she locates "in the margins" of the available documentation and
that constitutes "a spatial history of treason" (158). Her particular
quarry is the "long gallery" of the Tudor country house, an architectural space, "an accidental effect" of which "was its surprising
facility for sheltering private conversations" (168). The question
here is the extent to which the long gallery was symptomatic of a
growing cultural demand for "privacy," as indeed was the garden;
whether they were the consequence of an awareness of "the inhib-
iting effects of collectivity" (ibid.); and how the resulting tension
between "public" and "private" space informed the life of the
drama as well as the politics of the state. Orlin observes that plays
of the period are full of "witnessings, overhearings, and eavesdrop-
pings" (169), and that "while scenes of intercepted knowledge are
both fodder for comedy and necessary engines of drama, they are
also revelatory of larger social meanings and suspicions" (170).
This is a slightly modified, if not tendentious version of Henri Lefebvre's thesis in his groundbreaking book, *The Production of Space*
(1974, 1991), in which he notes the shift from feudal to capitalist
space as evidenced in an emerging urban geography. Lefebvre's use
of metaphor is germane to Orlin's argument: "Urban space was
fated to become the theatre of a compromise between the declining
feudal system, the commercial bourgeoisie, oligarchies, and communities of craftsmen. It further became *abstraction in action*—
active abstraction—vis-à-vis the space of nature, generality as
opposed to singularities, and the universal principle *in statu nas-
cendi,* integrating specificities even as it uncovered them" (Lefebvre [1991], 269). Orlin's contention that the long gallery, and its
proximity to the garden, was an architectural innovation facilitat-
ing what she calls "social privacy" (169) is empirically attractive
insofar as the evidence she presents points clearly in the direction
of a reconceptualization of social space. Her point is that in a culture in which it was still difficult to delineate the "public" from a
"private" sphere, privacy itself, or the desire for it, and the evident
containment of possible interlocutors, could provoke suspicion.
The condemnation of the Duke of Norfolk after the discovery of the
Ridolphi Plot rested on an allegation of "a suspicious intent to be

private" (188–89). Of course, we look at this allegation through the wrong end of the telescope, since one of our contemporary concerns is to protect our own privacy against the paranoid actions of a State determined to make public the most intimate of personal details. Orlin's witty conclusion that in the case of Norfolk "they had found a mind's construction in his space" (189), effects a telling metathesis in its recollection of Duncan's memorable formulation that "there's no art / To find the mind's construction in the face" (*Macbeth,* 1.4.11–12). The drawing together of "space" and "language" in such a way that space, like language, can be made to signify—"My subject is the signifying capacity of space" (188)—invites further consideration of the dialectical possibilities that emanate from their juxtaposition and the ways in which they intersect in the material and theatricalized world of early modern English politics.

The third section of the book moves away from some of the larger cultural questions concerned with the symbolically central aspects of marginality, and into the theater itself, taking its title from a chapter in Barroll's *Shakespearean Tragedy: Genre, Tradition and Change in "Antony and Cleopatra"* (1984). Jean Howard's "Staging Masculinities, National History, and the Making of London Theatrical Culture" reprises a topic and an approach that she and Phyllis Rackin broached in their jointly authored *Engendering a Nation: A Feminist Account of Shakespeare's English Histories* (1997). This book offers a four-chapter treatment of Shakespeare's First Tetralogy, and begins with the recognition that "the difficult transmission of patrilineal authority from one generation to the next is the subject of the history plays, but they marginalise the roles of the wives and mothers, centring instead on the heroic legacies of the fathers, the failures and triumphs of the sons" and that "the privileged scene of heroic history, the battlefield is a problematic place for women."[5] In her essay Howard articulates the same thesis, although with the kind of assurance that an acceptance of this thesis has conferred over a period of some ten years. She begins with the statement that the *Henry VI* plays stage "spectacular failures of the male dominated social order," and that in these apprenticeship pieces, Shakespeare experimented with soliloquy, with "emblematic scenes," and with interwoven plots. Of course, the recent resurgent flurry of attribution studies, allied with the modest claim that Shakespeare's intentions may have been "literary," may well force a readjustment of this veiled biographical perspective. But the claim that the dramatist was both "learning to delineate styles of stageable masculinity" and "not the collapse of an abstract, patriarchal social order—but individual men who hack, weep, or strut their way through the falling timbers of that large edifice" (199) can stand or fall, depending upon how the narrative of the dramatist's artistic "development" is perceived. This either/or logic, formerly an empowering strategy, but now an obstruction to any critical consideration of the binary thinking in which certain kinds of feminist criticism have become mired, is in danger of obscuring the densely intertextual nature of these plays, in particular, the ways in which they incorporate existing theatrical material into a complex historical (and generically over-determined) narrative. Dramatic characterization is not, it should be emphasized, entirely synonymous with the staging of "individual men," a point that Howard all but concedes in her speculation that Edward Alleyn may have played the role of Talbot if *1 Henry VI* was staged at the Rose by Henslowe. Her retelling of the Manningham story of Shakespeare's quip at the expense of the philandering Burbage, who had played Richard in *Richard III,* undermines the argument that what this tetralogy foregrounds is a practical theatrical learning process, or that what the audience saw was slices of social realism. Perhaps, as in her speculation that Will Kempe *may* have taken the role of Jack Cade in *2 Henry VI,* audiences may have warmed more to an erotics of performance, although we should take care not to graft our own assumptions about "celebrity" onto Shakespeare's actors. The Elizabethan theater was not Broadway, or at least, Broadway as we know it. Similarly, the hypothetical suggestion that Cade might have returned at the end of the play to perform a jig, and that this might have been "(an uncanny anticipation . . . of Falstaff's 'resurrection' in *1 Henry IV,* a part also arguably performed by Kemp)" (208), risks projecting onto Shakespeare's oeuvre the critic's own resourceful ingenuity. It would be difficult to dissent from the main feminist plank of Howard's argument, even though this is, perhaps, the most predictable part of her essay. Whether the theater—as both "popular" and marginal (200)—as evidenced in the Manningham or the Robert Greene anecdotes, reflected "popular images of the evolving theatre world" as both "a place of glamorous opportunity or a site of monstrous and socially destabilising ambition" (212) is a moot point, especially since these are not the only alternatives available. If the evidence of *Julius Caesar* or *Henry V* as possible candidates for the title of the play that opened the new Globe the-

ater in 1599 is anything to go by, then the players (and the dramatist) were working very hard, and perhaps, unglamourously, to
justify the identity of their collective, but still precarious, enterprise.

Raphael Falco's essay on "Charisma and Institution Building in
Shakespeare's Second Tetralogy" offers an account of how the Second Tetralogy handles "charismatic" and "institutional" authority
(215). "Charismatic authority" is a phrase borrowed (and revised)
from Max Weber that Falco uses as a means of analyzing "group
relations" in these four plays (215). His project is to investigate the
relations between the charismatic appeal of the ruler and the extent
to which it either generates the political instabilities over which it
then proceeds to exert a personal power, or hastens the onset of
"the so-called impersonal state" (219). His invocation of Quentin
Skinner, Stephen Greenblatt, and David Scott Kastan is designed to
clarify the difference between a sociohistorical usage of the concept
of "charisma," and a looser, literary usage. Falco cites approvingly
Greenblatt's thesis that in *Henry V* it is the king's provocation of
doubt that enhances his power: "For the enhancement of royal
power is not only a matter of the deferral of doubt: the very doubts
that Shakespeare raises serve not to rob the king of his charisma but
to heighten it, precisely as they heighten the theatrical interest of
the play" (cited, 219). Falco attaches to this thesis Kastan's refinement of this position, following Lacan, that "it is madness to believe that kingship resides magically in the person of the king
rather than in the political relations that bind, even create, king and
subject" and that it is Hal's "enabling knowledge" of this political
fact that authorizes "his impressive improvisations" (219). He
does, however, pull back from the implications of this New Historicist strategy since he sees all of Shakespeare's kings in this tetralogy
as "suffer[ing] from the conflict between an impersonal institution
of rule and the personal charismatic qualities that seem at times to
sustain their royal legitimacy," and he goes on to say that "we can
track the establishment of institutionalised authority through the
formation and breakdown of their charismatic group relationships"
(220). Falco is surely right to entertain "a robust scepticism about
seeing in Shakespeare's kings some sort of prototype of the conflict
between the charismatic and the impersonal state" (220–21), but
he goes further than that. What might it mean to say, as Falco does,
that "the charismatic conditions of the plays may not be reflective
of political realities" in this context? Moreover, can we slide off the

horns of this dilemma by reading into what are now regarded as "primarily literary representations . . . a kind of triangulation with the source material and Weberian theory"? It is Falco's contention that Weber addressed "ideal types" and that these were derived, not from actual political practice, but from "literary contexts" where, as in the case of Tragedy, "ideal types of charismatic authority" appear (221). Of course, the trouble is that in these plays the "ideal" and the "real" types appear, and if we were to go beyond the Second Tetralogy to *Macbeth* or *King Lear* we might find this complexity replicated and sophisticated further. "Charismatic authority" is a very useful category, but whether it provides a real key to these plays is another matter altogether. Indeed, it appears that Falco himself is unsure, since he needs to augment it with "one of the most provocative post-Weberian theories of charisma," Thomas Spence Smith's account of "entropy driven systems" (225). This returns the argument to something approaching a refinement of Greenblatt's position, in which the "mild chaos" that is the mode of being of "charismatic groups" is thought to provide "a criterion for control" that allows a leader to "extend or encourage a dissipative structure rather than gravitate towards stability, inasmuch as entropy guarantees a sharp dependency among followers" (ibid.). It is a moot point whether this kind of formalist structure is historically portable, especially since in the Second Tetralogy political crisis is generated by a *failure* of charismatic authority, by its appropriation, and by the attendant risks to the ideological fabric that is designed to sustain it. Here, of course, we would need to intercalate Weberian theory with the political theology of Ernst Kantorowicz, and beyond that with the debates about sovereignty of Carl Schmidt and Giorgio Agamben.

It is Falco's contention that Hal "resolves a great many unstable situations which he inherits from his father" because "he recognises the interdependence—or, again, intersubjectivity—that exists between himself and his followers" (231). He cites the Archbishop of Canterbury's account of Hal's transformation as evidence of "a distinctly charismatic authority of divine promise" that "like the charismata in 1 Corinthians 12, is made part of his *soma* at the moment that his mortal body becomes the immortal body politic" (232).[6] The contrast between Richard's appeal to his own "humanity" and that of Hal is well-taken (232–33), although little is made of anxiety surrounding Hal's success in *Henry V* or of the play's problem with the issue of representation itself. At a purely descriptive level we might agree that the "eroticization of Henry's persona charisma . . . heralds the transformation of his charismatic presence into the combined institutions of marriage, genealogical legitimation, and the rulership of England and France" (234), but this does not quite capture the larger ironies that we might, in retrospect, read into the play. What Falco earlier claimed of Hal, that he "provides the ideal model of charismatic administration" (225), reads only the play's manifest meaning, a meaning that a series of encounters, not least that with Williams and Bates, challenges. The Machiavellian plan, that Hal had confided to the audience in *Henry IV, Pt. 1* (1.2.192–210), is transformed in *Henry V* into a private admission of heavy responsibility; the "idol ceremony" (4.1.237) that requires the acknowledgment of charismatic authority through "adoration" (4.1.242) turns into a question: is it nothing more than "place, degree and form, / Creating awe and fear in other men, / Wherein thou art less happy, being feared, / Than they in fearing?" (4.1.243–46). It is precisely this kind of periodic questioning thrown up by the play's own nervousness about the business of theatrical representation that undermines its aesthetic teleology. "History" and wishful thinking are shown to be uncomfortable bedfellows; charismatic authority and "institution-building" are not shown in alliance; and the comic ending promises to be radically undercut by a descent into a political chaos to which the audience has already been privy: "Which oft our stage hath shown" (epilogue, l.13).

With Bruce Smith's essay, enigmatically entitled "Mona Lisa Takes a Mountain Hike, Hamlet Goes For an Ocean Dip," we move from the earnest and unwavering pursuit of a "thesis" to an altogether more playful style of exposition, and to a significant shift of methodology. In his book *The Acoustic World of Early Modern England* (1999), Smith briefly mentions the work of the maverick French thinker Michel Serres, and in particular Serres's claim that there is "no life without heat, no matter, neither; no warmth without air, no logos without noise" (cited, 9). Building on this, Smith now proposes in his essay a "historical phenomenology" (250) that he believes he can apply to *Hamlet* and to speculation about audience responses in Shakespeare's Globe, a building that "directed and propagated sound in distinctive ways" (242). Beginning from T. S. Eliot's description of *Hamlet* as the "Mona Lisa of Literature," Smith launches a comparison between the positioning against a background of the central figures in portrait and play respectively.

Speech and "presence," two concepts that are central to *Hamlet* and Hamlet, are raised in connection with the attempt to qualify Derrida's account of logocentrism by submitting it to a series of "historical contingencies" (241). To decenter Hamlet from *Hamlet* would be, argues Smith, to fail to acknowledge the articulation of the tension between language and context or between foreground and background. He contends that "to refuse Hamlet's rhetorical ploys, to decentre him among the sounds in which he exists, is the aural equivalent of telling Mona Lisa to go take a hike" (ibid.) in the sense that it would collapse the enigmatic portrait into its "background." The claim that the Globe theater "directed and propagated sound in distinctive ways" (242) is blandly phenomenological, although it gestures toward the affective delivery of language that in a theater is a much rougher process than the delineation of meaning in a static portrait whose mystery lies, in part, in its having been separated from the conditions of its own production. In a limited phenomenological sense Hamlet does struggle to "come to presence" but to claim simply that his physical surroundings are "full of dispersed sounds that only on occasion find a centre in a single speaker" (243) withdraws into an apolitical version of Kristeva's "semiotic chora." In the context of the play, "presence" and the political and ethical infrastructure that sustains it are a problem. The play is "about" both the formal and the *historical* grounding of language, and its circulation in the world renders the production of meaning a more hazardous task than a simple appeal to logocentrism would have us believe. Serres's championing of "prepositions" or "a relational way of knowing" (250) breaks radically with the "proposition" of orthodox analytical philosophy, or the "statement" of Foucauldian materialism. However, the extent to which "such a way of knowing recognises the embodiedness of historical subjects," and "attends to the materiality of the evidence they have left behind," *and*, at the same time, "acknowledges the embodiedness of the investigator in the face of that evidence" (cited, 250), is in Serres's writings a complex invitation to dissolve *disciplinary* boundaries, rather than to provide a blueprint for a reading of the dramatic action of *Hamlet*. Indeed, we may wonder to what extent Hamlet *undoes* the Cartesian subject/object couple, especially since the play poses it as a problem for which no clear solution is yet (historically) forthcoming. Moreover, the positioning of the hero "among," and that leads ultimately to an apparent oxymoron: "the materiality of air that calls

into question the distinction between subject and object" (251) and
his final relegation to "sea" and "air," is not easily sustainable as
a reading. For example, Hamlet's "The rest is silence" (5.2.363) is
immediately pulled back into an historical context, first by Horatio,
and then by Fortinbras, and examples from other plays should
place us on our guard against assuming that such apparent invitations to dissolution or isolation, or such "silences," can be read
apart from the politics that situate them. To place Hamlet in the formal world of "sound" is to miss the important point that the Messenger makes at 4.5.102–5 immediately before Laertes's entry,
about the *historical* and *practical* grounding of sound and the *fear*
of a return to primal chaos: "The rabble call him lord, / And, as
the world were now but to begin, / Antiquity forgot, custom not
known— / The ratifiers and props of every word." To read *Hamlet*
through the perspective glass of Prospero's apology for the insub-
stantiality of theatrical performance is to risk hijacking the play for
a phenomenology that is only tenuously historical, and at the same
time only superficially presentist. A "relational" approach to the
play must take into account its capacity to generate "passion" in an
audience. But returning the hero "to the sea of noise from which
he emerged" (252) abandons the task of attempting to explain the
various ways in which, in this play particularly, language *shapes*
"noise," and where "noise" is already part of a narrative, in favor
of rhetorical flourish.

The final three essays are grouped under the title of Barroll's first
book, "Artificial Persons." Smith's attempt to map out what in another theoretical register might have been called the "real" that ultimately resists representation, provides a neat bridge to Catherine
Belsey's essay "Psychoanalysis and Early Modern Culture: Lacan
With Augustine and Montaigne." Each of the three essays, in their
different ways, departs from Shakespeare, in order to encompass
Milton (Suzanne Woods's "Abdiel Centres Freedom"), and the
early modern preoccupation with the objects produced by technology (Barbara Maria Stafford's "Artificial Intensity: The Optical
Technologies of Personal Reality Enhancement"). Belsey seeks a
rapprochement between psychoanalytical theory and the historicizing texts of earlier epochs, and her piece is in some ways a response to Stephen Greenblatt's essay on "Psychoanalysis and
Renaissance Culture."[7] Greenblatt acknowledged the existence of
"complex forms of self-consciousness and highly discursive per-
sonhood in the West long before the sixteenth century"[8] but he

went on to argue that the best hope for a properly historicized form of psychoanalytic criticism lay in "the school of Hegelian psycho-analysis associated with the work of Jacques Lacan, where identity is always revealed to be the identity of another, always registered (as in those parish registers) in language."[9] The Hobbesian phrase "artificial person" had been for Barroll focused primarily in theatri-cal performance, but for Greenblatt it was extended to encompass an entirely theatricalized Renaissance culture. Belsey's concern is with Renaissance culture generally, although she is uncertain of the claim that Lacan's complex topographical account of the opera-tions of the symbolic order via language are "historical" in the "culturalist" way that Greenblatt thinks (258). Her solution is to uphold the formal aspects of Lacanian theory in order to demon-strate its effectiveness in dealing with the *reading* of "texts." This neatly sidesteps the problem of deciding whether psychoanalysis advocates a universal, or a historically relative, human condition, and concentrates on "an approach to the necessary condition of meaning" (ibid.). For Belsey the contribution of Psychoanalysis is "methodological rather than explanatory, a way above all of paying attention to the workings of the texts" (259). Not merely that, but the renewed emphasis upon "close reading"—a much closer read-ing than that advocated in New Criticism—would enjoin the cul-tural critic to employ the same procedures as the psychoanalyst "who listens for the slippages, lapses, and incoherences in speech of the analysand." The result of this "mode of interpretation" would be, Belsey insists, "more history, not less, and more nuanced history" that would not be hampered, either by a vague appeal to presentist concerns, or by the temptation to slide back into "the old reassuring cognitive totalities of the Elizabethan world picture and the early modern mind" (ibid.).

Belsey isolates the Freudian concern with human sexuality, and traces this back from St. Augustine, through Montaigne, to Freud and thence to Lacan. She argues that, like Augustinian theology, "psychoanalysis allots a central place to the conflict between law and desire," so that what in St. Augustine is an unruliness of the penis becomes in Psychoanalysis "the phallus as lawless, irrepress-ible, for ever in conflict with propriety." Thus her claim is that "Psychoanalytic castration re-enacts the Fall," and that sex is "the place where that loss is most evident" (261). Belsey points to a methodology, but she also offers an explanation and a narrative whose seductive coherence chafes against the nuanced "history" she advocates. Indeed, although in a post-structuralist world committed to the principle of fragmentation, "language is incapable of transmitting a full thematic content, a complete, coherent world picture, or a cognitive totality of any kind" (270), we cannot, as Belsey readily admits, do without some theoretical means of grasping "the contours of signification itself" (275). The difficulty she faces is in moving from the ideological contamination of a Freudianism steeped in biology, and from an explicitly sexual register, to an explanation that recovers from it the operations of "language," "culture," and law. Hers is a different kind of culturalist reading from that of Greenblatt, and one committed (in principle) to a materialist insistence upon the inextricable interdependence of "matter" and "spirit." Augustine, Montaigne, and Lacan are, in Belsey's carefully nuanced reading, "aligned against the division between matter and spirit that informs the dominant tradition of Western Philosophy" (271). Except that in her account a thematic narrative threatens to overwhelm what Jean-Joseph Goux calls "a *logic of the symbolisation process,* that is, a logic of the successive forms taken by the exchange of vital activities in all spheres of social organisation, a logic pertaining to phylogeny as well as to ontogeny. This logic enables us to conceive *the dialectics of history.*"[10]

What is glimpsed at tangentially in Belsey's rewriting of the brief of Psychoanalytical criticism—Goux's "regulated process of equivalents and substitutions which *cuts across* the separate registers of the general social body"[11]—is to some extent reprised in Suzanne Woods's analysis of the modern "state" as it is represented in Books 5 and 6 of Milton's *Paradise Lost,* in particular through the figure of the isolated loyalist Abdiel. Woods follows one of Barroll's own distinctive arguments to claim that the very patriarchal power that in structural terms informs the symbolic order is weakened in the early-seventeenth century whereby "the Crown (synonymous with 'the State')" found itself "in ideological opposition to those whom the Crown rules." Barroll's "polymorphic body politic," in which different interest groups such as the aristocracy, the gentry, and merchants, along with the Crown, "made up the early modern state by relating to one another within a general formation characterised by the constant mobility of power centering" (cited, 279), figures for Woods as the terrain upon which there developed a sense of individual autonomy that signified "personal and political freedom" (279).

It is Abdiel's resistance to Satan's rebellion that for Woods encapsulates the debate between what for Milton is "liberty" and "heedl-esse license" (281). Despite Milton's own dislike of monarchy, his own representation of himself as "a singular voice of conscience against the easily swayed mobs," and his depiction of the "coura-geous isolation" of Abdiel, indicates sympathy for a figure and a gesture that makes the angel "Milton's kind of rebel prophet" (283). Her reading of the theology implicit in this resistance is of a rather different kind from that proposed by Belsey. Milton, Woods argues, invites the reader to exercise "personal freedom" in interpreting this encounter as "a consistent reminder, if we choose to believe it, that it is possible to know good by knowing good, and that we do not have to fall into evil to know good" (288). Where Belsey would emphasize a constitutive dialectics that resides at the heart of the Fall,[12] Woods posits a concept of "presence" beyond signification that the exercise of "personal freedom" is designed to exemplify in Milton's poem. It is this "centering [of] individual freedom" that allows Milton to change "the cultural dynamics" by inviting the "individual reader and the individual hero to make choices founded on conscience and responsibility" (289). Of course, the question remains of precisely *how* such "conscience" and "respon-sibility" are produced in the ideology that informs the unconscious of the text.

Both Belsey and Woods, in their different ways, explore the dy-namic and shifting micropolitics of the early-modern period. Bar-bara Maria Stafford's essay "Artificial Intensity: The Optical Technologies of Personal Reality Enhancements" draws attention to particular aspects of early-modern technology and to the traces that various technological devices leave in visual art. Optic magni-fying glasses, "wonder cabinets," "magic lanterns," "perspective boxes," mirrors, and various anamorphic apparatuses capable of transforming human images, all contribute to the early modern definition of the "human" as being aligned with "the instrumental-isation of the biological self" (293). Stafford wants to depart from histories of "progress" which, she thinks, have served to obscure the "supernatural, wonder-inducing, and knowledge-producing evolution" as represented by this "optical instrumentation" (296). Stafford is on a mission to reinstate the "aura" of visual objects sep-arated from their context in a quotidian reality, as in a museum or an exhibition such as the *Devices Of Wonder: From the World in a Box to Images on a Screen* (293), to a serious consideration of these technological accomplishments as offering "the promise both to extend us prosthetically and to deliver transcendence" (296). It is the desire to perceive technological advances as capable of "delivering transcendence" that needs further elucidation here, especially in the light of how particular mechanical inventions mediate the natural world, replicate its features, and augment it, and in so doing, aim to return humanity to a lost perfection. Indeed, the juxtaposition of various objects such as "shells, gems, coins, sculpture, paintings, clocks and automata" may be perceived as "struggles to uncover general categories or cognitive patterns from myriad particulars," which "were signs of the turn towards empirical observation emerging in the sixteenth and seventeenth centuries" (297). Stafford's is a highly personal enthusiasm for the investigation and analysis of the material objects of culture that are designed to extend human potential, and she reads them as traces of those forces that "shape us" (304).

This essay offers a fitting conclusion to an impressive range of essays, that, taken collectively, pay a full and deserved tribute to Leeds Barroll's own intellectual achievement. Each essay is, in its own way, controversial, seeking to expand our knowledge of the early-modern period rather than simply to affirm a status quo. In precisely the same way that scholars have regularly returned to Barroll's own writings, so this collection, expertly edited by Lena Cowen Orlin, *performs* that role and invites readers to return, to debate, to challenge received knowledge, and to extend its horizons. These are, as the title suggests, "revisions," invitations to rethink, that are a fitting tribute to a lifetime dedicated to the prosecuting and encouraging of serious scholarship.

Notes

1. Michel Foucault, *The History of Sexuality Vol. 1: An Introduction,* trans. Robert Hurley (Harmondsworth: Penguin Books, 1978), 100ff.

2. Michel Foucault, *The Archaeology of Knowledge,* trans. A. M. Sheridan Smith (London: Tavstock? Publications, 1982) 31–33.

3. Cf. Will Fisher, *Materialising Gender in Early Modern English Literature and Culture* (Cambridge: 2006), 87.

4. See Cambridge University Press, Phyllis Rackin, "Misogyny is Everywhere." *A Feminist Companion to Shakespeare,* ed. Dympna Callaghan (Oxford: Blackwell, 2001), 42ff.

5. Jean E. Howard and Phyllis Rackin, *Engendering a Nation: A Feminist Account of Shakespeare's English Histories* (London: Routledge, 1997), 44.

6. Falco cites approvingly J. H. Walter's edition of *Henry V* that makes "the

appropriate connection to St. Paul's ecstasies" (232). Only in T. W. Craik's Arden 3 edition of the play is there a reference to St. Paul (*King Henry V* [London: 1995], 123n.29).

7. Stephen Greenblatt, "Psychoanalysis and Renaissance Culture," *Learning to Curse: Essays in Early Modern Culture,* (New York: Routledge, 1991), pp.131–45.

8. Ibid., 137.

9. Ibid., 142.

10. Jean-Joseph Goux, *Symbolic Economies After Marx and Freud,* trans. Jennifer Curtiss Gage (Ithaca: Cornell University Press, 1990), 24.

11. Ibid., 21.

12. See especially, *Shakespeare and The Loss of Eden* (Basingstoke: Palgrave Macmillan, 1999), 38ff.

REVIEWS

Environment and Embodiment
in Early Modern England
Edited by Mary Floyd-Wilson and
Garrett A. Sullivan, Jr.
Houndmills: Palgrave Macmillan, 2007

Reviewer: Theresa Krier

In 2004, the University of North Carolina hosted a conference called "Inhabiting the Body, Inhabiting the World," and the Shakespeare Association of America hosted a seminar called "Ecologies of the Early Modern Body," both organized by Mary Floyd-Wilson and Garrett Sullivan. Now we have two volumes of essays developed from these gatherings, grounded in the productive and provocative area of historical phenomenology—a special issue of *Renaissance Drama* called *Embodiment and Environment in Early Modern Drama and Performance* (n.s. 35, 2006), and the Palgrave Macmillan collection reviewed here. It's a book of strong, gratifyingly detailed essays, with a broad purview on many aspects of early modern life. John Sutton, coming from the philosophy of cognition, unfolds the early modern sense of the brain as spongy, disconcertingly able—like sponges—both to absorb and efface, in order to argue that "cognitive order and stability were not natural to the isolated brain, but were integrative achievements often distributed over tools and other people as well as the unstable nervous system" ("Spongy Brains and Material Memories," 16). Mary Thomas Crane walks with Andrew Marvell through "The Garden," arguing that he deploys his period's Aristotelian understanding of wonder as a cognitive passion to resist mid-seventeenth-century partisanship: wonder provides "a wonderfully flexible space where seemingly opposed doctrines and concepts remain suspended in a kind of playful equilibrium" ("Marvell's Amazing Garden," 35). In the most meticulous and beautifully crafted essay in the volume,

Elizabeth D. Harvey examines relations between psyche and soma in Donne's *Metempsychosis,* a poem that explores the notion of the tripartite soul through a narrative based on Pythagorean transmigration of souls ("The Souls of Animals: John Donne's *Metempsychosis* and Early Modern Natural History"). Steven Mullaney gives an account of the formation of Elizabethan drama in the generation of Kyd, Marlowe, and Shakespeare based on the historical changes and losses prompted by the English Reformation—in this case, the Reformation's sundering of the living from the community of the dead ("Affective Technologies: Toward an Emotional Logic of the Elizabethan Stage"). Katherine Rowe counterposes seventeenth-century tragedy, melodrama, and romance and their handling of contract to explore "the problem of forensic continuity of the self" (96) in a world anxious about fluxions of a humoral identity ("Inconstancy: Changeable Affections in Stuart Dramas of Contract"). Jim Egan ("The East in British-American Writing: English Identity, John Smith's *True Travels,* and Severed Heads") argues that Smith's marginalization of America in the *Travels* is a significant triangulation: "Smith was trying to show us precisely that English colonization of American space depends on a particular understanding of spaces to England's East" (104). David J. Baker, also taking up a travel narrative or rather its frontispiece ("'My Liquid Journey': The Frontispiece to *Coryat's Crudities (1611)*"), traces the page's comic excesses of depicted bodily matter and excreta with the suggestion that "the traveler is wittily dissected as a body in flux, seeping foreign stuff into the British body politic by various noxious means" (130). Gail Kern Paster's "Becoming the Landscape: The Ecology of the Passions in the Legend of Temperance" joins a distinguished line of scholarship on *The Faerie Queene,* Book II when she analyzes "the relations of body to environment, and of passions to their environmental surround," with a moving emphasis on the capacities of both environment and character for nurture, and the discovery of a human desire, as her title suggests, to fuse with landscape or natural elements. Katharine A. Craik ("'The Material Point of Poesy': Reading, Writing, and Sensation in Puttenham's *The Arte of English Poesie*") presses a claim for Puttenham's subtle articulations of relationships between poetry and feeling, the ways that poems move us and even move toward us. Tanya Pollard's "Spelling the Body" describes the force of magic spells as deriving from physical contact between written spells or prayers and the human bodies on which they were placed. Julian Yates's "Humanist Habitats; or, 'Eating Well' with Thomas More's *Utopia*" links the "net-work-models" underwriting all the projects of these essays to the original humanist project, insofar as both of these rely on technologies of the self to produce "different configurations of persons . . . [they are] ways of ingesting or introjecting various non-human entities . . . so that they are brought to bear on human relations" (193).

Threading through all the essays are variously implicit and explicit reflections on a multiform sense of the term "environment." An environment can be a cultural institution like the theater, in its capacity as "a critical affective arena" for addressing and enacting trauma (82); an environment might be a material medium, like the paper and inscriptions of spells placed against the body; it might be the geoclimatic world of winds and weathers ("the winds were in effect the body's passions out of doors," as Paster finely says [138]). Environment might name a differential genre system, like the structural relationships among melodrama, tragedy, and romance. An environment might be the brain's spongy, complex network or the dynamic network of humors, each of them mirroring environmental networks outside the body. An environment might be the open space outside the confines of the body, especially a space from which air, food, and stimuli enter our bodies and into which bodily matter returns. A crucial strength of this open-field approach to the notion of environment is that the mediating function of environment becomes salient, as when Sutton calls attention to the work of "culture, artifice, and moral practice" as "supplements which construct and maintain the biological processes that they simultaneously and deeply reform" (27), or when Crane describes how wonder and its cognate attitudes can mediate the individual's response to historical change in the revolutionary period.

The strategic advantages of this open-ended sense of environment notwithstanding, I want here to consider what still lies outside the terms of the book. What counts as environment shifts from essay to essay, as need arises. But the centrality of the human body (the human self) is less variable. It's a book structured around human fashioning and "somatic ecology" (3)—which sounds to me like a paradoxical phrase. For as Julian Yates suggests in his essay, many "non-human entities" of an ecological system tend to remain outside such a humanist or retro-humanist project of subject formation. Among them are Raphael's sheep in *Utopia*'s discussion of enclosure and farming, creatures who suggest to Yates an escape from his sense of an all-consuming humanism both in the sixteenth century and the twenty-first: "the ethico-political demand . . . may lie in trying to imagine what Utopia would entail for sheep. . . . what [Raphael's] momentary suspension of the discourse of species reveals is the way the enforcement of the human/non-human divide pre-empts the inclusion of all 'humans' as 'persons.'"

The creatureliness of these sheep complicates a range of otherwise fruitful dichotomies structuring this book. Floyd-Wilson and Sullivan are smart to address the predominance of dichotomies from the get-go; they are even optimistic about it: "we acknowledge the conceptual utility of thinking dualistically about body and environment. Doing so allows us to get an important purchase on many aspects of early modern thought" (3). They are right; dualisms work very well in these essays, in large part because the individual essays tend to move from a specified early modern dualism—microcosm and macrocosm, say—toward some new formulation that's become available in later discourses, as in the case of the word *ecology* itself.

The Introduction identifies four usefully dualistic early modern models of "transactions between body and environment" (3) examined in the collection. First is similitude, governed by "the overarching sense that the body resembles the world," as in the case of microcosm and macrocosm. Second is exchange, in which external objects (food, air) cross a threshold into the body and other objects cross over into the external world. Third is the counteractive model, in which "the body complexion is formed in opposition or through resistance to the environment," as in Stoicism's "withdrawal from an environment that too powerfully engages the passions" or in anxieties about the effectualness of regimen in managing the humoral body. Fourth is a dispersion or distribution model, in which "the embodied mind extends across the environment in its functional reliance on culture and artifice," or passions saturate a landscape. This taxonomy of motions and passages of the body in its negotiations with the world nicely demonstrates the intellectual-history aspect of the book's varied projects as they summon up Galen, Aristotle, Thomas Wright, Helkiah Crooke, and other encyclopedic writers of natural philosophy.

Floyd-Wilson and Sullivan take pains to ground their key terms within the context of historical phenomenology, which has "alerted us to the 'ecological' nature of early modern conception of embodiment—the way in which the body is understood as embedded in a larger world with which it transacts" (2). Ecology in this context is the drama of what happens inside the human body in early modern deployments of humoral physiology. From this point of view, the definitional open-endedness of *environment* appears as an impasse. The impasse arises because of the book's interest in the human, subject-formation side of the environment/embodiment equation, as distinct from what is outside the subject: landscape, animals, foreigners, farmers and shepherds, even women. This equation works as a dialectic of extraordinary force, along with a parallel dichotomy of inward and outward. It is the self that's inside, notwithstanding the gravitational pull of claims for somatic exchanges with the external world. Thus the notion of environment functions mostly in an indexical capacity, pointing toward anything that lies outside the zone of the human body's skin envelope. But how could such a powerful binary possibly be recast?

Much the liveliest aspects of the book become clear if we consider the degree to which these essays bespeak a gesture toward intimacy with the *quick* of things, to borrow a word that had broader and more intense significances than it does today: beings' vitality, mobility, energy, warmth. Hence the attention to the soma in essays devoted to articulating the latencies of proprioception, perception, sensation, affect, the fleeting consciousness of the lived.[1] Katharine Craik quotes Plutarch's observation that poems "come nere unto us, and touch the quicke," as if poems approach to make contact with the reader's own quick. Pollard's whole subject is the direct contact of written spells with the human body. For Rowe, a crucial aspect of genre differentiation is that genres variously model "the radical impressibility of affections," "the fact of being moved by the world as one moves through it" (93, 92). For Mullaney, a pathos of Elizabethan culture after the shocks of the English Reformation lies in his sense that "it's not just that Shakespeare's generation didn't know what to believe; they didn't know how to *feel*." The theater is a discovery that redresses this impoverishment.

In this book it is not only poems whose livingness—their ability to move, in both senses—might come near us, enlarge us, or move us. In key essays of the book, animals make unforgettable visitations, as with Yates's sheep who all too briefly warm up the emotional atmosphere of the essay. Paster's essay opens with a sober analysis of Spenser's bullock from the "Februarie" eclogue of *The Sheapheardes Calender,* who "venteth into the wynd:" "The etymological pun on Latin *ventus* makes the bullock's expelled breath an image of wind interacting with wind, of wind from within the body pushing back the wind outside, of microcosm and macrocosm converging and as the air." What reader could not be made joyful by this conjunction of patient scholarship and animal happiness, and by the approach of the bull's warm breath? When Paster's essay is paired with Harvey's piece on Donne's *Metempsychosis,* a poem in which a soul finds itself hosted variously by a swan, a mouse, an elephant, an embryonic wolf, and many others, we can perceive the stakes of a desire for nearness to animal vitality. For the poem assays "an inhabitation by the very beings that rational humanity seeks to disavow" (58). There are many reasons that our rational humanity might wish to disavow animal nature, of course; for Donne, one of them is that it's potentially painful to acknowledge the passions, agencies, and sufferings of other beings.

And there are other forms of nonhuman aliveness in this book. The first two pages of the introduction discuss the youth Verdant in Spenser's Bower of Bliss as exemplifying the concerns of the book to come. Verdant has been seduced by the enchantress Acrasia, and sleeps heavily throughout the episode that Floyd-Wilson and Sullivan discuss; he thus nicely fulfills his task of crystallizing issues of bodily regimen, temperance, the fluidity of the body, and so on. Nonetheless, he is most memorable for his investment with poetic figures insisting on his sheer livingness. As Sullivan says of Verdant in another context, he is "the perfect figure for undifferentiated (or undifferentiatable) vitality. . . . [he] exists at the intersection of the animal, vegetable, and human."[2]

Literary work has, from time to time, profited spectacularly from considering just such questions of livingness, immediacy, and the relation of animal life to human nature through anthropology; the instances of James Frazier and Clifford Geertz come to mind. In the present instance I want to draw on a brilliant series of essays on animism and totemism by anthropologist Tim Ingold, who considers definitions of aliveness available within Western intellectual history by tracing relationships among many beings in animic cultures, among them Lapp caribou herders and the Ojibwa of Canada. (Not coincidentally, the same essays take up what it means to have a body and to metamorphose bodily form.) What counts as life? Why do we think that life is contained within discrete objects in an inert or inanimate field? In the circumpolar cultures that Ingold studies, "Far from revealing the shape of a world that already exists . . . life is the temporal process of its ongoing creation" by all beings.[3]

Let me summarily take stock of . . . two approaches. The first posits a world "out there" full of objects, animate and inanimate. The life process of animate objects, being the expression of their essential nature . . . under given environmental conditions, is understood to be purely consequential, an "effect." Hence an additional principle, of mind or consciousness, has to be invoked to account for the powers of intentionality and awareness that we normally attribute to persons. In animic systems such as those of the Ojibwa, these powers are said to be projected onto non-human kinds. . . . [But] my argument has followed an alternative path. This has been to envisage the world from the point of view of a being within it, as a total field of relations whose unfolding is tantamount to the process of life itself. Every being emerges . . . as a locus of growth . . . within this field. . . . Thus the world is not an external domain of objects that I look *at,* or do things *to,* but is rather going on, or undergoing continuous generation, with me and around me. (107–8)

For life is not a principle that is separately installed inside individual organisms, and which sets them in motion upon the stage of the inanimate. To the contrary . . . life is a name for *what is going on* in the generative field within which organic forms are located and held in place. That generative field is constituted by the totality of organism-environment relations, and the activities of organisms are moments of its unfolding. . . . This means that in dwelling in the world, we do not act *upon* it, or do things *to* it; rather we move along *with* it. Our actions do not transform the world, they are part and parcel of the world's transforming itself. (200)

Ingold thus lets go of issues of "the subject." When these have gone, they leave not a vacancy but an unfolding field populated by many kinds of beings, energies, and forces. Of course literature has fields like this too, less concerned with fashionings and regimens of the human subject than with energies and forces encountering one another, weaving a web that *is* life unfolding. They occur in Lucretius and in Stoic allegories of myth, for instance, whereby—as Jon Whitman finely says—"the gods lose their personalities in the interests of science, but bequeath to the world that survives them their personal energy and dynamism."[4] They occur in literary work informed by ancient myth and natural philosophy on the elements (which turns out to be a very, very great deal of literary work, from antiquity to avant-garde fiction of the present). For Spenser and even for Shakespeare, elemental motion can prompt narrative movement; the motions of the elements are of narrative interest in

themselves. Elemental motion infuses character. That is, Spenser
and even Shakespeare don't always (or even often) begin with what
we now call the human subject; from the start they are invested in
characters shaped by or derived from mythic energies and forces,
allegorized representations of the passions, natural energies. What
would happen if an element became a character? It is perhaps unre-
markable to say that Spenser frequently asks this question—but
Shakespeare asks it too. Especially in his late plays, such a question
engages with a turn-of-the-century interest in the elements, motion
and space, dynamic materialisms and vitalisms.[5] Or again, such
fields of aliveness occur in medieval narrative, alongside the ubiquitous dualisms but perhaps most often in traditions that sit only
loosely, if at all, in relation to Christianity: in Scandinavian sagas,
in Celtic and Germanic folktale and heroic narrative, in the pervasive and influential European romance tradition that attests to mysterious, often shape-shifting life forms and energies alive
everywhere in the endless woods and seas. Fields of aliveness in
this sense occur frequently in Spenser's work, and it's telling that
Spenser plays a large role in *Environment and Embodiment in
Early Modern England.* (Gail Paster's essay in this volume was
given as a talk at an international conference on Spenser in 2006.)
This large, populous, unpredictable field of aliveness informs crucial moments in the book reviewed here. The essayists rethink the
very sense of being alive within a field of unfolding relationships
with other vital forces and beings who face us with the question of
what counts as a character, and therefore what counts as a narrative. They also confront us with questions about justice, as in
Yates's wondering what a utopia for sheep might look like, or in
Caliban's and Ariel's confronting Prospero's dicta.

Expanding literary terms like character and plot, hence literary
history broadly, must be a good thing. But it is not the only consequence of recasting the question of how we define life or livingness
or environment or ecology, in the work of historical phenomenology. One of the moving and (so far as I can tell) unremarked phenomena of this book is the anxiety that drifts through its pages
concerning the world's many, many objects and technologies, what
Emerson somewhere called "the fearful extent and multitude of objects." The sheer profusion of non-animate objects is felt as over-
whelming not just to early modern people but to contemporary
scholars, and I think this is symptomatic of the binaries underlying
the book's key terms. It's true that the early modern period does

find itself sometimes nearly driven mad by the penetrability of the senses in a world full of intromissive stimuli, driving beams, rays, and simulacra into the body. Floyd-Wilson and Sullivan put it first as "Renaissance anxiety about relations between body and environment" and "anxiety about the limits of regimen" (1, 2). Sutton's essay on the spongy brain speaks repeatedly of "the vast and uneven range of objects, props, and institutions used to scaffold and buttress activities of remembering, feeling, thinking, imagining, reasoning, communicating, and so on" and of the difficulty of analyzing "the multiplicity of relevant dimensions" (20, 23) as if inundated by such objects and entities in the constructed environment. He even adduces other scholars who challenge new historicism's attachment to glittering objects. Crane cites Jonathan Sawday's panicky description of "an endlessly repetitive interplay of metaphor, similitude, and comparison" in which "the body lay entangled within a web of enclosing patterns of repetition" (38), and she makes clear that Marvell's "The Garden" uses wonder as a defense against the sheer volume of "beliefs and causes" (50) besieging people in the mid-seventeenth century.[6] Baker's essay emphasizes not only the "surprising amount" and variety of "bodily filth" (118) in the frontispiece to *Coryat's Crudities* but also the chaos-inducing layout of the crowded engraving. The volume frequently reflects an additional sense of inundation from the fearful extent of explanatory systems circulating in the canonical texts, which are, after all, not only anatomical, philosophical, and medical but also encyclopedic: Galen, Aristotle, Hippocrates, la Primaudaye, the wonderful Bartholomaeus Anglicanus as mediated by Stephen Batman, Thomas Wright, Robert Burton, many others. What is being registered in this disturbance?

Yet once more, it seems to me, anxiety over heaps of objects is a displaced anxiety revolving around the issue of definitions of aliveness and acknowledgments of aliveness in other beings. At any rate this is how Spenser understands this very problem in *The Faerie Queene* II, a crucial poem for all the issues of this volume. In the genre that Spenser critiques through Book II, moralized epic-romance, knightly heroes are isolated and stranded in a world of relentlessly threatening forces, working hard to remain self-contained and self-preserved, little islands of firmly guarded humanity amid the beautiful, deadly flux of seductive objects in the world. The self against the world, the body and its senses resisting an environment of intromissive forces: this is the dualistic world in which Guyon, the protagonist of Book II, assumes that he lives. Yet everywhere around him are more various life forms, all offering models of more open and mobile ways of being in relation to environments. Moreover, Guyon's struggles to maintain poise against the onslaught of stimuli from the world's energies characteristically manifest as his resistance to thinking. Specifically, he resists perception of relations among objects and the forging of bonds with the external world. If thinking allows the psyche to create generative, mobile, ongoing meanings and links in a temporally unfolding field of beings, then it's no wonder that a felt exorbitant welter of objects elicits both intellective and affective resistance.

As Spenser's own work suggests, then, a move beyond body/environment dualisms might release the painfully perceived extent of objects in this book, by dissolving the defensive force-field around the humanist self. Literary documents and accounts of literary history, if read with an eye to elemental motions and perhaps to animic cultures, can do that work of dissolving binaries and linking the reader, and her intellectual and affective capacities, to the large field of other living beings. This is surely part of the *epistemological* energy informing both the early modern writers and the contemporary scholars represented in the pages of this book: the strongest links among its many discourses are epistemological. Its strongest early modern writers – Spenser, Donne, Marvell, More— are dedicated to mobility of thought and to investigating or expanding the possible range of relationships among thought, affect, experience, and knowledge. The quick of thought and feeling that they seek resides not in the human form but in the endless process of acknowledging manifold forms of life and affect (just what Guyon can't ever do), and generating productive links among them. Thus the kind of work in this book approaches the kind of historical science studies on the social and literary embeddedness of science. Among many others, one might think of Karen Edwards, Stephen Fallon, John Rogers, Elizabeth Spiller, Catherine Webster, all of whom not only take poetic history seriously for matters of the history of science, but who read natural philosophy with a literary eye. This kind of mobility seems precisely what Mary Floyd-Wilson and Garrett Sullivan hope for at the end of their introduction: they hope to dismantle "the usual [binary] categories of analysis," and though they privilege subjectivity, "we do so cautiously, with an eye to forming and sustaining approaches to history-writing that decenter humans" (11). This is not only epistemology, it is epistemophilia.

Notes

1. This move toward immediacy constitutes an interesting swing of the critical pendulum in its relation both to theory and to currents in new historicism. It would be worth examining in the light of other such moments, as in Leavisism or the work of Raymond Williams or John Berger, and the controversies that they stir up about experience, analysis, and mediation.

2. Sullivan, "Afterword," *Spenser Studies* 22 (2007), 283–84.

3. Tim Ingold, *The Perception of the Environment: Essays in Livelihood, Dwelling and Skill* (London: Routledge, 2000), 113.

4. Jon Whitman, *Allegory: The Dynamics of an Ancient and Medieval Technique* (Cambridge: Harvard University Press, 1987), 32–33.

5. The trajectory of Angus Fletcher's career is exemplary in this regard. It's not accidental that his first, magnificent books are about the movements of allegory in Spenser, nor that his early work on Milton's *Mask* is about movement; nor that his most recent, still magnificent, books are about an American poetry of environment and motion in early modern science and theater. See *The Prophetic Moment: An Essay on Spenser* (Chicago: University of Chicago Press, 1971); *The Transcendental Masque: An Essay on Milton's Comus* (Ithaca: Cornell University Press, 1972); *Allegory: The Theory of a Symbolic Mode* (Ithaca: Cornell University Press, 1982); *A New Theory for American Poetry: Democracy, the Environment, and the Future of Imagination* (Cambridge: Harvard University Press, 2006); *Time, Space, and Motion in the Age of Shakespeare* (Cambridge: Harvard University Press, 2007).

6. Sawday's remark comes from *The Body Emblazoned: Dissection and the Human Body in Renaissance Culture* (London: Routledge, 1995), 23.

Resurrecting Elizabeth I in Seventeenth-Century England
Edited by Elizabeth H. Hageman and Katherine Conway
Madison: Fairleigh Dickinson University Press, 2007

Reviewer: Carole Levin

Resurrecting Elizabeth I in Seventeenth-Century England is a superb essay collection that deals with historical memory and the uses of history as propaganda. This collection examines how Elizabeth's writings and images were used in the seventeenth century and demonstrates how some literature of that century reflected the queen. This collection grew out of a 2003 Shakespeare Association of America seminar. The editors then invited five additional scholars to contribute essays. Given the subject, there are a few surprising omissions among the contributors, most notably John Watkins, author of *Representing Elizabeth in Stuart England: Literature, History, Sovereignty.* The essays in the collection tie together in interesting ways. One theme that comes up a number of times is how the phoenix represented Elizabeth. Another is how Elizabeth's history—actual or created—was used to support or criticize Stuart politics. Elizabeth Hageman begins the collection with a strong introduction that presents the issue of how seventeenth-century writers recast images of Elizabeth in manuscripts and printed texts.

The first essay is one of the strongest. Katherine Duncan-Jones does not address the afterlife of Elizabeth but rather examines Elizabeth at the end of her life, analyzing the visit of the Venetian envoy, Giovanni Carlo Scaramelli, to the English court soon before the queen's death, and puts that visit within the context of the final two years of her reign. Duncan-Jones argues that these two years were the most culturally inventive and rich of Elizabeth's reign, though they were also years during which the people had grown completely disillusioned with their queen. It would only be after her death that their affection would be reclaimed and this fact opens the way for the rest of the collection.

In another strong essay, Steven May argues that Elizabeth I was an accomplished rhetorician and competent poet with her own literary legacy, but that legacy was countered in the seventeenth century by speeches and writings that were wrongly attributed to her. Instead of the seventeenth-century myth of Elizabeth being founded on her own writing, it was based both on third-person remembrances and a substantial body of what May refers to as "bogus discourse" (48). Part of the problem was that William Camden's history of Elizabeth used little of her own writings and also was published originally in Latin. The English translation was based on a French translation of the Latin, so the accuracy of any of Elizabeth's words is even more questionable. Elizabeth Pentland's essay is concerned with two 1620s' pamphlets, John Reynolds's *Vox Coeli* and Thomas Scot's *Robert Earle of Essex His Ghost,* published with *A Post-Script; or, A Second Part of Robert Earle of Essex.* These polemics present a martial Elizabeth who led her armies to victory. Pentland ties these representations to Elizabeth's Armada speech and *Book II* of Spenser's *Faerie Queene.* Pentland carefully analyzes how these pamphlets not only respond to the political situations of the time in which they were written, but show us much about the development of the myth of Elizabeth as it developed.

Alan Young discusses the image of the phoenix as one of the most powerful motifs of Elizabeth, giving a vivid description of the myth of the phoenix as it was disseminated in the sixteenth century. Young argues that while the phoenix was also used at the accession of James I, the powerful image did not become a major part of the iconography of the Stuart king, perhaps because James was so reluctant to present himself as Elizabeth's heir. The association of the phoenix with the new king was soon lost as the English people became disillusioned with James and the phoenix mythology faded. Georgianna Ziegler also discusses the phoenix image but within the context of the similarities of poetry written about Elizabeth I and her namesake Princess Elizabeth, daughter of James I who married Frederick, Elector Palatine in 1613. This is a particularly erudite essay that argues that there was a deliberate conflation of the identities of the two Elizabeths to evoke support for the Stuarts in the early years of James's reign. This conflation is especially significant because from the time she was a baby Elizabeth Stuart was, in Ziegler's words, "a site of contention between religious factions" (112). Ziegler carefully analyzes a number of poets; most interesting is her discussion of Aemilia Lanyer's *Salve Deus Rex Judaeorum.*

Lisa Gim provides another extremely fine essay. She discusses seventeenth-century women authors who used Elizabeth as a significant role model for women. Gim argues that Elizabeth had been able to occupy a number of different gender identities. While some were culturally acceptable, such as chaste virgin or mother to her country, others, such as learned scholar and authoritative prince, might be claimed on the part of her sex, that many women, not just Elizabeth, were exceptional. Gim focuses on the portrayal of Elizabeth in the work of Dutch educator and scholar Anna Maria van Schurman, who published in Latin, and the Puritan poet Anne Bradstreet. Gim demonstrates that this commemoration of Elizabeth allowed for belief in a transnational community of Protestant woman. Another very strong essay is Brandie Siegfried's, which deals with how Francis Bacon and Margaret Cavendish helped to reestablish Elizabeth's reputation, Bacon early in the seventeenth century and Cavendish later. Siegfried argues that both writers yoked their desires for fame and high reputation to carefully crafted nostalgia for Elizabeth. She brilliantly argues that the writings of these two authors demonstrate how the memory of the queen was believed to provide the possibility of reciprocity between the past and the future. Siegfried writes beautifully, and shows convincingly how Cavendish built on Bacon's work, but for Cavendish the image of Elizabeth allowed for the possibility of the attainment of social justice.

A number of the essays in the collection deal with seventeenth-century drama. Peter Hyland's beautifully written essay on *The Revenger's Tragedy* works as a response to and dialogue with Steven Mullaney's earlier famous essay, "Mourning and Misogyny." Hyland argues that though in 1603 people had tired of Elizabeth and cheered the prospect of having a king, this play written in 1606 and performed the following year demonstrates that there was a crisis of confidence in James only a few years into his reign, and only recently after the gunpowder plot. The audience would not only have made the obvious connection between Vindice's late mistress and the late queen, but would also have felt a strong nostalgia for Elizabeth. Hardin L. Aasand's essay is a thoughtful discussion of what he calls Ben Jonson's "provocative fixation" (95) on his dead queen that demonstrates how that fixation is a significant ingredient in his Jacobean masques.

Jonathan Baldo argues that James's greatest challenge when he became king of England was to make his new English subjects forget his famous predecessor. This became even more of a problem for James after the death of his popular son Henry in 1612. Baldo places the composition of Shakespeare and Fletcher's *Henry VIII* within this context. Kim Noling also looks at the play *Henry VIII* but as one of the sources for the late seventeenth-century play by John Banks, *Vertue Betray'd; or, Anna Bullen,* first performed in 1682. *Henry VIII* had been staged frequently since the Restoration, and Noling demonstrates the ways in which Banks's play is a direct response to Shakespeare's. Unlike the infant Elizabeth in the Shakespeare play, Banks inserts the child on stage and traces an alternative, maternal origin for English Protestantism. For Banks, unlike Shakespeare, Elizabeth is far more her mother's daughter than her father's. Erika Mae Olbricht continues some of the themes of the previous essay by discussing John Banks's play, *The Island Queens,* which creates a personal eroticized relationship between

Mary and Elizabeth that ends with Mary's execution. Davison manipulates Elizabeth into signing Mary's death warrant by making Elizabeth jealous of Mary's popularity. This play was written around the time of the Exclusion Crisis. Olbricht argues that when the story of Elizabeth and Mary Stuart was retold in this later period, the women's "femaleness" was more compelling than their competing religions.

Music is an important but often overlooked aspect of English Renaissance culture. Leslie Dunn takes a different angle in discussing Elizabeth's afterlife by looking at both Elizabeth as a musician and the music composed to celebrate her. Dunn discusses Thomas Morley's 1601 publication of *The Triumphes of Oriana,* a collection of twenty-five madrigals that all ended with the refrain "Long live fair Oriana," and then analyzes how these madrigals served as a model for tributes to Elizabeth throughout the seventeenth century, showing a connection between musical responses to the death of Elizabeth and the death of Mary II in 1694.

The collection closes with Susanne Wofford's fine essay that argues that significant aspects of Kapur's 1998 film *Elizabeth* were drawn from John Foxe's *Acts and Monuments* and Thomas Heywood's play, *If You Know Not Me, You Know Nobody.* While an interesting analysis, this essay offers few connections with the others in the collection. In the interests of full disclosure, in 2003 I published an essay I co-authored with Jo Eldridge Carney, "Young Elizabeth in Peril: From Seventeenth Century Drama to Twentieth Century Films," that also discussed Foxe and Heywood, and it would have been useful for Wofford to have addressed this in her essay.

The interest in Queen Elizabeth I appears to be unending. This book is to be commended for offering fine new ways of understanding the significance of how Elizabeth's image was represented in the seventeenth century. The essays help us understand how Elizabeth's memory was manipulated by politics just as it was commemorated by such women as Anne Bradstreet and Margaret Cavendish.

Collaborations with the Past:
Reshaping Shakespeare
Across Time and Media
By Diana E. Henderson
Ithaca: Cornell University Press, 2006

Reviewer: *Margaret Jane Kidnie*

Diana Henderson's engagingly written book explores four case studies of "diachronic collaboration" with Shakespeare in order to tease out what she describes as an ongoing process of "Shake-shifting." Debates around collaboration are by now well-established in Shakespeare studies, whether one thinks of contributors and processes associated with book production, cultural implications of early modern writing partnerships, or more philologically oriented attribution studies. The pressing question now is perhaps how far a conception of collaboration can be extended while still providing, whether in terms of theory or practice, a meaningful category of study. Highlighting the "contradictory history" of collaboration— the "mixed messages" the word inevitably carries after the Second World War—Henderson deliberately situates her examination of intertexts and borrowings within the "'uneasy' . . . dimensions of working with Shakespeare across time and media" (13). As her title suggests, the collaborations tracked in the book are as much with "the past" as with Shakespeare. Henderson implicitly resists a recent presentist trend that would refunction literature and history as sites for the exploration of current political interests, instead seeking, in a manner familiar for instance from the work of Robert Weimann, to tread an intermediary path that neither celebrates nor breaks with "the past." By maintaining this "difficult dance" between history and performance, one begins to perceive the past as multivalent rather than monolithic, and so "available for radical, sometimes magical shifting" (35).

Collaborations with the Past is structured as four chapters, with an introduction. The first half of the book focuses on two novels (*Kenilworth* and *Mrs Dalloway*), while the second section addresses a range of mostly filmic treatments of *Taming of the Shrew* and

Henry V. Henderson offers a rich, wide-ranging analysis of *Kenilworth* that opens with a persuasive account of the way the plot, themes, and characterization of *Othello* shape Sir Walter Scott's fictionalized account of Leicester's illicit first marriage and career in the court of Elizabeth I. The chapter increasingly moves beyond an account of Scott's literary borrowings and departures from the historical record as Henderson develops an argument for a revisionist reading of the novel's politics of "race" that interprets the Celtic borderlands (Scotland especially, but also Cornwall) occupying the othered space of Othello's blackness. Scott is thus presented as a writer more controversial and position-taking than literary history has allowed. The final part of the chapter offers a fascinating explanation of how Scott's stage "collaborators" popularized the novel for the nineteenth century—and so helped to set in place Scott's reputation for conservatism—precisely by draining it of its nationalist political agenda.

The second chapter moves from Victorian to Modernist "Shakeshifting" to explore Virginia Woolf's acknowledged indebtedness to *Cymbeline* alongside her unacknowledged structural borrowings from *Jane Eyre*. "A Fine Romance" provides Henderson the opportunity to question what might have seemed to Woolf a problematic inheritance from Victorian England, and how Shakespeare might have appeared a more amenable collaborator, both in terms of gender and historical situation, than Charlotte Brontë, Woolf's nearer literary contemporary. Henderson is clear from the outset of her study that other theorists of collaboration (she cites Jeffrey Masten, in particular) "would efface 'the author' more completely" than she does (1n1). What surprises somewhat about the *Dalloway* chapter, even in light of its psychoanalytic orientation toward resurrections and legacies of the mother, is the extent to which Henderson relies on biography and Woolf's presumed authorial reading strategies to make an argument for (occluded) influence. Thus, Septimus Smith "could hardly avoid evoking" the memory of Woolf's dead brother, Thoby (115), while for a writer already attuned to *Cymbeline,* "the latter part of *Jane Eyre* would be very hard to ignore" (135). There grows the uneasy awareness that this narrative of Shake-shifting— itself a critical collaboration with the past—constructs a view of Woolf as woman and intellectual that is especially indebted to a twenty-first-century readiness to find and diagnose the supposed symptoms of early twentieth-century feminist anxiety.

"The Return of the Shrew" opens the scope of investigation to

film, thus extending the analysis from novelists to other, more varied, creative collaborators. Henderson explores in turn the Pick-
ford-Fairbanks production, Jonathan Miller's BBC television
staging, Joe Papp's live production in New York's Central Park (subsequently televised as *Kiss Me, Petruchio*), and the Taylor-Burton
film, rounding out her analysis of this play's fortunes on film with
a discussion of the high school comedy *10 Things I Hate About You*.
With this chapter, Henderson returns to the troubling feminist politics of this early Shakespearean comedy, a topic she has explored
with such insight in previous publications. While remaining skeptical about the "pleasure" the play offers modern spectators, Henderson tries to push beyond ideology critique to "confron[t] the
more difficult task of understanding why we keep coming back,
and what keeps the comedy current" (158). Her tentative conclusion is that the attraction lies in the collaborative input each viewer
brings to a new film, especially the opportunity to refine and develop an independent critical interpretation among the "gaps" offered by "an always-already fractured narrative" (159). The
questions Henderson poses about the comedy's popularity are
pressing ones, but taken as a whole, this chapter on film performances of *Taming of the Shrew* feels less innovative than the other
chapters, ultimately offering a familiar cultural-feminist critique of
what are by now familiar, even canonical, examples of twentieth-
century filmed Shakespeare.

The book's closing chapter, to pick up Henderson's own terminology, offers something of a critical "swerve" as she seeks to recover historically resonant pasts that might have made *Henry V* (or
parts of it) particularly resonant for early modern English audiences. The analysis thus shifts from the situatedness of Shakespeare's later collaborators to Shakespeare's own production
moment, so keeping alive in a slightly different manner the "difficult dance" in which history and performance are engaged. Recov-
ering the nation building and gendered pasts allusively embedded
in the play through Shakespeare's fleeting reference to "Davy Gam,
Esquire" among the English warriors killed at Agincourt and his
inclusion (at least in the Folio text) of Queen Isabel among the
French court, Henderson demonstrates that these histories are
more problematic than one may expect. The stories of the French
queen and Davy Gam (or rather, to return to him the Welsh form of
his name, Dafydd ap Llywelyn) are well-known to historians, if not
Shakespeareans, and Henderson's contribution is to pin down

"how exactly the artwork transforms or thematizes the history" (207), so illustrating how Shakespeare, in terms of his own past(s), was himself a collaborator and "Shake-shifter." The chapter closes with consideration of Branagh's and Olivier's landmark films and the immense difficulties involved in making submerged histories available to modern spectators.

The critical strategies employed by *Collaborations with the Past* emphasize that "the past"—whether early modern, Victorian, Modernist, or our own—is always contingent and fractured, made to speak in particular ways by means of a wide variety of creative readings of Shakespeare. I remain unclear, however, how helpful "diachronic collaboration" is as a term to describe Henderson's methodology; to return to the increasingly widespread application of collaboration studies mentioned briefly in the opening paragraph, I question what is gained by describing Woolf's or Scott's peculiar forms of extended engagement with the works of Shakespeare as a form of "collaboration" with their author. The introduction, attuned to recent critical and theoretical trends in the field, promises something methodologically innovative but at certain key moments lacks theoretical bite. The analysis that constitutes the heart of *Collaborations with the Past* is probably most easily recognizable as participating in an ongoing critical project, once closely associated with cultural materialism, concerned to study the politics and continually changing histories of Shakespeare's plays in subsequent ages. The great merit of Henderson's research lies in the manner it pays particularly close, and often revealing, attention to how "borrowings" (whether forward or back in time) can function in sometimes unexpected ways.

Shakespeare's Entrails: Belief, Scepticism and the Interior of the Body
By David Hillman
Houndsmills: Palgrave MacMillan, 2007

Reviewer: Mary Floyd-Wilson

Shakespeare scholars will recognize the provocative assertions about selfhood and the body in David Hillman's new book *Shakespeare's Entrails* from significant essays of the late 1990s published in *Shakespeare Quarterly* and in *The Body in Parts,* a landmark collection he coedited with Carla Mazzio. In some subtle ways, the book feels belated, particularly in its insistence that the corporal language of the period has too often been read as "merely metaphorical" (2)—an issue addressed almost a decade ago by both Michael Schoenfeldt and Gail Kern Paster. But *Shakespeare's Entrails* also reminds us how profoundly Hillman's scholarship has shaped our discussions of early modern somatics.

The introduction, "Visceral Knowledge," takes up a quarter of the book and presents a complex array of shifting attitudes toward embodiment that Hillman finds expressed in late sixteenth- and early seventeenth-century English writing. In the early modern period, Hillman observes, we can see a move toward excarnation, as inwardness loses its "meaning as 'entrails,' gradually coming to mean 'interiority, inner essence'" (4). One angle on this decorporealization is the emergence of *homo clausus,* the "newly 'bounded' individual," as described by Norbert Elias, "severed from all other people and things 'outside' by the 'wall' of the body" (7). Unlike Janet Adelman, Peter Stallybrass, Paster, and others, who have identified similar fantasies of somatic autonomy with male selfhood, Hillman views this phenomenon as gender neutral. Deeply influenced by Stanley Cavell, Hillman contends that the "prominence of scepticism" in the period is "evidence for the centrality of *homo clausus*" (29). Scepticism in this story is "the drive to access the interior body of the other" (29). The emergence of anatomy, in particular, anticipated a post-Cartesian, mechanistic understanding of the body.

At times, tracking the rapidly "changing attitudes," "monumental shifts," and "increasing" or "waning" trends in thought that

Hillman cites proves a bit dizzying. Nor does Hillman wish to clarify which came first, the bounded individual or the penetrative drive. While the rise of skepticism functions as "evidence" of *homo clausus,*

> the fantasy of a closed body is precisely the spur which powerfully evokes a desire for (as well as, simultaneously, a fear of) laying open, the wish to see into the (now supposedly more than ever) hidden interior corporeal spaces. . . . The closure creates the need for more penetrative kinds of knowledge, which in turn evokes a terror and a desire to protect the boundaries of the body. (35)

The logical tautology at play here does not prevent Hillman from maintaining that the loss of older modes of embodiment generated anxiety and nostalgia, as represented most powerfully in Shakespeare's drama. In the introduction, Hillman establishes that *Troilus and Cressida* "counteract[s] the disembodied, over-rhetoricised status of the heroes" with its focus on entrails. *Hamlet* and *King Lear* enact "a struggle to recover the possibility of a meaningful kind of relating to otherness in a world growing nostalgic" for an open body. And *The Winter's Tale* "portrays the imagined recovery of a world in which language is accepted as emerging from the interior of the body and in which mutual corporeal inhabitation is a newfound possibility" (52).

All of Hillman's assertions regarding embodiment are stimulating; however, readers looking for dense historical support for his arguments may be disappointed. Aside from scattered references to Montaigne, Donne, and Bacon, the history of, and scholarship on, skepticism is bypassed. Hillman's representation of embodiment relies heavily on secondary sources rather than a deep archive of primary texts. But these objections strike me as minor when we acknowledge that Hillman's analysis of the period is driven more forcefully by psychoanalytical theory than historical evidence. Trained as a child psychotherapist before pursuing the study of literature at Harvard, Hillman invokes psychoanalytical theory with sophisticated grace. His stated aim in *Shakespeare's Entrails* is to "interweave historicist lines of enquiry with theoretical models, especially psychoanalytic ones" (3). Yet the book assembles very few primary sources from the early modern period to substantiate its claims. Instead, Hillman's admirable strength lies in analyzing early modern culture through lenses provided by his inspired read-

ings of Freud, Lacan, Kristeva, Starobinski, Winnicott, Wittgenstein, and Nietzsche.

To answer the question, in chapter 2, "The Gastric Epic: *Troilus
and Cressida,*" as to why Shakespeare would retell such an overdetermined story, Hillman turns to Nietzsche for an answer. Nietzsche's ideas clear away the obfuscation of idealizing and equate
"threatening truths" with our entrails (62). At the same time, his
philosophy acknowledges that a full comprehension of the body's
interior is impossible. Similarly, Hillman observes, Shakespeare's
Troilus and Cressida unveils the "distance between our proudly deployed language and the body's internal reality" (64). The play
functions as a reaction against the "historical process of textualis-
ing the body" (59) and expresses anger toward the "'excarnation' of
the world" (60). Emphasizing the play's obsession with eating and
digestion, Hillman asserts that the project of *Troilus and Cressida* is
"implicitly cannibalistic" (71). Read as an inversion of Montaigne's
essay "Of the Caniballes," the play "defamliarises (or disassimi-
lates) the epic ethos, infusing it with a 'cannibalism' which is seen
as 'savage strangeness'" (2.3.128) (76).

In chapter 3, "The Inward Man: *Hamlet,*" Hillman complicates
the long-held critical view that the play's representation of Hamlet's inwardness anticipates modern subjectivity by emphasizing
the tragedy's transitional status: *Hamlet* "hovers on the border between a pre-modern world of permeability and the regime of *homo
clausus*" (116). Cleverly citing the hardening of Old Hamlet's body
in the ghost's description of his murder as the emergence of *homo
clausus,* Hillman suggests that the closing of the "body of the father
. . . institutes the commencement of the regime of interiority" (89).
Refreshingly, Hillman challenges the tired notion (held by Freud,
Ernest Jones, and countless critics since) that Hamlet's desires are
Oedipal with a reading of the closet scene that demonstrates how
the prince desexualizes his mother even as he seeks to know her
insides. Inspired by Benjamin, Nietzsche, Wittgenstein, and Montaigne, Hillman finds the Hamlet of act 5 letting go of "the idea that
what lies beneath the surface is what counts" (110).

The fourth chapter, "The Body Possessed: *King Lear,*" proves in-
sightful and eloquent despite Hillman's noticeable struggle to differentiate his take on the play from influential readings by both
Adelman and Cavell. If Hamlet comes to embrace exteriority, Hillman argues, then *King Lear* depicts the necessity of accepting interiority, or rather, acknowledging "one's own interior and its

contents *as* one's own, including the existence of the other within oneself" (148). Taking up the play's themes of possession and exorcism, this chapter explores how *King Lear* treats "the relation to otherness within the body" as a "relation to human others" (145). At the conclusion of the book, Hillman turns to *The Winter's Tale* in a brief reading that identifies Leontes in the first half of the play as "steeped in the culture of *homo clausus* and its ambivalent sense of somatic closure" (164). The play's second half provides a fantasy of what "overcoming skepticism *might* look like, set in a world where full redemption is no longer possible" (169).

As the prior statement indicates, Hillman repeatedly characterizes the purported emergence of *homo clausus* as irredeemably melancholic in its costs. The Shakespearean corpus in *Shakespeare's Entrails* struggles obsessively to recognize, redress, or reformulate the losses that accompanied the advent of modernity's body. But readers can also sidestep the historical question as to which bodies are premodern, early modern, or modern and still find Hillman's interrogation of their shifting boundaries enlightening.

Foxe's "Book of Martyrs" and
Early Modern Print Culture
By John N. King
Cambridge: Cambridge University Press, 2006
and
Inventing Polemic: Religion, Print, and Literary
Culture in Early Modern England
By Jesse M. Lander
Cambridge: Cambridge University Press, 2006

Reviewer: Andrea Walkden

The remodeling of bibliography on the more demanding scale of cultural history has been proceeding apace with two new contribu-

tions from John N. King and Jesse M. Lander appearing recently
from Cambridge University Press. Both authors explore religious
literature published in England during the late sixteenth and early
seventeenth centuries: in King's case, the proliferating, protean text
of John Foxe's *Acts and Monuments,* commonly known as the *Book
of Martyrs;* in Lander's a range of works that recuperate the shaping
influence of post-Reformation polemic on literary history. That religious conflict galvanized the printing presses of Europe has long
been recognized and understood, but the gains of reconstructing
theological controversies not just across different works but across
different editions of the same work are still being measured. Such
painstaking scholarship, especially when in the service of large-
scale thinking, strengthens the connections between the history of
the book and the history of religion and situates both within the
broader political, cultural, and creative development of early modern England.

   A renewed interest in religious controversy has been to the benefit of John Foxe, whose magnum opus is the subject of King's erudite monograph, *Foxe's "Book of Martyrs" and Early Modern Print
Culture.* Tracing the publication history of the *Book of Martyrs* from
its inception through successive editions, abridgments, and appro-
priations between 1563 and 1684, King argues for the collection's
exemplary function "as a window" (3) through which to view the
expansive, and expanding, landscape of early print culture. To
complement his study's historical reach, and to signal his conceptual advance on the new bibliography, King introduces Robert Darn-
ton's model of a "communications circuit" (14) which connects
author, publisher, bookseller, and reader within a continual process of cultural, socioeconomic, and politicoreligious signification.
The progression of chapters follows this model, starting with the
book's conception and compilation of documentary materials
(chapter 1), moving next to its physical production and print history (chapter 2), and finally to the woodcut illustrations and paratextual materials that sought to direct the understanding of early
modern readers and, no less importantly, the response of readers
themselves in annotations, excisions, excerptions, even in the can-
dle wax and nutshells they left within the book's folds. (chapters 3
and 4). The result is a highly readable, generously illustrated, and
well-documented companion to the *Acts and Monuments* in all its
stages of production and across numerous editions, an indispensable resource for any scholar working on Foxe, on religious po-

lemic, on print technology in the hand-press era, or, indeed, on the cultural history of the book in early modern England.

Chapter 1, "The compilation of the book," opens with two claims: first, that Foxe is best viewed not as an author but as an author-compiler, tailoring existing manuscript and printed sources to the typographical and polemical aims of his larger narrative; and second, that the four editions printed in his lifetime consist "not of a single ever-expanding book, but of four distinctive constructions" (23), each exquisitely responsive to its own historical moment. These claims established, King reconstructs the editorial process from source to final version, emphasizing both the contribution of those who collected and verified accounts on Foxe's behalf and the influence of church histories and martyrologies already in print across Europe. Central to King's account is the interplay between scribal and print culture and its self-conscious exploitation by Foxe who, recognizing that the manuscript transcription and transmission of martyrological accounts lent authenticity to his printed narrative, took care to include the dramatic circumstances of their composition, circulation, and survival. Compiled from manuscript sources, Foxe's book is itself a source for those interested in reconstructing the scribal networks of imprisoned and persecuted martyrs.

Although chapter 2, "The *Books of Martyrs* in the printing house," begins with Foxe's continental education as a Marian exile, specifically, his association with two humanist printer-publishers, Wendelin Rihel in Strasbourg and Hieronymus Froben in Basel, its true protagonist is John Day whose technological and financial acumen saw the first four editions of the *Book of Martyrs* (1563, 1570, 1576, 1583) through the press and set new standards for the London printing trade. Documenting these early editions, King is especially fine at selecting material evidence—irregular pagination, narrower columns, smaller type font, and cramped text—that illustrates how Foxe's last-minute interpolations exercised the ingenuity of Day and his team of pressmen. Allying this bibliographical expertise to broader sociocultural considerations, King shows how the need simultaneously to attract two different groups of readers, those literate in Latin and those who were not, shaped the distinctive typographical conventions of the 1563 first edition, which used double columns for vernacular text printed in black letter, single columns for Latin text printed in italic type. Although much of this Latin material was deleted from the second 1570 edition, testifying to what King terms "the progressive vernacularity of the *Book of Martyrs*" (118), the work continued to grow, swollen by antipapal argument and invective whose inclusion struck a nationalistic chord with Foxe's English readership. Subsequent editions (1576, 1583, and, posthumously, those of 1596–97, 1610, 1631–32, 1641, and 1684), as well as several notable abridgments (1589, 1613–16), each sought to intervene within its own politico-religious moment, updating paratextual and prefatory materials to reposition the *Book of Martyrs* for new readers in a new age. Tracking these timely ideological adjustments, King's summary also highlights a broader shift in book manufacture and financing as master printers gave place to syndicates of booksellers who shared the expense and profits of publication. After the death of Day's son and business successor Richard (ca. 1606), the rights to the *Book of Martyrs* together with its distinctive woodblocks were acquired by the Company of Stationers whose shared ownership stands in pallid contrast to Day's entrepreneurial production methods and assumption of personal risk.

Woodcut illustrations, some drawn from Day's existing stock, but a majority (forty-five in total) commissioned for the first edition of the *Book of Martyrs,* are the subject of King's third chapter, "Viewing the pictures." King carefully describes how Foxe and Day laid out a "coherent pattern of illustration" (169), exploiting the dynamic interplay between text and image by inserting banderoles and cartouches (ribbon-like scrolls designed to bear inscriptions) that incorporated the martyrs' final words into depictions of their grisly deaths. Tending toward the formulaic, these embedded epitaphs enabled the woodcuts to function as both oral and visual stimuli, increasing the affect of the death scene itself. For the second edition, Foxe and Day embarked on a yet more ambitious pictorial program as they sought to ramp up the work's antipapal animus in the immediate aftermath of the revolt of the Northern Earls in 1569 and the excommunication of Elizabeth by Pope Pius V in 1570. Inaugurated by a spectacular three-leaf foldout titled "A Table of the X first Persecutions of the Primitive Church," an added sequence of woodcuts depicts the age-old conflict between crown and tiara, temporal power legitimately held and imperial pretensions to it. In brief, cogent analysis, King notes how different the Foxean illustrations are in their violent realism from either the beatific saints of Caxton's edition of *The Golden Legend* (1483) or the mannerist ones of the Catholic Counter-Reformation; how, as visual imagery, they aspire to remake the nature of sainthood itself.

But what did readers make of the illustrations and how did they react to them? King concludes his discussion of the woodcuts by surveying a range of responses, literate and non-literate, hostile and approving, from the formal rebuttal of the Jesuit Robert Parsons to the viewers who stabbed out the face of Edmund Bonner portrayed flagellating one victim in his orchard and burning the hand of another. Some readers scribbled in the margin, sketching their own portraits or practicing their signature; others added details to the illustrations themselves: a flag or beard or spurting blood. Still others supplemented image with text, identifying martyrs by name or filling in empty banderoles with their own choice of final words. The focus on audience continues into King's fourth and final chapter, "Reading the pages," which begins with Foxe's various attempts to shape readerly expectations in an array of prefatory addresses and finding aids and ends with records of individual reading practices, including those recorded in Nehemiah Wallington's commonplace book and in the diary of Lady Margaret Hoby. In between King raises the vexed question of access: how extensively was the *Book of Martyrs* read and by whom? Certainly, Foxe's envisioned audience was an inclusive one, encompassing laity and clergy, nobles and commoners, the wife at her domestic duties and, Erasmus-like, the ploughman at his plough. Surveying the available evidence, King concludes that Foxe's intentions for his book were generally met: the work was made widely available, if not through the state apparatus then through private bequests to parishes across the country, even finding its way into the George Inn at Norwich where it might be read in the anti-Puritan company of cakes and ale.

As this summary suggests, King carries his encyclopedic knowledge lightly, combining an impressive breath of information with a keen and patient eye for anecdotal detail. Although description takes precedence over argument, the study does promote the *Book of Martyrs* as a text designed (and redesigned) to travel across ideological and confessional boundaries, appealing to and provoking reactions from readers of quite different political and religious beliefs. In celebrating such diversity of readership, King at times underplays the sheer nastiness of sixteenth- and seventeenth-century confessional politics; his is a gentlemanly, domesticated *Book of Martyrs* shielded from the antipapal demagoguery it helped, and was no doubt calculated, to incite. Finally, and only fittingly for a book devoted to the history of the book, the study is handsomely produced, richly, but also judiciously, illustrated, and supplied with large margins, the better for its readers to indulge their own twenty-first-century predilections for doodles, annotations, and, it is to be hoped, manicula and pictorial art.

In *Inventing Polemic* Jesse Lander shares, and arguably sharpens, theoretical positions central to King's discussion, among them the need to complement an author-centered with a sociological and commercial approach to meaning and to weigh the specificity of the individual edition or "publishing event" (5) against the transtemporal pull of the canonical classic. But as his title suggests, Lander's reach is also more ambitious, aiming to show how "the consequential intersection of religious controversy and print technology" (1) produced polemic, a new category of writing that disturbed and ultimately reshaped the literary landscape of early modern England. This argument is pursued chronologically through individual case studies: two editions of Foxe's *Acts and Monuments* (1576, 1589), the Marprelate tracts (1588–89), the early quartos of *Hamlet* (1603–04), Donne's *Pseudo-Martyr* and *An Anatomy of the World* (1610–11), and Milton's *Areopagitica* (1644). Throughout, Lander's concern is to show how the discursive form of polemic is active within a wider range of genres than might be supposed, troubling the modern distinction between "the literary" and "the non-literary" in order to historicize its construction. For within his persuasive account of the centrality of polemical writing, Lander seeks to make a yet more consequential claim: that the ascendancy of new notions of literature as polite, decorous, and discriminating emerged in self-conscious opposition to the competing values of theological controversy, dogmatic, raucous, enthusiastic, over which they ultimately triumphed.

Lander begins his own battle of the books with a nod to Swift, but the focus of his first chapter returns his reader, and this review, to Foxe's *Acts and Monuments;* specifically, the contrast between two early editions in focus and polemical intent. Taking up the question of whether Foxe intended to promote England's exceptionalism as an elect nation, the chapter considers the divergent aims of the 1576 edition, which joined debate from within the Protestant community, and of Timothy Bright's 1589 *Abridgement,* which promoted Protestant unity in the face of recent Catholic propaganda and military campaigns. Read against each other, these two editions nicely illustrate Lander's main point: that a work need not always be dressed in the same controversial colors and successive versions require consideration on their own independent terms.

Chapter 2 turns to the Marprelate tracts, anti-episcopal polemic whose surreptitious printing on a private press within England coincided with that of Bright's patriotic *Abridgement* of 1589. Setting aside efforts to determine the historical identity of Martin, Lander focuses instead on the pamphlets' strategies of address and argument. Self-referential as to their own material form, the pamphlets attacked their opponents on material grounds, seizing upon printing errors and calculating paper costs with mischievous intent. They also pitched for a popular audience, appealing to readers uninitiated in the technicalities of formal theological debate in an ambitious attempt to win support for their reformist platform. That this attempt was cried down by conformists and Puritans alike suggests the degree to which it represented a new departure on previous publicity. Here, as elsewhere in his discussion, Lander reinforces the conclusions of Joad Raymond in *Pamphlets and Pamphleteering in Early Modern Britain* (Cambridge, 2003), a study surprisingly absent from his bibliography, arguing that the Marprelate tracts opened a popular front in theological controversy from which there would be no turning back.

Lander's third chapter will interest readers of this review for its bold recasting of the differences between the first (1603) and second (1604) quartos of *Hamlet.* Reorienting a discussion traditionally focused on issues of authorial intention, theatrical origin, or editorial practice, Lander concentrates on the competing fortunes of the two quartos, and of printed drama more generally, within the commercial marketplace. Marketing strategies, so Lander argues, bear upon textual content; a careful reading of variants demonstrates the divergent theological positions of the two quartos: Q1 hewing closely to a Calvinist consensus, Q2 espousing a more speculative, skeptical, and combative approach in "specific response to the problem of religious controversy" (112). By thematizing polemic the better to register its distance from it, Q2 successfully catered to an elite and literary readership, Q1, by contrast, to a popular and theatrical one. As such, the differences in audience between the two quartos stake out the terms of Lander's larger historical argument: that the category of literature consolidates itself through a repudiation of polemical culture, against which but also by means of which it comes to be defined.

In chapter 4 the focus moves from the beginning to the end of the first decade of the seventeenth century, a decade in which confessional conflict (the Gunpowder Plot in 1605 and the assassination of Henri IV in 1610) and political circumstance (the accession of James I and the Oath of Allegiance controversy) combined to create a charged polemical environment. Into that environment stepped John Donne with two very different works: one a religious polemic, *Pseudo-Martyr* (1610), the other an elegiac volume of poetry, *An Anatomy of the World* (1611). Taking issue with biographical or psychological explanations of Donne's embrace of print at this formative moment in his career, Lander turns to the material evidence provided by the books themselves, noting in each case Donne's willing, if often punning, investment in the conditions and possibilities of print publication. Perhaps more significantly, Lander also reverses the current terms of debate, asking not what print culture might tell us about Donne's authorial aspirations, but what those aspirations might tell us about the relationship among print, polemic, and poetry at the beginning of the seventeenth century. Persuasively situating *An Anatomy* within a larger "struggle over proper poetics" (176), Lander explains why Donne's volume was construed as a hostile act, asserting an elitism which, like Q2 *Hamlet,* defined itself through a rejection of "the interpretative certitude" (179) to which polemic routinely laid claim.

Readers, whether anticipated on title pages or voiced in reprisal, hold a prominent place throughout Lander's study which moves, in its fifth chapter, to the Restoration reception and revision of Milton's 1644 tract against prepublication licensing, *Areopagitica.* Both Charles Blount, a freethinker, and William Denton, an Anglican clergyman, follow Milton's argument in their responses to the lapse of the 1679 Licensing Act, but both also abandon its religious-charged rhetoric and millenarian expectations in favor of a more secular and protoliberal vocabulary of rights and interests. As a result, Milton's "polemic for polemic" (181), that is, a polemic that argues for the virtues of polemic as well as for a particular set of positions, marks "the zenith" (182) of public religious discourse as a positive good. Such optimism would no longer be forthcoming in the new public world of the Restoration.

The fortunes of polemical theology are reprised from a different angle in chapter 6 which traces the checkered history of Chelsea College, dedicated to the production of religious controversy, from its founding under James I through its long decline and eventual demise when its building and grounds were granted to the Royal

Society in 1669. Lander entertainingly plots the various projects to revive the mission of the College or appropriate its assets, including George Cottington's scheme to divert funding to the refurbishing of St. Paul's Church in the 1630s and Samuel Hartlib's reenvisaging of the College as a center for international Protestantism in the 1650s. But his broader purpose is to show how the College's history reflects larger cultural and intellectual shifts across the seventeenth century, notably the Restoration reaction against religious enthusiasm and the emergence of a secular political discourse. Although Lander is cautious about sounding the death knell of polemic prematurely, he considers these developments as definitive in the long term, a claim he elaborates in an epilogue discussing new paradigms of sociability and polite letters that carries his argument forward into the modern era. Intercepting recent work on the establishment of the English literary canon and on the cultural category of literature more generally, Lander shows how Shakespeare and Milton were purged of polemical taint prior to their enlistment in the higher echelons of artistic achievement. As such, the final curtain call belongs to Jacob Tonson and Samuel Johnson, the kingmakers of literary culture whose legacy the Arnoldian humanists would inherit and invent anew.

Inventing Polemic is a learned, provocative, and rewarding book. If the eloquence and density of its individual chapters defy easy summary so too does its vast and heterogeneous subject: the history of polemic, material, cultural, and intertextual, from the mid-sixteenth to the end of the seventeenth century. Faced with such a rich and unruly archive, Lander's adoption of the case study is a pragmatic choice but it can be faulted for reinforcing a small canon of male writers, raising polemic by association with them rather than through its broader practice, innovation, and influence. New readings of Shakespeare, Donne, and Milton are, of course, welcome but to claim that "Milton is perhaps the only canonical writer of English literature who is celebrated for his polemic" (180) is disingenuous, overstating the critical prejudice against controversial writing by ignoring, for example, the case of Andrew Marvell whose prose works have received recent magisterial treatment in a new edition by Yale University Press and whose career usefully spans the Restoration watershed that Lander identifies. Nor is it simply that there are texts, authors, and actors whose contributions Lander does not engage. The chapters on Shakespeare and Donne are exhilarating but also troubling in the neatness with which they

anticipate the historical conclusion toward which the study progresses; to locate the rejection of polemic and its corollary, the formation of the literary, within the second quarto of *Hamlet* and *An
Anatomy of the World* as well as across the later seventeenth century is to assert a strong teleological pull that makes the prescience,
the modernity, of these works practically a self-fulfilling prophecy.
Finally, Lander's focus on "publishing events" appears to the detriment of historical ones, specifically the English Civil Wars which
receive only passing mention despite their revolutionary influence
on print media and public life. To these criticisms, it might fairly
be objected that Lander has not set himself the task of offering a
comprehensive, or perhaps even a representative, survey but of
showcasing polemical insurrections where the literary critic has
not thought to look for them. And on these terms his study suc-
ceeds quite brilliantly, opening a controversial world to compelling
critical view.

Male Friendship in Shakespeare and his Contemporaries
By Tom MacFaul
Cambridge: Cambridge University Press, 2007

Reviewer: Nicholas F. Radel

Part synthesis and part interrogation of recent theoretical and historicist constructions of friendship in early modern England, *Male
Friendship in Shakespeare and his Contemporaries* usefully demonstrates some of the complexities of the discursive conception of
friendship as it made the transition from feudal or familial to affective models in the sixteenth and early seventeenth centuries. Focusing largely on Shakespeare, the book analyzes the interrelations
between friendship and a number of other discourses and social institutions such as brotherhood, sexual jealousy, service, politics,
fellowship, and loyalty. MacFaul situates friendship among these

other social relations to demonstrate the shortcomings of the Humanist idealization of male friendship.

In part, MacFaul responds to critics such as Lorna Hutson and Laurie Shannon, whose work suggests that idealizations of friendship as an affective space of equal relations between men in Humanist writings presaged new forms of early modern subjectivity. But he pursues the implications of their work in more text-centered or rhetorical directions than historicist ones. He echoes Hutson in suggesting that the rhetorical structures through which Humanists figured idealizations of friendship "opened up a space for considerable distrust" (15),[1] and he adapts Shannon's thesis that Humanist fictions of equality in male friendship created "a space in which the individual can feel sovereign" (20).[2] He varies both, however, by arguing (with some debt to Joel Fineman's reading of the *Sonnets*[3]) that the subjectivity Shannon sees emerging in idealizing Humanist discourses of mutual friendship is "fractured" (20) by drama's habit of presenting friendly characters in tense, agonistic relations that lead to alienated rather than sovereign senses of self—alienated because the subject becomes aware of himself through his difference from his friend.

Male Friendship in Shakespeare and his Contemporaries argues that "friendship, as an arena for self-assertion, is the means by which men in the best literature of this period, particularly in the works of Shakespeare, make themselves meaningful; but ultimately they have to accept that they are alone, that the framework of meaning is impermanent" (21). Friendship, in MacFaul's reading, is a symbiotic relationship that produces a "paradoxically interdependent sense of selfhood" (20). In a rigidly hierarchical society, friendship does not instantiate ideal equality so much as it brings into focus differences that reveal the limits of the sovereign self. Within the dynamics of drama, in particular, the symbiotic tensions of friendship help uncover the "peculiar individual shape" of particular characters (21), and MacFaul focuses on revealing these characters by analyzing their friendship relations.

Contrary to critics who emphasize the Humanists' reliance on Cicero's *De Amicitia,* MacFaul makes a claim for using Aristotle and Plato as model thinkers in understanding early modern friendship. Although he recognizes that Shakespeare (and many of his English contemporaries) may not have been directly familiar with texts by Aristotle and Plato, MacFaul argues that both perceive friendship as a dynamic process in which friends increase each other's moral well-being, sometimes to their own detriment. Aristotle valued difference in friendship, and while he recognized the ideal of equality, he also counted instrumental relations and purely pleasurable connections between people within the boundaries of friendship. Since ideal parity in friendship of the type Cicero valued was rare, MacFaul argues that the Greek model rather than the Roman one provides a better framework for conceptualizing the movable feast of affective male relations one finds in Shakespeare and his fellow dramatists.

Not surprisingly, *Male Friendship in Shakespeare and his Contemporaries* is organized into a series of chapters that explore the overlap between friendship and those social relations that MacFaul sees as defining male bonds in the period. The resulting close readings often seem useful both as a poetics of friendship and in terms of character analysis.

To provide only the briefest outline, MacFaul argues that the *Sonnets* explore an ideal parity of the type valorized by Humanists, but that Shakespeare reveals the strain between the speaker and the young man that expresses their emerging difference. He finds a similar strain in ideal, mutual friendship in plays such as *The Comedy of Errors, Much Ado About Nothing,* and *As You Like It,* among others, in which the claims of friendship and brotherhood compete. About these plays, MacFaul concludes that the "self-assertion of fraternal conflict is more vigorous and violent than that in friendship, but not entirely different in kind" (64). His chapter on love and friendship argues interestingly that friendship can involve bonds as stifling as those of brotherhood, a claim MacFaul supports through close readings of *The Two Gentlemen of Verona* and *The Two Noble Kinsmen.* He underwrites these readings with a careful analysis of John Lyly's *Euphues,* which, he argues, satirizes the friendship ideal extolled by Sir Thomas Elyot in his story of Titus and Gisippus in *The Boke Named the Governour.* Indeed, in many of his chapters, MacFaul anchors the discussion of Shakespeare to analysis of other major works, such as *Book IV* of *The Faerie Queene,* and any number of non-Shakespearean plays.

A chapter on service demonstrates that the equality of Humanist conceptions of friendship is belied by the discursive overlap, especially in drama, between servants and friends. MacFaul also locates the subtleties of the different subjectivities of Richard II and Prince Hal in the ways they handle the interactions between friendship and politics, and he comes, interestingly enough, to conclude that

Falstaff seems more estimable as a friend than Hal, despite the validity of the new king's politically astute dismissal of him. MacFaul
looks, too, at the stress created in several plays by competing
claims of fellowship and friendship, a point to which I will return
below. Finally, in his analysis of betrayals of male relationships in
Twelfth Night, Antony and Cleopatra, and *Othello,* among others,
he shows that "abandoning the Humanist ideal of friendship . . .
characters [such as Enobarbus and Iago] come to recognize themselves in differentiated interaction with others" (169). The contrast
between hero and friend in these plays makes us more acutely
aware of the dramatic limitations of identification with others.

Such conclusions about character as MacFaul reaches are not always strikingly original, and the book is dissatisfying in its failure
to engage more fully the enormous volume of (especially recent)
criticism on nearly every one of the plays and characters MacFaul
explores. Nevertheless, the analysis of character and rhetoric in
Male Friendship convincingly reveals friendship to be a dominant
factor in the creation of socially meaningful selves in the early period. MacFaul's multiple close readings of the varieties of meaning
to be found in the word *friend* counter understandings of friendship as a single, idealized force in a Shakespearean context. Consequently, the book's major contribution to scholarship may simply
be its demonstration that friendship depends upon those multiple
discourses and social institutions that otherwise define relations
between men in a dynamic, hierarchical culture.

But the book's strengths signal its weaknesses. MacFaul argues
that the dynamic nature of drama militates against static idealizations of friendship in the plays of Shakespeare and his contemporaries. But it is never wholly clear whether his book intends to
describe the ways drama, as a genre, necessarily envisions friendship as a dynamic process of identity formation or whether it intends to partake in the kind of historical poetics exampled by
Hutson or Shannon. Do Shakespeare's plays fail to instance Humanist idealizations of friendship because drama cannot instantiate a static relationship effectively or because the plays serve as an
ideological response to those idealizations? The last sentence of the
final full chapter of *Male Friendship in Shakespeare and his Contemporaries* points to the book's failure to resolve this tension: "Far
from promoting equalization, dramatic friendship is ultimately a
mode of recognizing and respecting human difference" (195). Is the
friendship MacFaul speaks of here a dramatic convention? Is it

merely a way of dramatizing friendship that bears little relation to material and ideological conditions in the world? Or do the conventions of friendship in drama perform a function in creating early modern subjectivity?

As a response to historicist critics of friendship in Shakespeare's England, MacFaul's book implies that he intends the latter conclusion. But in its habit of alluding to rhetoric and dramatic convention, it begs the questions it raises. "Friendship in Shakespeare's plays, even when it is most self-sacrificing in ethical terms," MacFaul writes, "is primarily a way of asserting an individual's dramatic importance and giving us a sense of his character" (12). Ultimately, one would like to hear more about how MacFaul understands the seemingly particular role friendship plays in the drama in relation to early modern subjectivities. Whatever the limitations of Hutson's and Shannon's books, both at least attempt to uncover a socially active function for the ideology of friendship. Even as it presents itself as an alternative to their methods, however, *Male Friendship in Shakespeare and his Contemporaries* seems to eschew a polemical argument with theoretical and historicist methodologies, which is not so much a virtue as an obfuscation.

The book is also curiously unsatisfying as a guide to large ideas about the friendship theme. At one moment in his late chapter on fellowship, MacFaul describes something of an overarching theme in his comments on *Timon of Athens.* He writes that Shakespeare's "most frequent technique when someone presses too hard at the concept of *true* friendship" is "to show its emptiness, and the bafflement of those who naively believed that there was something detachable from utility or pleasure at the core of friendship" (145). This clarifies MacFaul's sense that friendship in Shakespeare is largely instrumental. But it may imply as well that Shakespeare's plays and those of his fellow dramatists merely adopt a cynical perspective on idealist friendship, that their wisest characters see friendship as little more than an instrument of their own self-fashioning. If the goal of a thinker such as Shakespeare is primarily to disabuse us of idealism, why should we listen?

MacFaul's emphasis on the Aristotelian notion of *eudaimonia* and his analyses of, especially, servants and characters such as Falstaff provide evidence of bonds between men that are not wholly self-interested. But friendship for MacFaul is something of a chimera. It always means differently, even within similar contexts. So, in his chapter on fellowship, MacFaul writes that Benedick at the end of *Much Ado* seems "wiser," emerging from the "fellowship of men as a more serious, isolated character" (160), whereas he seems to fault *The Merchant*'s Antonio for seeking connection with Bassanio outside his gang of fellows and Hal for cynically manipulating Falstaff and his fellows. One wishes MacFaul had been willing to conceptualize more carefully and positively the larger social meanings of friendship in the plays as a whole rather than simply providing examples of how it functions symbiotically for individual characters in particular dramas.

Finally, one might be reasonably suspicious of MacFaul's admonishing critics who, in recent years, have explored the eroticism of male homosocial bonds in early modern England. When MacFaul raises the specter of male homoeroticism, he does so primarily to erase it: "If homoeroticism in the Renaissance is a normal component of friendship, then we must learn to treat it casually, avoiding the modern hysteria about sexuality" (18). A wise conclusion not to reify Renaissance sexuality, but treat it we must. Yet, despite MacFaul's citation of Alan Bray's complex work *The Friend* and Mario DiGangi's work on homoeroticism in friendship,[4] *Male Friendship in Shakespeare and his Contemporaries* almost wholly ignores the ways homoeroticism as well as sodomy overlap significantly with early modern male friendship. Aside from a useful discussion of *Twelfth Night*'s Antonio and Sebastian in connection with the *Sonnets* and the occasional comment on Palamon and Arcite, Volpone and Mosca, or Iago and Cassio, MacFaul treats this other important source of difference within male friendship entirely too casually.

Notes

1. Lorna Hutson, *The Usurer's Daughter: Male Friendship and Fictions of Women in Sixteenth Century England* (London: Routledge, 1994).

2. Laurie Shannon, *Sovereign Amity: Figures of Friendship in Shakespearean Contexts* (Chicago: University of Chicago Press, 2002).

3. Joel Fineman, *Shakespeare's Perjured Eye: The Invention of Poetic Subjectivity in the Sonnets* (Berkeley: University of California Press, 1986).

4. Alan Bray, *The Friend* (Chicago: University of Chicago Press, 2003); Mario DiGangi, *The Homoerotics of Early Modern Drama* (Cambridge: Cambridge University Press, 1997).

Angels in the Early Modern World
Edited by Peter Marshall and Alexandra Walsham
Cambridge: Cambridge University Press, 2006

Reviewer: Kristen Poole

At a crucial nexus in *Othello,* the protagonist admits his guilt, and he receives a response that leads to his recognition of Desdemona's innocence.

> *Othello.* She's like a liar gone to burning hell.
>   'Twas I that killed her.
> *Emilia.* O, the more angel she, and you the blacker devil!
>
> (5.2.138–40)

The student of English literature wishing to unpack these lines— theologically fraught as they are—is well-equipped to examine Emilia's contention that Othello is (like) the devil. Oceans of ink have been spent on analyses of the demonic in the early modern world. Devils, after all, lead interesting lives. They coerce people into doing naughty deeds. They can change themselves into toads or pigs. They have sex.

Angels, on the other hand. . . .

One is tempted to consider angels less intriguing. From a narrative perspective, they seem to have less to offer. If narrative is generated by conflict, and angels embody and seek to ensure spiritual harmony, then they are arguably of less interest to the storyteller. (Milton's war in heaven is an obvious exception to this.) From a historiographical perspective, angels also seem to be a dead end. If historiography is generated by documentation, the reams of evidence about the demonic produced around the sixteenth- and seventeenth-century witchcraft craze grossly outweigh the scattered reports of angelic visions and interventions. Since inhabitants of early modern Europe believed in both angels and demons, the copious literature on demonology is perhaps a symptom of a basic human (or at least, Western) tendency: we are more likely to write about (and to pray about, and to dramatize, and to preach about) what makes us afraid and unsettled than about what gives us comfort. (Or, such comforts are remembered in response to our fears.) Thus scholars of the early modern period have inherited more texts about the devil, who seemingly had the power to subvert neighbors, individual psyches, and the laws of nature, than about, say, guardian angels.

This preponderance of demonic evidence overshadows the fact that the sixteenth- and seventeenth-century supernatural world was as heavily populated with angels as it was with devils. Angelic presence was often presumed to be a ubiquitous feature of the cosmos. In a delightful image, one early modern commentator likens the presence of angels to those of "atoms," like specks of dust which become visible in a ray of sunlight. Angels, like demons, were understood to be standing beside us. The Mass, in particular, was a heightened moment of human-angelic interaction; sixth-century monks were warned against blowing their noses during the office "for fear of hitting the angels that stood immediately in front of them" (9). According to St. Benedict's Rule, angels were "God's ears and eyes" (9). This invisible, watchful presence continued into the Renaissance. In his *De civilitate morum puerilium* (1530), Erasmus admonished boys not to expose their private parts, "even if no witness is present. For angels are always present" (cited in Norbert Elias, *Civilizing Process*, 106). Angels were often portrayed as a sort of beneficent Big Brother.

In privileging the demonic over the angelic as a site of scholarly inquiry, then, we have overlooked an important element of early modern epistemology and daily existence. Peter Marshall and Alexandra Walsham help us to focus on the significance of angels in their excellent essay collection *Angels in the Early Modern World*. The fact that the editors can even give this anthology such a broad title indicates how unclaimed the topic is. And, as the sweep of "early modern world" indicates, this book takes the reader on a bit of a pan-European (and even transcontinental), pan-generic romp. The thirteen high-quality essays in the volume give us little snapshots of angels in a variety of contexts—political, theological, sociological, and aesthetic. As the editors state in their own masterful introduction, the book is not intended as a definitive study; it is presented "as a rough-drawn pioneers' map, rather than a definitive reference atlas" (3). All the more fun for the rest of us, since this collection indicates that there is fascinating territory out there waiting to be explored.

Many of the essays in this anthology will be of immense value to

literary scholars. The book opens with three essays that provide
more general information about angels: Peter Marshall and Alexandra Walsham's "Migrations of angels in the early modern world"
(perhaps the historian's rendering of the poet's "flights of angels"?);
Bruce Gordon's "The Renaissance angel"; and Philip M. Soergel's
"Luther on the angels." Marshall and Walsham begin by noting a
revived angelology among scholars of earlier periods: "Historians
are now less inclined to scoff than once they were: a thriving scholarly literature is demonstrating how attention to the form, function
and nature of angels illuminated a range of ontological and epistemological questions for thinkers in the apostolic, patristic and
medieval eras" (1). *Angels in the Early Modern World* takes this
scholarship forward. Angels did not disappear after the fifteenth
century; "on the contrary, they were often a focus of contention and
anxiety, a source of frictions and tensions that can help to expose
the fault-lines that criss-crossed early modern religion, society, politics and knowledge" (2).

In this introduction to the volume, Marshall and Walsham take
us on a whirlwind tour of angel history, from their biblical appearances to the hugely influential *On the celestial hierarchy* (ca. 500)
of the author known as Pseudo-Dionysius (the text which established the system of angelic taxonomy and hierarchy which persisted for a millennia), through Peter Lombard, Bonaventure, and
Aquinas (who, it turns out, never really did wonder how many
angels could dance on the head of a pin), through the Archangel
Michael's role as mediator between earth and heaven. The authors
then lead us through the complicated existence of angels in Reformation Europe: associated with the rejected saints' cults, angels
were perceived as part of a corrupted Catholic heritage, but their
scriptural credentials were impeccable. Angels thus became a site
of contested reformist theologies, a fact which contributed to their
theological, practical, and artistic resurgence in the Counter-Reformation that followed the Council of Trent.

Bruce Gordon's chapter on "The Renaissance angel" provides
something of an overview of fifteenth-century attitudes towards
angels through examining the writings of three major intellectual
figures: Nicholas Cusa, Marsilio Ficino, and Pico della Mirandola.
Gordon's conclusion sets the stage for many of the subsequent essays.

[The certainty of encountering angels] was a source of comfort and
brought a sense of continuity with previous generations, but in the de-

veloping world of Renaissance thought the consideration of angels marked a painful debate over what it meant to be human. Herein lay an irony not lost on the age: angels were humanity's greatest ally, yet, to assert its place as the divine image, humanity had to reclaim its higher calling above the angels. In a similar manner, control of the natural world, the very forum in which angels acted in human lives, meant, ultimately, the ability to control the angels themselves. In its many dimensions—artistic, theological and social—the engagement with angels bespoke a world shaped by tradition yet wrestling with new perceptions of the self that would invariably lead to the recasting of that same tradition. (63)

In the sixteenth century, the traditions of angelology were transformed by the Reformation, as Philip Soergel's essay explains. (One of the strengths of this essay collection is that many of the chapters flow from one to the next. While each is clearly its own free-standing piece with an idiosyncratic tone, the first six essays [with the exception of Cervantes's] read almost like a monograph, with the various chapters building upon each other.) Soergel briefly (too briefly, for those of us studying the English Reformation(s), more Calvinist than Lutheran) addresses Calvin's response to angels, appearing in a short section of the *Institutes* in which he validates their role in creation but debunks most of medieval angelology. He then turns to an extended consideration of Luther's evolving position on angels. As Soergel reiterates, the study of angels was hardly an abstract enterprise: "angelology had informed much scientific theory, performing explanatory functions about physical matter and the universe in the later Middle Ages similar to that performed by the theory of evolution in modern times" (69). Beliefs about angels were indicative of understandings of the natural and supernatural worlds. While initially exhibiting a medieval enthusiasm for angels, over the course of his lifetime Luther became more circumspect about angelic apparitions, and he came to deny that the motion of the planets is controlled by angels. Soergel maintains that Luther's writings on angels left "a divided legacy. For its theologians and officialdom . . . apparitions of angels became an increasingly remote possibility" (80). Given the biblical prominence of angels, however, they could not be discredited outright. Thus on the popular level, "in a narrow space between disfavour and outright prohibition, accounts of angelic apparitions continued to flourish in early modern Lutheranism" (82), even filling the void left by the rejected saints' cults.

The reformers' theologically ambiguous attitudes toward angels have an analogue in the beliefs and practices surrounding the deathbed, as Peter Marshall then goes on to explain in his own essay, "Angels around the deathbed: variations on a theme in the English art of dying." Building upon his previous work in *Beliefs and the Dead in Reformation England,* Marshall unpacks the complexities of the post-Reformation deathbed. "The theological revolution which in the mid-sixteenth century abolished the doctrine of purgatory and introduced the doctrine of predestination had immense consequences both for the symbolic representation of death and for its practical management" (83). Within the long-standing *ars moriendi* tradition (which continued to flourish in the sixteenth century), the deathbed was depicted as a scene of conflict between the dying person and demons, who would try to seduce the soul with spiritual doubts and torments; angels stood nearby to offer moral support in this battle, and would eventually transport the soul of the deceased to the bosom of Abraham. In Catholic theology, this final struggle with one's demons determined the fate of the soul in the afterlife. But reformist theologies—both the Lutheran emphasis on "faith alone" and Calvinist notions of predestination—"rendered nonsensical the idea of the deathbed as a place of final ordeal where salvation could be won or lost" (90). Based on "mature Protestant soteriology" (90) then, the vivid imaginings of the *ars moriendi* texts would seem to be neutralized, if not anathematized. However, both the biblical foundations for angelic care and the popular practices of deathbed ritual made "English Protestant attitudes towards angels in the later sixteenth and early seventeenth centuries . . . anything but straightforward" (91). The deathbed thus became a locus of complicated vectors of religious belief.

Such complexities were reflected in the aesthetic environs of sixteenth- and seventeenth-century England. Alexandra Walsham's chapter, "Angels and idols in England's long Reformation," takes us through the checkered history of representing angels pictorially. "In a climate ever sensitive to the perils of idolatry," she writes, "both devotion to and artistic depiction of these celestial beings could not but be surrounded by a degree of theological unease and anxiety" (134). Again we meet the central dilemma of the reformers' attitudes toward angels: associated as they were with medieval practices of devotion and intercession, they were "an uncomfortable reminder of the proscribed Catholic past" (134); yet their scriptural pedigree, for those who sought to ground their religion firmly in the Bible, warranted that they be taken seriously. Throw these factors into the mix with Protestant fears of superstitious idolatry, and we find a potent cocktail for theological conflict and disorientation. Over the course of the essay, Walsham takes us through two centuries of angels going up (on church walls, fonts, ceilings, windows, screens, etc.) and coming down—of beautifully rendered depictions of angels offered with pious devotion, and of these same portrayals being painted over and sawed or chiseled away in acts of faithful iconoclastic zeal.

This little cluster of essays (with the addition of Joad Raymond's chapter, discussed below) are probably of the most use to scholars of early modern English literature, not simply because they are the most immediately connected to the subject, but because of their quality and the wonderful ways in which they cohere and reinforce each other. Later chapters in the geographical neighborhood— Raymond Gillespie's "Imagining angels in early modern Ireland" and Owen Davies's "Angels in elite and popular magic, 1650– 1790" (focused on England)—are both interesting, but lack driving theses. Elizabeth Reis's "Otherworldly visions: angels, devils, and gender in puritan New England" provides a welcome counter-weight to the emphasis on the witch trials, with the cultural position of angelic interactions being similarly gendered, as women's experiences of angels were often assumed to be the result of de-monic delusions. The ability to discern the angelic from the de-monic is the subject of two other essays, by Robin Briggs and María Tausiet; the former of these studies the thought of Jean Bodin (fo-cusing primarily on demons, and thus feeling out of place in this volume), the latter offering an interesting analysis of a seventeenth-century case of demonic possession in a small village in the Pyre-nees. Fernando Cervantes's chapter on how European and indige-nous belief systems regarding angels merged in Spanish America is interesting, although it, too, feels misplaced and even token, and its placement between Marshall's and Walsham's own contributions is bizarre. Trevor Johnson's essay on the Jesuits' emphasis on guard-ian angels, which he argues was "a demonstration of its theology of the non-compelling but assisting operation of divine grace" (212), is an interesting exploration of how angels serve powerful func-tions as both metaphor and mechanism (212).

A crowning gem of this collection is Joad Raymond's essay, "'With the tongues of angels': angelic conversations in *Paradise*

Lost and seventeenth-century England." Admittedly, this reviewer may have been drawn to this essay by her own disciplinary orientation and a penchant for things Miltonic. That said, the essay is erudite and a complex argument is laid out with admirable lucidity. Addressing the speech of angels requires Raymond to move through theological debates over the nature of accommodation (how the numinous mysteries of God can be presented to and expressed within the limitations of human knowledge) to the more pragmatic aspects of speech (do angels have tongues?). Raymond discusses how Aquinas (building from the model of Pseudo-Dionysius) maintains an intensely vertical and one-directional model of human-angel communication; "though the medium of Aquinas' angelic communication is immensely powerful, the messages are very restricted: the strict hierarchy means that enlightenment is exclusively passed down from greater to lesser" (263). For some early modern commentators (building on Aquinas), angelic speech itself is correspondingly silent, as angels "impose their thoughts upon the mind" (267). By contrast, "the angels of *Paradise Lost* are genuinely and emphatically noisy. Speech and vocal communication constitute relationships, those mutual relationships that reject the strict hierarchies . . . attributed to the angelic orders. In conversing, a reciprocity is achieved that benefits both parties, that exalts both as the differences of a hierarchy are traversed and narrowed" (281). (While Raymond doesn't take his argument in this direction, this portrayal is a very short distance from the ideal society of free intellectual change Milton posits in *Areopagitica*.)

Within the context of this volume, Raymond's essay also feels token, the polite and obligatory inclusion of a literary scholar. But in demonstrating how Milton's poem is both "imaginative narrative and natural philosophy" (278), Raymond performs a bigger task than simply informing us of the properties of Miltonic angels. Raymond points out that Milton's treatment of angels in *Paradise Lost* corresponds with how he treats them in his systematic theology *De doctrina Christiana*. But with a difference. "Where this extends beyond *De doctrina,* this is not only because epic poetry permits latitude to the imagination, but because writing in the narrative form enables the theologian to develop critical arguments based on informed reconstruction. In other words, storytelling can be a means of discovering the truth" (277). (Raymond proceeds to trace this tradition in rabbinic exegesis.) The significance of this statement—at once bold and self-evident, at least to literary schol-

ars—is that it demonstrates the fallacy of modern divisions between poetry and history, or literary criticism and historiography,
or of fancy and fact. It provides an indigenous model, as it were, of
interdisciplinary scholarship. The poem ceases to be a mere representation of preconceived factual understandings or modes of
belief, and becomes a dynamic exercise in creating those understandings and beliefs. Given the great divide between early modern
engagement with the supernatural and our own, such attention to
the active role of literature in making truths offers a form of aesthetic historiography that fulfills a role that can't be satisfied by surveying wills and churchwardens' accounts. The early modern
poetic world provides a space for the convergence of historical,
theological, and literary interests that is not equaled in traditional
fields of social history. Perhaps Marshall and Walsham can be
coaxed into doing the sequel to this volume, one which teases out
the implications of a culture in which "real" and "imaginary" were
not antonyms.

Reading the Medieval in Early Modern England
Edited by Gordon McMullan and David Matthews
Cambridge: Cambridge University Press, 2007

Reviewer: Susan E. Phillips

In the last decade, medievalists and early modernists alike have increasingly traversed the institutional and historical boundary between their two fields, calling into question the teleological biases
built into periodization. Panels and conferences have brought these
two groups of scholars into more frequent conversation with one
another. Recent monographs have pursued early modern inquiries
through medieval antecedents, and have pushed medieval explorations well into the Renaissance, as critics transgress the conven-
tionally insurmountable barrier of the Reformation. And in the
ultimate sign of a shift in institutional and scholarly culture, the
University of Notre Dame Press now has a series devoted to such

boundary-crossing: Trans-Reformation Studies. Pre-Modern Studies has arrived at an exciting moment of literary and historical exploration, in which long held assumptions are being overturned and time-honored methods reinvented. The rich potential of this moment to radically shift the perception of medieval and early modern cultural practice is embodied by the essays in *Reading the Medieval in Early Modern England*.

Writing across the Reformation divide, the collection's contributors investigate the far-reaching consequences of periodization. The authors seek to reverse the Reformation's "revolutionary logic," which cast the Middle Ages as monolithic, repressive, and alien, and to expose the ways in which contemporary scholarly practice is informed and indeed structured by this logic. In their quest to uncover the continuities between the two periods, the essays in the collection do not simply trace the medieval origins of early modern texts and cultural artifacts; rather they reveal the surprising ways in which Reformation writers and their successors deployed the tactics, genres, tropes, and rituals of medieval culture to advance (and at times circumvent) Reformation practice. Examining medieval texts from early modern perspectives and early modern texts from medieval perspectives, the contributors practice what David Wallace, in the volume's afterword, calls "[r]everse chronological narration" (224), tracing early modern tropes, genres, and tactics backward in time to provide more expansive and international cultural histories.

The collection contains twelve essays by James Simpson, Deanne Williams, Larry Scanlon, David Matthews, Stephanie Trigg, Anke Bernau, Gordon McMullan, Bernhard Klein, Jennifer Summit, Cathy Shrank, Sarah Beckwith, and Patricia Badir, along with an afterword by David Wallace. Grouped into five categories—Period, Text, Nation, Geography, and Reformation—the essays treat "questions of periodisation, the technology of print, nationhood, visual and cartographic culture, and religion" (7). Individual essays take up a diverse range of texts and topics, from *Tamburlaine* and *Measure for Measure* to the travel itineraries and religious drama of John Bale, from devotional reading to cartographic innovation, from editorial paratext to unruly national icons. Despite, or perhaps because of this wonderful diversity, a persuasive narrative about continuity over rupture develops over the course of the collection and is particularly apparent in the five essays comprising the volume's two central sections on Nation and Geography. Indeed the collection as a whole is impressive in its cohesion. As the editors promise, the sections are interconnected, and the essays speak to each other not only within each grouping but also across the entire volume, creating a genuine scholarly conversation that is the collection's greatest strength.

James Simpson's provocative opening essay articulates a manifesto both for the volume and, more generally, for Medieval Studies. Lamenting that the field has become all too myopic, he argues that medievalists need to move away from the synchronic and interdisciplinary approaches of the past toward a diachronic history that centers itself in a discipline, while continually traversing, and in turn, historicizing the "historical rupture" (27) that has come to define the field. For Simpson, the Reformation, and in particular the 1534 Act of Supremacy, was nothing short of a "cultural revolution" in England that fundamentally altered "large tracts of the discursive landscape" (17) and that not only created the concept of the Middle Ages, but also initiated the tools and methods used to examine that period, most notably, the "rigidly philological historicism" (30) practiced by medievalists and early modernists alike in relation to the period. Following and reinforcing Simpson's essay, Deanne Williams's article traces the ruptures and continuities of the medieval/early modern divide in Robert Greene's play, *Friar Bacon and Friar Bungay,* arguing that the play both constructs the idea of the Middle Ages and offers a critique of that construction. Greene, Williams asserts, uses the play to "reflect upon the mental and imaginative processes of periodisation itself" (37), deploying a wide range of medieval and early modern generic conventions and rhetorical modes in order to demonstrate the inadequacy of representing historical moments. It is through these conflicting and competing modes and genres, Williams contends, that Greene "deconstructs the ideology of the Middle Ages" (46), calling into question a "linear and compartmentalised vision of history" (47).

Moving from tropes of periodization to tactics of publication, the two essays in the volume's second section, "Text," reexamine the paratextual features of two landmark early modern editions of medieval "auctors"—Thomas Speght's Chaucer and Robert Crowley's Langland—to reveal not radical misreadings or definitive entombments of the medieval past, but rather continuity and conversation. Echoing Simpson's lament about shortcomings of a synchronic historicism, Larry Scanlon argues that such an approach produces a "reified view of medieval culture" (53) as well

as a myopic interpretation of Langland, as a "quintessentially conservative, quintessentially medieval poet" (54). Scanlon's case in
point is the scholarly dismissal of Crowley's editions of *Piers Plow-
man* as the radical Protestant misreading of a thoroughly medieval
text. Although Crowley's editions certainly evince his Protestantism, Scanlon asserts, they do so in terms that are "primarily philosophical, poetic and political," rather than sectarian (58).
Analyzing Crowley's paratextual apparatus, Scanlon reveals that
Crowley's glosses, so often marshaled as evidence of radical misin-
terpretation, are in fact anti-aristocratic rather than anti-Catholic
(of the 495 glosses, he finds only 15 that are explicitly anti-Catholic). More surprisingly, Scanlon uncovers in those glosses the remarkable continuities between Crowley and Langland, namely a
shared apocalyptic vision and a common interest in the expansion
of vernacular literacy. David Matthews's essay complements Scanlon's by demonstrating the personal as well as political ends that
might be served by an early modern editor's embrace of a medieval
"auctor." Counter to earlier scholars who have declared that
Speght's 1598 edition represents Chaucer as "antique, ancient,
classic, canonised, and very dead" (75), Matthews argues that
Speght is "laying claim to a form of remembrance of Chaucer" (75)
by asserting that while Thynne and Stow's editions locked Chaucer
away, Speght's edition offers a "more transcendent Chaucer whose
spirit infuses poets and editors" (76). According to Matthews,
Speght uses his elaborate editorial apparatus (including an inventive Chaucer biography) not to distance Chaucer as a "medieval
primitive" but to refashion him as an idealized version of the Renaissance courtier, ultimately remaking Chaucer in his own image:
"it is the editor whom the poet comes to resemble" (87).

The three essays comprising the volume's third section, "Nation," explore the strategic deployment of medieval narratives of
national origins to justify early modern political and colonial ambitions. Stephanie Trigg's suggestive article explores the proliferation
of narratives surrounding the origins of the Order of the Garter. The
Order's cryptic motto and trivial emblem, Trigg argues, embody
"the mixed inheritance of the medieval past for early modernity,"
which can "confer both shame and honour" (105). Anxiety over
this ambiguous inheritance, she contends, compels early modern
antiquarians, heraldic experts, and historiographers not only to
cast aspersions on the veracity of medieval narratives but also to
generate new tales that replaced the eroticized and feminized story

of Edward's garter with a sober military narrative championing masculine reason and common sense. Early modern historiographers thus produced "the medieval period as a historical object worthy of study and dispute" (105), modeling the "rigorous philological historicism" that has come to define Medieval Studies. This approach, Trigg asserts, has prevented scholars from seeing what is really at stake in the Garter narrative: the power of the king's "evocative speech-act" (92) to make meaning. Anke Bernau's essay, like Trigg's, explores the gender politics at work in early modern narratives of origin, as she analyzes the gendered foundation myths circulated and revised in late medieval and early modern English national historiographies. Bernau investigates the contemptuous dismissal of medieval foundation myths based on the legends of two originary "British" women—Albina and Boudica—myths that were used in the medieval period both to fill the gaps left in Geoffrey of Monmouth's Brutus legend and to justify the Roman conquest of the British Isles. Each of these foundation myths tells the story of an unruly, monstrous, sexually perverse woman whose improper conduct can only be remedied by violent Roman colonization. Depicting a masculine order that overcomes "feminised savagery" (115), these female foundation myths, Bernau argues, became "instrumental in medieval and early modern English colonial ambitions" (116). Yet these myths, as Bernau demonstrates, also undermined that ambition: the "stubborn presence of originary monsters in early modern English national narratives works against their teleological momentum" (117). Gordon McMullan's essay dovetails nicely with Bernau's, taking up the premise that Roman colonization of Britain was often taken as a precedent for early modern colonial ambition in his investigation of the ways in which the early modern theater sought to interpret Elizabethan and Jacobean Britain through the reconstruction of the medieval past. Like Bernau, McMullan sees in these reconstructions an insistence on the "fundamentally divided origins and orientations of 'Great Britain'" (121), which playwrights exploit both to rehearse contemporary colonial tensions and to critique covertly contemporary colonial endeavors. British History, as it appears on the stage, is, for McMullan, a "colonial history, an ongoing narrative of the negotiation of national identity in the face of external imposition" (122), which he explores in relation to Middleton's *Hengist, King of Kent,* Brewer's *The Love-Sick King,* and Fletcher/Massinger's *The Sea Voyage.* Moreover, it is only in the context of this theatrical project,

McMullan persuasively suggests, that we can fully understand the oddities of Shakespeare's *Cymbeline.*

Following "Nation" seamlessly is the collection's fourth section on Geography, in which essays by Bernhard Klein and Jennifer Summit take up the question of how the early modern English nation mapped itself in the wake of Reformation destruction. Klein's article offers a detailed and rigorous analysis of the uneasy transition from the "affective power" (144) of medieval *mappaemundi* to the "disembodied, desacralised and entirely secular spaces of the New Geography" (144). He explores both the tension and the subtle and surprising continuities of this transition not only in cartographic material but also in what he describes as "[o]ne of the most flamboyant spectacles of cartographic hubris"—Marlowe's *Tamburlaine* (143). According to Klein, the affective power of the *mappamundi* resides in the "intimate relationship it entertains with the human body" (144) and it is precisely this affective power that Tamburlaine's bloody campaigns attempt unsuccessfully to destroy. For all the lasting success of the New Geography, Klein asserts, it could not immediately "displace the deep-rooted understanding that geography had to serve a moral purpose" (144). Summit's richly textured reading of the cartography and chorography of John Leland and his successors adroitly weaves together the concerns of the previous four essays. For Summit, Leland's *Itinerary,* so often read as the "inaugural work of Renaissance geography" (159), was less a product of "a newly awakened, classicised self-consciousness" than of the Reformation's "ongoing, politically driven struggle to redefine and contain the nation's own medieval past" (160). Summit stresses the importance of "reversing the direction of influence" (160)—of recognizing that later early modern geographers, such as William Camden and John Speed, constantly recur to Leland's Reformation agenda, rather than misidentifying Leland as a proto-Renaissance figure. Unpacking the "discovery of England" narratives espoused by early modern cartographers, Summit explores how these writers attempted to negotiate the fact that "in the wake of the Reformation it was impossible to experience the English landscape without also confronting physical evidence of the medieval past and the violence that historical change inflicted on it" (160). Ultimately, Summit contends, the "displacement of the medieval past in geographical representations" (176) provided a pattern for the acts of conquest that constituted new world exploration.

The volume's final section, "Reformation," applies the premise of the collection to questions of religious and devotional practice. Cathy Shrank's essay makes a number of interesting connections with earlier essays, particularly those of Scanlon, Matthews, and Williams, as she explores the paratextual features and generic borrowings of the dramatic corpus of John Bale, that ultimate "transitional figure" who straddles "the institutionalised chronological boundaries between 'medieval' and 'Renaissance'"(179). Contributing to the volume's developing argument about the ways in which early modern writers were dependent upon medieval modes and strategies, Shrank argues that Bale is a "Janus figure" (181), drawing on medieval motifs, conventions, techniques, and genres, even as he abjures what he refers to as the "horrible darkness" of the medieval past. However, as Shrank reveals, it is precisely through these medieval borrowings that Bale is able both to endorse and combine the religious and political processes of the Reformation, by repeatedly insisting upon the "primacy of the crown in religious affairs" (189). Sarah Beckwith extends Shrank's discussion of the Reformation's impact on the early modern stage in her exploration of the penitential politics in Shakespeare's *Measure for Measure.* Opposing critics who read Shakespeare's backward glances toward the Middle Ages as nostalgic or conservative, Beckwith investigates "the *radical* nature of Shakespeare's medievalism" (194) manifested in the play's "extraordinarily penetrating exploration" (193–94) of the transformation of medieval penitential practice into the idea of early modern repentance. For Beckwith, the abolition of auricular confession and the resulting excision of regular recourse to the ministrations and admonitions of the parish priest meant that penance became "more punitive, public and juridical" (197). It is precisely this devolution that the play critiques in the central figure of the Duke, who repeatedly and systematically exploits the discourse of self-knowledge as a device for gathering information. By deploying the figure of the deceiving friar to call into question not the church but the crown, Shakespeare, Beckwith argues, produces an "inversion of anti-Catholic theatre using its own techniques" (201). In the collection's final essay, Patricia Badir moves from public performance to private reading to investigate how Amelia Lanyer and Nicholas Breton used the medieval "reading Magdalene" to develop a "ghostly poetics of presence" (211) that allowed them both to explore the issue of spiritual affect and to "figure the palpable presence of an invisi-

ble god in an iconoclastic world" (207). Badir refutes earlier scholarship that dismissed sixteenth- and seventeenth-century maudlin
poetics as the eroticization and aestheticizing of late medieval corporeal piety, and demonstrates the more complicated and compelling functions of the maudlin aesthetic: the figuration of female
piety and reading as liberating the "authorial potential of the female imagination" (217). Like the other essays in the collection,
Badir's article demonstrates the continuities rather than ruptures
between the medieval and the early modern.

Reading the Medieval in Early Modern England has invaluable
lessons to teach about "the gendering of national myth making"
(14) and the origins of nationhood, the politics of penance and religion of mapmaking, the evolution of genres and contingencies of
editorial practice. Exposing and attempting to reverse the effects of
periodization, the contributors to this collection convincingly demonstrate that the continuities between the medieval and the early
modern are far more compelling and indeed persistent than the
ruptures that until recently dominated scholarly conversation. By
reading the medieval from the early modern and the early modern
from the medieval, these scholars reveal what "longer mappings of
human experience" (227) might accomplish for Medieval and Early
Modern Studies.

Shakespeare and the Nature of Love:
Literature, Culture, Evolution
By Marcus Nordlund
Evanston: Northwestern University Press, 2007

Reviewer: David Schalkwyk

In *Shakespeare and the Nature of Love,* Marcus Nordlund combines two things that go against the grain of contemporary Shakespeare studies: he gives *love* (rather than desire, or eroticism, or
sexuality) his full attention; and in focusing on the *nature* of love

he takes on "constructivist historicism," which holds that a concept like love is not based in nature at all, but is rather a historically variable construct. Both of Nordlund's moves are welcome. Love informs Shakespeare's work so thoroughly that it is due for proper exploration in its own right. And a fresh paradigm for the study of Shakespeare that goes beyond the current historicist/presentist divide is urgently needed.

It makes sense for Nordlund to tackle these two issues together. A good deal of the reason for love's neglect has been precisely its denigration by theoretical and political presuppositions. Offer a compelling new theoretical framework and love will shine again in restored splendor. This move is clearly attractive; but it is also impeded by great difficulties. *Shakespeare and the Nature of Love* has to do two very challenging things at the same time. It has to set out a sufficiently comprehensive account of, and argument for, a new theoretical framework for the investigation of love in general, and it also has to offer a wide-ranging analysis of sufficient complexity and depth of the *nature* of love in Shakespeare. Neither of these tasks is easy. The complexity of the second is not reduced by Nordlund's decision to cover widely different forms of love: not only romantic or sexual love, but also paternal and filial affection and, by implication at least, love as a form of social or political duty.

The size of the first task will be apparent from the nature of the new lens through which Nordlund views these forms of love in Shakespeare: a cultural-biological perspective based on evolutionary theory. Whereas evolutionary theory has established a firm foothold in the social sciences, it is not only undeveloped in literary studies but actively dismissed or passively overlooked by most as anathema. Its basic tenets oppose the most cherished literary critical preoccupations of the past three decades. Literary scholars generally hold a broadly constructivist view of human emotion and sexual identity. Darwinism posits a continuity derived from natural selection that would appear to many to be shamelessly essentialist. Against the Foucaultian view of short-term epistemic shifts and the more broadly historicist notion of cultural distance and difference, it assumes an extreme *longue durée* of adaptation against which cultural differences are no more than epiphenomena. And in contrast to Marxist denials of the existence of any transhistorical human qualities or essence, it makes no apologies for its belief in a fundamental human nature grounded in biological fact.

What's wrong with a bit of essentialism? Whereas most Shake-speareans can set the framework for their inquiry with a few cursory gestures and well-worn citations, anyone storming the citadel from Nordlund's position has to work very hard indeed. He or she needs to persuade a wary, if not a violently antagonistic, watch on the ramparts that the attacking forces are in fact the rightful heirs to the city. Any introductory, theoretical chapter is required not only to offer a compelling argument for its fundamental tenets, but also to muster and then condense a vast array of complicated evidence, which is itself in dispute among its adherents.

There is a great deal that is admirable about *Shakespeare and the Nature of Love.* It contains some fine analysis, it debunks arguments that have long gone unchallenged, its topic is urgent, and its theoretical perspective timely. I am going to forego detailed praise, however, and pay Nordlund the compliment of engaging critically with his argument.

Sex and chemicals

Let's begin with his theory in its most extreme form, expressed in a passage that explains love in the most uncompromisingly biological terms:

> As early as in 1983, Michael Liebowitz at Columbia University identified a link between romantic attraction and elevated levels of certain neurotransmitters, as well as a corresponding connection between calm loving feelings of attachment and the natural opiate serotonin. Later research has fleshed out the picture as follows (with apologies for inevitable simplification): the stage of attraction involves a cocktail of endogenous phenethylamine (PEA), norepinephirene, dopamine, and serotonin, while feelings of attachment or affiliation involve endorphins, oxytocin, and vasopressin. (209n41)

Nordlund writes this as a footnote. In his general argument he tends to distance himself from the simple reduction of love to certain levels of chemicals in the bloodstream. But his rhetoric nevertheless demonstrates in the starkest terms the difficulties of relating the findings of scientific experiments and the concepts of love and affection. First, the rhetoric of progress ("as early as 1983 . . . Later research has fleshed out the picture") appeals to an inexorable notion of scientific development consonant with the "knowledge" industry. We may not quite be able exactly to correlate feelings of affection and attraction at the moment, but pretty soon we'll be able to reveal, in precise chemical formulae, what love actually *is.* The second rhetorical (rather than "scientific") move involves the nature of that reduction in the ambiguity of that existential copula *is:* a causal explanation is affirmed through the no more than suggestive relational terms, "link," "corresponding connection," and "involves." The third lies in the imprecision of the concepts that are to be reduced. What exactly are we talking about here? "Romantic attraction," "calm feelings," "affiliation," or "love"? How do you delimit "romantic attraction" so that you can identify the cocktail that it produces (or that produces it)? How is it related to "calm feelings" and the much broader notion of "affiliation," and how are all these connected to the wider concept of "love"? If love is not a feeling but rather a disposition, since it subsists over a continuous period of time, then it exceeds the momentariness of "calm loving feelings of attachment," and so cannot be the product of equally temporary secretions of chemicals.

In his acute account of the limitations of experimental psychology and anthropology, William Reddy points out that "Western specialists who study emotion cannot even agree on what the term *emotion* means." He notes further that "George Mandler, in 1984, remarked, 'there is no commonly, even superficially, acceptable definition of what a psychology of emotions is about' . . . In 1996, Shaver et al. noted that 'No psychologist knows what anger, fear, or shame are independent of folk knowledge, and most studies of these emotions test hypotheses derived from tuition and everyday observation of self and others.'"[1] The evolutionary biologist or experimental psychologist is in no better position to tell us what love *is:* he or she has to use the same sense, available to all who speak a particular language, of its range of uses in the language as the basis for a hypothesis regarding the correlation (*not* the causal connection) between an isolated exemplum (under artificial, laboratory conditions, which are likely to change the emotion) and certain physiological events. Furthermore, none of these physiological occurrences can be said to be the emotion itself or its concept. We should therefore be skeptical of Nordlund's claim that "modern researchers in the life sciences have finally solved the conceptual problem that underlies" the paradox that "human nature is characterised by a paradox of sameness and difference" (9). Whatever experiments to correlate feelings of sexual attraction with chemical

cocktails in the blood may resolve, *conceptual* problems are emphatically not among them.

Paying nature and culture their dues

Despite Nordlund's enthusiasm for experimental research, he
counters brute constructivism with an evenhanded theory that he
calls *biocultural* criticism: not the reduction of feeling to chemistry,
but rather a position that aims to pay biology and culture their respective dues. The study of cultural artefacts must be "placed on
an evolutionary foundation" (5), but that does not mean that we
should ignore variations in culture and history. Darwinian theory
may show that love is a component of human nature everywhere
and at all times, but it also allows for variation in historical, individual, and cultural form and expression (10). This occurs when
cultures develop different ways of making individual subjects conform to social norms, either through the *hypercognition* (endorsement) or *hypocognition* (suppression) of what the human species is
"biologically disposed to do" (45). What our biology disposes us to
do is in turn determined by our adaptive history, through which
we have developed dispositions and emotions that "contributed to
genetic fitness" (33). Far from being the invention of the Trouba-
dours in twelfth-century France, romantic love has thus always ensured the survival of our species by providing a firm and lasting
attachment between mating partners that ensured the greater survival of the offspring. Because each partner had, and continues to
have, a different kind and degree of investment in caring for such
offspring, human brains and endocrinal systems have evolved to
differentiate degrees of attachment and distance across sex. This results in fundamental sexual difference. Since more was at stake for
them in rearing offspring, females had to be more choosy about
their liaisons; males are less, or at least differently, attached to both
offspring and partner. These divergent forms of behavior have their
locus in the endocrinal system, so men and women are necessarily
biologically different. To insist on their sameness is to override the
facts of biology with the false ideals of politics. But different does
not mean unequal, Nordlund hastens to add: "that human beings
must be identical in order to be equal is surely one of the most pernicious dogmas of our time" (43).

Aware of the political implications of his move, Nordlund hastens to draw a distinction between a description of human nature and the normative uses to which such a description may be put. To say, therefore, that our evolutionary history predisposes women to care to a greater extent than men for their children, or that men are more disposed to seek more partners to propagate their genes, does not imply anything about the way in which societies should structure and control the actual behavior of men and women. Let's come back to this claim once we have clarity on what exactly love is.

The definition of love

Nordlund recognizes that if we are to talk or write about love, we need to know what it is we are talking about. We need a definition of love. We can go about obtaining such a definition in two ways. We can either trace the way in which the word has been used (let's confine ourselves to Western usage) in a variety of societies on various occasions. If we did that, we would come up with a bewildering (but extremely rich) manifold of uses, some contradictory, some overlapping each other, some with apparently no connection except the signifier, and some with apparent, but very complicated, family resemblances. We would find no core or essence that holds all these uses together. Or we could just decide what love (or "romantic love") means, and get on with it. Not surprisingly, Nordlund chooses the latter course. He reminds us that "in Shakespeare's time the word 'love' was more semantically flexible than it is today, covering a wide range of phenomena from friendship to even non-emotive phenomena" (26), but he nevertheless assumes that beneath these "extraordinary number of senses" there lies a core, revealed by "Darwinism, materialism [in the non-Marxist sense in which all human phenomena are assumed to be materially caused], and evolutionary psychology" (27).

This move is derived from an assumption, fundamental to Nordlund's thesis, that if we want to know the nature of love, we need to discover the nature of the *lover*. The heart of the lover is encapsulated by Robert Sternberg's "love triangle": intimacy, passion, and commitment (23). These are, respectively, the desire to be in the presence of the love object, a yearning for union with the loved one, and the inclination to maintain the relationship over time. As a working definition of what Western societies have now come to expect of romantic love, this is as good a proposal as any—in fact, it seems no more (and no less) than common sense. But Nordlund also maintains that this emotion has persisted through its role in shaping genetic fitness for survival. Can we say that the definition of love is a biologically grounded, evolutionary programmed, universal set of human dispositions? Does it constitute the *nature* of love, in Shakespeare, or anywhere else?

Shakespeare and the Nature of Love presents a very selective sample of plays, but in striking and often very illuminating combinations. Parental love is treated in a comparative reading of *Titus Andronicus* and *Coriolanus;* filial love in *King Lear;* romantic love in a fruitful crossing of *Troilus and Cressida* and *All's Well That Ends Well;* finally, jealousy is explored in a combination of *Othello* and *The Winter's Tale.* The latter is an obvious pairing; the adjacent readings of the two problem plays are not.

Parental love

As is to be expected, Nordlund begins with a conception of the nature of parental love derived from evolutionary "investment theory." This holds that parental attachment will be differentiated in kind and intensity by the degree of investment (of energy, resources, emotions, and so on) that each parent would naturally be expected to make in the care and raising of offspring. Matters are not simple, however, as Nordlund is well aware. The fact that some mammals may instinctively protect their offspring does not mean, as he says, that "evolved psychological characteristics are not hardwired or inflexible and usually require adequate environmental input" (54). For the latter, there are always "individual exceptions to this rule" (54) and "nurturing itself needs to be nurtured" (58). Nevertheless, Nordlund urges us to accept that the "average woman will always have the edge on the average man in understanding children's needs and responding to them" (61). How does this express itself in Shakespeare's Roman plays?

Nordlund argues that in *Titus* and *Coriolanus* Shakespeare is engaging in a historically aware form of "dramatic anthropology," by which he tests "the impact of a specific culture on a central aspect of human nature" (63). The specific culture is the Roman concept of honor, "hypercognatized" by a set of social norms to trump the biologically natural, but in this case "hypocognatized," disposition to love one's children. Nordlund does not set up honor as a (false) cultural ideal against the (true) biological impulse to care for off-spring. Rather, honor is itself rooted in the biologically evolved nature of human beings as social creatures in order to regulate the behavior of individuals in line with the expectations or demands of the group. *Titus* exemplifies Shakespeare's insight into the fundamental demands of nature in the form of the biological imperative to love one's children against a distorting social elevation of another biological requirement, to the point at which the first is obliterated. *Coriolanus* rehearses the same tension, showing first the ways in which a cultural ideal can distort an individual's image of himself to the point at which all "natural propinquity of blood" is denied. But it concludes with the proper, but tragic, recognition of the natural impulse to parental and filial love, especially in the form of Aaron's deep commitment to his child.

This is a simplification of an argument that is not without subtlety and complexity. Nonetheless, there is a tension in Nordlund's treatment of nature and its relation to culture and the concomitant theoretical distinction between descriptive science and the normative or cultural uses of such description. He argues that it is not valid to object to a biologically grounded conception of human nature on the grounds of its debilitating political effects, because that confuses a descriptive truth with a normative rule. But Nordlund mobilizes the concept of nature precisely as a normative yardstick by which both the critical faults of "constructivists" may be judged and the insights of Shakespeare's plays gauged. Part of the aim of the elucidation of parental love as an evolutionary adaptation of the species as a whole in *Shakespeare and the Nature of Love* is to attack the historicist argument, exemplified by Lawrence Stone, that parental love was absent or highly attenuated in early modern England for cultural and environmental reasons.

There have been sustained attacks on Stone's argument, notably by David Cressy, but they are grounded on historical evidence rather than the universality of parental love. By offering no historical evidence other than his reading of Shakespeare's plays to counter Stone and his followers, Nordlund is using biology as a normative, not merely descriptive, instrument. Furthermore, it is also the yardstick that measures the profundity of Shakespeare's insights. Shakespeare's general method is to "deliberately violate a familiar aspect of human nature as a means of involving the audience emotionally and inviting us to reflect critically on the nature of human love" (5). In the two Roman plays, Shakespeare violates human nature as it manifests itself in our natural propinquity for parental love by subjecting it to the Roman cultural code of honor, in order to show us how *natural* parental love really is.

Love or duty

In *King Lear,* Nordlund argues, Shakespeare turns to the nature of filial love. We are too hard on Goneril and Regan, who are responding as long-suffering children to a waywardly senile father who has far too much power for his biological condition. Shakespeare's play is—as Emanuel Kant famously implied when he suggested that every old man is a Lear—more about the inescapable biology of "decaying brain tissue" than about broader, political struggles over land and power (106). As an explanation for the irrationality of the love test (which may be attributed as much to Shakespeare as to Lear) this may be as good as any. But it takes us away from what most recent critics see as the heart of the play, its concern with urgent, Jacobean questions of changing formations of ownership and political organization. The struggle over land and power involves the fraught relationship between "love and duty," concepts that Nordlund regards as mutually exclusive, certainly with little in common to explain their subsumption by the early moderns under the term love (89). In his view, love is the natural emotive disposition of intense attachment between parent and child, whereas duty is a nonemotive, culturally imposed obligation, which is always in danger of obliterating the emotional needs of love.

Nordlund certainly goes to the heart of at least one of the play's concerns in his recognition of the deep ambiguity or polysemy in the early modern uses of love as something signaling obligation, service, and loyalty—in which "deserving," "bonds," and "dues" are central—on the one hand, and an attachment to another kind of affect—traditionally associated with the heart—on the other. He is right to show how the language games associated with each of these concepts conflict and then disastrously cross each other in the love test. Self-regarding Goneril and Regan speak the conventional language of filial affection, whereas the genuinely loving Cordelia feels forced to adopt the language game of duty, bond, and obligation.

But I think Nordlund gets the relationship between love and duty wrong. He gets it wrong because he has already decided what is and is not love before he engages with the play. Love, by his account, is essentially a biologically grounded, private attachment residing in intense feeling, the result of aeons of selective adaptation to hostile environments. It cannot on this account be based on social notions of mutual obligation or service, which by his account are impersonal and devoid of emotion. The fact that Shakespeare's society used the same word to designate these two relations is by this argument no more than a homonymic accident. Their respective uses bear as little relation to each other as the place which cashes one's check and the margin of a river, both designated by the word "bank."

The notions of love as duty and service and intimate affection or attachment are, however, intricately and inextricably intertwined throughout Shakespeare's work and his society as a whole. We tend not to recognize this because relations of service and duty have changed unrecognizably in a postmodern, postcapitalist world, if they have not disappeared altogether. Despite his fine, attentive analysis of the opening scene, Nordlund all but ignores the Earl of Kent. Yet if there is any example of unconditional devotion in *King Lear* it is the king's servant, whose commitment stems from a powerful combination of obligation and love that unites reason and emotion in extremely complex ways. That devotion, furthermore, resists being reduced either to the secretion of particular hormones or the imperatives of genetic selection. First, Kent's love for Lear shows itself in a range of emotions, many of which appear to be mutually exclusive. Affection is tempered with anger and resistance in the opening scene; devotion and humility are followed by pity and rage; sorrow turns to the willing acceptance of death, all of which make up the complex contours of Kent's embodiment of love *and* duty. It is not sufficient to say, as Nordlund does, that "duty can be reunited with emotional experience only once it has been demoted from formal, contractual bonds" (115), and that "the word 'love' in Shakespeare's England was often used as a kind of *euphemism* for social allegiance rather than emotion" (154; emphasis added). If anything, Kent binds himself even more firmly to Lear as Caius. Nordlund ignores the degree to which formal, contractual bonds in the early modern period were indeed imbricated in "emotional experience" of various kinds, including love. He tends to speak of love as a fairly uniform set of emotional states—passion, desire, commitment, affection. But, like the emotional range that encompasses duty and obligation, it can range across anger, indignation, exultation, humility, uncertainty, resentment, and satisfaction.

Even if we could isolate the chemicals underlying these states and attitudes, they could not add up to love. Nordlund's failure to give full due to Shakespeare's equation of love and duty arises from the limitations of his modern biologically driven framework. It is difficult to conceive of obligation being part of the nature of love when evolutionary biology has no room for such a concept in its narrative of selective adaptation, and when life scientists have no way of measuring the concept of love as duty against a cocktail of chemicals in the blood.

Romantic love

What about romantic love? Readers will be struck by the fact that *Shakespeare and the Nature of Love* exemplifies this concept not through a romantic comedy like *Twelfth Night* or a tragedy such as *Romeo and Juliet,* but rather via the unlikely pairing of *Troilus and Cressida* and *All's Well that Ends Well.* This is a brilliant combination, and it brings out the best in Nordlund, who has a sharp analytical eye and an admirable capacity for exposing cant. It's by far the best chapter in the book. It is also the chapter that leans least heavily on the biocultural approach.

Central to Nordlund's argument is in fact the work of the historian, Irving Singer, whose three-volume study of love in the Western tradition from Plato to the present, *The Nature of Love,* seeks to offer an historical account of different conceptual manifestations of love.[2] "Bestowal" is the key term that Nordlund takes from Singer. It refers to the tendency of lovers to project value upon the beloved that is often not apparent to others. Freud's word for this process is "overvaluation," but that is too pejorative a use for something that can, as Hippolyta suggests, "grow to something of great constancy." This capacity was viewed very differently by Renaissance commentators, who tended to denigrate the irrationality of love's tendency to "see Helen's beauty in the brow of Egypt."

The value of Helen's beauty is itself put under intense pressure in *Troilus and Cressida.* Nordlund argues convincingly that the play condenses love's tendency to idealize or overvalue and the vulnerability of such valuation or bestowal to change over time. The bestowal of value trumps all notions of intrinsic value: "what's aught but as 'tis valued?" In *All's Well that Ends Well*, on the other hand, the problem is undervaluation. Young Bertram just won't see what is plainly apparent to everyone else in the court, and almost all critics of the play: that Helen is a paragon of beauty, virtue, intelligence, and, therefore, that it is not only irrational but also perverse not to want her as a wife and lover. Nordlund does a very good job at rescuing Bertram from his bad press and urging some sympathy for his predicament, at least before his attempt to seduce and then slander Diana. The cool responses of the four lords whom Helen approaches before she lights on him indicate that Bertram's lack of interest is not unusual or perverse. We should accord the young nobleman no less sympathy than we do Hermia, in *A Midsummer Night's Dream,* when she is forced to "choose love by another's eyes."

Nordlund's analysis of the king's attempts to force Bertram to love Helen focuses on a conceptual aspect of love that is almost obsessive in Shakespeare: love's peculiar relation to coercion and the will. The king can force Bertram to marry Helen, but it is in the nature of the concept that he cannot bend Bertram's will to love her. Moreover, Bertram himself lacks the power to make himself love Helen, even if he wished to do so. Love is notoriously willful, but it simultaneously escapes voluntary control. That is why it is potentially disruptive of social attempts to control and direct individual desire. One of Nordlund's major insights in his analysis lies in his diagnosis, again a conceptual one, that Helen's sexual obsession with Bertram prevents her from caring for him—her "romantic passion is so strong that it simply blocks her empathy for him. It makes her incapable of assessing either Bertram's point of view or the moral implications of her own actions" (152). This is an excellent point, and it depends, not on an evolutionary argument, but rather on a conceptual analysis that romantic love involves both passion and empathy. However, this very argument invalidates Nordlund's attempt to excuse Troilus's hasty and indifferent departure from Cressida on the morning after their consummation. He argues that it would have been dramatically inappropriate for Shakespeare to have staged *two* scenes in which Troilus is distraught at Cressida's loss. Perhaps so. But however passionate Troilus is about Cressida before their consummation, he shows very little empathy for her on the morning after his passions have been assuaged. This kind of transformation is the subject of much speculation in the philosophy of love and its relation to the vagaries of desire in the Renaissance, but since Nordlund pays no attention to historical conceptions of love, he lets it pass.[3] By Nordlund's own account, though Troilus desires Cressida, he cannot empathize with her position, and so he does not love her. This is where the heart of Trojan and Greek heartlessness may well lie: there is plenty of desire and will, indeed, "will in overplus," in both camps, but little or no love. What then, *pace* a whole tradition derived from Plato, is the difference between love and desire?

Love vs. desire

In his fine defense of the humanist concept of love, Tzevan Todorov (*The Imperfect Garden*—not, unfortunately, in Nordlund's bibliography), makes the capacity to bestow value upon the other central to his argument that such conferral of value is an indispensable aspect of a humanist notion of love in which the uniqueness and non-fungibility of the other is fundamental.[4] As Todorov puts it, what lies at the heart of humanist love is our capacity to transform the finite into the infinite in the singular person of the beloved, rather than instrumentalizing that person as a mere means to a higher ideal of truth and beauty. Todorov thus argues that the bestowal of value is not a fault of love, but is rather central to its very possibility, its miraculous capacity for transformation, and its difference from mere desire. He does not, however, claim that this is the *nature* of love, but rather that it marks the contours of a peculiar, historical concept of love in which the beloved is valued as an end rather than a means, and is therefore uniquely resistant to the substitution that underlies all notions of desire derived from Plato. Bestowal (or idealization or overvaluation) is precisely what characterizes the loved person who is loved for his or her uniqueness: it enacts the "finality of the *you*." This is a conceptual characteristic of "love-joy," as Todorov terms it, rather than "love-desire," which instead obeys the "diabolical" logic of endless dissatisfaction and replacement—of "lack."

Nordlund prepares the ground for his analysis of bestowal in the two problem comedies by characteristically appealing not to the philosophical history of the concept but rather to its evolutionary and biological foundations. Given the asymmetrical investment of males and females in the care of offspring, this argument goes, "it is only to be expected that the average man will be slightly more prone to 'idealize' a prospective sexual partner . . . while the average woman will have a greater incentive to prolong the courtship (which means more time for assessment and choice)" (132). When Shakespeare gives his heroines the power to choose their partners in his romantic comedies, then, all he is doing is recognizing this evolutionary imperative. But Nordlund's account of the biologically ingrained "tension between male desire and female choice" (132) is neither true to Shakespeare's depiction of male and female roles across the romantic comedies and tragedies (it encompasses *As You Like It* and *A Midsummer Night's Dream,* but not *Much Ado About Nothing, The Merchant of Venice, Twelfth Night,* or *Romeo and Juliet*), nor to the concept of bestowal. There is no evolutionary argument for the existence of bestowal in love, especially since it applies equally to both sexes. Indeed, there is no reason to suppose that, in evolutionary terms, the individual is any better at choosing an appropriate mate than the more mature, wiser members of the family or broader society. Nor is there a biological answer to the crucial *conceptual* question that Nordlund himself is driven to ask, whether it is possible to deserve or earn love. Is this (im)possibility biological, conceptual, or social and historical?

If we take the Elizabethan use of the term love to signify social allegiance (service, duty, reciprocal obligation) as more than a "mere euphemism," then the answer is a qualified "yes." Such an answer requires an acknowledgment of the range of affective investments that such relationships involved in a society in which nearly every form of relationship was, as Peter Laslett claims, "a love-relationship" not in spite of, but owing to the fact that it was in a relationship of service (and therefore duty and obligation).[5] Within the framework of a humanist concept of love, however, where bestowal of value is given as an (involuntary) gift, the response would be a qualified "no." Shakespeare's work contains both perspectives, often in tension. It is easy for us to recognise one of them but not the other because we are blinded by our own forms of social organization and personal experience to dissociate love and duty. This myopia is a historical accident, not a biological necessity. Historicism therefore reminds us that our inclination to regard the most prevalent use of love in the early modern period as a "euphemism" for emotion-free, social bonds misses an essential characteristic of Shakespeare's understanding of his age's concept of love. By denigrating this prevalent use, firstly as non-affective, and secondly as merely secondary or parasitic, Nordlund shows that his biocultural approach is blind to a major aspect of what we may call the nature of love in Shakespeare and his society. Ironically, that blindness is an effect of precisely the historical situation of evolutionary science.

I began by remarking on the hurdles faced by anyone who wishes to shift the center of gravity of current Shakespeare criticism. Despite his efforts to balance provocation with reasonableness, Nordlund doesn't manage to establish bioculturalism as a compelling alternative to historicism. The paradox at the heart of *Shakespeare and the Nature of Love* is that the issues that it tackles are in fact primarily conceptual rather than biological, and much of Nordlund's most trenchant analysis does not need his biocultural framework. The concept of love cannot be reduced to biological processes, chiefly because any biological test relies on the folk (and therefore historically bounded) notion of the concept (and its cognates) to establish the parameters of the biological argument. Nor can a speculative appeal to evolutionary adaptation encompass the complexity and variability of the expression of romantic love across historical and social conditions.

It is no coincidence that Nordlund ignores Petrarchan forms of desire, notoriously the subject matter of the romantic comedies and the sonnets. The peculiar combination of pleasurable pain in unrequited desire, and the concomitant tension between earthly pleasure and heavenly ideal in Petrarch himself, cannot be encompassed within a story told by Darwin. Certainly, Nordlund makes no attempt to do so. Courtly love may well have "seized upon a universal human potential" (48), but what is central to its story is the degree to which it resists what a later age might regard as the compulsions of species-specific genetic fitness: there is no obvious gain to the genetic fitness of the species to elevate heavenly love above carnal desire. When Nordlund analyzes Shakespeare's texts, he is often attentive to this bifurcated story. But he doesn't quite succeed in making the stories of biology and culture talk to each other. This is betrayed by a persistent diversion of register throughout the book. Bioculturalism should be able to find a unified mode of talking about these things, a way of transcending the divide between nature and culture in our discourses. But whenever Nordlund speaks of biology or evolution he adopts the peculiarly distanced, bloodless prose of pseudoscientism: human beings or people become the "human organism" or the "female mammal," society is reduced to the "group" or the "species," and reasons for moral actions are replaced by the search for evolutionary "causes." The new paradigm should be able to find a single language that does not betray in its vocabulary the reassertion of the divide between nature and culture that it seeks to bridge. Perhaps an entirely new language is needed, but it would need to encompass the old without reduction, otherwise it would lose touch with the forms of life from which the latter springs.

Reasons or causes?

The whole debate at the heart of *Shakespeare and the Nature of Love* could be said to turn on the philosophical question of whether the reasons people have for acting in particular ways can be reduced to explanations of their causes. Ludwig Wittgenstein believed that they could not; Donald Davidson held that they must be if any progress is to be made in philosophical understanding. To Wittgenstein the idea of progress was itself anathema. The task for him was to stop doing philosophy by eliminating the source of philosophical confusion: our habitual miss-takes on our language, in which we are equally at home and estranged. It is, as Freud would have said, *Heimlich*. I tend to stand with Wittgenstein. Rather than search for a single definition of love, to clear up confusions we need to pay closer attention both to the irreducible polysemy of the word and our habitual failure to acknowledge such difference, which may be seen in our tendency to think that when we talk of love we all mean one thing.

The compelling complexity of the texts that *Shakespeare and the Nature of Love* takes as its subject matter has more to do with their revelation of the conceptual spread of the central term than the material nature of referent, whether love or lover. When we talk of love, we could be referring to a state, an emotion, an attitude, a drive, or a disposition that unfolds across time and involves multiple, often conflicting states, emotions, drives, and attitudes. We could also be talking of a particular composition of chemicals in the blood. The tragedy of love lies in the fact that we never quite know what we are talking about, or what others are talking about when they use the word. Was this mess caused by natural selection working in tandem with hormonal secretions? That would not be tragedy but farce.

Notes

1. William R. Reddy, *The Navigation of Feeling: A Framework for the History of the Emotions* (Cambridge: Cambridge University Press, 2001), 11–12.

2. Irving Singer, *The Nature of Love,* 3 vols., 2nd ed. (Chicago: University of Chicago Press, 1984).

3. See especially, Leone Ebreo, *The Philosophy of Love,* trans. F. Friedeberg-Seely and Jean H. Barnes (London: Soncino Press, 1937), 18ff.

4. Tzevan Todorov, *The Imperfect Garden: The Legacy of Humanism,* trans. Carol Cosman (Princeton: Princeton University Press, 2002).

5. Peter Laslett, *The World We Have Lost,* 3rd ed. (New York: Charles Scribner's Sons, 1984), 5.

Secrets of Women: Gender, Generation,
and the Origins of Human Dissection
By Katharine Park
New York: Zone Books, 2006

Reviewer: Elizabeth D. Harvey

The frontispiece of Andreas Vesalius's 1543 *De humani corporis fabrica* is one of the most celebrated and frequently discussed images in the history of anatomy. Vesalius's book is usually seen as inaugurating the sixteenth-century revolution in dissection that propelled anatomy into its central place in medical knowledge. The frontispiece, which features Vesalius dissecting a cadaver, is crowded with onlookers who include not only the anatomist's contemporaries, but also such illustrious predecessors as Aristotle and Galen. The image captures Vesalius's radical departure from established procedure. Rather than representing the anatomical process as divided among *sector, ostensor,* and *lector* of anatomy, as it traditionally was, Vesalius embodies all three functions; he himself performs the acts of cutting, demonstrating, and explaining bodily structures. Conventional interpretations of the woodcut have made it into an icon representing a pivotal moment in the history of anatomy. But what has usually been eclipsed is the fact that the cadaver lying at the center of the frontispiece is female.

Katharine Park's important new book makes the gender and identity of the corpse Vesalius dissects the foundational moment of her study. Public dissections in the sixteenth century were usually medical; the partitioning and display of the body was used to teach and to further scientific knowledge. The gender of the body was relatively unimportant in this context because anatomy stressed the generic—what all bodies shared, not the features that made them distinct. Academic anatomies, which typically used the bodies of criminals as their subjects, worked to obliterate the identity of the cadaver. The criminal was already socially abject, and dissection eradicated the marks of social identity even further, first by cutting the body into parts, and then by turning these parts into nonproprietary organs and structures.

Park's book seeks to reverse this process of erasure. In order to accommodate gender, her first move is to enlarge the practice of dissection beyond the more academically oriented study of anatomy. She resituates anatomical dissection within a network of related practices: the embalming of the corpse in funerary custom, the preservation of a saint's body and the cult of relics, autopsies performed for forensic purposes, and, perhaps most interesting of all, the controversial performing of caesarean section. By positioning dissection within social networks, within kinship relations, and within the frameworks of religious beliefs, Park aims to restore "cultural coherence" to these practices. Because she locates her study in a historical sweep from the late thirteenth century to the mid-sixteenth century, Park also destabilizes the familiar narrative of the Vesalian anatomical revolution. This historical scope contextualizes medical anatomy within a much longer tradition, and it renders scientific curiosity one mode among others of exploring human interiority. *Secrets of Women* stands out among the many books on anatomy that have appeared in the past two decades. Its ability to name and identify the bodies that might otherwise disappear into the neutrality of the anatomical model and its capacity to analyze the undergirding ideologies through the lens of gender make it a vital addition to the field of anatomical research.

Park's account is richly textured. Anecdotes and narratives culled from Italian, often Florentine, archives, a close analysis of anatomical treatises, and an abundant array of images serve to ground her arguments in the specificities of time and place. Four of the five chapters employ a case history about the dissection of a woman's body, and two of these chapters focus on saints or visionaries. The conjunction of the discourses of sanctification and autopsy is one of the most fascinating aspects of this book: how does the body encode somatic signs of holiness, and how do the practices of dissection reveal them to ecclesiastical authority? Central to *Secrets of Women* is the idea that gender was elided in academic dissection, and that "women's secrets" figured the mystery of human interiority that lay at the heart, so to speak, of the anatomical quest. The Galenic foundation of Western medicine took the male body as generic, while female bodies were used for the knowledge that they could supply about women's sexual and reproductive organs. That the uterus was hidden inside the body and could be known only through dissection gave this organ a special symbolic power, for it came to represent both the origin of life and the enigmatic nature of the body's unknowable inside. Park explores the epistemological idea of secrecy, and her chapter on the anatomical history of women's organs details the assimilation of an oral, experiential, and usually female tradition of understanding women's "secrets" into the writings of learned (male) medical practitioners. Her account of this transition carefully divests itself of the nostalgia that has shaped some feminist analyses of this historical passage. Park recognizes the multiple factors that produced the shift, and she weighs both gains and losses attendant on it.

One of the strongest parts of the book is Park's analysis of maternity and the opening of the pregnant female body. Early modern patriarchal culture needed to regulate female sexuality and reproduction in order to sustain itself, and it is thus inevitable that generation would figure centrally. Because pregnancy earned a stay of execution for a convicted woman, the criminal bodies used for public dissection did not offer much knowledge about the female body's reproductive operations. However, autopsies, sometimes performed to ascertain the cause of death, or a caesarean section, conducted after the mother was deceased, provided information about women's propagative anatomy. Park examines these autopsies not only for what they reveal about medical knowledge but also for what they show us about contemporary ideas on lineage and kinship. The most compelling section of this chapter, "The Mother's Part," is Park's exploration of the narratives positioned at the interface of history and myth, those openings of the maternal body that bookend the Roman Empire: the caesarean delivery of Julius Caesar from his dead mother's womb, and Nero's crazed insistence that his mother, Agrippina, be killed and opened so that he might gaze at the organ that gave him life. These myths, according to Park, took on new resonance in the early modern period, especially as they were retold in relation to the emergent science of anatomy. Park's interest is not to examine the ethical controversies surrounding caesarean birth, although this would have been a welcome addition, but rather to suggest how the early modern reiterations of the myth shaped the new "empire" that emerged from Vesalian anatomical reform.

The final chapter of Park's book returns us to the Vesalian frontispiece. The structure of the book is suspended, for although Vesalius is invoked in the introduction and although the frontispiece is reproduced there, the intervening four chapters defer a full consideration of the image. Chapter 5, "The Empire of Anatomy," is the culminating moment in this revisionary book, and it effectively draws together the various strands of the historical argument Park has been making. She provides a narrative of the criminal woman who was executed and then simultaneously rendered unknowable and immortalized in the service of anatomical history. What little we know with certainty about her Vesalius tells us: the woman was middle-aged and unusually tall, she had given birth previously, she had claimed to be pregnant in order to escape hanging (a form of execution that itself indicated that she was unlikely to have been of noble birth), but that when her uterus was opened, the judgment of the midwives (that she was not pregnant) was confirmed. Park offers a conjectural narrative for the woman's last days, and the effect of humanizing the cadaver allows Park to speculate persuasively about why Vesalius chose a female corpse, particularly given that his understanding of the female reproductive system may be the weakest part of *De fabrica*. Park's analysis of the frontispiece aligns it both with Christian iconographic tradition (Mantegna's foreshortened Christ, Saint Anthony and the miser's heart) and with Roman myth. She argues that Nero and Caesar serve as intertexts to the Vesalian establishment of an anatomical empire. Vesalius's invocation of the Roman context resonated with Hapsburg mythology, and the dedication of *De fabrica* to the "divine Charles" supported Vesalius's ultimately successful bid to become an imperial physician in the Hapsburg Empire.

Park's intricate interpretation of the image makes gender not incidental but rather essential to the territorial claims that Vesalius makes about his reformation of anatomical method. Her central points are that imperial dominion has historically depended upon

the violent subjugation of female reproduction, and that this foundational moment in the history of anatomy instantiates a cognate
relationship between the male anatomist and his female object that
would continue to shape the scientific and anatomical gaze. Park's
thesis is not an unfamiliar one, for it draws on insights that would
be familiar to readers of Foucault and feminist history of science
and medicine. What is remarkable about *Secrets of Women* is the
wealth of historical detail that allows Park to situate Vesalius's ac-
complishment within a gendered framework. Her revisionary analysis of this anatomical icon urges us to reread the history of
anatomy differently, paying attention to what has been occluded in
the establishment of medical empire. *Secrets of Women* will certainly change our understanding of Vesalius and the history of anatomy, and its effects are likely to extend far beyond the field.

The Aesthetics of Antichrist:
From Christian Drama to Christopher Marlowe
By John Parker
Ithaca: Cornell University Press, 2007

Reviewer: Alison Shell

The notion that Marlowe's writing is atheistical is a long-standing
one; the counter-argument that it is religiously normative is almost
as familiar. In this study John Parker provocatively synthesizes the
two views, arguing with a wealth of documentation that Marlowe's
drama can indeed be seen as anti-Christian: in other words, opposed to Christianity but all too deeply implicated in it, even
springing from its fault lines.

In *The Theatre of God's Judgements,* Thomas Beard famously
wrote of Marlowe that he wrote books "affirming our Saviour to be
but a deceiver, and Moses to be but a conjurer and seducer of the
people, and the holy Bible to be but vain and idle stories, and all
religion but a device of policy." Dr. Faustus the magician and the

holy miracle-workers Moses and Christ have more in common than is often acknowledged, all three bearing a disturbing similarity to the Antichrist of Revelation, dangerous on account of his supernatural powers and his consequent ability to pass as Christ. Like an actor, Antichrist pretends to be what he is not.

Drawing inspiration from recent studies which have explored the deceptiveness of theatrical representation, such as Michael O'Connell's *The Idolatrous Eye,* Parker argues that "the figure of Antichrist encouraged premodern believers to see Christian transcendence as itself an effect of artistic representation, more stunning in proportion to the representation's actual vacuity." This was as evident at Mass as in drama, thanks to the Catholic doctrine of transubstantiation, whereby Christ's body is actually but invisibly present to the believer under the outward form of bread; it is no accident that much medieval drama is associated with the festival of Corpus Christi. Like Antichrist, the Eucharist can be seen as a revelation of absence, suggesting Christ and augmenting desire for Christ by virtue of what it is not; thus, though Antichrist is Christ's opposite and the Eucharist encapsulates his invisible presence, both point toward a state of affairs that, according to medieval and early modern thought, would receive typological fulfillment at the end of time.

Parker's range is exceptionally wide, spanning patristics and medieval drama as well as Marlowe and his age, and displaying a virtuoso familiarity with biblical commentary in several languages. Commentary on sacred texts is of its nature a way of pinpointing difficulties within them, so can act as a shortcut for those interested in heterodoxy, as well as displaying the extent of the commentator's own alertness to awkward questions. Some commentators gloss over embarrassing difficulties and overliteral readings; others welcome the opportunity to rebut them from within the fold, though as Parker points out, this needs to be done well. "It takes a dialectician of supreme talent working within this framework to prevent the history of the Eucharist from collapsing into nightmare, the endless repetition of past events, each as horrifying and fraudulent as the last: the miracle of Passover (a massacre), its recapitulation in the Last Supper (a death sentence), the reprise of that sad meal at Mass (a sacrifice), the mock consecration in Chester's play of the Antichrist (a lie)."

This quotation gives the flavor of Parker's authorial positioning, at once indignant and evasive. One is left asking whether he is made angry by bad Christianity or all Christianity, which may be a deliberate rhetorical gambit; if so, it is an appropriate one for a book dedicated to tracing the intimate relationship between Christian and anti-Christian discourse. One can respond, piously, by saying that Parker's argument would have acquired even greater finesse by giving more attention to the ethical charge of the Christian message: too obvious for medieval and Renaissance dramatists to spell out, maybe not obvious enough within this secular generation. The wonder-working similarities between Christ and Faustus may be striking, but one is out for self-aggrandizement and personal gratification, the other a radical altruism.

This tendency to ignore the benign messages and positive historical effects of Christianity also affects the other main strand of Parker's argument, the relationship between the deceptive Antichrist and money, with its pure power of representation and unparalleled ability to corrupt. In a chapter examining the notion of redemption as a quasi-commercial transaction and teasing out the history of the term "blood money," he writes that drama "could . . . apologise for the church's total collapse into worldly commercialism . . . even as these same rituals and dramas brought to bear on church finance a radical critique." This is partly fair. Though reformers disliked medieval religious drama about as much as the buying and selling of masses, perhaps they should not have done; consideration of figures like the Henrician playwright John Bale, whose dramatic indebtedness to his predecessors complicates his anti-Catholic satire, would have enhanced Parker's argument here.

But the notion of a totally venal church owes more to Reformation polemic than anything. Everyman does, in some sense, buy his salvation by giving money to the poor, but beneficiaries of charity in medieval England would have had cause to be grateful to his real-life counterparts. Then and now, the question of how charitable donations should be sourced is a complex one. But the medieval church unquestionably effected some redistribution of wealth by pricking people's consciences, and religious drama, where it advocates this, is symptomatic of the era's communal sense that charity toward the deserving poor is a good thing. Christian metaphors of buying and selling salvation, even when seen in terms of sacred parody, often lack finesse; but this is to look at them from a purely literary point of view, leaving aside questions of authorial intention and the instrumentality of the words themselves. If one sees the same metaphors as drawing attention to real-life suffering and its

possible alleviation, it is hard to be so dismissive. Critics of exceptional linguistic sensitivity—and Parker is certainly one such—
perhaps have a greater need than most to step back and consider
the historical situatedness of their subject matter. This learned and
stimulating book is also one which will leave some readers annoyed and unsatisfied; part of the reason is that, anti-Christianly
enough, its concentration on language draws our attention away
from referents, and gives us only a simulacrum of the real world.

Literature and Favoritism in Early Modern England
By Curtis Perry
Cambridge: Cambridge University Press, 2006

Reviewer: Alan Stewart

In early modern England, the powerful man or woman was *de ri-
gueur* accompanied by favorites. "The mightiest kings have had
their minions," Mortimer senior tells his nephew in Christopher
Marlowe's *Edward II,* listing a string of classical precedents. The
favorite's status inevitably mimicked the fortune of his master or
mistress: as the Player King in *Hamlet* notes, "The great man down,
you mark his favorite flies." These assumptions allowed the royal
male favorite to act as a key trope of anti-court sentiment, argues
Curtis Perry in his new book. The favorite becomes a figure whose
role provokes questions about "the uneasy intersection of the personal and the public in a political system traditionally organized
around patronage and intimacy," and throws light onto issues such
as personal monarchy, the early modern public sphere, the nature
and limits of prerogative, and the enfranchisement (or lack of) of
subjects. Perry argues that "the discourse of corrupt favoritism is
this period's most important unofficial vehicle for exploring constitutional unease concerning the nature and limits of personal monarchy within the balanced English constitution." Perry is known as
the author of *The Making of Jacobean Culture* (Cambridge University Press, 1997), and one might expect him to focus on James VI

and I, who serially replaced each pretty male favorite with a younger model, provoking scurrilous gossip across Europe. But in this study Perry noticeably widens his chronological range, to move from late Elizabethan through to Caroline texts, allowing him to take into account the different dynamics of female and male rulers with their male favorites.

The early modern royal favorite has previously been the domain of historians—perhaps the most prominent study being the collection of essays *The World of the Favorite* edited by J. H. Elliott and L. W. B. Brockliss (Yale University Press, 1999). It is true that Perry's work shares common ground with that of historians such as Thomas Cogswell, Peter Lake, Blair Worden, Linda Levy Peck, and especially Alastair Bellany. But Perry remains at heart a literary critic who believes that "the explanatory frameworks made available by a focus on favoritism can in numerous cases render intelligible literary texts that have been ignored hitherto or dismissed as second-rate, primitive, or simply bizarre." As a result, although he draws on trial reports, satires, polemics, and legal documents, the bulk of his readings is of plays, and his book reaches its logical teleological climax with an afterword concerned not with, say, the Civil War but with Milton's *Paradise Lost.*

Perry's key text, which acts as a leitmotif throughout the book, is the 1584 *Leicester's Commonwealth,* a Catholic attack on Elizabeth's favorite Robert Dudley, Earl of Leicester. The historical moment that produced this libel is significant, in Perry's analysis: despite the medieval examples of the favorites of Edward II and Richard II, "the all-powerful royal favorite does not really take its central place in literature's menu of prevalent stereotypes until the tail end of Elizabeth's reign." *Leicester's Commonwealth,* he argues, develops many of the consistent invective tropes that came to be used against Elizabeth's other favorites Sir Walter Raleigh, Sir Christopher Hatton, and Robert Devereux, Earl of Essex and James's favorites Philip Howard, Robert Carr, Earl of Somerset, and George Villiers, Duke of Buckingham. Devoting chapter 2 to the libel, Perry provides a thorough reading of the text, and then demonstrates its unacknowledged thematic links to well-known plays such as Kyd's *Spanish Tragedy* and Webster's *White Devil.* He goes on to examine the fertile print and manuscript lives of *Leicester's Commonwealth* itself, through to its 1641 reprinting during the Long Parliament's clash with Strafford, and the redaction of its themes in works by Thomas Scott, John Russell, and William Cavendish.

This structure is repeated for most of the book's chapters: a reading is offered of a central text, and then other, often more obscure texts are produced to interact productively with the ideas and concerns raised by the central text. It is a strategy that produces a "thick" reading of his chosen topics, at once erudite and convincing. The succeeding chapters interrogate the figure of the good favorite; the favorite's association with poison; and sexual libels that allege the "erotic incontinence" of the smitten monarch. Edward II is identified as the "central native exemplum of passionate and corrupting favoritism," and his treatment by Christopher Marlowe, Elizabeth Cary, and Francis Hubert is analyzed. The final chapter investigates the uses of Roman history to portray the favorite, in figures including Sejanus. While Perry does not shy away from familiar texts such as Sidney's *Arcadia,* Marlowe's *Edward II,* and Jonson's *Sejanus,* much of the pleasure of this book comes through its confident introduction and handling of a remarkable range of less familiar texts: from Lodowick Carlell's *The Deserving Favourite* (1629) to John Denham's *The Sophy* (1641).

My caveats about the book are minor: Perry is clearly more at home with drama than he is with Sidney's *Arcadia;* his work with manuscript sources is understandably tentative; and his work is narrowly English in focus. This is understandable—and presumably deliberate—but it rules out any helpful comparative inquiry into, for example, James VI's favorites in Scotland, or Henri III of France's much publicized relations with his *mignons,* the latter being a contemporary example with which English writers often drew comparisons when discussing Edward II in the late Elizabethan period. *Literature and Favoritism in Early Modern England* is an impressive and original achievement, striking especially for the thoroughness of its treatment of a subject over a considerable historical range, its very secure grasp of historical and political contexts and for its timely excavation of some lesser-known but fascinating texts. The favorite may be a familiar topic for English Renaissance literary studies, but Perry's book opens up the debate in new and interesting ways.

Cultural Politics—Queer Reading, 2nd ed.
By Alan Sinfield
London: Routledge 2005

*Shakespeare, Authority, Sexuality: Unfinished
Business in Cultural Materialism*
By Alan Sinfield
London: Routledge, 2006

Reviewer: Graham Hammill

As I was preparing to write this review, I happened to see a production of . . . *and they put handcuffs on the flowers,* Fernando Arrabal's gut-wrenching indictment of Franco's military dictatorship in
Spain, performed by a company called the Subversive Theater Collective. Arrabal's play focuses on the fantasies of four men imprisoned for political crimes and subjected on a regular basis to brutal
torture and humiliation. In order to elicit sympathy for the prisoners and heighten the audience's awareness of the horrors of imprisonment, the play was staged in the basement of an old abandoned
warehouse in a seedy part of town; instead of chairs, audience
members were seated on bales of hay; and (although this may have
been unintentional) during the performance bats were flying
around the basement. The performance notes made it clear that the
company was reviving Arrabal's 1969 play to rouse political sentiment against the Bush administration's treatment of prisoners at
Guantanamo Bay. But as I looked around the room, it was also clear
that the audience was made up of liberal professors, bohemian college students, and other left-thinking individuals eager to spend a
Saturday evening in a dank and somewhat scary basement, risking
the possibility of rabies, to see a play that confirms what all of us
already believe. Torture is degrading, dehumanizing, and morally
wrong. On its Web site, the Subversive Theater Collective calls this
one of its "most subversive productions of all time," but upon reflection, I think the performance was more an instance of preaching
to the choir.

I was left with a similar thought upon reading two of Sinfield's recent books, *Cultural Politics—Queer Reading* and *Shakespeare, Authority, Sexuality: Unfinished Business in Cultural Materialism.* Despite the pronounced radicalism that one expects from cultural materialism, the central claims of these two books confirm what left-leaning readers already tend to accept. Literature is politically and historically situated, and to say otherwise is to play a game of politics. It is much to Sinfield's credit that this position is so readily accepted because it demonstrates the far-reaching effect of his work and the work of his fellow travelers. The central tenets of cultural materialism have so powerfully displaced ideas about literature and criticism held by previous generations that to announce the cultural as political or that one task of critical interpretation is "the recovery of subordinated voices" (*SAS*, 25) is about as provocative as saying that torture is morally wrong. Sure, nuances and qualifications might need to be added, and there are certainly arguments to be had about what follows. But in the main such statements are not the dissident positions of young radicals but the hard-won axioms by which mainstream criticism now largely operates.

Sinfield seems bothered by this situation and frames *Shakespeare, Authority, Sexuality* with introductory and concluding chapters that address the relevance of cultural materialism for contemporary early modern studies. Almost twenty-five years after he and Jonathan Dollimore published *Political Shakespeare: Essays in Cultural Materialism,* the groundbreaking collection that fundamentally changed Shakespeare studies (for the better, in my opinion), the question emerges: has cultural materialism outlived its moment?

In Sinfield's assessment, cultural materialism has devolved into two distinct camps. On the one hand, anxiety over whether or not literary critics are doing history properly has lead to a renewed interest in literary history. On the other hand, interest in materialism has lead to what Sinfield calls "textual anthropology" (4), analysis of things like stage props, gendered tools (sewing utensils), and books and manuscripts as material objects. While acknowledging that each camp has produced valuable work, in both cases, Sinfield argues, "the political edge is blunted." It's not entirely clear how this works with the second camp, since Sinfield has little else to say about scholarship on material objects. But he does develop a brief critique of literary history, arguing that literary history is a

species of pastoral that posits history by retreating from and effac-
ing more politically pertinent problems, "[yearning] for a world before history, theory and politics" (39). The argument seems to me
to be somewhat overstated. There are countless examples in early
modern studies of literary histories that do not retreat from history,
politics, and/or theory. And there is also a familiar tradition of
Marxist criticism—think of Adorno, Benjamin, Bloch, or Jameson—which argues that literature is historical and political specifically in its refusal of the social. Literature inscribes history and
politics negatively rather than positively, and it's through literary
history that this negative inscription can be discerned. Because
Sinfield doesn't engage with that tradition, I think he misses a good
opportunity to refine and push forward some of his central claims
about cultural materialism and how it views the literary.

More pressing for Sinfield are challenges from Andrew Hadfield
and Ewan Fernie. Hadfield attempts to move beyond a somewhat
ossified model of dominance and dissonance by developing a
broader sense of political self-understanding in late sixteenth-century England. In response, Sinfield charges Hadfield with lacking a
sufficiently materialist account of concept-formation. For Hadfield,
Shakespeare was a republican. Hadfield sets out to prove that there
was a vital, if somewhat closeted discourse of republicanism in late
sixteenth-century England in order to argue that Shakespeare self-
consciously fashioned himself within this political tradition. Sinfield accepts half of Hadfield's position, arguing that republicanism
was an emergent discourse that runs throughout Shakespeare's
writings alongside his more conservative political vision. By rear-
ticulating this thesis in more explicitly materialist terms, Sinfield
is able to underscore the problem of agency. Because republicanism
is an emergent discourse, agency lies with Shakespeare's readers,
who are called upon to wrestle republican discourses from "the hegemonic critical tradition" that has occluded them (20). The point,
Sinfield argues, is not to claim Shakespeare for one or another political agenda but to make it apparent "that critics have always
done that" (199), that literary texts are always open to political re-
interpretation and appropriation. Cultural materialism is finally
more satisfying, then, because it offers a more accurate sense of history and a more accurate account of the agency of the critic in interpreting the past.

Fernie's attempt to supplement cultural materialism with spirituality is the second explicit challenge that Sinfield takes up—and,

to my mind, he responds much less successfully than he does in his critique of Hadfield. Fernie aims to bolster cultural materialism with political messianism, adding a more positive agenda to materialist critique. For Fernie, this doesn't mean that religion is the goal or outcome of political critique. Rather, he is interested in the role that messianic thinking plays in early modern figurations of the political, broadly conceived. Suspicious of this move, Sinfield rejects it on the grounds that religion is a tool of empire. For instance, Sinfield notes that George Bush explains his decision to invade Iraq as revelation from God; he concludes that "this must be one of the least propitious moments in history at which to get thoughtful academics to make a positive investment in religion" (198). However, I am left wondering why Shakespeare, who Sinfield tirelessly points out is used to further conservative cultural agendas, is a legitimate and urgent site of critical intervention while religion is not. As was the case with his critique of literary history, I suspect that some engagement with Jameson and the Frankfurt School might lead Sinfield to a more developed response.

Sinfield is quite candid about the provisional nature of his defense of the relevance of cultural materialism. As he somewhat disarmingly notes, a number of readers of his book in draft worried that he had not met his explicitly announced aim of developing and defending a cultural materialist reading practice. I tend to agree with these readers. Sinfield seems to me to engage in skirmishes over turf while avoiding more interesting engagements that might deepen cultural materialism as theory and practice. Nevertheless, the combination of cultural materialism and queer studies that Sinfield develops does invigorate cultural materialism in some pretty interesting ways. In the new introduction to the second edition of *Cultural Politics—Queer Reading,* Sinfield describes the chapters that follow (unchanged from the 1994 edition) as his attempt to bridge the two main phases of his work to date: cultural materialism and queer theory/gay and lesbian studies. The same can be said for *Shakespeare, Authority, Sexuality,* where Sinfield implicitly stages an engagement between cultural materialism and sexuality through readings of sexuality in Shakespeare and some of his contemporaries. Specifically, attention to sexuality leads Sinfield to reflect on, modify, and sharpen some claims about history and critical interpretation.

It's worth noting the distance traveled between the two books in this regard. In *Cultural Politics—Queer Reading,* Sinfield is primarily interested in positing ethnic and sexual subcultures as productive positions from which to develop and legitimate what he calls minority interpretations of texts. At times, these subcultures are clearly not the intended audiences. How, he asks, might Jews read *The Merchant of Venice* or gays read *Venus and Adonis?* And at other times, these subcultures clearly are at least one intended audience. How might gays read Auden's poetry against or alongside its reception by dominant English culture? In *Shakespeare, Authority, and Sexuality,* Sinfield presses the problem of minority reading into a more complex interaction between present and past. Contemporary readers tend to be scandalized or titillated by the often blatant homoeroticism of early modern literature, he argues, while we also tend to see heterosexual relations as more or less business as usual. But early moderns tended to see homoeroticism as the norm, while relations between men and women turn out to be the most scandalous, because, as Sinfield argues, women were expected to be the virtuous conduits through which property was transferred between men. This historical difference in expectations and assumptions leads Sinfield to ask two sets of questions simultaneously. First, how can we read relations between men and women in early modern texts in such a way that denaturalizes present-day, normative heterosexuality? That is, how can we read past anxieties over the role of women in such a way that calls into question a long durée of unchanging heterosexuality? And second, how can the relative disregard with which early moderns treated same-sex relations (what Laurie Shannon calls homonormativity) be used in support of present-day homosexuality, as a source of cultural pleasure and legitimation? Or, better, how do same-sex relations of the past project a future that would be unimaginable in the terms of the past? As Sinfield notes, this second set of questions shifts theoretical weight away from history to what he calls the unhistorical. Cultural materialism has a commitment to history, but at the same time "it is that underlying historical commitment that makes the manifestly unhistorical, self-consciously impertinent interpretation effective" (198). While the first set of questions grounds a critique of what Sinfield would most likely think of as patriarchal and heteronormative hegemony, the second set opens the space for the more positive, if also ongoing, project of inventing gay culture.

Shakespeareans and other early modernists are likely to find *Shakespeare, Authority, and Sexuality* more exciting for what it does rather than for what it says it does. Six of the eleven chapters in this book were published earlier as essays, and the entire book might best be characterized as essayistic. This is a book that explores, tests, and revises through interpretive practice. It is fascinating to watch Sinfield repeatedly engage with the figuration of gender and sexuality in early modern texts. Sinfield first introduces homonormativity in relation to anxious heterosexuality in a reading of *Poetaster*. Initially, Sinfield is interested in how Jonson opposes Horace, authoritative critic of the court, to Ovid, whose relations with Julia got him exiled. But at the very ending of the chapter, noting Horace's well-known vulnerability to pederastic desire—the love of young girls and boys—Sinfield concludes that Jonson need not address it because it was not worth addressing: "unlicensed cross-gender relations were regarded as more dangerous than private, same-gender liaisons" (51–52). This opposition between anxious heterosexuality and unregarded homonormativity continues through the following four chapters (chapters 4 through 7) as Sinfield analyzes the early-modern sex-gender system through readings of a host of plays by Shakespeare and Marlowe. His aim is not to adduce how people lived or imagined themselves to have lived, but to explore "contested representations through which early-modern society sought to explore its most troubling insights" (86). These chapters rely most heavily on Jonathan Goldberg, Bruce Smith, Valerie Traub, and to a lesser degree the cross-dressing debates of the late 1980s and early 1990s. Not surprisingly, then, in the system Sinfield elaborates misogyny buttresses masculinity while female-female relations remain a site of "improbable" eroticism, in the sense of unthinkable and therefore relatively unregulated (102). Meanwhile, boys become another "other" against which masculinity is defined, situated on the fault line between respectable manhood and erotic attachment. Sinfield gives his most impertinent and unhistorical interpretations in chapters 9 and 10. After showing how Marlowe, Sidney, and Barnfield express sexuality in the lyric (chapter 8), in chapter 9 Sinfield develops a reading of Shakespeare's *Sonnets* that attempts to mobilize what is most shocking for moderns against what he sees as most shocking or upsetting for early moderns. While the dark Woman is what would have been most provocative to Shakespeare's audience as the relation between the Boy and the dark Woman traverses class boundaries, Sinfield also argues that the Boy is not just an object of affection but makes advances upon the Poet who recoils because both want the same thing: "they are both tops" (170). And in chapter 10, Sinfield gives an impassioned reading of *Measure for Measure* in light of hate crimes against gays and lesbians, contrasting the state suppression of sexuality in Shakespeare's Venice with the problem of civil rights for gays and lesbians in the contemporary international community.

Readers coming to *Shakespeare, Authority, Sexuality* looking for new paradigms by which to think about either cultural materialism or queer theory in early modern studies are likely to be disappointed. Sinfield's explanations of cultural material—lucid as they are—do not substantially go beyond his earlier work. But readers willing to follow Sinfield's subtle, learned, and provocative interpretations will find this book to be rewarding indeed.

Murder after Death: Literature and Anatomy in Early Modern England
By Richard Sugg
Ithaca: Cornell University Press, 2007

Reviewer: Michael Neill

The dust jacket of Richard Sugg's handsomely designed book features a skeleton leaning upon a funeral monument, its head pensively supported by a bony left elbow, its right hand clasping a skull that is the object of its melancholy contemplation. The figure belongs to a set of engravings, generally attributed to Titian's pupil Jan Calkar, that were commissioned for the foundational text of modern anatomy, Andreas Vesalius's *De Humani Corporis Fabrica* (1543). The skeleton's unflinching gaze appears to parody the anatomist's studious investigation of bodily secrets; and on Sugg's cover, the gravely self-referential wit of the original conceit is nicely complemented by the inscription of the author's own name on the face of the tomb. Insofar, however, as this image, like many of the Vesalius illustrations, appropriates the medieval language of death to advertise the spiritual virtues of anatomical practice, it slightly misrepresents the thrust of Sugg's energetically materialist argument. Seemingly unaware of its decayed state, Calkar's skeleton mimics a popular *memento mori* trope, made famous by numerous Renaissance portraits featuring a Young Man with a Skull, and brought to striking theatrical life in *Hamlet* and *The Revenger's Tragedy.* Thus, even as it serves to exhibit the proper articulation of the human frame, the figure invokes a moralizing counterdiscourse to the scientific text it ostensibly illustrates. Sugg's primary interest, however, is less in the resonance of Calkar's illustrations than in Vesalius's text itself and in what it reveals about the role of his practice in developing a fully rational understanding of the human body.

Building on the work of Jonathan Sawday[1] and others, *Murder after Death* sets out to analyze "the impact of anatomy on English literature and culture" (2). Sugg uncovers a complicated process whereby the anatomist's knife progressively "despiritualized" the "cavities of the body," thereby engendering a discourse that "dislocated and problematized [the soul]" (208). Visual proof of this transformation, he suggests, can be discerned in the cold stylization of eighteenth-century anatomical illustration when compared to the arresting liveliness of the skeletons and flayed muscle-figures that adorn Vesalius's *Fabrica* (8–10). The process itself he traces through a remarkable range of literary texts, from Painter and Nashe to Shirley and Killigrew, that reveal how the discoveries of the new anatomy haunted the imagination of early modern England.

Although Sugg's argument is generally a convincing one, I think he significantly downplays the extent to which practitioners of the new science sought to legitimize themselves by exploiting the contemplative tropes of the *memento mori* tradition. It was not only preachers like John More who urged their readers to recognize in "some anatomy . . . (as in a glass) the original of Death,"[2] or dramatists like John Webster who envisioned the anatomy lesson as an enacted parable, designed "to teach man / Wherein he is imperfect" (*White Devil,* 3.2.97–98); for even propagandists of dissection like Caspar Barlaeus, in his treatise *On the Anatomical House which can be visited in Amsterdam* (ca. 1638), insisted that here— amid the carefully posed skeletal ornaments that turned anatomy theaters into museums of moralizing reflection—"you can learn the ways of death and a desire to shun death."[3] Vesalius himself had conducted his initial research by sifting through the bones stored in the cloister of Les Innocents in Paris, site of the most famous of all *Danse Macabre* murals, and his master work was assembled and printed in Basel, where a pair of equally elaborate *Totentanz* frescoes adorned cloisters on either side of the Rhine. In the *Fabrica* illustrations the iconography of these paintings is echoed by the way that Calkar's self-anatomizing musclemen are posed against a landscape which forms a continuous backdrop to the plates, as if inviting informed readers to envision the entire sequence as a reworking of the Gross Basel *Tod,* whose action trails across a similar landscape. Even Vesalius's great title page engraving—which Sugg interprets simply as a "creative image of early scientific investigation," celebrating the dissector's power to expose the secrets of the female body (111)—is rendered ambiguous by the oversized skeleton who presides over the scene of autopsy in the authoritative posture that once belonged to the lecturer of medieval dissections. It can hardly be a coincidence that in the second edition of the *Fabrica* (1555) the staff in the skeleton's right hand was replaced by the scythe of triumphant Death.

In Sugg's first chapter, "Between the Skin and the Bone: Anatomy, Violence, and Transition," he seeks to show how the new science, by replacing or absorbing older images of death, "reinvented not only notions of violence, but the very image of death itself" (13). His principal evidence here is Henry Chettle's tragedy, *Hoffman* (ca. 1603). Although Sugg is mistaken in supposing that "the vital role of anatomy in [this play's] sensationalism has previously gone unrecognised" (31),[4] his energetic analysis of *Hoffman*'s "strikingly dissective" imagery and its display of two hanging "anatomies" nicely illustrates what he describes as the "blurred boundaries between the anatomy theaters and play theaters" (26); and if he underestimates the extent to which this very blurring highlighted the didactic rhetoric of anatomical display, he is right to point out how in such spectacles "the tension between a degraded criminal specimen, and the divine artifice it was supposed to reveal [anticipates] potential conflicts between secular enquiry and sacred truths" (35). The coherence of Sugg's materialist argument is damaged, however, by a digressive excursion on the degree of realism required in Chettle's play: could the actors have decorated the stage with real bones? If they did, would such a display have struck the Master of the Revels as a too vivid emblematization of the play's critique of courtly corruption? Or, (assuming that actors, like anatomists, were likely to have sought the remains of condemned criminals) might he rather have approved such a shameful display for its deterrent value? It is certainly true that there was a significant overlap between anatomical performances and the histrionic violence of public executions; but it is difficult to believe that the Master's reading of the scenes is likely to have been much affected by such purely literal considerations. Arguably, moreover, the mere fact that the torture of Otho with a burning crown imitates "a known method of capital punishment in the Renaissance" (21) matters less than the way in which this detail transforms the Prince's monitory skeleton into a familiar image of King Death—thereby identifying Clois Hoffman, like Vindice in *The Revenger's Tragedy,* as the orchestrator of a perverted *Totentanz.*

Chapter 2 investigates the strange intersections of anatomy with that most pervasive of New World nightmares, cannibalism, touching on the uneasy similarities between savage anthrophagy and the European consumption of "mummy" in what Louise Noble has dubbed "medicinal cannibalism."[5] For Sugg, anatomy was "simply the best champion that European culture [could] summon to devour the cannibal," not just because it claimed cultural legitimacy for what was in essence merely "a[nother] form of ferocious bodily invasion," but because both were characterized by the same "strange desire for some absolute and immediate knowledge [of the other]" (60). At the same time, he suggests, "cannibalism must have acted as a convenient outer limit of savagery"—and one "which made anatomy seem mild by comparison." He illustrates his argument for the pervasiveness of this "ambiguous fusion of anatomy and cannibalism" (61) in the popular imagination with bizarre detail plucked from a variety of often unexpected sources, including *Twelfth Night,* Painter's *Palace of Pleasure,* and Shirley's *The Wedding.* Oddly missing from his discussion, however, are several plays in which dismemberment, evisceration, and cannibal feasting are on conspicuous display: Shakespeare's *Titus Andronicus,* Robert Wilmot's *Tancred and Gismund,* John Fletcher's *The Mad Lover,* and John Ford's *'Tis Pity She's a Whore.* There could be no better illustrations than these last three of the way in which the image of a lover's heart "ripped" from its body appears, in Sugg's words, "to match the psychology of anatomy and cannibalism with intriguing precision" (51). The posturing of Ford's Giovanni, in particular, when he displays his sister Annabella's heart impaled like the suffering heart of Jesus, shockingly travesties the way in which the anatomist becomes "a kind of priest, transforming degraded matter into a spiritually saturated object of wonder" (71). In terms that Sugg would immediately recognize (119), Giovanni presents himself as the celebrant of a cannibalistic Eucharist: "You came to feast, my lords, with dainty fare. / I came to feast too, but I digged for food / In a much richer mine than gold or stone / Of any value balanced. 'Tis a heart, / A heart, my lords, in which is mine entombed" (5.6.23–7).

To the extent that the heart was imagined as a locus of the most powerful and intimate emotions, or even of the soul itself, its evisceration epitomized that longing to discover the secrets of inner being to which the new science of dissection at first gave a satisfyingly material dimension. So it was that Montaigne, for example, could imagine his *Essays,* or Donne his *Devotions* as exercises in psychological self-dissection. "I wholly set forth and expose my self," wrote Montaigne of his book, "it is a *skeletos,* where at first sight appear all the veins, muscles, gristles, sinews, and tendons."[6] In the long run, however, the anatomist's scalpel served only to open up imponderable questions about the nature of interiority and, most disturbingly, about the physical location of the soul. In the *Fabrica* Vesalius had dismissed such speculation in a splendidly sarcastic disquisition on the occult belief in the *luz* or *Albadaran,* a bone the size of a chickpea, supposedly impervious to decay, from which the entire person of the deceased would be reconstituted at the day of judgment: playfully identifying it with "the inner ossicle of the right big toe," and observing that it "can in fact be broken and burnt just like other bones," Vesalius consigned the subject of the soul to the province of theologians, insisting that the metaphysics of immortality were no concern of the anatomical scientist.[7] A century later, however, Descartes would earnestly propose that the "principal seat of the soul" was to be discovered in the pineal gland, supported as it was "by the little branches of the carotid arteries which bring the spirits into the brain" (quoted 132). The remaining chapters of *Murder after Death* focus on the increasingly vexed relationship between the body and the inner self that Descartes vainly sought to resolve.

In "The Body as Proof" Sugg shows how dissection purported to discover in the condition of various internal organs evidence of what we would think of as psychological traits or particular emotional states: Queen Mary's famous vow that once she was "dead and opened" her physicians would discover "Calais lying upon [her] heart" was something more, he suggests, than a mere hyperbolic metaphor (100); while the size and softness of James I's heart, disclosed at his autopsy, appeared to reveal both his considerate nature and his timorous disposition (90). So when King Lear imagines how autopsy might reveal the cause of his daughters' "hard hearts" he means exactly what he says (105). Something close to Lear's fantasy is acted out in Middleton and Rowley's *The Changeling* (1622) —another text that Sugg might have discussed with profit. It is surely telling that in the figure of the madhouse keeper, Alibius, Rowley is thought to have caricatured the physician Helkiah Crooke, whom Sugg recognizes as a key figure in the early history of English anatomy. Crooke's *Microcosmographia* (1615), as Sugg reminds us, had provoked a violent controversy over its boldness in stripping away "the veil of Nature" and uncovering the "mysteries" of the female body, especially "the natural parts belonging to generation" (quoted p. 113). It is just such an unveiling that *The Changeling,* obsessed as it is with the existence of "secrets" hidden from "outward view" (1.1.158–59), seeks to dramatize: the play reaches an emblematic climax in the scene where the heroine, Beatrice-Joanna, opens her husband's closet to discover a sinister manual of scientific revelation that supposedly makes Alsemero "master of the mystery" (4.1.38). Entitled *The Book of Experiment, Called Secrets in Nature,* it threatens to expose the truth of her lost virginity; but the real master of mysteries is the disaffected servant to whom she has already surrendered her body. Deflores's remorseless excavation of Beatrice's hidden self culminates in the claim to absolute possession that he celebrates in a defiantly cannibalistic metaphor: "I have drunk up all, left none behind / For any man to pledge me" (5.3.170–71).

"Some women are odd feeders," Deflores opines early in the play (2.2.153); but in his world it is always men who desire the "knowledge . . . nearer, / Deeper, and sweeter" (1.2.12–13) that will give them power over women's bodies; and Sugg shows how anatomical dissection—as suggested by the triumphant display of a woman's opened womb on Vesalius's title page—provided a particularly rich vehicle for male fantasies of penetrating the mysteries of womanhood and female sexuality. Ironically, he suggests, the ultimate effect of acting out such fantasies was to undo them by revealing the gross materiality of the human subject. Thus by the time we reach Killigrew's Restoration comedies *The Parson's Wedding* and *Thomaso,* the male characters' elaborate rhetorical dissections of women's bodies reduce each of them to "a set of fetishized parts . . .

revealing only surfaces" (122, 129). Something even more reductive, it might be argued, had already happened to Annabella's body
in 'Tis Pity: when Giovanni bursts into Soranzo's banquet flourish-
ing her eviscerated heart, he believes himself possessed of the arch
"secret" with which the play has been so preoccupied. But the extreme overdetermination of the icon he has fashioned results in a
collapse of meanings, so that for his baffled audience the organ on
his knife stands for nothing more than itself—a piece of bleeding
meat.

   In "The Split Body" Sugg traces the efforts of a succession of
thinkers, including John Donne and his friend, the royal chaplain,
Joseph Hall, to rescue what Giovanni destroys by distinguishing between the material reality of "that fleshy part which is in the centre
of the body" (Hall, quoted p. 143) and the figurative truth of the
human "heart." Citing Tourneur's D'Amville in *The Atheist's Tragedy* as an example of the vicious despair to which "deluded materialism" could bring the disciples of "dissective notions of truth"
(146), he discovers in Donne "an attempt to recover a congenial
version of the corporeal, with its lingering unfathomed mystery,
from the cold hands of the dissectors" (151). For Sugg, Donne's
writing marks a turning point in the effort to preserve an idea of the
religious body. "The gulping whirlpool of the mind," he concludes,
with characteristic eloquence, "the springing of faith or emotion,
[that was] once proved so insistently and creatively through anatomy, would increasingly have to be proved against it" (158–59).
The desperate need for such probation provides the context for the
final chapter on "Vivisection, Violence, and Identity" where Sugg
explores the impact of Harvey's work on the circulation of the
blood and the advent of the Royal Society. As Katharine Maus and
others have done, he approaches the conduct of public executions,
especially the brutal dismemberment of hanging, drawing, and
quartering, as a species of vivisection; but beyond the mere demonstration of hidden guilt, he conjectures that in the executioner's
display of the eviscerated heart to his dying victim, we can recognize a darker version of the anatomist's drive for knowledge: "a
slightly different, but no less liminal, desire than that for intellectual control: namely, that of knowing death itself, in that pure, authentic moment of disbelieving terror which causes the dying to
flash a reflected gleam of the next world, fleetingly, into this one"
(171). Moving through a brilliantly extended discussion of Jack
Wilton's terror of vivisection in Nashe's *Unfortunate Traveller*,

Sugg goes on to look at how Michael Drayton's evocation of a "music of the self—the rhythms, murmurings, pulses, and whispers of fluid which the infant does not feel, but actually is—"helps to explain "something of the stubborn link between truth and interiority—that involuntary recourse to the finality of our gut feelings and rooted certainty of our bones" (199). Then, in a somewhat abrupt and speculative forward leap, he turns to the Marquis de Sade's *Justine* for a demonstration of the way in which, by the end of the eighteenth century the body has been comprehensively demystified, yielding up a core that "will tell us about itself, and nothing more"; ultimately, he concludes, "the body becomes the new soul, just as science becomes the new religion" (205). Well, perhaps: but I am not convinced that the process is quite so clear, so uniform, or so coherent as (out of rhetorical necessity, I suppose) Sugg makes it appear. Unrecognized in his history of body and soul, is the disturbing figure of Thomas Lovell Beddoes, the romantic poet and dramatist, whose preoccupation with death and the puzzle of immortality led him to the study of anatomy. In 1849, at the age of forty-six, apparently unhinged by what he discovered (or failed to discover) in the anatomy theaters of Germany and Switzerland where he had developed and practiced his art, Beddoes opened an artery with his anatomist's scalpel. He could hardly have chosen a more fitting scene for this last exemplary gesture—he died in Basel, the city where Vesalius had published his revolutionary *Fabrica,* and where in 1805 the authorities had demolished the last of its great *Totentanz* frescoes. Beddoes firmly believed that "the study of anatomy [and that] of the dramatist . . . are closely, almost inseparably allied" and that a tragedy might best be constructed as "a living semiotical display, a series of anthropological experiments developed for the purpose of ascertaining some important psychical principle."[8] At his death Beddoes left behind just such an experiment in tragical anatomy—his own (fittingly unfinished) masterpiece, an elaborate pastiche of Jacobean horror, entitled *Death's Jestbook.* It might provide the starting point for the sequel to *Murder after Death* which the last sentence of Richard Sugg's fascinating and beautifully produced[9] study seems to promise.

Notes

1. Jonathan Sawday, *The Body Emblazoned: Dissection and the Human Body in Renaissance Culture* (London: Routledge, 1995).

2. John More, *A Lively Anatomie of Death* (1596), sig. B3v.

3. Cited in William S. Heckscher, *Rembrandt's Anatomy of Dr Tulp* (New York: New York University Press, 1958), 114.

4. This aspect of the play is discussed in "The Stage of Death: Tragedy and Anatomy," chapter 2 of my *Issues of Death: Mortality and Identity in English Renaissance Tragedy* (Oxford: Clarendon Press, 1997), 136–38.

5. See, e.g., Louise Noble, "'And make two pasties of your shameful heads': Medicinal Cannibalism and Healing the Body Politic in *Titus Andronicus*," *ELH* 70 (2003): 677–708.

6. Michel de Montaigne, *Essays,* trans. John Florio, ed. J. C. Harmer, 3 vols. (London: Dent, 1965), 2.6.60.

7. Andreas Vesalius, *On the Fabric of the Human Body,* book 1, chapter 28, trans. William Richardson and John Carman (San Francisco: Norman Pub., 1998).

8. H. W. Donner, ed., *The Works of Thomas Lovell Beddoes* (Oxford: Clarendon Press, 1935), 609.

9. However carefully prepared, no book can be entirely free of small slips and misprints: Cornell University Press, as far as I can tell, has been meticulous with this one. It therefore seems especially unfortunate that the comprehensive index manages to confuse the playwright of *The White Devil* with the modern historian Charles Webster.

Colorblind Shakespeare: New Perspectives on Race and Performance
Edited by Ayanna Thompson
New York: Routledge, 2006

Reviewer: Arthur L. Little, Jr.

In the very last critical words in *Colorblind Shakespeare,* Peter Erickson in an endnote about Denzel Washington as Don Pedro in Kenneth Branagh's film of *Much Ado About Nothing* (1993), asks, "How could we be colorblind if the camera fixes on the coincidence that the character excluded from the marital festivity is played by the actor who just happens to be black?" (248). Is colorblindness, ideally the practice of casting plays and films without regard to race or ethnicity, even or ever desirable? Ayanna Thompson has gathered a distinguished group of scholars and theater practitioners to explore as well as expose the depths of such questions while studying the production history of color-blind and nontraditional casting, and thinking about the cultural and theoretical implications of such casting practices for contemporary readings of Shakespeare. A talk given at Princeton in 1996 by the African American playwright August Wilson serves as a kind of Ur-text or ground zero for the volume and for many of its contributors. According to Wilson, "Colorblind casting is an aberrant idea that has never had any validity other than as a tool of the Cultural Imperialists. . . . It is inconceivable to them that life could be lived and even enriched without knowing Shakespeare" (1). Directly or indirectly responding to Wilson are the fourteen essays, including an introduction by Thompson and a foreword and afterword by Ania Loomba and Peter Erickson, respectively. While all the essays are not equally up to the task of the volume, overall the collection—divided into three well-conceived parts, "The Semiotics of (Not) Viewing Race," "Practicing Colorblindness: The Players Speak," and "Future Possibilities/Future Directions"—is an exciting one and opens up important avenues for future research, especially for the field of Shakespeare and race studies and the field of performance studies, and at least one of the essays should be required reading for Shakespeareans more generally.

The collection begins with Ania Loomba making the kind of incisive and culturally and theoretically astute arguments readers have come to expect from her ever since her own groundbreaking study of Shakespeare and race and on through her work on Shakespeare and postcoloniality. Predicating her opening remarks on the anecdotal and moving on to broader critical concerns, she bares the cultural and disciplinarian stakes of the collection and concludes that "to pay attention to colorblind casting of Shakespeare is to do nothing less than to engage in the most vital discussions about identity, performance, and the politics of contemporary multiculturalism" (xvii).

As the title of Thompson's introduction makes clear, "Practicing a Theory/Theorizing a Practice" (chapter 1), the collection is invested in both the practice of colorblindness and the theorization of the practice. The introduction provides an informative and cogent historical and theoretical introduction to color-blind and nontraditional casting, and scholars who have only a passing or disparate knowledge of these practices will especially find the introduction a rich and suggestive starting place. The first part of her chapter provides a useful historical overview, beginning with an all-black production of *Richard III* in 1821 by the African Theater in New York, a company of former slaves and sons of former slaves, and with reflections on several performances by the nineteenth-century black actor Ira Aldridge, who played several of Shakespeare's major protagonists—Shylock, Macbeth, and Lear among them—in "white face." She discusses in greater detail Joseph Papp and the New York Shakespeare Festival, the official institutionalization of color-blind casting, and the place where several prominent actors and actresses of color began their careers. The historical coverage of the introduction really stops with Papp, which is difficult to explain given that many of the essays in the volume are concerned with what may be considered a post-Papp or post-color-blind era. Also, I would like to have seen Thompson extend the section of her introduction that looks specifically at the issue of colorblindness in Shakespeare (this is the shortest section of her introduction). Arguing that "including a discussion of the Shakespeare effect into this analysis [of colorblindness] adds yet another layer of complexity" (18), only begins to set the stage for what should be a more thorough engagement with issues of Shakespeare and colorblindness, evocative perhaps of the kinds of cultural terrain delineated in the foreword. Notwithstanding, the introduction does a superb job laying the groundwork for many of the contributors' broader questions.

Angela C. Pao's "Re-casting *Othello* in Text and Performance" (chapter 2), which opens part 1, "Viewing Race," is especially interested in the role of race in the casting of *Othello* after Othello began to be routinely played by black actors; she examines Anglo-American productions from the 1970s through the 1990s. Her essay makes the interesting observation that one way the question of race in the play has gotten resituated has been by casting Iago and Emilia as black. With a stronger theoretical frame, Pao could have moved her essay to a more meta-critical level, allowing her to distinguish her voice further from that of some of the theater practitioners and reviewers she quotes and enabling her more definitively to discuss the kinds of critical and reception problems posed by nontraditional casting. As Pao herself asserts (although she leaves the moment a discrete one in her essay), "The implicit assumption that racialized attitudes are a relevant factor only when members of different races are placed in direct opposition overlooks the structural and systemic nature of racism and its durable and pervasive effects which are not suddenly called into being at moments of interracial contact" (36). There is, too, a lost opportunity with Pao's wonderful essay, which (given its place in the volume) could have served as a beacon for the rest of the collection by explicitly taking up the question of what a color-blind *Othello* would look like and what lessons may be taken from this as the volume contemplates colorblindness and nontraditional casting and the casting of white actors in Shakespeare more generally.

Sujata Iyengar's "Single-Sex Shakespeare" (chapter 3) would perhaps prove even more resonant with respect to the volume were it to come later, after the volume had established a more extensive semiotics for thinking about colorblindness more discretely; her essay argues that colorblindness or color-conscious casting cannot be separated from questions of sex and gender. She is particularly interested in critical responses to three Shakespeare plays produced with same-sex casts. By focusing the main of her critical evidence on the published reviews of these productions, Iyengar expertly teases out some of the ways sex, gender, and race are deeply entwined in each other's signification processes. However, I found some of her editorials or apologies distracting and potentially undermining of the cultural force of her argument, such as when she counters her own argument about how *systemic* racism and sexism persist despite what may or may not be a particular production's intentions by adopting the more personal conservative framing of racism and sexism in opposition to her own critical reading when she adds, "I am sure that such associations were far from the minds of those casting and performing in the production" (64). Notwithstanding, the essay is steeped in a wealth of cultural material that Iyengar uses quite perceptively and convincingly.

Courtney Lehmann's "Faux Show: Falling into History in Kenneth Branagh's *Love's Labour's Lost*" (chapter 4) is one of the gems in this collection. It's critically, theoretically, and historically rich and sustained by a verve and turns-of-phrase that make the essay not only scholarly accomplished but a pleasure to read. Putting to effective and nuanced use a range of thinkers—Richard Dyer, Paul Gilroy, Arthur Knight, Toni Morrison, and Slavoj Žižek, among others—Lehmann studies and culturally situates the workings of colorblindness (and "colordeafness") in Branagh's Shakespeare films. She argues, mostly quoting Branagh himself that "Branagh claims to have been so 'transfixed' by his brother's impersonation of a 'blacked-up American minstrel' that his decision to become an actor was 'ignited' by the mask of burnt cork, which embodies the

performance of racechange [*sic*] to which he has dedicated himself
ever since" (82–83). Even though her readings of Branagh's *Much
Ado* (1993) and *Hamlet* (1996) are very cogent and right on, her analytical brilliance and incisiveness are most evident in her discussion of *Love's Labour's Lost* (2000), the essay's dominant critical
focus. Branagh transforms Shakespeare's play into an "integrated"
1930s musical—"integration" denoting the enfolding of the musical numbers into the diegesis and having nothing ostensibly to do
with race or culture. Colorblindness in Branagh's film comes in the
form of the black British actress Carmen Ejogo (Maria) and the
black Birmingham native Adrian Lester (Dumaine), who are point-
edly not coupled together in this comedy of couples. She argues
that the film's mise-en-scène, set in 1939, is dominated by a "faux
history": "In fact, it is almost as if the invocation of 1939 is, in fact,
a decoy aimed at forestalling the film's inevitable 'fall into history'" (76), most specifically the historical realities of the gestapo,
but, she adds later, closely reading the "Let's Face the Music and
Dance" moment in the film, "More historically accurate than he
ever intended to be, Branagh's rendering of this scene suggests the
cultural leaps that could convert Dumaine, decades later, into an
Emmet Till" (85). Throughout, she insists on underscoring the
roles of heterosexuality and whiteness in Branagh's filmic utopias.
Lehmann's is one of the essays that deftly and convincingly shows
how unexamined colorblindness can potentially turn Shakespeare
into a "faux show" of whiteness.

More polemical than many of the essays in the collection, Lisa
M. Anderson's "When Race Matters" (chapter 5), questions the via-
bility of colorblindness in the United States, contending that colorblindness "ultimately signifies assimilation" (91) and "requires
that we ignore three hundred years of history or . . . render them
meaningless" (91). Focusing on a 2001 production of *Macbeth* at
the Globe Theater in London and a 1996 production of *Richard III*
in Chicago, she essentially elaborates on the point that the *Macbeth*
production "had its difficulties" and the *Richard III* production
"was actually disturbing" in their respective use of color-blind
casting. There are some distracting problems with the essay. She
argues, for example, that Richard pursues Anne while she accom-
panies "her dead husband's body to burial" (98)—it's the body of
her father-in-law—and she posits that the foundation of Western
theatrical representation of "blackness as pathological" begins in
the nineteenth century (92). It's much earlier. Like several other es-

says in the volume, she does read with cultural suspicion how re-viewers often show no explicit evidence of seeing the race of nonwhite players, a phenomenon itself worthy of an article-length study. Outside its polemical frame, Anderson leaves her produc-tion critiques rather inconclusive.

Despite the mention of color-blind casting in her opening sen-tence, Krystyna Kujawinska Courtney's "Ira Aldridge" (chapter 6) is really a study of archival materials related to the nineteenth-cen-tury Shakespearean actor Ira Aldridge's reception on the European Continent. But the essay does intrigue with its knowledge and anal-ysis of the cultural and political use of Aldridge in Russia and Po-land, and the antagonism and deep distrust between the two countries. It argues quite convincingly that Russia's and Poland's responses to Aldridge figure him as "not only one of the best and most effective emissaries of Shakespeare, but also a compelling representative of the antislavery movement and an effective ambas-sador for the politically, socially, and culturally abused" (118). Courtney's essay is certainly an accomplished and fascinating essay, especially for those interested in Aldridge or the Continent's receptiveness to Shakespeare in the nineteenth century, but its in-clusion here is somewhat risky given the purported emphasis of the collection; and without Courtney further contextualizing her argu-ment, I'm not convinced its inclusion here does a service to either the volume or the essay.

The two essays in part 2, "The Players Speak," are from the point of view of two theater practitioners, the second in the form of an interview conducted by Thompson herself. These are important es-says, rightly placed at the center of the collection, and their inclu-sion a very innovative and smart choice on the part of Thompson. The volume benefits from these contributors not only because it brings two extremely well-situated theater practitioners into the conversation but because these essays challenge and help to stretch the parameters of academic discourse. In the first of these, "My Own Private Shakespeare" (chapter 7), Antonio Ocampo-Guzman, Colombian-born director, actor, educator, and member of Shake-speare & Company in Lenox, Massachusetts, discusses colorblind-ness from both professional and personal perspectives. He also provides the volume's most sustained analysis of Latino actors' ex-periences with both colorblindness and colordeafness. Ocampo-Guzman is quite professionally and personally exposed in his essay, a difficult achievement in either instance. As he repeatedly returns to his quandary that "if Shakespeare is a paragon of human creativity, we all have a right to access him from our own identities" (132), he performatively shows himself accepting and rejecting a kind of Bloomian insistence on Shakespeare's claim to the human. Ocampo-Guzman's voice should stand as a paradigmatic one for this collection that exhibits in its best moments that as a cultural practice (in the theater and outside it) colorblindness at its best can only *signal* a discursive (and real) site where societal participants can grapple with their understanding of the relationship between race and humanness.

After reading Ocampo-Guzman's essay, there's much that sounds familiar in Thompson's interview with Timothy Douglas, "In the Blood" (chapter 8). Like Ocampo-Guzman, Douglas is a director, actor, and educator, and was affiliated with Shakespeare & Company; he is perhaps best known for having directed the world premiere of August Wilson's *Radio Golf* (2005). Douglas is well-suited for this collection, since his work, according to Douglas himself, is made of "50 percent dead white playwrights and 50 percent living black playwrights" (137). The Douglas piece is more cultural critique than personal narrative, even though, like Ocampo-Guzman, he does synthesize the two; however, the interview is less focused on Shakespeare. Like Ocampo-Guzman, Douglas finds himself not quite willing to accept or reject colorblind or nontraditional casting practices. Perhaps the most unique contribution Douglas makes to this collection is his focus on the logistical difficulties faced by theater practitioners (whether actors or directors) involved in colorblind or nontraditional casting.

Richard Burt's "Middlebrow Multiculturalism" (chapter 9) opens the third part of the collection, "Future Directions," and proffers more vitriol than analysis and at times devolves into self-parody, as he seems, incredibly, to argue that racism is now more an issue for Leftist academics than it is for American (popular) culture, and that race has become "*relatively* insignificant in Shakespeare performance" (emphasis added, 169). His real vehemence seems to be directed at the field of Shakespeare and race studies. Whether urged on by paronomasia or color illiteracy, much of the first half of Burt's essay means to incite, as when he counters arguments about the existence of "white male anxiety" by exclaiming, "Similarly, arguments that the *black bodies* of actors playing Othello are being *exploited* because they are commodified have no *purchase*" (emphases added, 166). The second half of the essay in which he discusses several 1950s television episodes and then moves inexplicably to a 2002 television episode overwhelms with myopic description. Nevertheless, with the inclusion of this latter episode he does articulate, quite rightly, the need for future studies to examine colorblindness and nontraditional casting (in and outside Shakespeare) in a post-9/11 culture.

Like Ocampo-Guzman's essay, Margo Hendricks's "Gestures of Performance" (chapter 10) broadly concerns itself with the (de)humanizing possibilities of color-blind casting. Hendricks argues that as theater scholars and practitioners look forward, it's important that they pay closer attention to some of the gestural ways racialized bodies populate Shakespearean stage and screen. Using three film adaptations, Hendricks discusses how race is not only about perceived physical characteristics but gestures that can signal a particular ethnic position, no matter the perceived race or ethnicity of the actor. Throughout, Hendricks makes some highly astute observations, as when she points out that racially or ethnically coded gesturing is even demanded of actors of color presenting what is thought to be a racial or ethnic heritage he or she presumably already owns. Hendricks is at least partly right when she argues that "race must be made visible if race is to have cultural and ideological weight" (201), but she overstates the significance of gesturing, I think, when she concludes that "race in Shakespearean performance has no meaning until it is gestured" (201). Given the kind of forthright cultural critique mounted by her essay, her final sentence—that gesture, like language, turns "performing Shakespeare's playtexts [into] exciting possibilities" (202)—seems rather evasive and overly amelioratory.

Using a range of theatrical and filmic representations of Cleopatra in addition to Shakespeare's as well as a memoir by the Australian actress Zoe Caldwell, Celia R. Daileader's "White Actresses on the Interracial 'Classic' Stage" (chapter 11) filters the issue of color-blind and multicultural casting through ongoing Western questions regarding Cleopatra's race and offers some poignant cultural commentary along the way. In many respects her essay complements Hendricks's quite well, since Daileader is really concerned here with the ways various gestures may be read as (de)racializing Cleopatra. Like a few other contributors to this volume, she takes into critical and theoretical account the relationship between race and gender. Even though the essay is only tangentially invested in colorblindness as its constitutive topic, it includes one of the most potentially racially coded moments around which to construct an essay for this volume: the black actress Claire Benedict, who was the understudy to the white actress Clare Higgins playing Cleopatra in the 1992 RSC season, had to replace her for one night (208). Other than an intriguing endnote, Daileader doesn't pursue any analysis of this moment; had she done so, Daileader, with her iconoclastic vantage (217) and highly intelligent verve, could have stolen the show. Notwithstanding, the essay sustains a quick and impressive critical wit and will certainly be of interest to those of us engaged in the cultural study of Cleopatra.

Francesca T. Royster's "Whiteness, Terror, and the Fleshwork of Theatre in a Post-Colorblind Age" (chapter 12), a gem, a brilliant piece of scholarship, not only spans the intellectual, critical, theoretical, and cultural range and depth of the volume but is the essay that most demonstrates the exhilarating possibilities that future collections could and should pursue. As her essay commandingly and cogently shows, the liberal idealism of color-blind casting has evolved into the more responsive and responsible realism of conceptual casting, that is, as she defines it, "the race or ethnicity of the actor might deliberately cut against the grain of the role to make a sociopolitical or aesthetic statement about identity and history" (228). Royster offers the volume's most intoxicating and accomplished reading of nontraditional casting, a reading that works seamlessly with her reading of the Chicago Shakespeare Theater's 2003 production of Edward Hall's *Rose Rage,* his nearly five-hour-long condensation of *Henry VI* parts 1, 2, and 3, that he premiered in London in 2001, and opened in New York in 2004. Hall introduced conceptual casting with the Chicago production, and through Royster's critical acumen the Chicago production becomes a deliberate and challenging meditation on the staging of white manhood. "The extreme physical violence of the War of the Roses" (221), particularly as staged by Hall, provides Royster with a rich site for analyzing what she sees as the "heroic whiteness of English history," the "fictional whiteness of the theatrical space," and the "'honorary' whiteness" that some bodies are allowed to interpellate (221). She argues that Hall's production "links early modern English history to the history of making 'other' bodies into flesh in other moments in history" (222); she calls this process "fleshwork." If, as Royster argues, "flesh is the physical material of human existence at the very boundaries of the social and the human" (227), then her reading of flesh massages that cultural dialogue that goes on between the raced and the human subject. Because of the perspicacity, sheer intelligence, and nuance with which Royster reads Hall's production as itself a critique and historicization of colorblindness and Western commercial (Shakespearean) theater's trafficking in others' flesh as a way to perform white subjects, especially in a post-9/11 United States, Royster's essay should be required reading for anyone interested in Shakespeare, race, or contemporary performance.

The collection ends with Peter Erickson's very powerful and balanced afterword in which he argues, as have many of the contributors, that "conventions of blackface and colorblind casting are accorded a suspension of disbelief that is not just willing but eager. The escapist impulse behind this eagerness deserves critical scrutiny" (242). But Erickson's afterword is no mere summation of the essays coming before. It is a well-informed, well-honed, and heartfelt critique, and an address to fellow Shakespeareans, an insistence that we desist deluding ourselves about a Shakespearean theater that is "a pristine space hermetically sealed off from ordinary social discourse" (242).

There is much that Thompson's collection accomplishes and much that it does not, but as the essays in the volume show, especially those that really foreground and directly take up the issue of color-blind Shakespeare, a study of colorblindness on the Anglo-American Shakespeare stage is no less a study of multiculturalism in England and the United States. Erickson titles the penultimate section of his afterword, "Putting the Argument on Stage" (243–44), but I want to take Erickson a step further: "Putting the Argument to Shakespeare Scholars and Shakespeare Students." It's worth noting that most of the scholars of color in this volume articulate having "personal" knowledge of some kind of racial or ethnic posturing that shape them as researchers and teachers. I would venture that they understand this because they too have audiences—colleagues and students—and are aware, joyfully, painfully, or some complex mix of these, of their own negotiations in the construction of color-blind *and* nontraditional Shakespearean spaces. However, Shakespeareans of color as well as white Shakespeareans must carry out more historically and theoretically informed discussions about the workings of race in our discipline and our classrooms; there is no immunity here. And it would be productive to see this conversation happening across multiple critical and cultural terrains. Whatever may be the individual foibles of the contributors to this volume, they have given us a substantial and excellent collection to begin the conversation.

Shakespeare in French Theory: King of Shadows
By Richard Wilson
New York: Routledge, 2007

Reviewer: Christopher Pye

Richard Wilson's *Shakespeare in French Theory: King of Shadows* is not simply an application of French theory to Shakespeare's plays, although it does bring the writings of Pierre Bourdieu, René Girard, Michel Foucault, and Jacques Derrida to bear on the works in genuinely compelling ways. Wilson seeks instead to trace the forms of "mutual acculturation" between Shakespeare and French thought, the ways in which the plays have haunted the theory as much as the theory transformed the plays. And that dialectic is marked, Wilson notes, by a central irony. While French theory has underwritten the iconoclastic strain in Anglo-American criticism, a version of Bardolatry not entirely distinct from the Romantic tradition has been at the core of some of the most radical dimensions of French thought, particularly its political thought. Whether construed as Gothic threat or as embodiment of an anodyne cultural multiplicity, Shakespeare has been affiliated in the French intellectual tradition with possibilities of heterogeneity. That emphasis on the culturally and temporally disruptive *arrivante* has force, not just in relation to the outright monoculturalism of traditional Shakespeare criticism, but also in relation to New Historicism's tendency to discover in the works "power's ode to itself," as well as to the strain of Anglo-American critique that amounts, in Wilson's words, to "one long campaign to arraign the plays as guilty by association with the European colonialism, slavery, and pogroms they foretold" (244).

While the book thus explicitly sets itself against the political tenets or assumptions of New Historicism—sometimes agonistically so—one may be equally struck by its methodological commonalities with that critical mode, though Wilson might prefer to see this as an affiliation with cultural materialism. For a work zeroed-in on "high theory," the book is notable for its intensely topical character, whether that's a matter of finding the perilous circumstance of Catholics in *King Lear*'s cliff scene, or an equivalency between Brutus and Lenten butchers "licensed to kill in March" (188). That cultural immersiveness is inflected by Wilson's attention to the temporally disjunct—anachronistic, anticipatory—status of the Shakespearean text; the book hears in the plays, for instance, the sacrificial foundations of the Roman city-state, as well as the charged political circumstances of post-Revolutionary England. And, while one can query the relation between the topical mode and the book's larger theoretical framework (I'll return to the issue), Wilson's mixed method produces for the most part a tremendous sense of critical possibility. Indeed, *Shakespeare in French Theory* is an intelligent, edgy, and impressively wide book, capacious in the range of critical voices it mobilizes often toward new ends, in the depth and sure-handedness of its theoretical reference, and in the sheer richness and inventiveness of its historical contextualizing.

The book is divided into two parts, the first tracing Shakespeare's effects within French critical thought, the second bringing the theory to bear on a handful of plays. The first chapter traces the intriguing story of Shakespeare's French reception, and especially the response to the Bard's "monstrous elasticity" (33). The account moves from the poet's status as "sordid affront to absolutist ideals of claret" during the Enlightenment, to the unstably valorized "gothic" Shakespeare of the Revolution, to the frisson of his ghostly returns among the French Romantics (Berlioz) and anti-Bourgeois modernists (Hugo), to his role in the psychic negotiation of the postwar era for figures like Gide, Lacan, and Girard, to his outright liberatory potential for Lyotard, Deleuze, Derrida, and Cixous. Although the account affirms Shakespeare's Rorschach-like availability to varied interpretive and political ends, the emphasis falls on the play's demotic possibilities, and on Shakespeare's status as historical revenant; the point is not simply that Shakespeare is put to different uses, but that he inhabits French modernity like an alien and returning form. In that regard, Marx, and particularly the Marx of *Eighteenth Brumaire*, remains (paradoxically) the exemplary figure.

The second and third chapters consider Shakespeare in relation to two seminal theorists, Michel Foucault and Pierre Bourdieu. In "Prince of Darkness," Wilson brings Foucault to bear on *Measure for Measure* by offering a corrective to Foucault's own account of the chronology of modes of power. Taking the "visual taxonomies" of Bridewell prison as his central historical exhibit, Wilson makes the case for an earlier transition from spectacular punishment to an internalizing disciplinarity based on voyeuristic authority, and thus to a power founded not on "the mere containment of opposition, but the positive production of resistance" (108). Although such an argument is anticipated by prior analyses of the "hidden monarch" motif in Shakespeare, Wilson's account is richer in its contextualizations and more theoretically comprehensive. And in its claims for the play's knowingness about such structures, the chapter offers a valuable corrective to the strain of Foucauldian critique (and not just of the New Historicist stripe) that sees the subject as nothing but a blindly inscribed effect of power.

The Bourdieu chapter—"The Management of Mirth"—is based, again, on a chronological corrective, a convincing transposition of Bourdieu's argument for the modern emergence of aesthetic autonomy to the early-modern context, in this case as a way of unraveling a significant sociological riddle. Why Shakespearean drama's strong alignment with aristocratic personages and values given the actual class profile of the London theater-going audience? Wilson argues that the symbolic transformation through which artists sought to free themselves from bourgeois demands by claiming the autonomy of the work begins with Shakespeare "as a strategy to exchange the economic capital earned in the public playhouse for the cultural capital awarded by the princely patron" (131). Wilson's argument here is important for the way it suggests a mode of political reading able to accommodate, unlike much cultural materialist analysis, Shakespeare's investment in disinterestedness and the complexity of his relation to the aesthetic status of the work.

"The Kindly Ones," the first of the chapters of applied analysis, explores questions of power and censorship in *Midsummer Night's Dream*. Combining Bourdieu's account of aestheticization with Foucault's analysis of disciplinary self-management, the chapter explores the euphemization of the violence, or potential violence, at the origin of the work, a negation of grounds figured both in the ameliorative self-effacement of the author and the etherealization of the taboo and threatening figure of patron Queen. It's a dispersed chapter, but also one of the most evocative, with a beautiful extension of Foucault's account of the ghost presence of the royal patrons in Velásquez's *Las Meninas* to Elizabeth's ambivalently valorized lunar manifestations in the play. "A Bleeding Head Where They Begun," on *Julius Caesar,* is underwritten by Walter Benjamin's famous dictum that there is no document of civilization that is not also a document of barbarism. Wilson focuses on the reiterative character of such foundational violence, the eternal recurrence manifest in the uncanny temporality of a play which at once hearkens back and prophetically anticipates, variously, the founding of Rome, the Revolution to come, Christ's sacrifice, and the equivocal returns of the Eucharistic act during Shakespeare's own ambiguous theological moment. The political valence of such reiterations arises from the loss of distinction they imply between the returns of theater and the returns of history as such.

The focus on cultural violence continues in "Bloody As the Hunter," a sustained reflection on the cultural meaning of the off-stage duel scene in *Twelfth Night,* a scene evident only in what we might have taken to be its comic aftereffects. For Wilson, the scene figures "the bloody rites of passage" at the core of the play's cultural logic—its proximity to the operations of "blood sacrifice." According to Wilson, the scene alludes in precise ways to the Raleigh-Cecil-Essex feud (210). But the duel should also be read, as sociologists have suggested, in light of the larger conflict between an imperiled aristocracy and the emergent juridical class associated with state and monarchy, "the epochal battle between gown and sword . . . in which an elite threatened by 'pen gents' . . . vented its violence upon itself" (223). That self-violence in itself functioned as an affirmation of the logic of blood-sacrifice associated with a vanishing conception of the body politic.

"When the Cock Crows" reflects on the messianic turn in recent writing on *Hamlet.* If the play has a strong eschatological cast, it anticipates an end which nevertheless arrives, as Cixous formulates it, "too early, too late, and never at the right time" (239). And if it is the end of history that's at stake, that end nevertheless incessantly reinscribes itself within historical time. Such indeterminate immanence—the very condition of historicity—has, again, a notable topical specificity for Wilson: "something distressing has entered peripheral vision with the Jacobean Quarto that was not there in the Elizabethan text, and will be censored from the Folio" (237). That something is the accession of James, an event to which Wilson attaches the play's generalized foreboding. The epilogue—"Making Men of Monsters"—returns by way of Derrida to Shakespeare's heterogeneity, an openness to the European and non-European Other based not on tolerance but on radical hospitality, that condition, in Derrida's words, of being open in advance to "whomever arrives as an absolutely foreign *visitor,* as a new *arrival,* non-identifiable and unforeseeable, in short, wholly other." Wilson gives that prospect a local habitation and name by aligning Shakespeare, not with Carnival, a practice associated with enforcing solidarity against the stranger, but with Mumming, a custom "which symbolized the imperative of kindness to strangers by enacting the right of even the uninvited to cross the threshold of the house" (247).

That recognition of Shakespeare's radical cultural and historical openness is in Wilson's account what French theory offers to our understanding of the playwright; it is certainly what distinguishes *Shakespeare in French Theory* from those modes of materialist history which find in the texts nothing but a reinscription of dominant ideologies. But what distinguishes Wilson's work in relation to prior engagements between Shakespeare and the French school? Although the book opens with reference to Joel Fineman's claim that it is Shakespeare's attentiveness to the "languageness of language" that gives the work its uncannily anticipatory relation to post-modernity, Wilson's own mode is less marked by linguistic or formal preoccupations than by its assumption of the possibility of a relatively unproblematic conjunction between theory and topicality, the assumption that Derrida and Chartier can occupy a common methodological ground.

That's the source of the book's extraordinary richness. It may also be where the most interesting theoretical questions arise, questions prompted by different moments in Wilson's own argument. What, for instance, is the relation between the autonomization of the work Wilson describes in the Bourdieu chapters—the (historical) process through which the Shakespearean work "retreats from the world of referentiality into the empty 'nothing' of its own aesthetic void"—and the often relatively direct referential character of Wilson's own claims? Is the aesthetic turn simply a refusal of the truth of the work's referential dimensions? Wilson's association between Shakespearean heterogeneity and "the play of the signifier" suggest the need for a more complex account of the relation between form and reference. Although the book assumes relative transparency between the two registers, the duel, for instance, may have a very different meaning as a literary construction than it does as a sociological phenomenon; indeed, the manner in which the exorbitancies of a play like *Hamlet* resolve themselves into the specular structure of the duel may suggest the degree to which the work's own mimetic status—its "semblable"ness—is bound up with such an encounter, a structure and function Lacan brings to the fore.

The problem of reference occurs with particular acuteness, I think, in relation to what may be the book's dominant preoccupation: the fact of cultural violence. One of Wilson's central claims is that the scene of culture's foundational violence is, in fact, reiterative and always already contested—no origin at all. At the same time, particularly when he reads the works as an exposé of the unacknowledged barbarism at the heart of early modern civilization, Wilson understands such violence to convey something like a "face to face" encounter with the truth of culture (164). Thus, the fact that the Huguenots "disinterred, cooked, and ate the relics of saints"—a case of "sacred metaphor becom[ing] profane reality"— amounts to an instance of the "savage exception" "prov[ing] the revolutionary rule" (191). A certain violence may indeed lie at the foundation of culture, but the status of that violence remains a significant question. Does literature euphemize the brute if indeterminate fact of founding violence, a process the Shakespearean text demystifies? Or is the very luridness of such scenes in the plays and perhaps in the critical writing as well a sign of the role they play in the process by which texts seek to posit their own ground and thus secure their claims to reference? How one decides that uncertainty is intimately bound up with how one reads the political and theoretical dimensions of Shakespeare's work.

Index